Humanitarian Logistics

Humanitarian Logistics

Meeting the challenges of preparing
for and responding to disasters

Edited by
Peter Tatham and
Martin Christopher

KoganPage

First published in Great Britain and the United States in 2018 by Kogan Page Limited

2nd Floor, 45 Gee Street	c/o Martin P Hill Consulting	4737/23 Ansari Road
London	122 W 27th Street	Daryaganj
EC1V 3RS	New York, NY 10001	New Delhi 110002
United Kingdom	USA	India
www.koganpage.com		

© Peter Tatham and Martin Christopher 2018

ISBN   978 0 7494 8144 5
E-ISBN 978 0 7494 8145 2

British Library Cataloguing-in-Publication Data

A CIP record for this book is available from the British Library.

Library of Congress Control Number

2018003916

Typeset by Integra Software Services, Pondicherry
Print production managed by Jellyfish
Printed and bound in Great Britain by CPI Group (UK) Ltd, Croydon CR0 4YY

CONTENTS

11   Humanitarian logistics – the functional challenges facing field offices 226

12   Supply chain improvement at ShelterBox: a case study of the application of lean principles and techniques in a disaster relief organization 242

LIST OF FIGURES
AND TABLES

ABBREVIATIONS

Introduction

4PL	fourth party logistics
CRED	Centre for Research on the Epidemiology of Disasters
CTPs	Cash Transfer Programmes
GDP	gross domestic product
H-CLOP	humanitarian common logistic operations picture
HL	humanitarian logistics
HLA	Humanitarian Logistics Association
IDPs	internally displaced persons
JIT	just-in-time
LMMS	Last Mile Mobile Solutions
SKUs	stock keeping units
UN	United Nations
UNHCR	United Nations High Commissioner for Refugees
UNHRD	United Nations Humanitarian Response Depot
VMI	vendor-managed inventory
WATSAN	water and sanitation
WFP	World Food Programme

Chapter 1

ALNAP	Active Learning Network on Accountability and Performance
CCIC	Canadian Council for International Cooperation
CHS	Core Humanitarian Standard
DAC	Development Assistance Committee
ECB	Emergency Capacity Building
EFQM	European Foundation for Quality Management
GAP	Global Accountability Partnership
Groupe URD	Urgence, Réhabilitation, Développement
HAP	Humanitarian Accountability Project
HAP-I	Humanitarian Accountability Partnership International
IFRC	International Federation of Red Cross and Red Crescent Societies
NGOs	non-governmental organizations
OCHA	Office for the Coordination of Humanitarian Affairs

ODA	official development assistance
OECD	Organisation for Economic Co-operation and Development
PVO	Private Voluntary Organization
SCHR	Steering Committee for Humanitarian Response
SCOR	supply chain operations reference
UN	United Nations
UNDP	United Nations Development Programme

Chapter 2

CERF	Central Emergency Response Fund
CHFs	Common Humanitarian Funds
CTPs	cash transfer programmes
ERFs	Emergency Response Funds
IFRC	International Federation of the Red Cross and Red Crescent Societies
NGOs	non-governmental organizations
OR	operations research
UN	United Nations

Chapter 3

CIDA	Canadian International Development Agency
DFATD	now known as the Department of Foreign Affairs, Trade and Development
ECHO	European Civil Protection and Humanitarian Aid Operations
EFSVL	Emergency Food Security and Vulnerable Livelihoods
ICTs	information communication technologies
KYC	'know your customer'
LMMS	Last Mile Mobile Solutions
NGOs	non-governmental organizations
UNHCR	United Nations High Commissioner for Refugees
WFP	World Food Programme
WV	World Vision

Chapter 4

3DP	3D printing
ABS	acrylonitrile butadiene styrene

BLOS   'beyond line of sight'
CTPs   cash transfer programmes
DCA   Danish Church Aid
FAA   Federal Aviation Administration
FDM   fused deposition modelling
FSD   Swiss Mine Action
HCAs   hybrid cargo airships
IATA   International Air Transport Association
ICAO   International Civil Aviation Organization
ITAR   International Traffic in Arms Regulations
LALE   'low altitude, long endurance'
NDMO   National Disaster Management Organization
OCHA   UN Office for the Coordination of Humanitarian Affairs
RPAS   remotely piloted aircraft systems
UAS   unmanned aerial systems
UAVs   unmanned aerial vehicles
UNHRDs   United Nations Humanitarian Response Depots
VTOL   vertical take-off and landing
WASH   water, sanitation and hygiene
WFP   World Food Programme

Chapter 5

ECHO   Civil Protection and Humanitarian Aid Operations
                department
IFRC   International Federation of Red Cross and Red Crescent
                Societies
IHOs   international humanitarian organizations
INGO   international non-governmental organization
JIT   just-in-time
LRT   logistics response team
LSPs   logistics service providers
MSF   Médecins Sans Frontières
UNHCR   United Nations High Commissioner for Refugees
UNHRDs   United Nations Humanitarian Response Depots
UNICEF   United Nations Children's Fund
UNOPS   United Nations Office for Project Services
WFP   World Food Programme
WHO   World Health Organization
WV Canada   World Vision

Chapter 6

BINGOs	big international non-governmental organizations
GOs	governmental organizations
HDR-SCM	humanitarian and disaster relief supply chain management
NGOs	non-governmental organizations
SCI	supply chain integration
SCM	supply chain management
SCs	supply chains
UN	United Nations
UNCERF	United Nations Central Emergency Response Fund
UNHRD	United Nations Humanitarian Response Depot

Chapter 7

API	active pharmaceutical ingredients
ART	antiretroviral therapy
ARV	antiretroviral
AU	African Union
CSIR	Council for Scientific and Industrial Research
DMISA	Disaster Management Institute of Southern Africa
DRM	disaster risk management
EM-DAT	Emergency Events Database
ERP	enterprise resource planning
EU	European Union
FFA	Forest Fire Association
GIMPA	Ghana Institute of Management and Public Administration
IDP	integrated development plan
IS/IT	information systems/information technology
ITU	International Telecommunications Union
MSG	Meteosat Second Generation
NDMC	South African National Disaster Management Centre
NDMIS	National Disaster Management Information System
NEPAD	New Partnership for Africa's Development
NGOs	non-governmental organizations
PDMCs	The Provincial Disaster Management Centres
PEPFAR	US President's Emergency Plan for AIDS Relief
PMTCT	prevent mother-to-child transmission
SAC	Satellite Application Centre

UN	United Nations
UNDP	United Nations Development Programme
UNISDR	UN Office for Disaster Risk Reduction

Chapter 8

CHP	combined heat and power plants
EU	European Union
NESA	National Emergency Supply Agency
NESO	National Emergency Supply Organization
NGOs	non-governmental organizations

Chapter 9

CIPD	Chartered Institute of Personnel and Development
HL	humanitarian logistics
HLCF	humanitarian logistics competency framework
NGOs	non-governmental organizations
NVQs	National Council for Vocational Qualifications
PTD	People that Deliver
SATs	standard attainment tests

Chapter 10

CRED	Centre for Research on Epidemiology of Disasters
DCs	distribution centres
MREs	meals ready to eat
UNHRD	United Nations Humanitarian Response Depot
WFP	World Food Programme

Chapter 11

3PL	third party logistics
ERP	emergency response preparedness
EU	European Union
IDPs	internally displaced people
KPIs	key performance indicators
NGOs	non-governmental organizations
PoCs	persons of concern
UNHCR	United Nations High Commissioner for Refugees
WIM	warehousing and inventory management

Chapter 12

BPM	'big picture map'
DRVCA	disaster response value chain analysis
HQ	headquarters
IFRC	International Federation of Red Cross and Red Crescent Societies
KPIs	key performance indicators
NFIs	non-food items
NGO	non-governmental organization
SRTs	ShelterBox response teams
UK	United Kingdom
UNHCR	United Nations High Commissioner for Refugees
UNHRDs	United Nations Humanitarian Response Depots
VCA	Value chain analysis

Chapter 13

CDEM	civil defence and emergency management
CRC	Christchurch Response Centre
DESC	Cabinet Committee on Domestic and External Security Coordination
DFID	Department for International Development
DPMC	Department of the Prime Minister and Cabinet
ECC	Emergency Coordination Centre
EM	Emergency management
EMIS	Emergency Management Information System
EOC	Emergency Operations Centre
FEMA	Federal Emergency Management Agency
FMCG	fast moving consumer goods
HL	humanitarian logistics
IT	information technology
MCDEM	Minister's Office
NGOs	non-governmental organizations
NSS	National Security System
NZTA	New Zealand Transport Agency
SCM	supply chain management
WFP	World Food Programme
WoG	'whole of government'

Chapter 14

BRAT	basic rapid assessment tool
CFW	cash for work
CHL	Certificate in Humanitarian Logistics
CILT	Chartered Institute of Logistics and Transport
CRED	Centre for the Research on the Epidemiology of Disasters
CSR	corporate social responsibility
CTP	cash transfer programme
CTP	cash transfer programming
ESUPS	Emergency Supplies Prepositioning Strategy
HLA	Humanitarian Logistics Association
INGOs	international NGOs
KPIs	key performance indicators
LSPs	logistics service providers
NFIs	non-food items
NGOs	non-governmental organizations
OCHA	United Nations Office for the Coordination of Humanitarian Affairs
SCRM	Supply chain risk management
UAVs	unmanned aerial vehicles
UN	United Nations
UN DESA	United Nations Department of Economic and Social Affairs
UNCTAD	United Nations Conference on Trade and Development
UNHRDs	United Nations Humanitarian Response Depots
VfM	value for money
WFP	World Food Programme
WHS	World Humanitarian Summit

Chapter 15

3D	three-dimensional
BINGOs	big international non-governmental organizations
CTPs	cash transfer programmes
ERP	enterprise resource planning
ERUs	emergency response units
EU	European Union
GRI	Global Reporting Initiative
ICT	information and communications technology

IPs	implementing partners (sometimes called cooperation partners or CPs)
ISCRAM	Information Systems for Crisis Response and Management
ISO	International Organization for Standardization
SKUs	stock keeping units
UNGM	United Nations Global Marketplace
UNICEF	United Nations Children's Fund
WASH	water, sanitation and hygiene

LIST OF CONTRIBUTORS

Professor Anthony Beresford is a Professor of Logistics and Transport in the Cardiff Business School, Cardiff University. He was awarded his PhD in Environmental Sciences at the University of East Anglia in 1982 for research that focused on climate change in East Africa. He has subsequently travelled widely in an advisory capacity within the ports, transport and humanitarian fields in Europe, Africa, Australasia and North America. He has been involved in a broad range of transport-related research and consultancy projects including: transport rehabilitation, aid distribution and trade facilitation for the United Nations Conference on Trade and Development (UNCTAD) and for, for example, the Rwandan Government. His cost model for multimodal transport has been widely used by United Nations Economic and Social Commission for Asia and the Pacific (UNESCAP) Corridors in Southeast Asia, Africa and elsewhere. He has also advised both the United Kingdom and Welsh Governments on road transport and port policy options. More recently, he has been working on humanitarian supply chain operations in the context of man-made emergencies and natural disasters. He is a member of the Cardiff-Cranfield Humanitarian Logistics Initiative, a research group exploring operational and strategic aspects of humanitarian and emergency response.

Professor Paul S N Buatsi is the Managing Consultant of Omega Strategic Resources Ltd (Accra, Ghana). He is a Professor of Marketing and International Business with research interest in humanitarian logistics. He is a former Chief Director of the Ministry of Education (Ghana), Dean of the Graduate School of Business at the Ghana Institute of Management and Public Administration (Accra, Ghana), and the founding Dean of the KNUST School of Business, Kwame Nkrumah University of Science and Technology (Kumasi, Ghana). He is a founding member of the HUMLOG Group (Helsinki, Finland).

Professor Paul Childerhouse is the Director of Logistics and Supply Chain Management at Massey University. He obtained his PhD in 2002 for his research into supply chain integration and market orientation whilst at Cardiff University. His major research interests are in supply chain networks and relationships. He is practitioner focused and enjoys auditing and advising organizations on how to improve their supply chain practices. He has published over 50 articles in quality journals including: *Journal of Business Logistics, Journal of Operations Management, Supply Chain Management: An international journal, International Journal of Production Economics* and *OMEGA*.

Tatenda Chingono is a PhD student at the University of Johannesburg in the Faculty of Engineering and the Built Environment, Department of Quality and Operations Management. He has conducted research in logistics, supply chain management, life cycle assessments and sustainability. He has a Master's in Operations Management from the University of Johannesburg. He is also a Contract Lecturer for Logistics, in the Department of Transport and Supply Chain Management, College of Business and Economics Studies.

Professor Martin Christopher is Emeritus Professor of Marketing and Logistics at Cranfield School of Management. His work in the field of logistics and supply chain management has gained international recognition. He has published widely and his recent books include *Logistics and Supply Chain Management* and *Marketing Logistics*. Martin Christopher co-founded the *International Journal of Logistics Management* and was its joint editor for 18 years. He is a regular contributor to conferences and workshops around the world. Martin Christopher is an Emeritus Fellow of the Chartered Institute of Logistics and Transport. He is also a Fellow of the Chartered Institute of Purchasing and Supply and a Fellow of the Chartered Institute of Marketing. In 1988 he was awarded the Sir Robert Lawrence Gold Medal for his contribution to logistics education, in 1997 he was given the USA Council of Logistics Management's Foundation Award and in 2005 he received the Distinguished Service Award from the USA Council of Supply Chain Management Professionals. In 2007 he was appointed a Foundation Professor of the UK Chartered Institute of Purchasing and Supply, and in 2008 he was awarded the Swinbank Award for Lifetime Achievement by the same Institute.

Gerard de Villiers is a Professional Transportation Engineer who specializes in transport economics, freight logistics, humanitarian logistics and supply chain management. He was appointed Global Supply Chain Director of World Vision International in April 2007 where he established a global office for supply chain management. His position changed to Chief Logistics Officer and after four years he joined Arup as Logistics Specialist in their Johannesburg offices in May 2011. Gerard has various local and international postgraduate qualifications and teaches part-time at the University of Pretoria in supply chain management as well as the University of Lugano in Switzerland in humanitarian logistics. He was Honorary Professor in the Department of Business Management, Faculty of Economic and Management Sciences at the University of Pretoria from 2009 to 2011.

Laura Eldon is an Advisor on applications of information communications technologies (ICT) in Oxfam's Humanitarian Response and Longer-Term Resilience Building programmes. She has worked on a number of initiatives including developing new and innovative methodologies around protection information gathering in Jordan and the Philippines, leading cross-departmental streams of work focusing on mobile data collection and geographic information systems (GIS), and project managing a collaboration with World Vision to pilot their Last Mile Mobile Solutions (LMMS) digital beneficiary management technology. She works across Oxfam's Global Humanitarian Team to drive forward the organization's ICT in humanitarian programmes strategy.

George Fenton is a Freelance Humanitarian Operations Consultant and also Executive Director and co-founder of the Humanitarian Logistics Association. He has been the catalyst for several humanitarian innovations and partnerships, including digital cash transfers and market-based programming. His passion is to constantly seek new challenges and use his academic, commercial and aid sector networks, broad humanitarian operations experience and versatility to improve the delivery of global health and humanitarian assistance. Working at senior levels within a large international aid organization over the past decade, George led and managed operations, information management and supply chain teams to ensure successful multi-million dollar responses to major global humanitarian crises. He co-founded the global Fleet Forum, an initiative designed to promote humanitarian transport knowledge sharing, road safety and capacity development, and played a leading and influential role in developing the concept of the Humanitarian Response Network for disaster coordination. George also co-founded the East Africa Inter-Agency Working Group for disaster preparedness, which links with the United Nations Office for the Coordination of Humanitarian Affairs (UN-OCHA) contingency planning initiatives.

Captain Shaun Fogarty MNZM is the Director of Strategic Engagement for the New Zealand Defence Force. He has 30 years' experience as a military logistics professional specializing in humanitarian logistics. He has seen operational service in the Former Yugoslavia, East Timor, Afghanistan and the Middle East. In 2013 he obtained his Master of Logistics and Supply Chain Management (distinction) at Massey University. He also has a Master of Management (Defence Studies) from Canberra University. His major research interests are in disaster response and humanitarian logistics.

Walter Glass is the Deputy Director of Logistics and Supply Chain Management at Massey University. Walter has been involved in postgraduate supervision for over 25 years. He is a Fellow of the Chartered Institute of Logistics and Transport and a member of the CILT International Education Standards Committee. Walter Glass recently received the CILT President's Appreciation Award for Excellence for his leadership during the international response to the Vanuatu Cyclone. Walter regularly publishes academic journals, government technical papers and articles in applied professional magazines, including *China Quality*. His current interests are blockchains and humanitarian supply chain collaboration.

Dr Ira Haavisto is the Director of the Humanitarian Logistics and Supply Chain Research Institute (HUMLOG Institute) at the Hanken School of Economics. Her main research interests are in performance management in the supply chain, access and last mile problems in humanitarian supply chains and she has published articles, book chapters and conference papers in these areas. She has several years of experience in conducting academic research at Hanken School of Economics at the Department of Supply Chain Management and Social Responsibility and as part of the Humanitarian Logistics Research Institute.

Dr Hanna Harilainen is a Senior Lecturer at the Haaga-Helia School for Applied Sciences in Finland, where she teaches in entrepreneurship, business planning, sourcing, supply chain management, sustainable supply chain management, logistics, marketing and negotiations. Her research interests are in sustainable supply chains and supply chain risk. Her doctoral thesis, 'Managing supplier sustainability risk', won an award in 2014 from the Fund for Promoting Finnish International Trade.

Dr Irina Harris is a Lecturer in Logistics and Operations Modelling at Cardiff Business School, Cardiff University. Irina's background is in computer science and, as part of the Green Logistics Project, her PhD focused on multi-objective optimization for strategic and tactical network design from economic and environmental perspectives. She has extensive knowledge of logistics modelling, transportation and optimization through work with industry and other academic partners. Irina's research interests range from logistics networks and operations modelling to collaborative partnerships and sustainable supply chains, with a focus on data analysis and evaluating trade-offs related to different objectives. Her recent work includes the application of information systems and technology to the business and logistics environments.

Professor Graham Heaslip is Professor of Logistics and Head of the School of Business at Galway-Mayo Institute of Technology (GMIT),

Ireland. Prior to joining GMIT Graham was Associate Professor of Logistics at UNSW, Australia. Graham completed his PhD studies in the area of civil military cooperation/coordination at the Logistics Institute, University of Hull, for which he was awarded the James Cooper Memorial Cup for best PhD in logistics and supply chain management by the Chartered Institute of Logistics and Transport. Prior to entering academia Graham spent 14 years working in the Irish Defence Force. Graham's research interests are broadly in the intersections between global logistics/supply chain management, humanitarian logistics and organizational management development.

Dr Hlekiwe Kachali is a Practitioner and Researcher in the system dynamics of disaster resilience and recovery and humanitarian logistics. Her interests in system dynamics, disaster recovery and resilience led to her undertaking doctoral work on the key elements of disaster recovery and resilience after the Christchurch earthquakes. Hlekiwe now works in the areas of emergency management, disaster risk reduction, humanitarian logistics, emergency telecommunications, global flows, conflict dynamics, mine action and information management in emergencies. She has a Bachelor of Engineering (BEng) in Computer Engineering from Finland and a Master of Engineering (MEng) in Systems Engineering from Australia, and has over 15 years' experience in the telecommunications industry.

Jihee Kim is a PhD student in logistics and operations management at Cardiff Business School, Cardiff University. Her research is being funded by the Economic and Social Research Council (ESRC). She was awarded an MA in Management from Durham University in 2010. Prior to this she had worked in several organizations including the Korean National Assembly, Samsung, LG and Korean Air. Her research interests involve cooperation, coordination, collaboration, supply chain integration and partnerships in humanitarian and disaster relief supply chain management (SCM). In particular, she seeks to understand the suitability of the key assumptions of business SCM for the analysis of humanitarian SCM.

Anna Kondakhchyan is an Advisor on applications of information and communications technologies in Oxfam's Humanitarian Response And Longer-Term Resilience Building programmes. Anna's particular focus is on use of technologies in cash transfer programming, exploring effective programme design and set-up to enable greater impact, quality and transparency. Anna previously led a global roll-out of a supply chain automation and process standardization initiative at Oxfam.

Professor Gyöngyi Kovács is the Erkko Professor in Humanitarian Logistics at the Hanken School of Economics, and is the Subject Head of Supply Chain Management and Social Responsibility. The former Director of the

Humanitarian Logistics and Supply Chain Research Institute (HUMLOG Institute) and a Founding Editor of the *Journal of Humanitarian Logistics and Supply Chain Management*, she has published widely in humanitarian logistics and sustainable supply chain management.

Dr Cécile L'Hermitte is a Lecturer in Supply Chain Management at the University of Waikato. After having worked for 10 years in the banking industry as a specialist in international business, both in France and in Germany, she completed an MBA in Maritime and Logistics Management and undertook research work in humanitarian logistics. She completed her doctoral research project at the Australian Maritime College/University of Tasmania where she explored the concept of organizational capacity building and the critical role played by an organization's systems, structure and culture in supporting agility in humanitarian logistics operations.

Professor Paul D Larson is the CN Professor of SCM at the University of Manitoba. Currently, Paul is also Distinguished Senior Fellow/Professor in Supply Chain Management and Social Responsibility at Hanken University. From 2005 to 2011, he served as Head of the SCM Department and Director of the Transport Institute at the University of Manitoba. The Institute for Supply Management funded his doctoral dissertation, which won the 1991 Academy of Marketing Science/Alpha Kappa Psi award. From 1979 to 1981 Paul worked with the Ministry of Cooperatives in Fiji, as a United States Peace Corps Volunteer. Dr Larson serves on the Editorial Review Boards of the *Journal of Business Logistics, Journal of Supply Chain Management, International Journal of Physical Distribution & Logistics Management*, and the *Journal of Humanitarian Logistics and Supply Chain Management*. On 18 February 2017, for the second time, he stood at Uhuru peak, Tanzania, the 'roof of Africa', as a climber with the Larson-Scott Kilimanjaro expedition.

Magnus Larsson is a Doctoral Candidate at the Hanken School of Economics in Helsinki. He is passionate about sustainability in humanitarian supply chains and his research focus currently is on transport emissions in humanitarian response. He has several years of experience working with humanitarian logistics in the field.

Rebecca Lewin MSci is Director of Logistics and Procurement at Plan International, covering a portfolio of more than 50 countries. Her responsibilities span a global supply chain, including more than 3,000 vehicles, over 600 physical premises and spend of more than €400 million a year. Rebecca's role takes her from Latin America, to West Africa, to Asia and the Pacific and varies from supporting the operations of long-term development projects to rapid onset humanitarian crises. Prior to taking this position, Rebecca has worked in the INGO sector for over a decade after graduating from University College London with a Masters in Astrophysics. Her sector roles have included positions at Merlin, Oxfam and with the Global Logistics Cluster at WFP. Rebecca is a sector specialist on cash and markets based programming and the links therein to humanitarian supply chains and, last year, was among a delegation representing logistics at the World Humanitarian Summit in Istanbul. Rebecca's publications include co-authoring the paper 'Delivering in a moving world' (2016), outlining a number of future humanitarian trends and their intrinsic interdependence to supply chain, and supply chain actors. Rebecca's other achievements include leading the innovative interagency partner capacity building project PARCEL (www.parcelproject.org) and the development of the resource page for cash and markets information (www.logcluster.org/cashandmarkets). Rebecca is a member of the Humanitarian Logistics Association, Women in Logistics UK and has recently been elected to be one of three international non-governmental organization (INGO) representatives on the Strategic Advisory Group of the Global Logistics Cluster.

Professor Charles Mbohwa is a Professor of Sustainability Engineering in the Faculty of Engineering and the Built Environment at the University of Johannesburg. He holds a Bachelor of Science in Mechanical Engineering Honours from the University of Zimbabwe, Master in Operations Management and Manufacturing Systems from the University of Nottingham and a PhD from Tokyo Metropolitan Institute of Technology in Japan. He was Vice-Dean of Postgraduate Studies Research and Innovation in the Faculty of Engineering and the Built Environment at the University of Johannesburg from 2014 to 2017. He has published more than 350 papers in peer-reviewed journals and conferences, 10 book chapters and three books.

Darren Moss joined ShelterBox in 2014 as Procurement Manager and became Operations Director in January 2016. Prior to ShelterBox he spent 30 years working for Texas Instruments in a wide variety of roles, including Supply Chain Process Re-Engineering Manager, Procurement and Logistics Management and as an Equipment Engineer. He also spent five years in the oil and gas industry working as a Consultant on projects including the implementation of the Bribery Act, supplier performance and through to full supply chain re-engineering projects.

Dr Stephen Pettit is a Reader in Logistics and Operations Management at Cardiff Business School. In 1993 he was awarded a PhD from the University of Wales and he has worked at Cardiff Business School since 2000. He has been involved in a range of transport related research projects and his most recent work has focused on humanitarian aid logistics and supply chain management. Stephen has written a large number of journal papers, conference papers and reports primarily on port development, port policy and the logistics of humanitarian aid delivery. An example of Stephen's published output, 'Critical success factors in the context of humanitarian aid supply chains' has been widely cited. His work has been extended through collaboration with Cranfield University in the Cardiff-Cranfield Humanitarian Logistics Initiative, a research group focused on operational and strategic aspects of humanitarian and emergency response.

Professor Karen Spens is the Rector of the Hanken School of Economics, as well as a Professor of Supply Chain Management. A Founding Editor of the *Journal of Humanitarian Logistics and Supply Chain Management*, she has published extensively in logistics and supply chain management, particularly in health care and humanitarian supply chains.

Isabell Storsjö is a Doctoral Candidate in the subject Supply Chain Management and Social Responsibility at Hanken School of Economics. She worked as researcher in the CAIUS project under the HUMLOG Institute. Isabell's research interests include supply chain strategy, service supply chains, public and private service networks, the justice system, interaction in networks, disaster preparedness, and procurement.

Professor Peter Tatham is the Professor of Humanitarian Logistics at Griffith Business School, Queensland, Australia. Prior to entering academia, he served for 34 years as a logistician in the (UK) Royal Navy, reaching the rank of Commodore (1*). In addition to investigating the challenges of achieving agile defence and business logistic systems, his main research field is that of humanitarian logistics and, in particular, the use of emerging technologies in the preparation and response to natural disasters and complex emergencies. He is a member of the editorial boards of the *Journal of Humanitarian Logistics and Supply Chain Management*, the *International Journal of Physical Distribution and Logistics Management*, and the *Journal of Defense Analytics and Logistics*.

Dr David Taylor worked for 15 years as Senior Research Fellow at the Lean Enterprise Research Centre, Cardiff Business School, where he carried out a wide range of projects in different industry sectors aimed at introducing lean methodologies for the improvement of supply chain activity. Since leaving Cardiff University in 2010 he has focused on the humanitarian sector and worked as a consultant with a number of organizations in Africa, India and Europe. He led the ShelterBox project as an Associate Consultant with LCP Consulting Ltd.

Dr Fuminori Toyasaki is a Member of the Faculty of the Decision Science area in the School of Administrative Studies, York University, Canada. In the humanitarian logistics area, he has researched the interaction between non-profit organizations' finance systems and their operations. His publications include articles in *Production and Operations Management, European Journal of Operational Research, International Journal of Production Economics, International Journal of Production Research, Annals of Operations Research, Transportation Research Part E, Journal of Natural Disaster Science* and *Journal of Managerial Psychology*.

Dr Alain Vaillancourt is a Lecturer in Operations and Supply Chain Management at Coventry University and is affiliated to the HUMLOG Institute. His research area specializes in humanitarian logistics and supply chains with publications on disaster policies, logistics competencies and a thesis on material consolidation. Dr Vaillancourt also has practical field experience in humanitarian logistics with non-governmental organizations and United Nations agencies both working as Consultant and as a Logistic Manager.

Professor Tina Wakolbinger is Professor of Supply Chain Services and Networks and Head of the Research Institute for Supply Chain Management at WU (Vienna University of Economics and Business). She conducts research in the area of sustainable and humanitarian supply chain management. In her research, she explores the impact of relationships, information and financial flows on supply chain operations. Her publications include articles in the *European Journal of Operational Research, International Journal of Production Economics, Annals of Operations Research, Naval Research Logistics* and *International Journal of Production Research*. She serves as senior editor of the Disaster Management Department of Production and Operations Management. She is a member of the Board of the EURO Working Group on Humanitarian Operations.

Dr Mark MJ Wilson specializes in supply chain management practice and research. With a PhD from Lincoln University, he has over 37 years' industry experience in integrated supply chain systems at operational and strategic levels. Mark is currently teaching supply chain management at degree and masters levels as well as supervising a number of PhDs. Publishing in international journals, such at the *International Journal of Operations and Production Management, Engineering Construction and Architecture Management* and international conferences, Mark's current research agenda focuses on: supply chain management theory, inter-organizational governance, complex networks and agribusiness supply chain systems as well as disaster response and humanitarian logistics.

Introduction

PETER TATHAM AND MARTIN CHRISTOPHER

As we began to prepare this introduction to the third edition of *Humanitarian Logistics*, almost inevitably the first question that came to mind was whether or not the title of the book remains valid. Is meeting the (supply chain) challenge of preparing for and responding to disasters still unfinished business, or have we moved to a situation where the focus is more on the last segment of the 80:20 rule? Unfortunately, we believe that, whilst there have been some clear advances, considerable – albeit in some cases different – challenges remain. However, we also get the sense that there have been some solid improvements, and that there are more on the way. Thus, our overall conclusion is that the whole area of humanitarian logistics (HL) theory and practice is moving firmly in the right direction, and the resultant aim of this edition of the book is to shine a light on some of the darker areas of the HL challenge that have yet to be subject to detailed consideration. In doing so, we hope to encourage further practitioner and academic research that will help those working in the field to deliver improved outcomes more swiftly and at less cost.

That said, the core problem of balancing supply with demand in as efficient and effective a way as possible remains the ultimate challenge. On the demand side the '6W' problem of 'who wants what, where, when and why?' reflects the reality of operations that frequently take place in a confused and swiftly changing environment. Indeed, the inevitable departure of a large swathe of the population away from a disaster area (combined, in some cases, with a movement into the affected area by those who anticipate the emergence of job opportunities) continues to make the estimation of demand size (and its sub-sets with differential needs relating to, for example, age and gender) a continuing challenge. Whilst in theory the huge rise in the availability of mobile phone systems and the internet will help mitigate or overcome this, sadly these systems cannot be relied on, as evidenced by the impact of cyclones in Vanuatu (March 2015) and Fiji (February 2016) which, in both cases, resulted in the destruction of the cell phone tower serving the affected area, making the needs assessment process far more challenging.

On the supply side, the almost inevitable consequence of any emergency or disaster is the degradation of roads and bridges, with the associated impact on the resupply routes. However, even here, there are potential solutions on the horizon with the advent of the emerging generation of helium filled airships that can lift significant quantities of material from, for example, a United Nations Humanitarian Response Depot (UNHRD) and deliver these directly to the affected area – including, if necessary and appropriate, by landing on water and offloading onto a beach or dock. Indeed, arguably, the greater use of Cash Transfer Programmes (CTPs) represents another way of overcoming the supply challenge in that, by one means or another, traders will find a way to get their goods to the customers – especially those who have the means (through a CTP) to pay for them.

A further observation is that the raw number of natural disasters recorded by the Centre for Research on the Epidemiology of Disasters (CRED) continues to fall from the high point of 437[1] in 2005 to 301[2] in 2016, and this must give one some cause for optimism. However, almost inevitably, the impact of such events is disproportionately felt by those countries least able to manage them and this is reflected by the succinct observation of Matthew Kahn[3] that the per capita gross domestic product (GDP) is a key indicator of disaster casualty rates. Furthermore, the impact of complex emergencies such as those within the Middle East (and the associated refugee crises affecting much of Europe) is a stark reminder that there is a much broader challenge than simply that of overcoming the forces of nature that requires the support of the humanitarian logistician.

With this introduction in mind, this volume seeks to understand the nature of the challenges facing those who are involved in the management of the logistics of disaster relief, and to offer some potential solutions that can be developed in the near and longer term. Many of those contributing have spent considerable periods thinking about such issues, be this in a commercial, a humanitarian or a military context. We aim, therefore, to try to bring these perspectives together as a means of offering ways in which particular aspects of this complex and evolving problem might be tackled. In doing so, we have retained some 50 per cent of the chapters published in the second edition, but invited these authors to update their thoughts in line with developments over the last three years. At the same time, we have introduced a number of new chapters that are designed both to increase the level of input from the practitioner community and also to focus on a number of subjects that have received only limited consideration previously. Examples of the latter include the support for complex emergencies and for natural disasters in high-income countries. Sadly, this does not mean that the issues that no longer feature in the book have been solved – rather that their relative importance has, to our editorial eyes, diminished slightly, albeit we would wish to stress the 'relative' qualifier that has guided our thinking.

But why focus on logisticians? The answer is simple – be it in the context of a rapid or slow onset disaster or emergency – the imperative is to procure and move the required materiel water, food, shelter, clothing, medicines, etc, from point A to point B in the most efficient and effective way possible. But although simply stated, the reality is hugely complicated and, indeed, costly – not least because of the difficulty of forecasting when and where the next crisis will occur. It is unsurprising, therefore, that recent estimates would suggest that some 60–80 per cent of the expenditure of aid agencies is on logistics,[4] within which we include the procurement, transport into the affected country, warehousing, and internal and 'last mile' distribution processes. Given that the overall annual expenditure of humanitarian agencies is of the order of $20 billion, the resultant logistic spend of some $15 billion provides a huge potential area for improvement, and consequential benefit to those affected by such disasters/emergencies.

In light of these almost self-evident observations, it is really quite surprising that, until relatively recently, the challenges facing the humanitarian logistician have not attracted serious consideration by the academic community at large. Certainly a number of important contributions have been made, with one of the earliest by Douglas Long and Donald Wood[5] being published in 1995; however, it is clear that the South East Asia tsunami of 2004 really provided the catalyst for the current sustained level of interest. Not least, the publicity surrounding this catastrophic event underlined the importance of the logistic challenge as exemplified by the reported comment of a European ambassador who observed in the immediate aftermath of this disaster that: 'We don't need a donors' conference, we need a logistics conference'.[6]

Fortunately, however, the tide does seem to be turning, with a general recognition of the importance of research within the field as evidenced by the launch in 2011 of a dedicated academic outlet – the *Journal of Humanitarian Logistics and Supply Chain Management* – and the associated increase in literature focusing on the area. Thus, for example, a review indicated that 228 papers were published in the period 1980–2012,[7] of which over 100 appeared in the five years from 2008 to 2012. Separately, an informal bibliography maintained by one of this book's editors[8] now exceeds 80 pages of A4 paper. To this must of course be added the wealth of practitioner literature to be found within both the reports of aid agencies and in the 'lessons learned' – which, arguably, should be re-named 'lessons identified' – analysis that has followed each major event.

But, of course, the challenges of humanitarian logistics have a number of key aspects that clearly differentiate them from those of the commercial world. First and foremost amongst these is the massive uncertainty surrounding, in particular, rapid onset events. Thus, whilst we know that such events will unquestionably occur, their timing and location is hugely difficult to predict with any significant degree of certainty. Second, the humanitarian field faces the challenge of a decoupling of financial and material flows. As a result, aid agencies are placed in the difficult position of having to second-guess the needs of the beneficiaries who are frequently solely focused on the business of staying alive – and yet, at the same time, the agencies must satisfy the increasingly demanding governance requirements of the donor community. Therefore, whilst many management gurus would argue strongly that the voice of the customer should always be paramount in an organization's thinking, the absence of clarity over the identity of the humanitarian logistician's customer remains unhelpful and can lead to perverse behaviour. Third, almost by definition the infrastructure surrounding the disaster will be devastated to a greater or lesser extent. Thus, generic prescriptions such as the substitution of information for inventory face a particular challenge in this environment. Finally, of course, the price of failure in terms of unnecessary loss of life or prolonged hardship is significantly greater than that of reduced profits.

However, in the seven years since the first edition of this book was published there have been a number of important advances in thinking. First, the recognition that, from a logistic perspective, rapid onset disasters go though a number of phases, each of which potentially requires a different logistic response. Thus in the initial (emergency) period of one to two weeks there will only be limited availability of demand information from the affected area and, as a result, a 'push' approach may be entirely appropriate. This also reflects the relatively limited range of material, equipment, etc that is needed to provide the necessary life-saving response. For example, the Oxfam equipment catalogue is of the order of 300 stock keeping units (SKUs), which is two orders of magnitude less than the equivalent for a large supermarket chain that may run to 30–40,000 SKUs.[9] In the light of the potential mass movements away from an affected area, the issue in this phase is, therefore, more about how many people/family units are to be found in a particular geographic location and the associated 'last mile' delivery challenge in the face of a severely disrupted logistics and communications infrastructure.

After the first two weeks, it is likely that needs assessments will have been completed and that a clearer picture of the requirements is available – leading to the ability to employ a significantly more targeted 'pull' approach. At this point, in order to reduce the potential of inefficient overlaps and/or life threatening gaps in the response, the benefits of improved inter-agency coordination are becoming clearer. However, whilst the World Food Programme (WFP) logistics cluster is making an increasingly effective impact on driving coordination across the United Nations (UN) family and more broadly, there remains a strong case for greater effort in this regard. In a commercial context major players have recognized the benefits of the development of a multi-source overview of their supply network, which enables them to intervene proactively in order to meet the emerging demand picture. It is strongly argued, therefore, that the development of such a 'humanitarian common logistic operations picture' (H-CLOP) is increasingly becoming a necessary next step on the path from operational humanitarian logistics to strategic supply network management.

The development of the H-CLOP concept does, however, imply the need for a far greater level of pan-agency process integration than is currently the case. Historically, there has been a marked reluctance to share data with other agencies for a number of reasons – not least because, in part, they can be perceived as competitors for donor funding. This is slowly changing, especially across the larger agencies, as demonstrated by the use of the same software supply chain management systems by multiple organizations. But, in doing so, it raises the larger question of whether a system of certification of agencies (and, by implication, their logistics teams) should be introduced – not least because, at the operational level, such a certification process could incorporate more standardized policy/process/procedural requirements that would, in turn, lead to greater efficiency and/or effectiveness in the response process.

By extension, the development of such common processes would become the basis on which education and professional curricula could be developed and which would, in turn, not only enhance the professional status of the humanitarian logistician, but also help to reduce the burden of training for new staff as well as for implementing partners within a given country or region. Importantly, such an approach already exists in the related context of the international search and rescue community, and is being developed by the UN's health cluster that is overseen by the World Health Organization. In parallel, the Humanitarian Logistics Association (HLA) is actively developing a body of knowledge that is designed to assist those carrying out the key logistic functions (especially those who are new to this role) whilst at the same time assisting in the development of a commonality of practice.

With these opening remarks in mind, we propose to begin by exploring the challenge of how to manage supply networks when future requirements are manifestly uncertain – which is, of course, one of the most challenging aspects of humanitarian relief programmes.

Managing supply networks under conditions of uncertainty

One of the distinguishing features of modern supply networks – both in the world of business as well as in the humanitarian arena – is that they are characterized by uncertainty and, hence, unpredictability. For some time now, commercial supply network managers have been accustomed to the idea that they can no longer rely on the traditional rules and techniques that have allowed them to plan ahead with a degree of confidence.

Thus, although conventional supply network management typically assumes a degree of stability with planning horizons that extend some months into the future, the last few decades have seen a considerable increase in turbulence in the wider business environment. Demand can no longer be easily forecast and supply conditions have become more volatile in almost every industry. As a result of this uncertainty new business models have emerged to enable organizations to make the transition from the classic 'forecast driven' approach to a much more 'event' or 'demand' driven capability.

Organizations doing business in turbulent markets have learned that one of the key elements to ensure survival is 'agility'. This can be defined as the ability to respond rapidly to unexpected changes in demand or supply conditions – and, indeed, to changes in the wider business environment.

It can thus be argued that the logistic capabilities required by aid agencies and others to deal successfully with large scale, sudden onset disasters are not dissimilar to those required in commercial organizations faced with rapidly changing conditions. There is, therefore, an excellent opportunity to learn from the experiences of companies who have become adept at responding rapidly to unpredictable events.

Because all organizations are part of a wider network of suppliers, intermediaries and customers, it is important to recognize that agility is not just about achieving internal responsiveness, but rather about how the end-to-end supply network can become more agile. Thus, the concept of agility has significant implications for how organizations within the supply/demand network relate to each other, and how they can best work together to maximize the efficiency and effectiveness of the network as a whole. It has been suggested[10] that there are a number of key prerequisites to the design and management of such agile supply networks. Specifically, the concept of agility implies that they are demand or event driven, they are network based, they are process oriented and they are virtually integrated through shared information.

Demand and event driven

Traditional management practice has been based upon the principle of planning ahead, usually based upon a forecast. In conditions of turbulence and unpredictability, however, the challenge is to create a capability to facilitate a rapid response to events as they happen. A fundamental enabler of demand/event driven responsiveness is time compression. Much of the time that is consumed in supply networks could be termed 'non-value adding time'. In other words it is time when nothing is happening to achieve the goal of the 'right product in the right place at the right time'. Sometimes this non-value adding time is incurred because of cumbersome planning and decision-making processes. At other times it may arise because of queues at bottlenecks, or because of inadequate coordination across the different stages in the supply network. As a result, many commercial organizations have transformed their responsiveness by a strong focus on what has been called 'business process re-engineering'[11] whereby every underpinning process in the supply network is put under the spotlight with the intention of squeezing out as much non-value adding time as possible.

Demand and event driven supply networks are also often characterized by their strategic use of inventory and capacity. Conventional wisdom is often driven by the desire to follow 'lean' principles of reducing inventory and eliminating idle capacity. Agile supply networks, on the other hand, recognize that in conditions of uncertainty – both on the demand side and the supply side – a certain level of 'slack' is essential. Ideally, such strategic inventory is held as far upstream as possible and in a generic form to enable 'risk pooling' – in other words, rather than disperse the inventory in its final form and run the risk of having the wrong product in the wrong place, it is held centrally, shipped and configured on a just-in-time (JIT) basis. Clearly this approach will incur a cost penalty compared to the 'leaner' alternative, but that is the price of responsiveness.

Network based

One way that organizations can enhance their agility is by making use of the capacity, capabilities and resources of other entities within the network. It could be financially crippling for one organization to have to carry enough capacity and inventory to, for example, cope with any demand eventuality. However, if close working relationships can be established with other organizations who can provide access to their own resources then a real opportunity exists for creating high levels of flexibility in the supply network.

A good example of how network partners can enable a more agile capability in the commercial world is provided by the Spanish clothing manufacturer and retailer Zara. Because Zara competes in a market characterized by unpredictability and short product life cycles, the need for agility is high. One way that Zara achieves this agility is by making use of a network of small, independent workshops that do the final sewing of many of their products. Zara has established strong working relationships with these suppliers and regards them as part of their 'extended enterprise'. These external workshops reserve capacity for Zara even though they will not know the precise requirements until a few days before the garment is to be manufactured.

In other cases, organizations can benefit by sharing resources across a network even with competitors. Thus, for example, petrol companies such as Shell, BP and Total will often share refinery capacity, whilst in the airline industry different airlines will pool their inventory of service parts and position these strategically around the world. In a similar way, the armed forces of the NATO countries use a common parts identification system that facilitates an equivalent approach.

Indeed, in the world of humanitarian logistics, such a resource sharing model has recently been created to enable access to a common inventory, with the UNHRD network which is coordinated by the WFP in Italy being a case in point. In a similar way, the water and sanitation (WATSAN) cluster and associated non-governmental organizations (NGOs) that operate in this space have recently agreed to both standardize and pool their equipment resources.

Process oriented

One feature of organizations that can respond rapidly to unpredictable events is that they have achieved a high level of cross-functional working. Most conventional businesses tend to be organized around functions, eg the production function, the distribution function, etc. This type of organizational structure may be administratively convenient, but it often leads to an inwardly focused 'silo' mentality. It also means that there are usually multiple 'hands-offs' from one department to another. The end result is that the decision-making process is lengthy, and that lead times are extended.

The alternative is to break down the silos by adopting a cross-functional team-based approach that reflects the key business processes – particularly the supply network processes. Processes are the horizontal, market-facing sequences of activities that create value for customers. In the context of supply networks they include such key underpinning processes as order-to-delivery, capacity and demand management, and supplier management. For each of these processes a 'process owner' should be appointed whose task is to bring together a cross-functional team and to seek to create a seamless and more rapid achievement of the process goals. Thus, for example, the order-to-delivery process will consider how a customer's requirement can be met in shorter time frames with more reliability by 'project managing' the order from the moment it is captured until it is delivered. Usually when processes are managed in this way, opportunities for process simplification and improvement quickly become apparent.

Furthermore, if the supply network is to work effectively across multiple independent entities, it is critical that processes are aligned across organizational boundaries. A good example of such process alignment is provided by the concept of vendor-managed inventory (VMI). Under a VMI arrangement, the sales outlet (say a supermarket) does not formally place an order on the supplier; rather they provide the supplier with regularly updated information (easily extracted from the point of sale systems) on the rate at which the customer's inventory of the product in question is being depleted. The supplier then automatically replenishes the inventory. It is akin to a closed-loop supply network process.

Virtually integrated

By definition, for globally networked supply networks to achieve high levels of agility there must be a corresponding level of *connectivity*. Historically, such connectivity may have been achieved through ownership and control – a state often described as 'vertical' integration. Today, the likelihood is that the supply network will be fragmented and dispersed with each entity independent from the other. However, the need for integration is still as vital as ever, but now the essential integration is not achieved through ownership and control but rather through shared information and collaborative working. This type of connectivity is often called 'virtual integration'.

The underpinning idea of virtual integration is that an agile capability can be enabled through enhanced visibility. Ideally all parties in the network should share information in as close to real time as possible. This information will include the actual requirement from the field (demand), current inventory dispositions, the supply schedule and event management alerts.

Many traditional supply networks have poor upstream and downstream visibility with little shared information. Hence they are prone to mismatches of supply and demand at every interface – a situation made worse by the so-called 'bullwhip' effect which amplifies disturbances in the demand signal as orders are passed up the supply network. Bullwhips can be dramatically reduced or even eliminated if the different echelons in the supply network can be linked through shared information.

The barrier to improved visibility is, however, no longer technological. The tools exist to enable the highest levels of connectivity in even the most fragmented global network. The real challenge is the reluctance that still exists within some organizations to share information across boundaries – be these internal or external. The most agile supply networks are typified by a mindset of collaborative working with other partners in the network based upon a spirit of trust and shared goals.

Lessons from best practice

It may sometimes seem banal or inappropriate to ask the question 'what can humanitarian logistics learn from best practice in the commercial sector?' Whilst there can be no question that the challenge of saving lives is significantly more important than improving on-the-shelf availability of consumer products in a retail outlet, we would argue that there are lessons that can be learned and through which humanitarian logistics practice can be improved.

We have suggested that the key connection between the worlds of commerce and humanitarian logistics is that of uncertainty, and we have highlighted how, to a certain extent, such uncertainty can be conquered through agility. But one of the biggest remaining barriers to supply network agility is complexity. In a global supply network this complexity comes in many forms, but one of its most potent manifestations is in the multitude of nodes and links that constitute the network.

As Figure 0.1 suggests, what are often referred to as 'supply chains' are not really chains; rather they are networks or webs of interconnected and

Figure 0.1   There are two generic categories of risk

• Supply chains comprise nodes and links

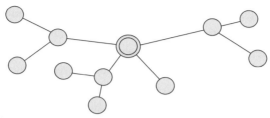

• Nodes – organizational risk
• Links – connectivity risk

interdependent entities. The resulting complexity can be considerable, and unless a means is found of managing across these nodes and links the system will be prone to disturbance and disruption. The challenge is to synchronize activities across the network so that a more agile response to changes in demand can be achieved. One idea that is attracting attention is the concept of supply network 'orchestration', and a good example of such orchestration is provided by the Hong Kong based company Li & Fung.

Li & Fung work on behalf of clients, mainly retailers, who are seeking to source products made to their own specification. Thus, for example, the global retailer Wal-Mart might decide that for the next winter season in the USA they want to introduce a range of low-priced ski wear. Acting on their behalf, Li & Fung will identify the appropriate designers, they will source the different fabrics, fasteners and zips, they will contract with appropriate manufacturers, and manage the whole supply network from raw materials through to Wal-Mart's stores. Li & Fung's capability as an orchestrator comes from their specialist knowledge of the industry, their longstanding relationships with suppliers, and their information systems that enable them to coordinate and synchronize the flows of material and product across a complex network.

Sometimes the supply network orchestrator is termed a lead logistics provider or a fourth party logistics (4PL) provider, and companies like DHL, UPS and Fedex are increasingly taking on this role on behalf of global corporations. For example, Cisco, one of the world's leading suppliers of communication network equipment, use UPS to coordinate a large part of their global network of contract manufacturers, distribution service providers and component suppliers to enable a high level of synchronization in what has become a very volatile marketplace. Again, this synchronization is greatly enabled by real time information that is shared across the partners in Cisco's global network.

One important feature of humanitarian emergencies is that every one is different. Hence it has to be recognized that the conventional 'one size fits all' approach to supply chain management clearly does not apply. Even within a specific emergency, the likelihood is that, as the focus moves from the immediate relief effort through to eventual reconstruction, the nature of the supply chain response will need to change. Thus in the early stage where time is critical the emphasis will be on agility but later when cost effectiveness is the objective then 'lean' becomes the watchword.

The implication is that humanitarian relief supply networks must be configured to meet the specific contingencies of the prevailing situation. Meeting this challenge requires a high degree of what has been termed 'structural flexibility'.[12] Structural flexibility refers to the capability of a supply network to adapt rapidly to changing conditions and environments. It is a step beyond the idea of agility previously referred to – rather it suggests an ability to reconfigure the entire end-to-end supply network as and when required. To facilitate this capability it is important that access to appropriate capacity and assets be easily obtained. In a commercial setting this access is often achieved through collaborative arrangements with other organizations – even, sometimes, with competitors. It is also increasingly commonplace to find assets being shared between supply chain partners rather than being reserved for exclusive use. Equally, it is often seen to be preferable to rent those assets rather than to own them.

However, structural flexibility is as much about 'mindset' as it is about tangible assets. It implies a willingness to work closely with other players in the supply network, to share information and to invest in systems with a high degree of interoperability. This is an idea that is slowly gaining ground in the commercial world as uncertainty and turbulence continue to be the hallmarks of the 21st century business environment. We would argue that a similar transformation in the way we think about supply networks could be of great benefit in the humanitarian logistics arena.

The way forward

From the above discussion, a key thread running through the development and operation of agile and flexible supply networks is a focus on synchronization enabled by shared information. Clearly there are other enablers of agility and flexibility, such as process alignment and collaboration across inter- and intra-organizational boundaries, but 360° visibility appears to be the critical element. Given that meeting the challenges facing the humanitarian logistic community would seem to demand the ultimate in agile response, it is heartening to recognize that, as reflected in the contributions contained within this book, this message is now gaining traction and that there is a growing commitment to breaking down the barriers to much closer collaboration across organizational boundaries.

In approaching the challenge of developing this volume on humanitarian logistics, as editors we were especially keen to present as diverse a set of perspectives as was practicable and, as indicated earlier, to focus on areas that had not previously been discussed in any level of detail. In particular, we believed that an improved understanding of the challenges and solutions could be gained by garnering contributions both from a geographically diverse community and, critically, from practitioners (as distinct from academics).

Thus, in line with our theme that there are potential lessons that humanitarian logisticians can develop from emerging business best practice, *Professor Paul Larson* from the University of Manitoba, Canada, explores these issues more fully in Chapter 1. In particular, Paul reflects on the potential for an approach that considers the application of commercial and academic models of process management and process improvement to the humanitarian logistics network. In doing so, Paul reviews a number of alternative methods and approaches that are used within both the for profit and non-profit sectors and their applicability to the humanitarian logistic challenge and, hence, ways in which the efficiency and/or effectiveness of the logistic preparation and response activities might be improved.

In Chapter 2 *Professor Tina Wakolbinger* (WU, Vienna University of Economics and Business, Austria) and *Dr Fuminori Toyasaki* (York University, Canada) reflect on a key challenge facing the humanitarian logistic system as a whole. This emanates from the basic structure of the system for funding the preparation and response mechanisms, and its significant complexity, which is driven, at least in part, by its multiple goals. Tina and Fuminori go on to analyse the potential impact of emerging trends, particularly in relation to fundraising, and also to suggest a number of key areas for further research.

As has been discussed at some length in the opening section of this chapter, a robust and comprehensive end-to-end communications system is one of the key ingredients underpinning the advances in commercial supply network management. Unsurprisingly, this is equally true of humanitarian logistics systems; however, persuading NGO management to invest in such a 'back office' (as distinct from 'front line') function has proved extremely difficult – notwithstanding the weight of evidence from other fields. Perhaps this reflects the very nature of NGOs where the absence of the profit motive removes a key indicator that will inform strategic decision making. Nevertheless, a number of major NGOs are making a concerted effort to improve the information systems supporting their supply networks, and the resultant experience of implementing the Last Mile Mobile Solutions (LMMS) platform are explored in Chapter 3 by two members of Oxfam GB's 'ICT in Programme' team, *Laura Eldon* and *Anna Kondakhchyan*.

Taking this the technology theme forward in Chapter 4, *Professor Peter Tatham* from the Griffith Business School in Australia, *Professor Graham Heaslip* from the Galway-Mayo Institute of Technology in the Republic of Ireland and *Professor Karen Spens* from the Hanken School of Economics in Finland offer a perspective on the potential impact of a number of novel concepts, and how these might be utilized to support the work of the humanitarian logistician. Specifically, they consider the potential benefits and challenges inherent in the use of three-dimensional (3D) printing, remotely piloted aircraft systems (otherwise known as 'drones'), hybrid cargo airships and cash transfer programmes.

Chapter 5, written by *Professor Graham Heaslip* from the Galway-Mayo Institute of Technology, represents the final scene-setting element of this book. In this chapter Graham reflects on the multiple ways in which the provision of services is being undertaken within the sector. In doing so, this chapter underlines the opportunities for improvements in efficiency and effectiveness that agencies can leverage by adopting a customer (as distinct from product) focused mindset, and the consequential use of an approach that embraces the concept of 'service dominant logic', which implies that value is defined by, and co-created with, the customer.

In line with the approach to this book that has been outlined earlier, Chapter 6, authored by *Jihee Kim, Dr Stephen Pettit, Professor Anthony Beresford and Dr Irina Harris* of Cardiff University, Wales, consider the challenges of integrating the supply chains across the multiple players who respond to a humanitarian crisis. Drawing on a series of interviews with senior humanitarian logisticians, the authors analyse how the integration challenge may be best mitigated.

Professor Charles Mbohwa and *Tatenda Chingono* of the University of Johannesburg, South Africa, and *Professor Paul Buatsi*, the former Dean of the Kwame Nkrumah University of Science and Technology in Ghana, have kindly contributed Chapter 7, which emphasizes the enormity of the challenges facing those working as humanitarian logisticians in Africa and, arguably, these are mirrored in many developing countries. Indeed, the absolute level of improvement generated by even limited advances in the practice of supply network management underscores the importance of working with local agencies and individuals to deliver transformational change in a way that is appropriate to the specific geographic and cultural context.

In Chapter 8 *Dr Hlekiwe Kachali* and *Isabell Storsjö* from the HUMLOG Institute at Hanken School of Economics, Finland reflect on the challenges of procurement in a developed country (Finland). They reflect on the ways in which the public procurement processes can be used to improve the civil preparation for disasters as a contribution to, and enhancement of, society's overall preparedness capabilities in respect of such events.

If one were to summarize many of the themes that this book has touched on at this stage, one might use the single word 'professionalization', and this is the subject of Chapter 9 contributed by *Professor Graham Heaslip* from the Galway-Mayo Institute of Technology, *Dr Alain Vaillancourt* from Coventry University, England, *Professor Peter Tatham* from Griffith Business School and *Professor Gyöngyi Kovács* from the HUMLOG Institute. These authors offer a detailed examination of the competencies that are needed by humanitarian logisticians at various stages in their career. This represents a significant step forward in the development of a model in which the ability for individuals to move more seamlessly between humanitarian organizations can be achieved.

Gerard de Villiers, formerly Chief Logistics Officer of World Vision International, introduces the concept of centre of gravity analysis in Chapter 10. Using a case study of Africa, he demonstrates how this technique can be used to provide an initial estimation of the most appropriate location for a major response hub. This technique can be easily carried out using simple spreadsheets and has clear potential to improve the efficiency and effectiveness of a humanitarian response.

The issue of responding to complex emergencies is the subject of Chapter 11 written by *Dr Ira Haavisto* and *Magnus Larsson* from the HUMLOG Institute, *Professor Peter Tatham* from Griffith Business School, *Dr Hanna-Riitta Harilainen* from the Haaga-Helia University of Applied Sciences, Finland, *Dr Cécile L'Hermitte* from the University of Waikato, Waikato Management School, New Zealand and *Dr Alain Vaillancourt* from Coventry University. These authors discuss the findings of their research in the field offices of the United Nations High Commissioner for Refugees (UNHCR) and draw attention to a number of key challenges faced when operating in direct support of refugees and internally displaced persons (IDPs) in a number of countries. The authors particularly emphasize the need for further research that focuses on such operational problems (rather than at the more strategic level, as is the norm in the academic literature to date).

Chapter 12, authored by *Dr David Taylor* and *Darren Moss* of the international disaster relief charity ShelterBox, provides a detailed discussion of the challenges facing this organization in responding to disasters and emergencies, and a clear example of the application of a well-known academic model – that of 'lean thinking' – to the humanitarian context. The authors discuss not only the specific issues faced by this organization, but also how these were overcome using the lean methodology.

Chapter 13 considers the particular challenge of responding to disasters not in a low or middle income country, but rather in New Zealand. Written by *Dr Mark Wilson* of Lincoln University, New Zealand, *Shaun Fogarty* of the New Zealand Defence Force, and *Walter Glass* and *Professor Paul Childerhouse* of Massey University, New Zealand, this chapter presents the results of a major review of the effectiveness and efficiency of the logistic function in the aftermath of the 2011 earthquakes in Christchurch, New Zealand. Through this, it offers a number of areas in which the authors believe that changes to the status quo would significantly improve the HL element of the preparation and response to such events.

Chapter 14 is the second of those penned by practitioners, in this case two highly experienced logisticians: *George Fenton* who is the Executive Director and a co-founder of the Humanitarian Logistics Association and *Rebecca Lewin* who is the Director of Logistics and Procurement at Plan International. These authors explore the changing nature of the role of the humanitarian logistician, and the new skills that will be required as they strive to deliver the right products and services at the right cost to the right place at the right time. By considering the global changes that are underway in respect of each of these 'four rights', the authors offer a vision of the future role of the humanitarian logistician and present an agenda for change within both the aid community at large, and for an aid organization's logistics department and its individual members.

The final chapter has been written by *Professor Gyöngyi Kovács* from the HUMLOG Institute. Universally acknowledged as one of the thought leaders in the humanitarian logistic field, she has risen to the editors' challenge of peering into the mythical crystal ball in order to discern and capture the emerging trends. In doing so, she has first reflected on the accuracy of the predictions that she made when penning a similar concluding chapter to the first and second edition, before reflecting on what other developments have taken place in the last three years. Finally, she offers a new set of thoughts over where the theory and practice of humanitarian logistics is heading. In doing so, not only has she touched on many of the key themes that have been considered in the chapters of this book, but she also highlights a number of emerging challenges.

Endpiece

Finally, we would like to reiterate the observation that we made at the end of the second edition in which we noted that, in inviting contributions to this book, we were keen to stress that authors were at liberty, if not positively encouraged, to offer unusual or controversial viewpoints. Inevitably, therefore, the book will continue to contain perspectives that can be contrasted or may even be thought to be in downright opposition. We have not sought to ameliorate these conflicting viewpoints – indeed, to do so would seem to imply a degree of arrogance as it would suggest that we are aware of the correct and proper approach to a particular challenge. Certainly this is not the case; rather, we hope that this volume will provide some tangible assistance to those tasked with prosecuting the enormously complex business of humanitarian logistics. However, what we would claim is that we have yet to meet a 'wicked problem' in this field that cannot be at least partially tamed through the application of prescriptions drawn from the commercial environment.

Notes

1 Guha-Sapir, G, Hoyois, P and Below, R (2016) Annual disaster statistical review 2015: The numbers and trends, *Centre for Research on the Epidemiology of Disasters* [Online] http://cred.be/sites/default/files/ADSR_2015.pdf

2 CRED (2016) 2016 preliminary data: Human impact of natural disasters [Online] http://cred.be/sites/default/files/CredCrunch45.pdf

3 Kahn, ME (2005) The death toll from natural disasters: The role of income, geography and institutions, *The Review of Economics and Statistics*, 87(2), pp 271–284.

4 Tatham, PH and Pettit, SJ (2010) Transforming humanitarian logistics: The journey to supply network management, *International Journal of Physical Distribution and Logistics Management*, 40(8/9), pp 609–622.

5 Long, DC and Wood, DF (1995) The logistics of famine relief, *Journal of Business Logistics*, 16(1), pp 213–229.

6   Shane, S and Bonner, R (2005) UN chief urges immediate aid for tsunami-torn countries, *New York Times*, 6 January 2005.

7   Leiras, A, de Brito, I, Peres, EQ, Bertazzo, TJ and Yoshizaki, HTY (2014) A literature review of humanitarian logistics research: Trends and challenges, *Journal of Humanitarian Logistics and Supply Chain Management*, 4(1), pp 95–130.

8   The informal bibliography is available from the website of the HUMLOG Institute at Hanken School of Economics, Helsinki, Finland. Available at: https://www.hanken.fi/en/about-hanken/organisation/departments-and-subjects/department-marketing/humlog/bibliography

9   Fernie, J and Sparks, L (2004) *Logistics and Retail Management*, Kogan Page, London.

10   Christopher, MG (2016) *Logistics and Supply Chain Management*, 5th edn, Pearson Education, London

11   Hammer, M and Champy, J (1993) *Re-Engineering the Corporation*, Nicholas Brenley Publishing, London.

12   Christopher, MG and Holweg, M (2011) 'Supply chain 2.0': Managing supply chains in the era of turbulence, *International Journal of Physical Distribution and Logistics Management*, 41(1), pp 63–82.

Process improvement

01

A matter of life or death for non-governmental organizations

PAUL D LARSON

...for how long will NGOs remain a legitimate humanitarian actor?

(Kent *et al*, 2013)

Abstract

As planet earth hosts ever more natural disasters, armed conflicts and mass migrations, the need for humanitarian relief seems to be without end. Humanitarian logistics continues to be 'big business', with overall budgets for non-governmental organizations (NGOs) running far into the billions of dollars. In the midst of such chaos, some analysts are questioning the relevance, and even the survivability, of NGOs. This chapter focuses on the operational issue of process improvement, with special reference to the possible role of standards. However, the pressure on NGOs is not only about 'doing things right' in the operational sense, ie the question of 'how' are things being done? The pressure also includes the question of 'why' are things being done? This question is beyond process improvement and any possible role of standards. This is about missions and strategic directions, about 'doing (the) right things'. An NGO's answers to such questions may be the difference between (organizational) life and death.

Introduction

Disaster brings tremendous suffering and loss of life. In 2015 there were 376 natural disasters that killed nearly 23,000 people worldwide, affected more than 110 million others, and caused US $70.3 billion of economic damages (Guha-Sapir *et al*, 2016). That same year, more than 1 million migrants and refugees entered Europe, over two-thirds of them fleeing conflicts in Syria, Afghanistan and Iraq. After a disaster, or during a war, humanitarian agencies respond, racing against the clock to save lives and ease suffering. Service quality, including timely delivery, means the difference between life and death.

The United Nations Office for the Coordination of Humanitarian Affairs (OCHA) estimated that humanitarian agencies would require $22.2 billion to meet the needs of 92.8 million people in 33 countries – from Afghanistan to Zimbabwe – during 2017. This is a dramatic increase from the $2.7 billion called for in the inaugural inter-agency humanitarian appeal launched in 1992. The last quarter century has seen a tremendous surge in the frequency and magnitude of humanitarian disasters (United Nations Office for the Coordination of Humanitarian Affairs, 2016).

Official development assistance (ODA), ie development aid from the 29 Organisation for Economic Co-operation and Development (OECD) Development Assistance Committee (DAC) member countries, rose to a new high of US $142.6 billion in 2016. The amount includes aid spent on refugees in donor countries. It also reflects an increase of 8.9 per cent compared to 2015, adjusting for exchange rates and inflation. The United States alone contributed US $33.6 billion. Measured in real terms (ie correcting for inflation and currency fluctuations), ODA has doubled since 2000 (OECD, 2017).

As shown above, providing disaster relief and development aid services is 'big business'. The quality of these services is in the eyes of the beholders or stakeholders, including beneficiaries, donors, relief and aid workers, implementing partners, host governments, etc. This chapter updates an earlier review of selected humanitarian quality and accountability concepts (Larson, 2014), and covers recent developments among the NGOs. There continues to be a variety of approaches to quality assessment (and process improvement) being used or recommended for use in the humanitarian community, many involving standards. Since 2014 there have been important developments in the area of humanitarian service standards – along with continuing questions regarding the need (Purvis, 2015). Meanwhile, the legitimacy of large, international NGOs is being questioned by multiple stakeholders (Doane, 2016; Kent *et al*, 2013).

Humanitarian logistics

A variety of process management and quality improvement tools are used in the commercial sector (Larson and Kerr, 2006). While business logisticians work with established actors and predictable supply and demand, humanitarians deal with unknown or ever-changing actors and unpredictable supply and demand (Kovács and Spens, 2007). Unlike businesses, aid agencies often receive unsolicited and unwanted supplies as donations, eg high-heeled shoes in the desert. These mistakes increase logistics costs and compromise service quality, such as timely delivery of service. This is an especially demanding environment for process management.

Compared to business logisticians, humanitarians face greater challenges in working with a diverse group of stakeholders, including beneficiaries, donors, implementing partners, host governments, militaries, suppliers, etc. Further, the coordination of many different aid agencies, suppliers, and local and regional actors, all with their own operating procedures and unique missions and cultures, can be difficult. There is considerable duplication of effort and little standardization of procedures in the humanitarian sector.

While 'time is money' to the business logistician, time is life (or death) to the humanitarian. Humanitarians seek social impact rather than profit, though they must be mindful of donor desires and budget limits. Humanitarian agencies serve beneficiaries in need and rely on donors as a source of funds. In contrast, businesses both serve and are funded by paying customers. Humanitarian supply chains must be flexible and responsive to unpredictable events, as well as efficient and able to maximize the reach of scarce resources. More effective delivery can save the day; greater efficiency means serving more people in need. The most pressing challenge may be to balance the seemingly conflicting objectives of service quality, flexibility and efficiency (Larson, 2014). This is process management.

Humanitarian NGOs perform two broad types of activities: relief and development. While *relief* focuses on short-term provision of goods and services vital to the survival of victims after a disaster, *development* offers long-term aid, working towards community self-sufficiency and sustainability (Beamon and Balcik, 2008). The United Nations Development Programme (UNDP) (2004) notes important interplay between development aid and disaster relief. Disasters can compromise or even nullify years of development work. In turn, aid efforts often have considerable impact – both positive and negative – on the likelihood and severity of future disasters.

Table 1.1 Development aid vs. disaster relief

	Humanitarian Logistics Context	
Aspect	**Development Aid**	**Disaster Relief**
Uncertainty	Low	High
Time Frame	Long	Short
Approach to Risk	Proactive	Reactive
Objectives	Improve lives; reduce poverty	Save lives; ease suffering
Funding Model	Empowerment	Charity
Supply Chains	Lean	Agile

Table 1.1 contrasts development aid and disaster relief across several aspects of humanitarian logistics. Aid workers operate in environments of relatively low uncertainty, over a long time frame. Broadly, prominent among their objectives are those of improving lives and reducing poverty. The relative stability enables such supply chains to adopt a proactive stance to risk and a lean approach to logistics. On the other hand, relief workers face high uncertainty within a rather short time frame. Risk management tends to be reactive, and supply chain agility is critical in attempting to save lives and ease suffering day by day.

Process management

Humanitarian NGOs face unique challenges in achieving process excellence. Their work is complex, unpredictable and intensely people-oriented. Much of the decision making favours local autonomy over centralization. Further, there is no profit motive; workers are dedicated to helping people, not making money. These factors foster bureaucracies with multiple hand-offs, reviews and approvals, yielding long lead times, poor quality and high costs (Parris, 2013).

Blecken (2010) reports a lack of process modelling and management, along with inadequate measurement of supply chain performance among humanitarian organizations. Forty-eight per cent of his survey respondents had no written documentation of supply chain processes, whilst another 32 per cent had partial documentation. For logistics improvement, he recommends a variant of the supply chain operations reference (SCOR) model (APICS, 2017).

Schulz and Heigh (2009) develop a *balanced scorecard* for the International Federation of Red Cross and Red Crescent Societies (IFRC). It consists of four perspectives: (1) customer service; (2) financial control; (3) process adherence; and (4) innovation and learning. The scorecard contains standard measures, includes staff development, and should be attractive to donors. However, it appears to exclude direct contact with beneficiaries.

SGS, a Swiss company, offers an NGO *benchmarking* service, including neutral, third-party certification audits. Promoted as an impartial assessment of an NGO's level of compliance with international best practices, it assesses performance against 101 indicators, selected from existing codes and international standards. Indicators are organized into four categories: best practice dimensions (eg integrity management, human resources, fundraising, operations); contributors' expectations; management components; and continuous improvement (SGS, 2017).

World Vision International has used a *lean six sigma* approach for process improvement in East Africa, as a means of getting better outcomes with existing funds, staff and other resources (Parris, 2013). The lean approach is about eliminating waste, providing value and letting downstream needs 'pull' supplies towards beneficiaries. Six sigma utilizes problem-solving tools to identify and eliminate unnecessary variation. Both techniques document, standardize and measure performance for the purpose of continuous improvement.

The need for standards

According to John Telford, 'the most deadly killer in any humanitarian emergency is not dehydration, measles, malnutrition or the weather. It is bad management' (Hulm, 1994). Although standards alone cannot cure bad management, there are at least three reasons humanitarian NGOs may find them useful: high staff turnover, donor reporting requirements and the critical nature of service to beneficiaries.

The sector faces high staff turnover (Loquercio *et al*, 2006; Thomas and Kopczak, 2005), which reduces the effectiveness of programmes and leads to the loss of lessons learned after any given project or disaster. Enabling new staff to become rapidly operational can lessen the consequences of turnover. Standardized tools and policies allow people to quickly get up to speed or switch from one project to another. Standardized orientation and training provide staff with the information, tools and contacts to help them contribute to the mission from day one. An investment in standardized training and certification could build a pool of logistics personnel with common skills and vocabulary, promoting professionalism and collaboration.

According to Hofmann (2011), interest in process certification is likely to remain high given the pressures on aid organizations to demonstrate value for money. Donors want to know how their money is being spent; that NGOs are committed to accountability, along with efficient, effective humanitarian action (Anonymous, 2007). In Canada, the Humanitarian Coalition was formed in 2005. Today, its members are seven of the largest Canadian NGOs. Among its goals is providing 'leadership in accountability to stakeholders': the Canadian public, donors, peers and beneficiaries. Coalition members have a history of involvement in developing and signing on to international codes of conduct and standards (humanitariancoalition.ca).

Standards can help establish accountability. While accountability to donors is very important, it should not supersede accountability to beneficiaries, ie people affected by disasters (Oxfam, 2006). Evaluations of the response to the 1994 Rwanda genocide and the 2004 Indian Ocean tsunami highlighted the variability of humanitarian response quality (Cosgrave, 2013), and led to a call for accreditation/certification 'to distinguish agencies that work to a professional standard in a particular sector' (Telford *et al*, 2006: 23).

Verboom (2002a) offers some more reasons the sector needs quality standards. There has been a tremendous proliferation of NGOs and humanitarian aid organizations in recent years. Standards can help separate the good ones from the others. Related to this is an infiltration of fake 'humanitarian' organizations with hidden political, religious or commercial agendas. The sector is also under increasing scrutiny from donors, host governments and other stakeholders. There is an ongoing call for greater professionalism. These arguments overlap with practical drivers of self-regulation (Obrecht, 2012), especially the matter of stakeholder trust as well as concerns about possible restrictive regulations from host governments.

Tamminga (2013) asks: 'How can we assure affected communities and other stakeholders that humanitarian organizations can be trusted to reliably apply humanitarian principles, quality standards and good practices?' Should organizations obtain certification to show they meet minimum requirements of capacity and commitment to humanitarian principles to work in a crisis situation? Similar questions were asked by the Steering Committee for Humanitarian Response (SCHR), an alliance of nine of the world's largest humanitarian NGOs and networks, in 2012–2013 (www.schr.info).

A recent *State of the Humanitarian System* report identified 4,480 organizations in 2014, with total humanitarian spending of over \$35 billion and around 450,000 professional aid workers. However, the sector is dominated by a small group of large organizations: the United Nations (UN) humanitarian agencies, the IFRC, and 'the big five' international NGOs – Médecins sans Frontières, Save the Children, Oxfam, World Vision and International Rescue Committee (Stoddard *et al*, 2015; Taylor *et al*, 2012). To reduce chaos in the crowded field, Tamminga (2013) argues a standard approach is needed, with mandatory (rather than voluntary) compliance.

Standards in humanitarian relief

A brief history

Griekspoor and Sondorp (2001) provide a concise history of quality improvement initiatives in humanitarian assistance. During the 1980s there was substantial growth in the number of NGOs, the amount of money coming from donors and media attention. More NGOs implies an increase in performance variability. More media attention exposes performance issues. The OECD humanitarian assistance budget reached US \$3.5 billion in 1994, a tenfold increase from 1980.

An evaluation of the humanitarian response to the 1994 Rwanda crisis raised concerns about the quality of service delivery. The report estimated there were 100,000 avoidable deaths due to poor performance of the relief agencies. It concluded that a lack of standards and weak systems of accountability were partly responsible for many of these fatalities (ODI, 1995). *Of course, the killers were also partly responsible*. In 1994 the first voluntary code of conduct was developed by the Red Cross movement and various NGOs.

In 1997 the Active Learning Network on Accountability and Performance (ALNAP) was established to promote learning in the humanitarian sector. Members were drawn from the 'four pillars' of the international humanitarian system: bilateral donors, the UN, the IFRC and the NGOs. Also in 1997, the Sphere Project was launched; the Humanitarian Ombudsman Project, which became the Humanitarian Accountability Project (HAP) in 2000, commenced; and People in Aid published their Code of Best Practice. In 2003 People in Aid released an update of the Code.

SCHR was the original sponsor of the 1998 IFRC Code of Conduct, establishing ethical standards for organizations involved in humanitarian work. In 1997 SCHR and InterAction launched the Sphere Project to set minimum standards in humanitarian aid (www.schr.info/about/). After more than 700 people from 228 relief organizations in 60 countries came together and considered humanitarian best practices for over three years, the original Sphere Project handbook was published in January 2000 (Collins and Griekspoor, 2001). The handbook was revised in 2004 and 2011, with a further revision in 2018.

According to Bugnion (2002), the Sphere Standards and the Code of Conduct for the Red Cross and NGOs were among the 'most widely used' quality management tools at the turn of the century. He appraises various strengths and weaknesses of these two tools, along with the HAP Standards, InterAction Private Voluntary Organization (PVO) standards (www.interaction.org), People in Aid, ALNAP, the European Foundation for Quality Management (EFQM), ISO 9000, Groupe URD (Urgence, Réhabilitation, Développement), and the balanced scorecard.

In 2003 HAP became Humanitarian Accountability Partnership International (HAP-I). HAP-I includes external audit and certification of compliance with the HAP 2010 standard. The 2010 standard replaced an earlier (2007) edition. However, of the 86 HAP-I members, only 15 were certified as of August 2012 (Cosgrave, 2013).

Released during late 2014, the Core Humanitarian Standard (CHS) on quality and accountability brings together elements of the IFRC Code of Conduct, the People in Aid Code of Good Practice, the HAP Standard, the Sphere Handbook Core Standards and the Groupe URD Quality COMPAS. The People in Aid Code focused on standards, accountability and transparency, with special reference to the quality of human resource management practices. The CHS is slated to replace the Sphere Handbook Core Standards (Sphere, 2015). It is an attempt to harmonize standards, while adhering to fundamental humanitarian principles: humanity, impartiality, independence and neutrality. The merger of HAP and People in Aid created the CHS Alliance, launched 9 June 2015 in Nairobi (CHS Alliance, 2015).

Types of standards

Based on interviews with humanitarian field staff members, Bhattacharjee (2007) compares the core principles or benchmarks of the four 'most important' standards: the Sphere Standards, One World Trust's Global Accountability Partnership (GAP) Standards, the HAP Standards, and ISO 9000. The Advanced Training Program on Humanitarian Action report, *Humanitarian Quality and Accountability Initiatives*, specifies 'the most known' initiatives to be ALNAP, HAP, People in Aid and the Sphere Standards (Advanced Training Program on Humanitarian Action, 2014).

Standards to assure quality and accountability and to improve processes in humanitarian aid can be placed into three categories: codes of conduct or good practice; formal humanitarian standards; and ISO 9001.

Codes of conduct

The Code of Conduct for the International Federation of Red Cross/ Red Crescent Societies and Non-Governmental Organizations (NGOs) in Disaster Relief outlines ten principle commitments that NGOs should adhere to in disaster response work. The 1994 Code of Conduct is based on ten core principles. To paraphrase, the core principles focus on prioritizing and delivering aid only on the basis of need, independent of political or religious perspectives. In addition, in delivering aid, agencies are to respect local culture and customs, develop local capacities, and attempt to reduce future vulnerabilities. The core principles also address accountability, to both beneficiaries and donors (IFRC, 2017).

The People in Aid Code of Good Practice focuses on standards, accountability and transparency, with special reference to quality of human resource (HR) practices. The code's overall guiding principle is: 'People are central to the achievement of our mission.' The 2003 code provided guiding principles to help aid agencies improve the quality of practices across these areas: HR strategy; staff policies and practices; people management; consultation and communication; recruitment and selection; learning, training and development; and health, safety and security (PIA, 2006). Connected to each practice are qualitative indicators pertaining to documented policies and procedures, as well as staff training.

More comprehensively, the Canadian Council for International Cooperation (CCIC) Code of Ethics and Operational Standards outlines principles and provides operational standards, including compliance procedures and practices. The code covers partnerships, governance, organizational integrity, finances, fundraising and communication to the public, management practices and human resources. It is guided by the following six general principles: human rights, accountability, transparency, fairness, cooperation and sustainability (CCIC, 2009).

These codes are invaluable guides to various humanitarian practices. However, they all fall short as tools for process improvement. The latter two codes, People in Aid and CCIC, lack direct consideration or involvement of beneficiaries.

Humanitarian standards and certification schemes

A standard is a reference point against which something can be evaluated. For a standard to become widely recognized as a mark of excellence, it needs to be developed via consensus building involving all relevant stakeholders. Most standards measure excellence in terms of: *product specifications* (assessing outcomes or deliverables); and/or *process specifications* (measuring methods and the management of activities).

The Sphere Project's Humanitarian Charter and Minimum Standards in Disaster Response aims to improve quality of assistance to people affected by disasters and improve the accountability of humanitarian agencies to their donors, beneficiaries and other stakeholders. It is driven by the humanitarian imperative: 'action should be taken to prevent or alleviate human suffering arising out of disaster or conflict,' along with the *rights* of affected people: to life with dignity, to receive humanitarian assistance, and to protection and security (Sphere, 2011).

The 400-page Sphere Handbook includes six core standards: people-centred humanitarian response; coordination and collaboration; assessment; design and response; performance, transparency and learning; and aid worker performance (see Appendix 1, page 39). Under each core standard, Sphere gives: *actions* or suggested activities and inputs to help meet the standard; *indicators*, ie signals that show whether the standard has been attained; and *guidance notes*, including points to consider when applying the standard, actions and indicators in different situations. Sphere also espouses minimum standards for four specific humanitarian sectors: water supply, sanitation and hygiene promotion; food security and nutrition; shelter, settlement and non-food items; and health action (Sphere, 2011).

Collins and Griekspoor (2001) note several concerns about the Sphere Standards. First, the standards tend to apply to ideal, less complex, situations such as relief camps, which may prevent relief workers from adapting them in more complex situations. Second, politicians and others could use the standards to obscure their responsibility as to the cause of a crisis. Third, the standards could foster unrealistic expectations while ignoring constraints, leading to adverse publicity, liability and reprisals. The revised 2011 Handbook partly addressed these concerns.

Dufour *et al* (2002) outline several additional concerns about the Sphere approach. While it offers minimal standards for four critical sectors, it is not comprehensive. It also seems to assume certain conditions: access to victims, cooperation of local authorities, reasonable security and sufficient resources. What if these conditions are not met? Standards need to consider context (eg arctic vs tropical climate; peace vs war). Sphere's universal standards (eg 15 litres of water per day) could be inappropriate. Each disaster or event may require a customized approach.

The HAP 2010 Standards in Humanitarian Accountability and Quality Management was a most comprehensive, ambitious certification scheme. Tamminga (2013) called it the most advanced of existing certification mechanisms. The HAP Standards measures accountability and quality commitments made by aid agencies. They also assess management systems used and services provided by its members. The Standards define accountability as 'the means through which power is used responsibly' (HAP, 2010).

The HAP Standard Principles include the first four (out of seven) IFRC principles: *humanity*, *impartiality*, *neutrality* and *independence* (IFRC, 2015). To these, HAP (2010) added six additional principles, focused on listening to and serving beneficiaries, including *transparency* and *complementarity* within the aid community.

To achieve HAP certification, a NGO had to show that it met six benchmarks: establishing and delivering on commitments, staff competency, sharing information (with its stakeholders), participation (of beneficiaries), handling complaints (from all stakeholders), and learning and continual improvement. While the benchmarks cover all stakeholders, the clear focus was on beneficiaries and workers. Attached to each benchmark were a series of specific requirements and means of verification (HAP, 2010).

The HAP Standards were promoted as a complement to the People in Aid Code of Good Practice, the Sphere Standards, the Emergency Capacity Building (ECB) Project, Groupe URD, and the ALNAP in Humanitarian Action, as well as various national self-regulatory schemes focusing on accountability and quality in the non-profit sector. As noted above, HAP and People in Aid merged to create the CHS Alliance.

The CHS outlines nine commitments NGOs could use to 'improve the quality and effectiveness of the assistance they provide' and to establish 'greater accountability to communities and people affected by crisis' (CHS, 2014). It goes beyond the Sphere Core Standards by adding an element on *budget monitoring* and emphasizing *two-way communication* with beneficiaries. While building local capabilities is more prominent in the CHS (vis-à-vis the Sphere Standards), staff safety and security are more explicit in the Sphere Core Standards. The CHS also focuses heavily on accountability to the beneficiaries and their communities. Still, there are specific elements that focus on aid workers (commitment 8), donors (commitment 9) and implementing partners/NGOs (commitment 6). Appendix 2 (page 40) lists the nine commitments and corresponding quality criteria that comprise the CHS. For each commitment, there is a list of key actions and organizational responsibilities.

ISO 9000

ISO 9001 sets out criteria for a quality management system. It has been implemented by over 1 million organizations in more than 170 countries (www.iso.org). The ISO 9000:2015 standards are based on the following seven quality management principles: (1) customer focus, (2) leadership, (3) engagement of people, (4) process approach, (5) improvement, (6) evidence-based decision making and (7) relationship management (ISO, 2015).

Verboom (2002a) discusses the pros and cons of ISO 9000 in the humanitarian aid sector. On the plus side, it is an internationally recognized standard for quality management systems. It also focuses on accountability to downstream customers (beneficiaries), promotes evaluation and learning, and encourages compliance with quality principles. Finally, ISO 9000 is not rigid, it allows for flexible solutions to unique problems. However, it may be perceived as a tool for business or as a marketing gimmick, and it can create extra paperwork and bureaucracy.

Medair may be the first humanitarian NGO to gain ISO 9001 registration. Its core values are: integrity, hope, compassion, accountability, dignity and faith (see www.medair.org). Medair considers quality to be *the process by which an organization continuously improves its work to deliver services that meet the needs of people it assists, in accordance with their values, cultural standards and dignity.* SGS performed Medair's ISO audits (Verboom, 2002b).

To gain certification, Medair established a quality policy, documented their processes, and developed feedback mechanisms for beneficiaries, staff, donors and other stakeholders. At first, staff members were concerned ISO 9001 would mean more paperwork and that it would not be useful in the field. These objections were overcome, and Medair realized several advantages of implementation, including: enhanced accountability, organizational learning, greater efficiency and effectiveness, beneficiary involvement, standardization of procedures, and institutional knowledge (Verboom, 2002b).

The Cambodia Trust earned ISO 9001 registration around the same time as Medair. Its vision is: 'Creating possibilities and exceeding expectations for a future without limitations.' The Trust was established in 1989 in the United Kingdom. It operates rehabilitation centres in Cambodia for victims of anti-personnel mines and other amputees, as well as schools of prosthetics and orthotics. It is also in Sri Lanka, Indonesia, Myanmar and the Philippines (www.exceed-worldwide.org).

Processes involved in the ISO project include: financial reporting, work procedures for device manufacture, staff training, patient treatment and liaison. Among the benefits of ISO 9001 at Cambodia Trust are: enhanced accountability (to beneficiaries and donors), increased ability to build local capacity, and to transfer and manage knowledge (via process documentation and the quality manual). ISO 9001 was adopted, in part, to ensure sustainability of the organization once the operation is transferred to local Cambodian staff. The organization credits ISO 9001 certification with facilitating growth and opening donor doors (Walsh, 2005).

Dufour *et al* (2002) question the usefulness of ISO 9000 and suggest it may be cumbersome. Will it work in the volatile, uncertain, unstable world of humanitarian relief? Will ISO standards get in the way of flexibility? They argue that it may be useful for administrative processes and logistics, but may not be useful in the field. ISO is not necessarily a rigid standard. It could be adapted to unique environments. Like all standards, ISO may be more useful at headquarters rather than in the field. Of course, much of logistics happens in the field.

Issues about standards

Alexander (2005) suggests standards would help assure the quality of emergency preparedness, enhance accountability and enable impartial evaluation of effectiveness. However, he also recognizes a primary argument against standards – rigidity, and the possible loss of flexibility. Hilhorst (2002) asks some tough questions about humanitarian aid standards: Do standards compromise independence? Are standards an entry barrier? Do standards stifle creativity and improvisation? Are they inflexible? Should standards be mandatory or voluntary? Should conformance be verified by external agencies or only subject to internal review? Griekspoor and Sondorp (2001) concur that standards could undermine flexibility in response to local conditions – and threaten NGO independence.

Dufour *et al* (2002) discuss two challenges in adopting a quality approach in humanitarian relief. The first is 'cultural' – how could people working to help other people possibly do something wrong? The second is 'technical' – emergencies are fraught with insecurity and complexity. The first challenge could be overcome by stating the case that most things can be done better – and doing better means helping more people. The second challenge calls for NGOs to involve their people in process improvement, and to understand uncertainty and variability in their environments.

NGOs are concerned that certification schemes could increase donor and host government control over humanitarian operations, undermine principled humanitarian action and reduce the effectiveness of relief (Hofmann, 2011). Then there is the matter of costs. Certification costs include administrative overhead, costs to create documentation, compliance costs and cost to compensate the registrar or certifying organization (Cosgrave, 2013).

Despite these challenges and costs, the NGOs seem to have an obsession with standards as the path to quality and accountability. However, there are signs humanitarians are ready to expand their toolkit. The October 2013 paper, *Professionalising the Sector: A proposed certification model for humanitarian organisations*, released by SCHR, states that: 'Certification is just one of many different, complementary approaches to promoting greater quality, effectiveness and accountability; it should not be seen as a solution to all issues facing humanitarian organizations' (SCHR, 2013).

Do standards suit all NGOs?

Standards may be a better fit for certain NGOs, based on characteristics such as organizational size, uncertainty faced in field and organizational culture (eg values and mission). These are contingency factors that impact NGO strategy and performance (see Haavisto, 2014). Use of standards may be more likely (and likely to be more effective) at: larger NGOs; NGOs operating in more certain environments (ie development aid vs disaster relief); and NGOs embracing a 'Wilsonian' tradition, as opposed to a 'Dunantist' or faith-based tradition (Stoddard, 2003).

The organizational size and environmental uncertainty effects have been studied and discussed in the literature on quality management practices (eg Sila, 2007). The effect of uncertainty can be somewhat complex. Stable environments may ease implementation and administration of standards, but standards could be more valuable in taming unstable environments, if possible. (While development aid work occurs in relatively stable environments, disaster relief tends to take place amidst considerable uncertainty.)

Regarding organizational culture, having a strong, faith-based agenda may serve as a substitute for formal quality or process improvement standards. These NGOs are primarily inspired and guided by their faith.

Thus, secular NGOs may be more likely to implement formal standards compared to faith-based NGOs. Within the secular realm, NGOs with a 'Wilsonian' mission (named after President Woodrow Wilson) might be especially attracted to standards. These organizations favour rule-based coordination, emphasizing service delivery over a short-term horizon. On the other hand, 'Dunantist' NGOs (named after Red Cross founder Henry Dunant) are more independent – and probably less drawn to standards. They emphasize advocacy and adopt a long-term horizon (Stoddard, 2003).

Must NGOs improve to survive?

Doane (2016) notes the legitimacy of international NGOs is being questioned by many stakeholders – from donors and host governments to their own workers and local implementing partners. She also argues that 'it is unlikely that NGOs will survive, at least in their current form, without a direct full-frontal assault on the sector'. According to Mikolajuk (2005), aid 'often does more harm than good'. Without careful planning and a long-term perspective, the charity model of financial and food assistance to the needy can perpetuate dependence, build entry barriers for local agriculture and business, and spawn economies of theft and corruption. From Cambodia to Rwanda, food aid has been diverted to the killers, the people who created the need for aid in the first place.

Strategically, like most organizations, an NGO is trying to 'do right things', as defined by its mission. For an NGO, this typically means delivering aid, feeding people, easing suffering and saving lives, all while remaining neutral and impartial. Process improvement in general – and standards in particular – cannot help NGOs determine what the 'right things' are. When, if ever, should neutrality and impartiality be sacrificed in favour of feeding people? Is it ever 'right' to work with greedy human traffickers or corrupt government officials? While these can be difficult questions, NGO survival may depend on the answers to such questions, in a chaotic world of increasing accountability and transparency.

On the other hand, standards can help an NGO become more efficient and effective or 'do things right' – whatever the 'things' are or the mission is. This is about stretching budgets, feeding more people in the face of limited funding, conserving scarce resources, eliminating waste, improving beneficiaries' living conditions, adhering to donor reporting requirements, etc. Like any other organization, NGO survival depends prominently on operational efficiency and effectiveness (Stoddard, 2003). Operationally, well-designed and -implemented standards can make a difference, for example by improving NGO responsiveness (Jahre and Fabbe-Costes, 2015).

In summary, humanitarian NGOs could be increasingly vulnerable, both strategically (Mikolajuk, 2005) and operationally (Doane, 2016; Stoddard, 2003). Standards can help with the operational issue, but not on matters of strategy. As they look to the future, NGOs are advised to consider the following action items:

1 Become proactive, as opposed to reactive, in the face of disaster. Try to anticipate natural and man-made disasters. Link short-term disaster relief to long-term development aid (Larson, 2011; Mikolajuk, 2005; United Nations Development Programme, 2004). By minimizing the likelihood and/or severity of disasters, NGOs can maximize the impact of development aid efforts.

2 Move towards an empowerment model of development aid and disaster relief (Bartle, 2007). This includes building local capacity and collaborative aid networks (Bealt and Afshin Mansouri, 2017). Though not always possible, it is always better if disaster relief can be led by empowered, local actors following humanitarian principles.

3 Exercise great caution in compromising organizational mission or principles. This relates to the issue of cultural relativism versus ethical imperialism (Donaldson, 1996). When working in a nation or region that condones or even embraces gender inequality or corruption, what is an NGO to do? Are there contexts in which gender inequality is 'right' – or is it always wrong?

4 Develop and state the 'business case' for process improvement, including use of standards. Ideally after reflection and discussion on the first three items, NGOs are advised to estimate costs and benefits of process improvement. Are any additional administrative costs and likely loss of flexibility worth the probable improvements in efficiency and effectiveness?

There seems to be growing pressure on the NGOs to 'do right things' and to 'do things right'. Doing things right is largely an operational issue. The question is 'how' do we do the things that we do? Doing (the) right thing is more a strategic matter. Now, the question goes beyond how to 'why' do we do the things that we do? If the NGOs are indeed in jeopardy, answers to these questions may be the difference between (organizational) life and death.

References

Advanced Training Program on Humanitarian Action (ATHA) (2014) *Humanitarian Quality and Accountability Initiatives* [Online] http://www.atha. se/content/humanitarian-quality-and-accountability-initiatives

Alexander, D (2005) Towards the development of a standard in emergency planning, *Disaster Prevention and Management*, 14(2), pp 158–75

Anonymous (2007) *Humanitarian Assistance Guidelines*, Ministry for Foreign Affairs of Finland

APICS (2017) SCOR Framework [Online] http://www.apics.org/apics-for-business/ products-and-services/apics-scc-frameworks/scor

Bartle, P (2007) *From Disaster to Development*, Community Empowerment Collective [Online] http://cec.vcn.bc.ca/cmp/modules/dis-int.htm

BBC (2016) Migrant crisis: Migration to Europe explained in seven charts, 4 March [Online] http://www.bbc.com/news/world-europe-34131911

Bealt, J and Afshin Mansouri, S (2017) From disaster to development: A systematic review of community-driven humanitarian logistics, *Disasters*, Overseas Development Institute

Beamon, BM and Balcik, B (2008) Performance measurement in humanitarian relief chains, *International Journal of Public Sector Management*, 21(1), pp 4–25

Bhattacharjee, A (2007) *Common Humanitarian Accountability Framework for IWG Agencies*, Inter Agency Working Group: Emergency Capacity Building Project (ECB2)

Blecken, A (2010) Supply chain process modeling for humanitarian organisations, *International Journal of Physical Distribution & Logistics Management*, 40(9), pp 675–92

Bugnion, C (2002) *Analysis of 'Quality Management' Tools in the Humanitarian Sector and their Application by the NGOs*, ECHO – Partners' Annual Conference, Brussels, 14–15 October

CCIC (2009) *Code of Ethics and Operational Standards*, Canadian Council for International Cooperation, Ottawa [Online] http://www.ccic.ca/_files/en/ about/001_code_of_ethics_booklet_e.pdf

CHS (2014) *Core Humanitarian Standard on Quality and Accountability*, CHS Alliance, Groupe URD and the Sphere Project

CHS Alliance (2015) The CHS Alliance launches, 9 June [Online] https://www. chsalliance.org/news/latest-news/the-chs-alliance-launches

Collins, S and Griekspoor, A (2001) Raising standards in emergency relief: How useful are Sphere Minimum Standards for humanitarian assistance? *British Medical Journal*, 323, pp 740–42

Cosgrave, J (2013) Standards: A stick to beat us with? 14 February [Online] http://pool.fruitycms.com/humanitarianstandards/Standards-a-stick-to-beat-us-with-John-Cosgrave-Feb-2013.pdf

Doane, D (2016) The future of aid: Will international NGOs survive? *Guardian*, 23 February [Online] https://www.theguardian.com/global-development-professionals-network/2016/feb/23/the-future-of-aid-will-international-ngos-survive

Donaldson, T (1996) Values in tension: Ethics away from home, *Harvard Business Review*, September–October, pp 48–62

Dufour, C, de Geoffroy, V, Grünewald, F, Levy, K, Maury, H and Pirotte, C (2002) Did someone say quality? Contributions to a debate [Online] http://www.urd.org/

Griekspoor, A and Sondorp, E (2001) Enhancing the quality of humanitarian assistance: Taking stock and future initiatives, *Prehospital and Disaster Medicine*, 16(4), pp 209–15

Guha-Sapir, D, Hoyois, P and Below, R (2016) *Annual Disaster Statistical Review 2015: The numbers and trends*, Brussels: Centre for Research on the Epidemiology of Disasters (CRED)

Haavisto, I (2014) *Performance in Humanitarian Supply Chains*, Hanken School of Economics

HAP (2010) *The 2010 HAP Standard in Accountability and Quality Management*, Humanitarian Accountability Partnership, Geneva

Hilhorst, D (2002) Being good at doing good? Quality and accountability of humanitarian NGOs, *Disasters*, 26(3), pp 193–212

Hofmann, C-A (2011) NGO certification: time to bite the bullet? *Humanitarian Exchange Magazine*, 52 (October) [Online] http://www.odihpn.org/humanitarian-exchange-magazine/issue-52

Hulm, P (1994) UNHCR: Bureaucracy, nurse, and scapegoat, *Crosslines Global Report*, 31 October [Online] http://reliefweb.int/node/25792

IFRC (2015) Promoting the fundamental principles and humanitarian values [Online] http://www.ifrc.org/en/who-we-are/vision-and-mission/principles-and-values/

IFRC (2017) Code of conduct [Online] http://media.ifrc.org/ifrc/who-we-are/the-movement/code-of-conduct/

ISO (2015) *Quality Management Principles*, International Organization for Standardization [Online] https://www.iso.org/iso-9001-quality-management.html

Jahre, M and Fabbe-Costes, N (2015) How standards and modularity can improve humanitarian supply chain responsiveness: The case of emergency response units, *Journal of Humanitarian Logistics and Supply Chain Management*, 5(3), pp 348–86

Kent, R, Armstrong, J and Obrecht, A (2013) *The Future of Non-Governmental Organisations in the Humanitarian Sector: Global transformations and their consequences*, Humanitarian Futures Programme, King's College, London

Kovács, G and Spens, KM (2007) Humanitarian logistics in disaster relief opera-tions, *International Journal of Physical Distribution & Logistics Management*, 37(2), pp 99–114

Larson, PD (2011) Risky business: What humanitarians can learn from business logisticians—and vice versa, Chapter 1 in *Humanitarian Logistics: Meeting the challenge of preparing for and responding to disasters*, ed MG Christopher and PH Tatham, Kogan Page, London, pp 15–31

Larson, PD (2012) Strategic partners and strange bedfellows: Relationship building in the relief supply chain, Chapter 1 in *Relief Supply Chain Management for Disasters: Humanitarian aid and emergency logistics*, ed G Kovács and KM Spens, IGI Global, Hershey, PA

Larson, PD (2014) An improvement process for process improvement: Quality and accountability in humanitarian logistics, Chapter 1 in *Humanitarian Logistics: Meeting the challenge of preparing for and responding to disasters*, 2nd edition, ed PH Tatham and MG Christopher, Kogan Page, London, pp 19–39

Larson, PD and Kerr, SG (2006) *Integration of Process Management Tools in Warehousing: Activity-based costing (ABC) and ISO 9000*, WERC Watch, Summer, Warehousing Education and Research Council, Oak Brook, IL

Loquercio, D Hammersley, M and Emmens, B (2006) Understanding and address-ing staff turnover in humanitarian agencies, Humanitarian Practice Network, Overseas Development Institute, London

Mikolajuk, C (2005) Thanks, but no thanks, *Harvard International Review*, 26(4), pp 32–35

Obrecht, A (2012) *Effective Accountability? The drivers, benefits and mechanisms of CSO self-regulation*, Briefing No 130, One World Trust, London

ODI (1995) *Joint Evaluation of Emergency Assistance to Rwanda, Study III: Humanitarian aid and effects*, Overseas Development Institute (ODI), London

OECD (2017) Development aid rises again in 2016 but flows to poorest countries dip, 11 April [Online] http://www.oecd.org/dac/development-aid-rises-again-in-2016-but-flows-to-poorest-countries-dip.htm

Oxfam (2006) *Oxfam International Policy Compendium Note on Humanitarian Accountability*, December [Online] http://www.oxfam.org

Parris, A (2013) Improving processes for good in East Africa, *The TQM Journal*, 25(5), pp 458–72

PIA (2006) *Code of Good Practice in the Management and Support of Aid Personnel*, People in Aid

Purvis, K (2015) Core Humanitarian Standard: Do NGOs need another set of standards? *Guardian*, 11 June [Online] https://www.theguard-ian.com/global-development-professionals-network/2015/jun/11/core-humanitarian-standard-do-ngos-need-another-set-of-standards

Santarelli, G, Abidi, H, Klumpp, M and Regattieri, A (2015) Humanitarian supply chains and performance measurement schemes in practice, *International Journal of Productivity and Performance Management*, 64(6), pp 784–810

SCHR (2013) *Professionalising the Sector: A proposed certification model for humanitarian organisations*, Steering Committee for Humanitarian Response [Online] www.schr.info

Schulz, SF and Heigh, I (2009) Logistics performance management in action within a humanitarian organisation, *Management Research News*, 32(11), pp 1038–49

SGS (2017) NGO benchmarking [Online] http://www.sgs.com/en/public-sector/monitoring-services/ngo-benchmarking

Sila, I (2007) Examining the effects of contextual factors on TQM and performance through the lens of organizational theories: An empirical study, *Journal of Operations Management*, 25(1), pp 83–109

Sphere (2011) *Humanitarian Charter and Minimum Standards in Humanitarian Response*, The Sphere Project

Sphere (2015) *The Core Humanitarian Standard and the Sphere Core Standards: Analysis and comparison*, The Sphere Project, March

Stoddard, A (2003) Humanitarian NGOs: Challenges and trends, *HPG Briefing*, Overseas Development Institute, London, July

Stoddard, A, Harmer, A, Haver, K, Taylor, G and Harvey, P (2015) *The State of the Humanitarian System*, Active Learning Network for Accountability and Performance in Humanitarian Action (ALNAP), London

Tamminga, P (2013) Certifying humanitarian organisations, *Monthly Developments Magazine*, 31(3), pp 21–23

Taylor, G, Stoddard, A, Harmer, A, Haver, K, Harvey, P, Barber, K, Schreter, L, and Wilhelm, C (2012) *The State of the Humanitarian System*, ALNAP – Active Learning Network for Accountability and Performance in Humanitarian Action, Overseas Development Institute, London

Telford, J, Cosgrave, J and Houghton, R (2006) *Joint Evaluation of the International Response to the Indian Ocean Tsunami: Synthesis report*, London: Tsunami Evaluation Coalition, London [Online] http://www.alnap.org/pool/files/889.pdf

Thomas, AS and Kopczak, LR (2005) *From Logistics to SCM: The path forward in the humanitarian sector*, Fritz Institute

United Nations Development Programme (2004) *Reducing Disaster Risk: A challenge for development*, UNDP, New York

United Nations Office for the Coordination of Humanitarian Affairs (2016) *Global Humanitarian Overview 2017* [Online] https://reliefweb.int/report/world/global-humanitarian-overview-2017-enarzh

Verboom, D (2002a) Can ISO 9001:2000 aid the humanitarian aid sector? *ISO Management Systems*, September–October, pp 25–29

Verboom, D (2002b) Medair believed to be first humanitarian aid organisation worldwide to achieve ISO 9001:2000, *ISO Management Systems*, September–October, pp 30–36

Walsh, E (2005) ISO 9001:2000 supports humanitarian aid NGO's expansion in Asia, *ISO Management Systems*, March–April, pp 27–29

Appendix 1: Sphere Core Standards

1 *People-centred humanitarian response* – People's capacity and strategies to survive with dignity are integral to the design and approach of humanitarian response.

2 *Coordination and collaboration* – Humanitarian response is planned and implemented in coordination with the relevant authorities, humanitarian agencies and civil society organizations engaged in impartial humanitarian action, working together for maximum efficiency, coverage and effectiveness.

3 *Assessment* – The priority needs of the disaster-affected population are identified through a systematic assessment of the context, risks to life with dignity and the capacity of the affected people and relevant authorities to respond.

4 *Design and response* – The humanitarian response meets the assessed needs of the disaster-affected population in relation to context, the risks faced and the capacity of the affected people and state to cope and recover.

5 *Performance, transparency and learning* – The performance of humanitarian agencies is continually examined and communicated to stakeholders; projects are adapted in response to performance.

6 *Aid worker performance* – Humanitarian agencies provide appropriate management, supervisory and psychosocial support, enabling aid workers to have the knowledge, skills, behaviour and attitudes to plan and implement an effective humanitarian response with humanity and respect.

(Source: http://www.spherehandbook.org/)

Appendix 2: The Nine Commitments and Corresponding Quality Criteria (QC)

Communities and people affected by crisis …

1 … receive assistance appropriate and relevant to their needs.

QC: Humanitarian response is appropriate and relevant.

2 … have access to the humanitarian assistance they need at the right time.

QC: Humanitarian response is effective and timely.

3 … are not negatively affected and are more prepared, resilient and less at-risk as a result of humanitarian action.

QC: Humanitarian response strengthens local capacities and avoids negative effects.

4 … know their rights and entitlements, have access to information and participate in decisions that affect them.

QC: Humanitarian response is based on communication, participation and feedback.

5 … have access to safe and responsive mechanisms to handle complaints.

QC: Complaints are welcomed and addressed.

6 … receive coordinated, complementary assistance.

QC: Humanitarian response is coordinated and complementary.

7 … can expect delivery of improved assistance as organizations learn from experience and reflection.

QC: Humanitarian actors continuously learn and improve.

8 … receive the assistance they require from competent, well-managed staff and volunteers.

QC: Staff are supported to do their job effectively, and are treated fairly and equitably.

9 … can expect that the organizations assisting them are managing resources effectively, efficiently and ethically.

QC: Resources are managed and used responsibly for their intended purpose.

(Source: CHS, 2014, *Core Humanitarian Standard on Quality and Accountability*, CHS Alliance, Groupe URD and the Sphere Project, p 9)

Impacts of funding systems on humanitarian operations

TINA WAKOLBINGER AND FUMINORI TOYASAKI

Abstract

Funding systems and financial flows play an important role in humanitarian operations. They directly and indirectly affect the scope, speed, effectiveness and efficiency of disaster response. Despite their importance, constraints imposed by funding systems are often not considered in models of humanitarian supply chains. This chapter explores the interdependence of financial flows and material flows in humanitarian relief operations. Specifically, this chapter demonstrates how the structure of funding systems and the characteristics of financial flows impact humanitarian operations. Based on insights concerning the link between funding systems and humanitarian operations, we analyse the expected impact of new trends in fundraising, and we provide recommendations concerning future research projects, including topics such as joint fundraising appeals and cash transfer programmes (CTPs).

Introduction

The occurrence and impact of natural disasters are expected to strongly increase in the future (Thomas and Kopczak, 2005). In order to respond to increasing needs, improving the efficiency of response systems is essential

(Altay and Green, 2006; Oloruntoba and Gray, 2006). Due to the realization of the need to improve response systems, the area of humanitarian supply chain management emerged. Humanitarian supply chain management is typically defined as 'the process of planning, implementing and controlling the efficient, cost-effective flow and storage of goods, materials, and money, as well as related information from the point of origin to the point of consumption for the purpose of alleviating the suffering of vulnerable people' (Thomas and Kopczak, 2005: 2). Logistics plays an essential role in humanitarian supply chains. Reducing inefficiencies in humanitarian logistics operations can, thus, lead to large costs savings.

Inefficiencies in humanitarian operations have many causes. Current funding systems are one of the causes that have been cited in the literature (Thomas and Kopzcak, 2005; Jahre and Heigh, 2008; Gupta *et al*, 2016). Funding systems limit the scope of humanitarian response, and they directly and indirectly affect the speed, effectiveness and efficiency of disaster response. The impact of funding systems is increasing as aid agencies are currently facing multiple changes and challenges in their environment: increasing demand for disaster relief, increasing numbers of aid agencies leading to more intense competition for donations, increasing earmarking of donations, increasing use of CTPs, new funding mechanisms such as the Central Emergency Response Fund (CERF), Common Humanitarian Funds (CHFs), Emergency Response Funds (ERFs) and the emergence of joint fundraising initiatives furthermore, donors are more demanding in terms of performance, accountability, quality, and impact (Thomas and Kopczak, 2005; Beamon and Balcik, 2008; Street, 2009).

Burkart *et al* (2016) provide a literature review of papers addressing the funding–humanitarian supply chain interface and a framework for categorizing the articles. The authors show that the number of publications has been increasing in recent years but that more research is necessary to fully capture the impact of funding on humanitarian supply chains.

In this chapter we explore the interaction between funding systems and humanitarian relief operations from the perspective of a non-profit organization. The chapter is organized as follows: first, we provide an overview of the structure of humanitarian funding systems. Then, we describe how the characteristics of financial flows impact the efficiency and effectiveness of humanitarian operations and we show how incentives provided by donors can lead to misallocation of resources. Based on insights concerning the link between funding systems and humanitarian operations, we offer our perspective on the expected impacts of recent trends in fundraising and we provide recommendations concerning future research projects.

Structure of funding systems

Funding systems typically involve multiple stakeholders with diverse objectives. The structure of the humanitarian funding system and the number of stakeholders involved impact the characteristics of funding flows and the power of the stakeholders. Furthermore, these affect the percentage of donations that reach beneficiaries since intermediaries typically keep a percentage of the money as transaction costs and, thereby, reduce the amount of money that can be used for beneficiaries (Walker and Pepper, 2007).

Funds to deal with the effects of disasters usually come from public or official sources. Traditionally, governments provided a big portion of funds; therefore, they had a strong influence over the sector (Thomas and Kopzcak, 2005). In recent years, however, contributions from foundations, individual donors and the private sector have increased in importance (Thomas and Kopzcak, 2005; Kovács and Spens, 2007).

Donors need to decide how to allocate their money. Funds are either given directly to providers of aid or they are channelled through intermediaries (Macrae, 2002). Brokers can help overcome with the problems of matching donors and humanitarian organizations (Stapleton *et al*, 2010). Providers of aid include international aid agencies, local non-governmental organizations (NGOs) and community-based organizations (Oloruntoba and Gray, 2006). International aid agencies can be divided into three categories: entities operating under the United Nations (UN) umbrella; international organizations such as the International Federation of the Red Cross and Red Crescent Societies (IFRC); and global NGOs (Thomas and Kopczak, 2005). Intermediaries include the World Bank, international organizations and NGOs (Macrae, 2002).

CTPs are increasingly employed in humanitarian response as a substitute or complement to in-kind aid. CTP transfers purschasing power directly to beneficiaries in the form of currency for them to obtain goods and/or services directly from the local market (Falaga Sigala *et al*). Currently, 7 per cent of the humanitarian assistance is in cash but there is an international effort to increase the usage of cash in humanitarian interventions (European Commission, 2017). For a successful implementation of CTP, humanitarian organizations' collaboration with donors, the private sector (especially financial institutions), local authorities and national governments is indispensable. Despite the growing interest in CTPs from practitioners, academic literature is still limited in this area (Doocy and Tappis, 2016; Burkart *et al*, 2016). A systematic literature review on CTPs from Doocy and Tappis (2016) for the International Initiative for Impact Evaluation indicates that only nine studies were in peer-reviewed publications, and none of these focused on the private sector's role. We expect to see more research papers that address the relevant issues.

Administrative costs involved in fund allocation play an increasingly important role in donors' allocation decisions. These considerations led to increasing amounts of resources being allocated to new funding mechanisms such as CHFs (Street, 2009). Furthermore, networks of international aid agencies are being established that collaborate in fundraising; examples include Agire in Italy, Consortium for Emergency Situations in Belgium, Samenwerkende Hulporganisaties in the Netherlands, Aktion Deutschland Hilft in Germany, the Humanitarian Coalition in Canada, and the NGO Center for International Cooperation in Japan (Toyasaki and Wakolbinger, 2018).

The advantages of joint fundraising include a reduction in excessive competition for funds, reduced information costs (Rose-Ackerman, 1982), and reduced solicitation costs due to economies of scale in fundraising (Weinblatt, 1992). Disadvantages include reduced discretion in the allocation of funds, concerns over a possible loss of market share (Westhead and Chung, 2007) and of independence (Chua and Wong, 2003; Nunnenkamp and Öhler, 2012). Since financial considerations are very important in encouraging aid agencies to participate in a joint fundraising organization (Chan 1998 in: Chua and Wong, 2003), allocation rules applied by the intermediary strongly determine its desirability for aid agencies.

Besides deciding how to allocate money, donors and intermediaries also need to decide on restrictions that they impose on the use of financial funds and reporting requirements. Accountability is of increasing concern to many donors, and this has led to increases in reporting requirements for aid agencies. Donors who want to ensure that their resources are used for the donor intended purpose need to consider the impact of their restrictions with respect to the use of their resources. While more restrictions allow for greater control, they are also potentially reducing the effectiveness and efficiency of aid agencies' operations, as the next section shows.

Impacts of financial flows on disaster response

Financial flows are an important input in humanitarian supply chain operations and, as a result, humanitarian operations are strongly affected by the characteristics of funding flows (Development Initiatives, 2009a). When analysing the impact of financial flows, traditionally, much emphasis has been put on the total amount of donations received. However, speed and timing, fluctuation and predictability, and flexibility of funds also influence the efficiency and effectiveness of disaster response, and, hence, these characteristics strongly impact the value of donations from the perspective of an aid agency.

Volume

While funds available for humanitarian relief are growing, they are not large enough to cover humanitarian need (Development Initiatives, 2009b). Given the increasing need for disaster response, this situation is not likely to change. Aid agencies need to compete for the resources that are available. The amount of funds that an aid agency receives determines the scope of the relief operations that an aid agency can conduct. Large amounts of donations provide aid agencies with the opportunity to take advantage of economies of scale and to gain influence and negotiation power with suppliers.

Furthermore, large amounts of resources provide aid agencies with visibility to donors. Due to the importance of financial funds, a large literature on fundraising strategies and issues exists. Traditionally, fundraising issues have been analysed by researchers in the area of economics. Only later have they also been addressed by papers in the area of operations research that highlighted, for example, implications of fundraising mechanisms, auditing (Privett and Erhun, 2011) and information disclosure (Zhuang et al, 2014) on the behaviour of donors and humanitarian organizations.

When analysing the impact of increased donation amounts, it is important to distinguish between donations that are earmarked and donations that are not. Earmarking/restricting donations means that donors put conditions on their gifts and select what projects or activities to fund within the recipient organization (Barman, 2008). In the case of earmarked funds, increasing donation amounts is not always desirable for aid agencies, as too much money can be allocated to certain emergencies. This is especially true for emergencies with high media attention that receive large amounts of earmarked donations that cannot be sensibly spent within the allocated time frame. In these situations, aid agencies sometimes discourage donors from donating money, eg Doctors without Borders discouraged donors from donating money for the 2004 Indian Ocean earthquake and tsunami.

Fluctuation and predictability

Fluctuations in funding levels can be observed in funding from both private and government donors. Private donation levels are strongly impacted by the amount and type of news coverage (Bennett and Kottasz, 2000; Tomasini and Van Wassenhove, 2009). For example, the 2004 Indian Ocean earthquake and tsunami led to a huge response from the donor community, while other emergencies that were neglected by the media received few resources. In the case of government donations, money that has been pledged is not always delivered. In the refugee crises in Darfur, Western Sudan and after Hurricane Mitch, for example, aid agencies only received a third of promised funds (Oloruntoba, 2005).

Strong fluctuations with respect to donations make it difficult for aid agencies to efficiently use their resources. A sudden inflow of financial resources might overload an aid agency's capacity to handle these resources, while very limited donations might force an aid agency to reduce valuable resources and capacities. Kovács and Spens (2007) divide disaster relief operations into three phases: preparation, immediate response and reconstruction. Adequate funding for the preparation stage strongly determines how quickly and efficiently an aid agency can respond to a disaster (Jahre and Heigh, 2008). Strong fluctuations in the occurrence and impact of disasters, as well as availability of financial resources, make it difficult for aid agencies to determine the adequate amount of capacities to build and resources to acquire.

Speed and timing

Once a disaster occurs and an aid agency decides to provide aid, an immediate response is critical and time delays can lead to loss of lives (Kovács and Spens, 2007; Beamon and Balcik, 2008). How quickly an aid agency can respond to a disaster depends on how well it is prepared. However, it also depends on how quickly the aid agency is able to receive money to set up operations.

Some aid agencies have resources that they can use to pre-finance their operations before they get aid from outside sources (Development Initiatives, 2009a). The IFRC, for example, has a Disaster Relief Emergency Fund. The Fund is used immediately after a disaster and allows the IFRC to respond quickly in many emergencies, for example in the case of the Gujarat earthquake in 2001 (Chomilier et al, 2003). Aid agencies that do not have the financial resources to pre-finance their operations need to wait until they receive the aid before they can respond, resulting in costly time delays in their response.

While many donors are aware of the importance of quick aid, they are also increasingly concerned about financial accountability. The increasing desire for financial accountability slows down the process of releasing funds from official sources, which can take up to 40 days (Walker and Pepper, 2007).

Flexibility

Aid agencies receive earmarked and non-earmarked donations. Government aid is often earmarked with respect to regions and use. Private donations are also often earmarked for a certain disaster; however, they are typically not earmarked in terms of how an aid agency needs to spend the money, and private donors are typically willing to reallocate donations if the need arises (Development Initiatives, 2009a). Earmarked donations reduce aid agencies' flexibility in their allocation decisions. Aid agencies might be forced to allocate money and resources to emergencies, activities and projects that provide little benefit to them. Interest in the operations research (OR) community on the topic of earmarking and its implications on efficiency, service levels and operational performance has been increasing recently (Burkart *et al*, 2017 and references therein).

Allocation to emergencies

Private as well as government donors frequently earmark donations with respect to the emergency that it should be used for. Resources are often allocated not according to need but according to donors' preferences, which are frequently driven by media attention in the case of private donors and political and strategic considerations in the case of government donors. A lot of resources, for example, were used to respond to the 2004 Indian Ocean earthquake and tsunami.

Too many resources allocated to one area not only takes resources away from being used in other areas, but they can also lead to increased competition, increased prices and wasted resources (Van Wassenhove, 2006; Beamon and Balcik, 2008). Furthermore, donations and equipment that are earmarked for certain areas also restrict aid agencies' flexibility concerning their allocation and reallocation of resources (Besiou *et al*, 2012). Postponement strategies have been shown to potentially lead to large cost savings in humanitarian supply chains (Oloruntoba and Gray, 2006; Jahre and Heigh, 2008), but earmarked donations severely restrict the use of postponement strategies.

Allocation to resources and activities

Donor funding tends to focus on direct programme and project inputs and does not provide enough funding for disaster preparedness, infrastructure, information and logistics systems (Gustavsson, 2003; Thomas, 2007; Beamon and Balcik, 2008). IFRC, for example, found it challenging to obtain funds for disaster preparedness and capacity building (Chomilier *et al*, 2003). Besides too little funding for the preparation phase, there is also often too little funding for the long-term phase of reconstruction (Kovács and Spens, 2007).

Resources need to be available in the right amounts in each of the disaster relief phases: preparation, immediate response and reconstruction. A very strong focus on short-term relief leads to a lack of planning, capacity building and investment in infrastructure and employee training as well as a lack of long-term reconstruction (Kovács and Spens, 2007; Oloruntoba, 2007; Perry, 2007; Beamon and Balcik, 2008; Goncalves, 2008; Jahre and Heigh, 2008). Lack of planning leads to high competition for available resources, overuse of expensive and unsafe transportation modes and high supply chain costs (Oloruntoba, 2007; Jahre and Heigh, 2008). Not enough investment into areas such as computer systems and employee training leads to wasted time, reduced efficiency, and increased costs (Perry, 2007; Beamon and Balcik, 2008).

Aid agencies also benefit from flexibility concerning changing the allocation of resources at any time. The situation in the emergency areas frequently changes. Hence, it is important to be able to change the allocation of resources accordingly, but donors' increasing desire for financial accountability has led to a large amount of funding being allocated against requests for proposals which has, in turn, strongly limited aid agencies' flexibility in their allocation decisions (Walker and Pepper, 2007).

Volume, speed, fluctuation, predictability and flexibility of funds from different donors and intermediaries determine how desirable they are for aid agencies. Private funds, for example, are typically preferable to official funds with respect to the speed with which they are available as well as the flexibility with which they can be used (Development Initiatives, 2009a). However, not every aid agency values these characteristics equally. The speed of financial flows, for example, is typically more important for small organizations that do not have enough money to pre-fund activities than for large organizations with funding reserves. Also, the importance of these characteristics differs with respect to the phase of the disaster relief. Speed of aid provision, for example, is crucial for immediate disaster relief, and private funds are, therefore, often used in this phase.

Jahre and Heigh (2008) provide a table of preferred funding models for each disaster relief phase differentiating between earmarked and non-earmarked as well as long- and short-term funds, and in doing so highlight the importance of flexibility and speed in the response phase of disaster relief. Table 2.1 provides an overview of the main objectives of fund management and their associated challenges with respect to the characteristics discussed in this section.

Table 2.1   Main objectives and challenges in fund management

Disaster Response Phase	Main Objectives	Challenges
Preparation Phase	Forecast costs and needs for various disaster scenarios Allocate resources to prepare for future disasters and disaster response	Uncertainty concerning future needs Volume: Shortage of funds because of donors' lack of interest
Immediate Response Phase	Quickly secure adequate amount of funds for disaster response under limited information concerning need	Speed: Slow disbursement of government funds Predictability: Strong role of media and strong fluctuation in private funds Flexibility: Increasing earmarking of private and government funds Volume: Too little or too many funds depending on media response
Reconstruction Phase	Allocate funds to long-tem projects considering need, impact and cost effectiveness Consider interaction between reconstruction phase and immediate response phase, especially for areas where emergencies occur frequently	Volume: Shortage of funds because of donors' lack of interest Predictability: Reallocation of funds if new emergencies arise Coordination: Different organizations and funding sources for disaster relief and long-term development

SOURCE Jahre and Heigh, 2008

Aid agencies need to determine the optimal portfolio of funding sources based on the characteristics of funds from different sources, their specific needs, the type of disaster they respond to, as well as the phase of the disaster response. Some previous papers analyse the importance and trade-offs between some of these characteristics. For example, Toyasaki and Wakolbinger (2014) analyse the trade-off between size and flexibility, while Jahre and Heigh (2008), Balcik and Beamon (2008), Martinez *et al* (2011), and Besiou *et al* (2012) highlight the importance and value of flexibility. Further exploration of the trade-offs between these characteristics is clearly an important area for future research projects.

Incentives provided by donors

As the previous section highlights, donors can directly influence how their donations are used. Besides this direct impact, donors also indirectly influence how aid agencies use their resources. When aid agencies make decisions concerning resource allocations, they need to consider how these decisions impact donors' perception of their work and future donation streams.

Donors are interested in making sure that their donations are used in the best possible way; however, they cannot directly measure the impact of their donations (Tatham and Hughes, 2011). While current efforts exist to measure the performance of aid agencies, this is not an easy task due to the intangibility of services offered and the characteristics of humanitarian operations (Beamon and Balcik, 2008). Since donors cannot directly observe the quality of an aid agency's work, they need to rely on indicators of the quality of aid agencies' operations. Examples of indicators that are currently used are visibility, fundraising cost percentage and overhead costs. These indicators have the potential to provide aid agencies with incentives for inefficient resource allocations.

Visibility

Aid agencies that want to make sure that their efforts are noted by donors, especially private donors, need to focus their activities on emergencies and activities with high donor visibility. Aid agencies' desire for visibility leads them to provide aid in areas with a lot of media coverage, as these are typically areas that receive a large volume of aid (Oloruntoba, 2007). Furthermore, it leads aid agencies to focus their activities on the response phase, since it provides more possibilities for activities with high visibility than the preparation phase (Jahre and Heigh, 2008), and it also encourages aid agencies to participate in projects and activities with high donor visibility, for example provision of water as opposed to infrastructure development. In addition, the need to be visible to donors can also reduce collaboration and coordination between aid agencies (Tomasini and Van Wassenhove, 2009) since aid agencies want to emphasize their own contribution.

Financial indicators

Government and private donors increasingly focus on financial accountability. In the case of government donors, this leads to slower disbursement of donations and reduced flexibility for aid agencies, as discussed in the previous section. Private donors who want to make informed decisions when donating money can base their decisions on information provided by organizations such as Charity Navigator, Give Well, CharityWatch and BBB Wise Giving Alliance. These organizations provide rankings of aid agencies based on a multitude of financial and non-financial factors. Financial indicators that are used include overhead costs and fundraising cost percentages.

However, the problem with both indicators is that they are currently not consistently defined and measured, and that data quality is often low. Furthermore, these indicators are influenced by many different factors, eg NGOs that receive official funds typically have lower fundraising costs but higher administrative costs than comparable aid agencies without official funds (Nunnenkamp and Öhler, 2012). Hence, a detailed and often costly analysis is necessary in order to receive valid information about an organization's financial efficiency. In addition to these general problems, each indicator also has its unique associated problems.

Overhead costs include support activities. By supporting aid agencies that have low overhead costs, donors encourage them to focus on the response phase and they discourage them from allocating sufficient amounts of money to the preparation phase with all the negative consequences discussed in the previous sections. Furthermore, competition to lower costs might lead to under-reporting of administrative expenses (Krishnan et al, 2006).

The fundraising cost percentage is defined as total fundraising costs divided by total funds raised. This indicator is typically reported by aid agencies. It represents the percentage of donations that cannot be directly used for disaster relief activities. Donors and policy makers generally prefer aid agencies that have a low fundraising cost percentage (Sargeant and Kaehler, 1999; Hopkins, 2002). However, when looking at fundraising cost percentages, one must consider that dollars raised for 'unpopular' emergencies typically require more fundraising activities than fundraising for 'popular' emergencies. Trying to reach a low fundraising cost percentage might encourage aid agencies to focus their fundraising activities on 'popular' emergencies. Hence, this might lead to a further emphasis on emergencies that already receive a disproportionate amount of aid. This problem is further exacerbated by the increasing amount of private funds that are earmarked for certain disasters, as well as donors' increasing willingness to enforce these allocation decisions.

A strong focus on visibility and financial accountability can provide aid agencies with incentives to use their resources in an inefficient way. It can potentially encourage aid agencies to provide aid for emergencies that are already crowded with relief groups, and it can also encourage them to focus on short-term objectives instead of long-term goals. That said, donors are starting to realize that visibility and financial indicators do not always reflect the quality of an aid agency's work. However, given that better indicators are still largely missing, the development of improved measurement for aid agencies' performance, need in different regions, the impact of improvements in logistics systems and time value of money, are of utmost importance. Furthermore, a stronger focus on programme effectiveness instead of financial efficiency is necessary (Lowell *et al*, 2005).

Summary and recommendations

Due to the increasing demand for disaster relief and limited resources, it is important that aid agencies use the available resources in the best possible way. Currently, misallocation of resources reduces the efficiency and effectiveness of humanitarian operations. Resource misallocations are partly caused by aid agencies' difficulty in determining the optimal allocation of resources. Aid agency workers are often not aware of the value of logistics and information systems and, therefore, do not invest enough in these areas. Researchers in the area of OR/MS are working on projects that highlight the value of logistics operations and information systems. Furthermore, while models have been developed that help aid agencies in allocating appropriate resources to different phases and activities in humanitarian operations, very often these models do not consider financial constraints. The inclusion of financial constraints into such models of logistics operations, and analysing their impact, are of key importance.

Resource misallocations are also partly caused by funding systems and they will not disappear until funding systems are improved and donors are educated about the consequences of their decisions. Donors provide resources for aid agencies and, hence, have a strong influence on aid agencies' allocation decisions. On the one hand, donors can directly impact allocation decisions by earmarking donations for certain emergencies or activities. On the other hand, they can provide incentives that guide aid agencies towards a certain decision. Currently, donors frequently explicitly and implicitly provide incentives for aid agencies' behaviour that results in too many resources being allocated to direct response instead of the preparedness and reconstruction phases, and also to excess resources being provided for those emergencies that have gained media attention while others are largely neglected.

Aid agencies, UN agencies and donors are, however, aware of the shortcomings of current funding systems. They are re-evaluating their previous approach to humanitarian funding and they are trying to improve the system through many programmes such as the Good Humanitarian Donorship (2003) Initiative. On the other hand, some new trends such as the increased influence of rating agencies that often base their analysis on inconsistent data and overemphasize financial indicators (Lowell *et al*, 2005) appear to, at least in part, be worsening the situation as they have the potential to further misdirect funds. Other new initiatives such as joint fundraising can contribute to providing sound fundraising systems as they can contribute to lowering competition and excessive fundraising efforts. However, even in the case of joint fundraising initiatives, they can worsen the situation if they are not carefully implemented (Toyasaki and Wakolbinger, 2017).

Operations researchers and operations research tools could significantly contribute to establishing sound humanitarian funding systems. The number of publications in this research field has strongly increased over previous years (Burkart *et al*, 2017), but further research is necessary to truly capture key elements and stakeholders of funding systems, their characteristics and impacts. System dynamics models can highlight the interaction between money and product flows as well as trade-offs between short-term and long-term goals (Goncalves, 2008; Besiou *et al*, 2011). Principal-agent models (Seabright, 2001) can also provide insights that indicate how to improve the alignment of the interests of the different stakeholders in humanitarian supply chains.

Development of indicators of need and quality of response (Beamon and Balcik, 2008) can reduce information asymmetries between donors and aid agencies, and they can contribute to improving the quality of aid agency evaluations and rankings. Optimization models can highlight the trade-offs between different characteristics of funding flows and they can allow aid agencies to create appropriate funding portfolios. The effects of competition and collaboration in fundraising activities have been described and analysed in the economics literature (Rose-Ackerman, 1982; Bilodeau and Slivinski, 1997) and they are currently analysed in the operations research literature (Toyasaki and Wakolbinger, 2017). Further research is necessary concerning the benefits and drawbacks of joint fundraising modes and the effects of allocation rules. We expect to see more research papers in the future that address these issues.

Acknowledgement

This work was partially funded by a Summer Research Grant from the Fogelman College of Business and Economics, University of Memphis, and a Start-up Fund at Faculty of Liberal and Professional Studies, York University. This support is gratefully acknowledged.

References

Altay, N and Green, WG III (2006) OR/MS research in disaster operations management, *European Journal of Operational Research*, 175(1), pp 475–93

Balcik, B and Beamon, BM (2008) Facility location in humanitarian relief, *International Journal of Logistics: Research and Applications*, 11(2), pp 101–21

Barman, E (2008) With strings attached, *Nonprofit and Voluntary Sector Quarterly*, 37(1), pp 39–56

Beamon, BM and Balcik, B (2008) Performance measurement in humanitarian relief chains, *International Journal of Public Sector Management*, 21(1), pp 4–25

Bennett, R and Kottasz, R (2000) Emergency fund raising for disaster relief, *Disaster Prevention and Management*, 9 (5), pp 352–60

Besiou, M, Stapleton, O and Van Wassenhove, LN (2011) System dynamics for humanitarian operations, *Journal of Humanitarian Logistics and Supply Chain Management*, 1(1), pp 78–103

Besiou, M, Pedraza-Martinez, AJ and Van Wassenhove, LN (2012) The effect of earmarked funding on fleet management for relief and development, INSEAD working paper 2012/10/TOM/ISIC

Bilodeau, M and Slivinski, A (1997) Rival charities, *Journal of Public Economics*, 66, pp 449–67

Burkart, C, Besiou, M, Wakolbinger, T (2017) The funding–humanitarian supply chain interface, *Surveys in Operations Research and Management Science*, 21(2), pp 31-45

Chomilier, B, Samii, R and Van Wassenhove, LN (2003) The central role of supply chain management at IFRC, *Forced Migration Review*, 18, pp 15–18

Chua, VCH and Wong, CM (2003) The role of united charities in fundraising: The case of Singapore, *Annals of Public and Cooperative Economics*, 74(3), pp 433–64

Development Initiatives (2009a) Public support for humanitarian crises through aid agencies, United Kingdom [Online] www.globalhumanitarianassistance.org/Projects.htm [accessed 21 April 2009]

Development Initiatives (2009b) GHA Report 2009, United Kingdom [Online] www.globalhumanitarianassistance.org [accessed 21 October 2009]

Doocy, S and Tappis, H (2016) Cash-based approaches in humanitarian emergencies: A systematic review, 3ie Systematic Review Report 28, International Initiative for Impact Evaluation (3ie), London

European Commission (2017) Guidance to partners funded by ECHO to deliver medium to large-scale cash transfers in the framework of 2017 HIPs and ESOP, Ref. res (2017)516771 - 31/01/2017

Goncalves, P (2008) System dynamics modeling of humanitarian relief operations, working paper, MIT Sloan Research Paper No 4704–08

Good Humanitarian Donorship (2003) 23 principles and practices of good humanitarian donorship [Online] www.goodhumanitariandonorship.org [accessed 10 June 2010]

Gustavsson, L (2003) Humanitarian logistics: Context and challenges, *Forced Migration Review*, 18, pp 6–8

Hopkins, BR (2002) *The Law of Fundraising*, Wiley, New York

Jahre, M and Heigh, I (2008) Does failure to fund preparedness mean donors must prepare to fund failure in humanitarian supply chains?, in *Beyond Business Logistics*, ed V Autere, AH Bask, G Kovács, K Spens and K Tanskanen, NOFOMA conference proceedings, Helsinki, Finland, 265–82

Kovács, G and Spens, KM (2007) Humanitarian logistics in disaster relief operations, *International Journal of Physical Distribution & Logistics Management*, 37(2), pp 99–114

Krishnan, R, Yetman, M and Yetman, R (2006) Expense misreporting in nonprofit organizations, *The Accounting Review*, 81(2), pp 399–420

Lee, HW and Zbinden, M (2003) Marrying logistics and technology for effective relief, *Forced Migration Review*, 18, pp 34–45

Lowell, S, Trelstad, B and Meehan, B (2005) The ratings game, *Standford Social Innovation Review*, 3(2), pp 38–45

Macrae, J (2002) The bilateralisation of humanitarian response: Trends in the financial, contractual and managerial environment of official humanitarian aid – a background paper for UNHCR [Online] www.odi.org.uk/resources/download/3197.pdf [accessed October 10, 2009]

Martinez, AP, Stapleton, O and Van Wassenhove, LN (2011) Field vehicle fleet management in humanitarian operations: A case-based approach, *Journal of Operations Management*, **29**(5), pp 404–21

Nunnenkamp, P and Öhler, N (2012) Funding competition and efficiency of NGOs: An empirical analysis of non-charitable expenditure of US NGOs engaged in foreign aid, *KYKLOS*, **65**(1), pp 81–110

Oloruntoba, R (2005) A wave of destruction and the waves of relief: Issues, challenges and strategies, *Disaster Prevention and Management*, **14**(4), pp 506–21

Oloruntoba, R (2007) Bringing order out of disorder: Exploring complexity in relief supply chains, in *Proceedings 2nd international conference on operations and supply chain management: regional and global logistics and supply chain management*, ed U Laptaned, Bangkok, Thailand

Oloruntoba, R and Gray, R (2006) Humanitarian aid: An agile supply chain? *Supply Chain Management*, **11**(2), pp 115–20

Perry, M (2007) Natural disaster management planning: A study of logistics managers responding to the tsunami, *International Journal of Physical Distribution and Logistics Management*, **37**(5), pp 409–33

Privett, N and Erhun, F (2011) Efficient funding: Auditing in the nonprofit sector, *Manufacturing and Service Operations Management*, **13**(4), pp 471–88

Rose-Ackerman, S (1982) Charitable giving and 'excessive' fundraising, *The Quarterly Journal of Economics*, **97**(2), pp 193–212

Sargeant, A and Kaehler, J (1999) Returns on fundraising expenditures in the voluntary sector, *Nonprofit Management and Leadership*, **10**(1), pp 5–19

Seabright, P (2001) Conflicts and objectives and task allocation in aid agencies: General issues and application to the European Union, in *The Institutional Economics of Foreign Aid*, ed B Martens, Cambridge University Press, Cambridge

Stapleton, O, Van Wassenhove, LN and Tomasini, R (2010) The challenges of matching private donations to humanitarian needs and the role of brokers, *Supply Chain Forum: An International Journal*, **11**(3), pp 42–53

Street, A (2009) Review of the engagement of NGOs with the humanitarian reform process, synthesis report commissioned by the NGOS and Humanitarian Reform Project

Tatham, PH and Hughes, K (2011) Humanitarian logistics metrics: Where we are, and how we might improve, in *Humanitarian Logistics: Meeting the challenge of preparing for and responding to disasters*, ed MG Christopher and PH Tatham, Kogan Page, London

Thomas, AS (2007) Humanitarian logistics: Enabling disaster response, Fritz Institute, San Francisco, CA

Thomas, AS and Kopczak, LR (2005) From logistics to supply chain management: The path forward in the humanitarian sector, white paper, Fritz Institute, San Francisco, CA

Tomasini, R and Van Wassenhove, LN (2009) *Humanitarian Logistics*, Palgrave Macmillan, Hampshire, UK

Toyasaki, F and Wakolbinger, T (2014) An analysis of impacts associated with earmarked private donations for disaster relief, *Annals of Operations Research*, **221**(1), pp 427–47

Toyasaki, F and Wakolbinger, T (2017) Strategic decision-making about fundraising: Comparison of competitive and joint fundraising modes, under review

Van Wassenhove, LN (2006) Humanitarian aid logistics: Supply chain management in high gear, *The Journal of the Operational Research Society*, **57**(5), pp 475–89

Walker, P and Pepper, K (2007) Follow the money: A review and analysis of the state of humanitarian funding, background paper for the meeting of the Good Humanitarian Donorship and Inter Agency Standing Committee, 20 July, Geneva [Online] www.reliefweb.int/rw/lib.nsf/db900SID/AMMF-75MGSC/$FILE/Tufts-July2007.pdf [accessed on 1 June 2010]

Weinblatt, J (1992) Do government transfers crowd out private transfers to non-profit organizations? The Israeli experience, *International Journal of Social Economics*, **19**(2), pp 60–66

Westhead, R and Chung, M (2007) Aid coalition formed: Care Canada, Oxfam, Save the Children team up to cut down on donor fatigue, but other agencies fear loss of market share, Toronto Star, 1 January, Toronto

Zhuang, J, Saxton, GD and Wu, H (2011) Publicity vs impact in nonprofit disclosures and donor preferences: A sequential game with one nonprofit organization and N donors, *Annals of Operations Research*, forthcoming

Introducing information communication technologies into humanitarian programming

LAURA ELDON AND ANNA KONDAKHCHYAN

Abstract

The rapidly evolving digital landscape is radically transforming the ways in which aid agencies, and the communities with whom they work, can interact. Oxfam believes that information communication technologies (ICTs) offer a huge cross-cutting opportunity to amplify and improve the effectiveness of the organization's work. From monitoring water points to delivering electronic vouchers through mobile phones, and digitalizing protection surveys, Oxfam has been harnessing the use of ICTs to enhance the quality, accessibility and efficiency of our programming. Yet, the path from experimentation to widespread adoption and organizational support for new tools and technologies can be a challenging one to navigate, often opening up a myriad of interlinked considerations, concerns and opportunities. Taking the example of beneficiary[1] information management and the introduction of World Vision's Last Mile Mobile Solutions (LMMS) digital registration and distribution management platform, we will explore the application of Oxfam's 'innovation pyramid' based on a model developed by Gartner Inc. that takes the introduction of new tools through from 'systems of innovation' to 'systems of differentiation' and subsequently 'systems of record.'

Figure 3.1   Oxfam's 'innovation pyramid'

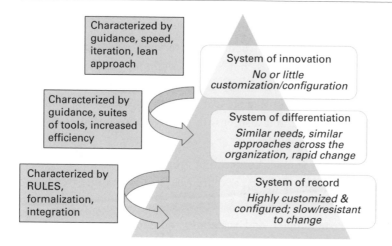

Introduction

Recognizing the enabling role of ICTs[2] in improving the quality and effectiveness of Oxfam's work, the organization has invested in a dedicated ICT in Programme team to support the use of new technologies in programme activities. This team acts as a bridge between the Information Systems (IS) department and International Programme and Humanitarian teams, fulfilling a 'business analyst' function that supports opportunities for innovation and creativity that build on best practice and the roll-out of proven approaches. Making space to pilot new approaches, the team works to hand over proven methodologies or systems to IS for mainstreaming as appropriate.

Grounded in the belief that ICTs can only ever act as an *enabler*, and also recognizing that solutions will only work when responding to concrete programme needs, Oxfam's approach focuses on a number of key principles relating to the successful use of ICTs in programme activities.[3] These include:

1 **ICTs are not an end in themselves, but need to be integrated into existing programmes:** The use of ICTs in a specific programme will not determine its humanitarian or development outcomes; these will be directly linked to the set of activities and services provided by the programme and not to its delivery channel. In advising whether to apply ICTs to a specific programme, Oxfam focuses on effective design, systems thinking and the

explicit value-add of using ICTs, which could include increasing its outreach, reducing its running costs, increasing efficiencies, promoting accountability of stakeholders or improving its monitoring and evaluation activities.

2 **Build on existing ICT infrastructure and services where possible:** We will avoid bespoke solutions, but utilize common, existing tried and tested solutions. Aligned with Oxfam's Information Systems Enterprise Architecture Strategy, this principle can greatly help reduce implementation and support costs, and also ensure that we avoid proliferation of technology for technology's sake.

3 **Keep the technology simple:** Low-tech or 'appropriate' solutions tend to reduce costs, improve reliability, and are easier to source and frequently easier to use.

4 **Plan for the sustainability and scalability:** Planning for sustainability (financial, ecological and social) and scalability will be integrated in the initial design of the solutions; we design for the future, not the now.

5 **Listen to the end-users to understand their needs, habits and risk factor and to maximize ownership and control over services:** Through all initiatives we commit to significant, continued stakeholder engagement, to understand needs, habits and risk factors, and to maximize control and ownership over ICT solutions.

6 **Handle data responsibly:** Not currently formally included in the ICT in Programme team principles, but consistent with Oxfam's Responsible Programme Data Policy (Oxfam, 2015a). All ICT-related activities must be designed in accordance with Oxfam's Responsible Programme Data Policy, and will respect relevant privacy and data protection principles and ethics. This includes placing significant focus on communities' dignity and rights as well as data security.

Oxfam's approach to scoping, trialling, supporting and mainstreaming the use of ICTs in programme activities has gone through an evolution over the past five years. With a current portfolio of tools relating to areas ranging from mobile data collection, digital registrations, data analysis, mapping and case management through to electronic cash and vouchers, initiatives have come about through a variety of means. In some cases these have been initiated by the ICT in Programme team who have identified a common challenge being faced at field levels, in other instances they have been driven by specific field activities, funding calls or opportunistic moments relating to collaboration with other actors.

Oxfam's early experience introducing the use of ICTs into programme activities focused, for example, on the use of mobile survey tools to support existing paper-based data collection exercises such as assessments and monitoring activities. With the relative freedom of senior endorsement to test and pilot, yet without a formally defined process to follow, this was crucial in developing and refining a more structured approach to innovating, scaling and mainstreaming ICT-enabled tools. As formal pilots and field-based initiatives grew, demonstrating clear added value in terms of speed and accuracy of data collection, so did demand. The ICT in Programme team played a key coordination role in liaison with country teams, providing support and capturing learnings about both their needs and experiences with mobile survey tools and guiding activities through to what we now think of as a 'Systems of Differentiation' phase. Crucially, working closely with the Protection team on a number of mobile survey initiatives (Oxfam, 2015b) helped lay the foundation for much of Oxfam's subsequent work on responsible data (Oxfam, 2017a).

As momentum grew, guidance developed on different tools and best practice usage was refined with two tools identified to be mainstreamed as 'Systems of Record', rooted in an acknowledgement that no one single tool could address all of Oxfam's diverse programme needs (Oxfam, 2016). This approach also sought to empower programme teams to identify the best software for their needs and thereby engender greater buy-in at the local level and increase the likelihood of long-term sustainability. Working closely with the IS department to narrow down tools and bring them into the internal service catalogue of supported tools prompted the team to adopt the 'innovation pyramid' model as a framing tool for the introduction of ICTs. While engagement with mobile surveys first prompted this framing, subsequent and parallel exploration of the use of ICTs to support improved capture and management of beneficiary data proved key in further refining this approach.

Innovation

As with many humanitarian agencies, Oxfam had long been faced with the 'last mile problem' – the ability to measure reach, accountability and impact at the critical stage of humanitarian aid delivery where essential goods and services reach people affected by disasters – at the agency level and as a sector. Traditional reliance on paper-based processes to register individuals and manage the distribution of aid was seen to contribute to a number of challenges related to transparency, wasted time, human error, fraud and dignity. In a context of increasing use of digital technologies, a number of tools started to emerge with the aim of helping agencies answer the following questions:

- Did we target the right people with the right aid?
- Did the aid reach the intended beneficiaries? If so...
- Was the aid effective and did it make a difference?

This movement to digitalize beneficiary registration and distribution management activities positioned itself not only as a way to save time and increase the efficiency and effectiveness of the overall process, but also to cut down on fraud, to improve the beneficiary experience, have faster and better disaggregated reporting with fewer input errors, and to increase accountability to all stakeholders. Investment in such tools formed a strong alignment with Oxfam's organizational objectives and its ICT in Programme principles, addressing a clear existing need with the potential to integrate with programme activities to add value. Crucially this area offered the ability to increase accountability and improve the quality of aid provision at the last mile of humanitarian activities.

In January 2013 a member of Oxfam's Emergency Food Security and Vulnerable Livelihoods (EFSVL) team was approached by World Vision (WV) to discuss whether Oxfam would be interested in piloting their Last Mile Mobile Solutions (LMMS) digital beneficiary registration and distribution management software as part of a WV proposal to the Canadian International Development Agency (CIDA) (now known as the Department of Foreign Affairs, Trade and Development (DFATD)), which sought to scale usage to multiple agencies. World Vision's proposal was budgeted to cover all costs relating to equipment, training and the bulk of technical support, and made provision for a coordination fund to be used by Oxfam to support participation in the collaboration. Given the longstanding reliance on predominantly paper-based processes at the 'last mile', which can create manifold challenges, this formed an opportunistic platform from which to pilot the use of a new technology that sought to increase accountability and *impact*, at low cost and risk to Oxfam.

Last Mile Mobile Solutions is a standalone technology solution that registers beneficiaries digitally and issues barcodes that can be scanned at distributions points to bring up detailed records, linking to a live updating database of stock levels and projects. The system is designed to eliminate reliance on paper-based systems for distributions, to automatically calculate accurate cash, food and non-food rations, and deliver faster computer-generated reports to stakeholders. As such LMMS supports aid delivery to beneficiaries and strengthens control over inventory during distributions in the field. This includes improved procedures on delivery of aid through photo verification of households or proxies authorized to receive assistance.

Collaborating with World Vision to trial their LMMS technology had clear alignment with Oxfam's strategic aims. Significantly, such an opportunity also aligned with the organization's key principles relating to 'buy not build', collaboration with wider sector actors, and prioritizing synergies with existing processes. Following internal consultation, it was agreed that taking part in the CIDA-funded grant to trial LMMS would provide Oxfam with an opportunity for significant learning from programmatic, logistics, accountability and ICT perspectives at minimal cost to the organization. Given the complex nature of the collaboration involving multiple countries, time zones and stakeholders, this project offered the opportunity to trial what was seen as a new, flexible model of working in which overall coordination rested with the ICT in Programme team, but with significant input and ownership sitting with key stakeholders including the global EFSVL team, Logistics, IS and country teams. In part, this structure was also agreed as it acknowledged the cross-sectorial nature of the technology, and its compatibility for multi-sector distributions. Sitting firmly at the systems of innovation stage of Oxfam's 'Innovation Pyramid', it was agreed that this piloting of new technology required a great deal of flexibility and autonomy in order to explore its relevance for Oxfam.

The significant anticipated benefits from participating in the project included the opportunity for the Global Humanitarian team to utilize technology that would:

- reduce reliance on paper-based processes;
- generate time savings during beneficiary registration, distribution and reporting;

- increase the accuracy and disaggregation of data;
- streamline logistics for distributions with greater accountability to beneficiaries and all project stakeholders;
- be able to track beneficiaries over time and support Oxfam's resilience programming;
- have the potential to be able to link to government social protection schemes;
- have the potential to avoid duplication of beneficiary targeting with other agencies.

In addition, this opportunity provided a number of other significant benefits:

- It provided a platform to generate valuable learning from using this technology that could be applied across multiple sectors and help inform Oxfam's wider approach to digital registration technology and beneficiary data protection. This included drawing useful comparisons with similar initiatives such as a home-grown project in Bangladesh.
- There was the potential to share learnings more widely across the Oxfam confederation, especially relevant given the *importance of collaboration with affiliates* at a country deployment level.
- There was minimal cost for Oxfam other than staff time, given provision made under the CIDA proposal to cover all costs relating to hardware, software, training and the bulk of technical support, and the creation of a coordination fund for Oxfam's exclusive use.
- Building a strong partnership with World Vision provided a practical and realistic way for Oxfam to help influence the product development roadmap.
- WV's previous work developing and testing the LMMS tool provided Oxfam with a controlled risk environment and the opportunity to learn from them about 'pain points' when looking to scale up this type of technology.

Pilot project experiences under the CIDA grant

Following dialogue with country teams, the Philippines and Niger were identified as locations in which to conduct pilot projects. In the Philippines it was agreed to pilot the tool as a preparedness measure by registering households in flood-prone areas such as Pampanga where Oxfam has both responded in the past and anticipated future distributions. The newly released Android-based version of LMMS (with additional functionality) was also piloted and rolled out as part of the Typhoon Haiyan response in northern Cebu in early 2014. In Niger, LMMS was piloted as part of the European Commission's European Civil Protection and Humanitarian Aid Operations (ECHO) funded series of cash distributions from June to October 2013.

Oxfam's experience piloting LMMS proved to be very positive, with significant time savings and improved quality of service delivery. For example, in the Philippines, Oxfam's use of LMMS as part of its Typhoon Haiyan response resulted in time savings of approximately 47 per cent for registration (233 staff days for 14,000 beneficiaries). As part of the wider CIDA-funded grant, an accountability study was carried out by World Vision in Niger and the Philippines in which beneficiaries expressed a sense of relief that the system ensures distributions are not open to being tampered with, and thus ensures transparency in distributions (eg cannot claim with a stolen card, nor a case of first come first served). Women in Niger spoke of having such faith in the system that they would arrive on time for a distribution and not hours in advance for fear that not getting to the front of the queue would mean that they would miss out. Owning a card with a photo gave them a sense of confidence that no imposter could stand in for them, and they reported that people had stopped trying to beat the system because they couldn't.

In a similar way to the experience with mobile surveys, interest in the use of LMMS began to grow as roaming Humanitarian Support personnel took their experiences from deployment to deployment, and HQ-based advisors became more aware of the potential benefits of digitalizing these crucial processes. Alongside the CIDA-funded pilots in the Philippines and Niger, the Myanmar country team successfully included budgeting for LMMS in a funding proposal to CIDA, and other locations such as Mali and Ethiopia began to actively seek funding to engage with the tool. Whilst the 'innovation' of digitalizing beneficiary information management and distribution activities was clearly gaining traction and addressing an important need, the ad hoc nature of new deployments highlighted the need for Oxfam to streamline its approach and consider the options relating to further investment in LMMS and its engagement with the wider digital beneficiary management space as a whole.

Aware that a number of agencies had developed their own tools, such as the World Food Programme's (WFP) SCOPE and United Nations High Commissioner for Refugees' (UNHCR) PROGRES, there were a number of unanswered questions about investing in a single platform. For example, it was not clear whether those, such as WFP, developing proprietary solutions would require funded programmes to make use of their software, even if teams were already trained on and using a different model. As organizations looked to wider usage of their solutions, business models were still being developed, leading to a lack of clarity about the wider costs and implications of engagement. Given the increasing numbers of tools making their way on to the market and into the field, there was a push from donors to consider interoperability and to ensure that systems are able to talk to each other. While many agencies had spoken of the need to ensure some degree of theoretical compatibility between systems, this had not been knowingly tested. This prompted Oxfam to prioritize engagement in consortia grants that centred around how the different systems being developed complement each other (or not), and ways of maximizing their use to ensure effective management of information from beneficiary to delivery of assistance and back to donors for reporting.

Beyond the questions relating to how different tools 'talked' to each other and the specific functionality they offered, was also the need to consider potential inter-agency usage, and the opportunities posed by beneficiaries being registered once, by just one actor, facilitating a better experience for them, whilst also allowing for greater efficiencies on the part of different agencies. Bigger questions remained about data security and openness to the process change, as well as the trust required between agencies to collaborate in such ways. As with many ICT-related initiatives, what began as a relatively simple, contained set of pilots, opened up a number of wider, interlinked conversations covering data protection and security, collaboration, integration with e-transfer technologies, digital identity standards and even biometric technology for identification and authentication.

On LMMS specifically, it was agreed that before any further decisions about its wider application across Oxfam could be made, the following questions needed to be further examined:

- To what extent could key partners work with World Vision in contributing to software development to suit their own organizational needs? To what extent could there be multiple ownership of this software, balancing the need for customization against the benefits of more rigid consistency?

- Given that LMMS was originally designed for food distributions and given the amount of cash transfer programming the sector (and Oxfam) engages in, it was felt that the LMMS roadmap needed to include the ability to link to banks, mobile phone companies and other elements of the cash delivery infrastructure. How does LMMS compare to other similar software packages such as SCOPE created by WFP? And will non-governmental organizations (NGOs) become increasingly obliged to adopt specific software packages depending on their donor relationships?

- Wider questions also exist about the applicability of LMMS for sudden onset emergencies as well as activities in slow onset responses. Do we want to focus our attention and resources on a particular type of scenario? Where can we best make use of this technology to maximize the benefits?

- What resources would be required internally to make this work? Do we need dedicated support? Would there be changing requirements in people's job descriptions to do this?

- Going forward, given that LMMS cuts across so many functions, who should 'own' this process within Oxfam? How could we ensure a more streamlined effort to engage with LMMS and similar systems?

- Who could Oxfam identify as 'internal champions' of LMMS globally? How should we resource their ability to be deployed to other countries to support?

Scaling up

Building on these initial pilot experiences and also the growing demand, Oxfam was at a crossroads: on the one hand, pilots had confirmed that there was a real need for this type of technology with most pilot locations keen to continue utilizing it. The tool has been deployed in the Philippines, Mali, Niger, Ethiopia, Iraq and Myanmar. Field teams would engage directly with the LMMS team at World Vision International and through word of mouth, and new country programmes were keen to come on board (the ICT in Programme team facilitated links directly with WV whilst maintaining oversight of a growing portfolio of activities). The marketing and outreach efforts that the ICT in Programme team had invested at the start had now reached a tipping point where managing demand for LMMS (as well as wider mobile data collection tools) with the existing team capacity became a challenge. On the other hand, and from a global perspective, it was clear that Oxfam was at risk of being stuck in a perpetual pilot mode, foregoing many of the potential benefits of streamlining its approach to beneficiary registration and distribution, and building internal capacity for end-user training and functional support.

In the summer of 2015, just under two years from when Oxfam first engaged with LMMS, a learning review was commissioned to examine what had and had not worked well from the perspective of stakeholders as diverse as programme managers and officers, Headquarters-based advisors, IT and information security specialists. This process enabled Oxfam to formulate a clear roadmap for the next steps of its engagement with digital beneficiary information management processes. Key lessons from the innovation phase that would have a bearing on the design of the scale-up strategy and further tool deployments included:

- The tool added most value for programmes with a repeat distribution component (food, NFI direct cash, cash for work).
- With pre-positioning of kit and investment in training, the tool could be used from phase one of an emergency; however, it fared better in a slow-onset context or in the second phase of a response.
- It did not prove cost effective for use in blanket distributions or where digital registration has significant risks for the population being registered.
- Where vulnerability criteria for programme participant targeting are complex and highly variable (for example, in protracted crisis responses such as the Syria response), the tool lacked flexibility.
- Training should ideally be immediately followed by field deployment.
- Training can be provided internally by trained Oxfam staff, reducing the cost of and reliance on WV support.
- The system can be operated by Oxfam staff and partners, and is fully localized for use in French and Spanish.
- Kit procurement is best done locally and internally.
- There should be a light-touch advisory service to help teams assess the suitability of LMMS for a specific programme context.
- Process guidance should be provided, so that roles and responsibilities during registration and distribution are understood.
- The scope of a deployment must be discussed with, and understood by, implementation teams from programme management levels through to thematic leads and IS support.

The latter two points, borne out of Oxfam's experience using LMMS in the first phase of the Nepal Earthquake Response, in particular stressed the importance of getting the 'human process' surrounding technology implementation right, and of the continuous need to manage stakeholder expectations. But more on this later...

The business case developed on the back of the review argued that the moment was right to scale the use of this technology across Oxfam's humanitarian programmes, and with reference to the Innovation Pyramid model, take it through to the System of Differentiation stage. This would allow for the implementation of the following digital processes:

- beneficiary registration (field);
- ID card printing and distribution (office, field);
- distribution planning (office);
- actual distribution (field);
- post-distribution monitoring and reporting (field and office).

Using rather conservative estimates, the business case set the goal of deploying LMMS technology in at least four countries every year for the following three years, targeting highly relevant contexts in Oxfam's humanitarian programmes, alongside deployments in rapid-onset contexts using pre-positioned LMMS kits. It further argued that the investment would be consistent with the programme expenditure data, highlighting a twofold increase in spend on programmes requiring beneficiaries to be registered in order to receive assistance in the form of food, cash or other non-food items. We also had data from studies conducted during the innovation/pilot phase, clearly indicating that, by going digital in this high-risk area of operation, Oxfam could reach more vulnerable people faster and dramatically reduce commonly identified distribution risks such as double-dipping.

Benefits we could predict from the scale-up – based either on the data from the early pilots or Oxfam's experience with rolling out Helios (Blansjaar and Fraser, 2014) – were:

- financial return through efficiencies via streamlined and planned process;
- improved beneficiary experience and strengthened two-way accountability;
- improved programme quality through better targeting of community needs over time;
- structured process with a digital audit trail against which Oxfam can monitor and measure its performance;
- reduction in potential for fraud during beneficiary registration and distribution.

Importantly, the business case warned against maintaining the status quo, arguing that if Oxfam decided not to formalize its commitment to LMMS, countries would continue ad hoc investment in developing their own solutions or buying them off the shelf, and these may be either not appropriate for Oxfam or too expensive to implement. Oxfam would also remain vulnerable to issues arising from audits around compliance and value for money, with consequent reputation and financial implications.

Having recently released its responsible data policy (Oxfam, 2015a), Oxfam was also acutely aware of the increased urgency of ensuring safe handling of beneficiary data across the entire data life cycle, and the importance of facilitating the use of tools that had been thoroughly reviewed to ensure compliance.

At the time, Oxfam was in an advantageous position of being able to adopt the technology of its own choice.[4] We were keen to continue collaborating with World Vision, with whom we were aligned in the future vision of agencies coordinating and safely sharing beneficiary registration data for more effective and timely humanitarian responses. It was also clear, however, that for the scale-up phase to be effective, we had to tackle three key aspects:

1 Defining new terms of partnership with World Vision as the 'owner' of the tool and ultimately the service provider.

2 Working closely with Oxfam's internal IT team to transition LMMS into a fully supported service.

3 Developing a sustainable model for training and functional support.

Following the investment decision, a six-month project phase set out to address these diverse concerns. The decision to invest was not insignificant as Oxfam was a year into an organizational transformation process known internally as Oxfam2020. Thus, anticipated key users of the LMMS from the Humanitarian teams across 17 different Oxfam affiliates were in the midst of a merger into a Global Humanitarian team, with significant amounts of organizational resource and management attention dedicated to the process.

Both organizations were in uncharted territory – at the purely pragmatic level, the WV LMMS team were providing a service to Oxfam. To our colleagues in the Information Systems Service Management team this meant agreeing an unambiguous service level agreement through which Oxfam, as the customer, could monitor the provider's performance. Yet, there was also an important strategic partnership dimension. Both organizations were keen to continue collaborating for a shared common good – to be able to jointly shape the tool, share training and deployment resource, and where appropriate coordinate with other players and share registration data for more impactful responses. It is fair to say that the negotiations around the licence agreement and service terms, skilfully guided by Oxfam's Service Management experts with input from both WV's and Oxfam's legal teams have been a learning and further trust-building experience. It was a nine-month marathon, with a win–win outcome: Oxfam now had an unlimited licence for the use of LMMS across its programmes for a period of three years, moving away from a server-based model used in the pilot; WV LMMS team had secured its first external customer, increasing their internal leverage for further product development and boosting their small internal team's capacity to test and improve the tool further.

In parallel with these negotiations, internal negotiations with the Information Systems colleagues to transition LMMS into a suite of tools and services within Oxfam's support IS portfolio were just as important. The questions that in the previous pilot phase could be deferred or worked around, such as, for example, how could all subsequent LMMS installations and future upgrades be managed, or how would Oxfam ensure secure storage/transfer and disposal of the data collected, or how could support calls be filtered internally, had to be resolved. In this negotiation, the appointment of an IS project manager, who took the lead in intra-departmental navigation of the service transition process in close collaboration with the LMMS product lead with a good grasp of field realities and the tool itself, helped enormously. So did the formation of the LMMS Project Governance Board with senior representatives from Humanitarian, Internal Audit, IS and International Programmes departments.

With the benefit of hindsight, we can now acknowledge that both the internal and external negotiation phases, with their many frustrations over delays, were key steps in the change journey from the pilot mentality of the innovation phase towards scaling up into a 'System of Differentiation', where process was perhaps just as valuable as (if not more so than) the negotiated outcomes.

The third question the scale-up project set out to address was, 'How can we develop a sustainable training and functional support model for LMMS?' For this we drew heavily from the organizational experience rolling out Oxfam's Programme Information and Supply Chain Management processes and systems. For example, although we had access to WV learning materials, we knew it was important to link these with Oxfam's accepted terminology and field ways of working. We also knew, from previous deployments that some learning materials (for example, visual 'how to' guides relating to the most frequent transactions) are more valuable and easier to maintain than others. Additionally, we knew that given the endemic challenges of high staff turnover and shortages of tech-savvy staff in some of our more remote operational environments, we needed to build internal capacity for first and second line functional user support and training. To this end, a permanent beneficiary information management lead role was established and supported during the project phase by a dedicated LMMS trainer.

Eighteen months since the scale-up decision was made and twelve months after the 'project phase' of the scale-up ended, Oxfam:

- Has saved tens of thousands of dollars from the centralized service model compared to one in which each country would secure the service directly from WV.

- Is using LMMS in eight country programmes with an average number of four servers per country. Thanks to the work of the project team to develop robust process guidance and more streamlined implementation support, Nepal is up and running with the LMMS service after the initial thorny deployment in the aftermath of the 2015 earthquake.

- has been able to influence the LMMS product development roadmap with feedback loops from deployed locations. The house-to-house offline registration functionality known as LORA (so named for Laura Eldon, who was the Oxfam focal point for LMMS during the early innovation phase), and more recent changes to the reporting aspects of the tool developed with colleagues from the Oxfam Philippines programme that speed up the 'know your money' (KYC)[5] verification process for programme participants, serve to prove the merits of collaboration and of adopting a partnership approach with World Vision.

Is it mainstream yet?

Thinking back to the Innovation Pyramid model introduced earlier, where is Oxfam now in relation to the 'last mile problem' it set out to begin to address with the introduction of LMMS? Has the technology fulfilled its promise as an enabler of a more streamlined and planned aid delivery process? Has it strengthened two-way accountability between Oxfam and the people it works with? Have we been able to target community needs better over time with insight offered by technology? Unsurprisingly, these are hard questions to answer unambiguously.

We have some insight from a learning review of a multi-year learning and experimentation initiative SHINE (Oxfam, 2017b) which, with the generous support from the Swedish International Development Agency (Sida), sought to explore how use of ICTs might enable better quality humanitarian responses (Oxfam, 2017c). In particular, in Ethiopia, where the LMMS-based ways of working were introduced, staff who were initially sceptical about the move away from the traditional paper-based approach soon realized that LMMS is very flexible: it can accommodate projects with different objectives and different modalities. Also, the system does not always require internet connection – this is crucial, especially in remote areas. With the new system, once beneficiaries have been registered, it takes minimum time and effort to search data and to edit and update information. Opportunities for data manipulation are minimized, and it is straightforward to generate reports for donors.

In addition to the obvious benefits for Oxfam, the new system has had a positive impact on the individuals it supports. In the context of Ethiopia, as was made clear during focus group discussions, affected communities have valued being given the ID cards. According to participants, having a card gives them a sense of security as people were previously unsure about the payment they would receive. One man said that 'The card is a confirmation that we will get our payments.' The system provides people with a secure means of receiving cash, and gives them the dignity of choice – ensuring they can buy what they need, when they need it.

During the ongoing 2017 drought response in Ethiopia, Oxfam has incorporated LMMS into its Cash Based Intervention in the Somali region, drawing upon the benefit of ICTs speeding up and simplifying delivering humanitarian aid. As a result, ICT-enabled beneficiary registrations and distributions have been adopted and implemented as part of Oxfam's large-scale response. As of the end of May 2017, all drought response zones in the Somali region were using LMMS. In order to make this happen, Oxfam provided various training sessions to key local implementing partners and their staff on the use of LMMS, and deployed an additional six LMMS servers to ensure the effectiveness of this approach. Having been introduced in Ethiopia on a pilot basis more than three years ago, the Ethiopia country team has now scaled its use to all relevant humanitarian programmes.

Has LMMS now moved down the pyramid into a System of Record? This last question is perhaps the easiest to answer. LMMS sits firmly within a suite of tools fully supported by Oxfam's internal Information Systems department; the country on-boarding process has been streamlined, and we continue to expand our internal pool of staff who are able to deliver new training and support existing sites. It thus has many characteristics of a System of Record.

Yet, as Oxfam's international programmes streamline their use of beneficiary registration and distribution technologies, new questions are emerging around responsible digital identity management for crisis-affected populations and also how biometric and blockchain-based technologies might be used to improve response outcomes and transparency at the last mile. The ICT in Programme team is actively engaged with these questions, along with many of Oxfam's peer agencies and private sector partners. The Innovation Pyramid is back at work – with the hope of one day turning the last mile problem into a working link in the chain of humanitarian aid delivery.

Notes

1 As an organization, Oxfam has endorsed the use of 'people we work with' over the term 'beneficiary' to address issues relating to imbalances of power and to highlight the active participation of many communities with whom we work. For the purposes of this chapter, we have continued to use the term 'beneficiary' for clarity about the specific process this activity sought to address.

2 By ICTs in this context we mean technologies that support specific elements of development and humanitarian programmes, and not enterprise-wide solutions, with a routine process standardization objective.

3 A full list is available at: http://policy-practice.oxfam.org.uk/our-approach/ict-in-programme; also see http://digitalprinciples.org/.

4 It is not uncommon in the sector for donors to insist that their implementing partners utilize particular technology solutions. Whilst this is valid as an approach, it does come with its own set of challenges around process and technology interoperability and staff capacity.

5 Know your customer (KYC) is the process of a business identifying and verifying the identity of its clients. The term is also used to refer to the bank and anti-money laundering regulations that govern these activities.

References

Blansjaar, M and Fraser, S (2014) Information technology in humanitarian supply chains, in *Humanitarian Logistics*, ed M Christopher and P Tatham, 2nd edition, Kogan Page, London

Oxfam (2015a) Oxfam responsible program data policy, 27 August [Online] https://policy-practice.oxfam.org.uk/publications/oxfam-responsible-program-data-policy-575950

Oxfam (2015b) Typhoon Haiyan: Community research into the relocation of internally displaced people in the Philippines, 15 May [Online] https://policy-practice.oxfam.org.uk/publications/typhoon-haiyan-community-research-into-the-relocation-of-internally-displaced-p-552930

Oxfam (2016) Mobile survey toolkit, 27 July [Online] https://policy-practice.oxfam.org.uk/publications/mobile-survey-toolkit-617456

Oxfam (2017a) Responsible data management training pack, 29 March [Online] https://policy-practice.oxfam.org.uk/publications/responsible-data-management-training-pack-620235

Oxfam (2017b) SHINE [Online] https://policy-practice.oxfam.org.uk/our-work/humanitarian/shine

Oxfam (2017c) ICTs in humanitarian response: A learning review of a three-year, five-country programme, 13 April [Online] https://policy-practice.oxfam.org.uk/publications/icts-in-humanitarian-response-a-learning-review-of-a-three-year-five-country-pr-620256

Technology meets humanitarian logistics

04

A view on benefits and challenges

PETER TATHAM, GRAHAM HEASLIP AND KAREN SPENS

Abstract

This chapter considers how a number of relatively novel technological concepts – three-dimensional printing (3DP), remotely piloted aircraft systems (RPAS), hybrid cargo airships (HCAs) and cash transfer programmes (CTPs) – can potentially be used to support the work of the humanitarian logistician. In each case the concept will be outlined, and its potential benefits and challenges discussed.

Introduction

At the macro level, the challenge facing the humanitarian logistician is broadly similar to that found in a business context, namely getting supply to equal demand as efficiently and effectively as possible. However, of course, those preparing and responding to natural disasters and complex emergencies face greater complexity on both sides of the equation. In respect of demand the '6W' problem of 'who wants what, where, when and why?' reflects the inherent uncertainty in the environment of such events where there is frequently a paucity of data in relation to, for example, the population locations and demographics, as well as the actual impact of the event and, hence, the needs of those affected. On the supply side, the physical destruction of roads, bridges and communication systems together with the influx of multiple responding organizations has the potential to result in excess supply in some locations, and paucity in others.

Given these multiple challenges, the aim of this chapter is to reflect on the potential benefits and challenges of a number of developments that are being increasingly used in the 'for profit' sector, and consider how they might be applied to support the work of the humanitarian logistician. The four concepts that will be discussed are: 3D printing, remotely piloted aircraft systems, hybrid cargo airships and cash transfer programmes, each of which will now be considered in turn.

3D printing

The basic approach employed by 3DP (which is also referred to as rapid prototyping, rapid manufacturing or additive manufacturing) is that it builds an item by adding layer upon layer. As a result, 3DP can be distinguished from traditional production methods that typically involve the use of injection moulding techniques or the removal of material from a large block.

Furthermore, although the technique has been in existence since the early 1990s, the development of new and improved approaches is changing what is possible to be created as well as the economics of the process. Thus, whilst multiple 3DP technologies exist, this chapter will consider the use of fused deposition modelling (FDM) as this is ideal for printers that are easy to operate, have a low cost, are easily transported and can utilize a range of source materials. As a result, FDM printers are well suited for a role in supporting the humanitarian logistician.

Most basic level FDM machines operate by heating a single filament of material, such as acrylonitrile butadiene styrene (ABS), which is a strong, stable engineering grade polymer that is suitable for multiple end use applications. The filament is then extruded in a continuous feed (like a glue gun) and, at the same time, the bed of the 3DP moves slowly downwards thereby allowing an object to build. Such machines start at around the size of a desktop printer and are thus easily transported. They are also relatively inexpensive, with entry level machines priced at about US $750 and, reflecting Moore's Law, the capability of such machines is quickly growing whilst, at the same time, the cost for a given capability is reducing. In addition, FDM machines that can use multiple raw materials at the same time are becoming available, and there is also a growth in the range of source materials that can be used for different applications.

That said, single filament FDMs are the least problematic of the current range of printers to operate as they do not require a sealed print environment and can, subject to constraints around wind strength, dust and changes in humidity, be used in an outdoor environment. Equally importantly, they are not expensive to run with the filament costing around $40/kg and, as the workings are easily accessed, they are also the easiest printers to maintain, adjust on site, and/or repair if damaged in transit. As a result, such relatively simple systems can be used to build complex objects such as pipes and connectors that can then be used in water, sanitation and hygiene (WASH) projects in order to, for example, replace a broken component.

In an ideal world the printer should be supported by an uninterrupted power supply as a component must be printed in one continuous process, and this can take as long as 12 hours for a large or complex item of equipment. Thus, in a humanitarian context, it may be necessary to provide either a dedicated mini-generator or a battery back-up in the case of power failures. Importantly, however, whilst such a power failure may result in a need to restart the print process, it will not damage the printer itself.

3DP – a humanitarian logistic perspective

As indicated in the introduction to this chapter, faced by a lack of clarity in the demand side of the equation, the humanitarian logistician is frequently forced to use an inefficient push-based approach in which the answer to the 6W problem has been guesstimated in advance. However, the use of 3DP eases this challenge in a number of ways:

1 It enables the use of a single raw material from which multiple items can be created to meet an identified need. This reflects the concept of logistic postponement (Christopher, 2016) and avoids the requirement to transport items into, and warehouse them within, the field location on a 'just in case' basis, which often sees them lying unused in a warehouse.

2 The reels of raw material (such as ABS) require limited packaging and have a high mass to volume ratio when compared to finished goods. This makes them more efficient to transport – an important consideration in a humanitarian context.

3 Given the remote location of many humanitarian operations, the lead time for the provision of spare parts can be lengthy, with delays of up to six months for some countries having been encountered. Thus, whilst a 3DP time of up to 12 hours may sound excessive, it is clearly a significant

improvement over the time needed for a component to be sourced from outside the country in which the field operation is being conducted.

4 The use of 3DP could help mitigate incompatibilities between the equipment supplied by different non-governmental organizations (NGOs), which, according to de Leeuw *et al* (2010), can be a particular challenge where WASH equipment is involved.

5 The 3DP technology also allows for the design of components that are not constrained by the limitations of mass production techniques. For example, it is relatively simple to incorporate in-line filtration in to a printed part when using an FDM machine, whereas this is difficult to achieve if injection moulding is used as the production method.

Management of the overall process

Unfortunately, and perhaps inevitably, the benefits of 3DP technology have already been misused – for example, to produce miniature firearms. Perhaps more realistically, there is clear potential for a well-intentioned but over-enthusiastic, individual to 'print' an item that malfunctions and thus causes injury or worse.

To overcome such challenges, a hub-and-spoke management model is proposed. In essence, a field logistician identifies a requirement and then provides the details to a technical hub. This can be achieved by means of photographs, written descriptions or even a 3D scanner. Once the requirement has been received, the team at the hub can develop a prototype ensuring that, for example, its design and the materials used are appropriate, that suitable risk mitigation strategies have been considered, and that mechanical engineering and logistic considerations have been taken into account.

After the prototype has been tested and found to be 'fit for purpose', the design can be passed electronically to the field location and 3D printed. The resulting component can then be subject to local testing as necessary to ensure the integrity of the print process before the component is fitted and its performance monitored.

In the first instance this process is likely to require that a set of core components be developed, but as the use of 3DP becomes more widespread it is anticipated that a bank of open-access designs will be created. These can then be modified to meet the particular requirement without the loss of structural integrity. For example, whilst a standard water pipe bend might be 90°, a site-specific layout may call for a pipe with an angle of 75° or 120°.

In this case, the standard design held on the computer can be manipulated to achieve the required dimensions, and an appropriately redesigned model printed off in a relatively short time.

Summary

In summary, subject to any unforeseen challenges emerging, there would appear to be no reasons in principle why the benefits of 3DP should not be transferable from the 'for profit' to the 'not for profit' environment. Indeed, arguably, the basic process has even greater potential in this latter context. For example, a 3DP house has been created in Amsterdam that uses sustainable materials such as recycled plastics as the source material. In a similar vein, it is suggested that wood chippings or even the rubble from destroyed buildings could be ground down to provide the source material input to a 3DP process. Thus, the challenge of the 2010 Haiti post-earthquake debris removal, which was estimated to take 1,000 trucks 1,000 days (Booth, 2010), could actually lead to the onsite development of new dwellings with significant reductions in cost and overall environmental impact.

Remotely piloted aircraft systems

This section of the chapter discusses the potential use of remotely piloted aircraft systems (RPAS) to support the work of the humanitarian logistician. In doing so, it will be noted that there are multiple words/acronyms used to describe such systems, including unmanned aerial vehicles (UAVs), unmanned aerial systems (UAS) and drones. Thus, in order to avoid confusion, the term RPAS will be used as this reflects the nomenclature adopted by the International Civil Aviation Organization (ICAO), and also emphasizes the end-to-end nature of such a system.

The potential benefits of RPAS operations have been emphasized by the United Nations (UN) Office for the Coordination of Humanitarian Affairs (OCHA) which, in a recent report discussing their use in a humanitarian context, observed that '[the] move from speculation to reality raises challenging questions around ... how best to integrate [RPAS] into humanitarian response' (OCHA, 2014: 3).

Indeed, that the question is now a case of 'how' and not 'if' has been reinforced by recent research undertaken by the organization Swiss Mine Action (FSD) in which a survey of 194 humanitarian organizations, donors, UN agencies, national governments, private businesses and other respondents was undertaken. The results can be summarized in the authors' observation that 'A majority of survey respondents [66 per cent] expressed confidence that [RPAS] have the potential to strengthen humanitarian work, and that [RPAS] can greatly enhance the speed and quality of localized needs assessments, while a significant minority [22 per cent] viewed the use of [RPAS] in humanitarian work unfavourably' (Soesilo and Sandvik, 2016: 3).

Using RPAS to support the humanitarian logistician

First, it is clear that RPAS are becoming relatively commonplace, with 270 companies in 57 countries reported as manufacturing such aircraft (OCHA, 2014). These range from very small platforms that cost about US $100 to high-end military systems that are the size of a small executive jet and cost around US $130 million, with Table 4.1 offering a summary of three exemplars.

Table 4.1   Rotary, fixed wing and hybrid exemplar RPAS

	Rotary Wing RPA	Fixed Wing RPA	Hybrid RPA
Exemplar	DJI Inspire	Aerosonde Mk 7	Latitude HQ –160 B
Endurance	15–30 mins	10+ hrs	15 hrs
Cruising Speed	70–80 kph (40–45 kts)	90–110 kph (50–60 kts)	70 kph (40 kts)
Ceiling	4,500 m (14,750 ft)	4,500 m (14,750 ft)	4,268 m (14,000 ft)
Wingspan	0.559 m (1.63 ft)	3.6 m (5.6 ft)	3.81 m (12.6 ft)
Overall Length	0.559 m (1.63 ft)	1.7 m (5.6 ft)	2.44 m (8 ft)
Max Gross Take-off wt	4.6 kg (10.14 lb)	25 kg (55 lb)	43 kg (95 lb)
Max Payload Weight	1.7 kg (3.74 lb)	4.5 kg (10 lb)	5.44 kg (12 lb)
Launch	Vertical	Catapult or from roof of a 4*4 driving at an appropriate speed	Vertical
Landing	Vertical	Belly landing or catch net	Vertical

SOURCE   DJI: http://www.dji.com/inspire-1/info#specs; Aerosonde: http://www.uavglobal.com/aerosonde-mk-4-7/ and http://www.textronsystems.com/what-we-do/unmanned-systems/aerosonde; Latitude: https://latitudeengineering.com/products/hq/

Faced with this broad range of potential systems, it is insightful to consider what might be valuable attributes to support the work of the humanitarian logistician. In summary, it is argued that such RPAS should:

- not be within the regime covered by the International Traffic in Arms Regulations (ITAR) or be an otherwise restricted system;

- have a sufficiently long endurance to allow it to operate throughout daylight hours and also, if possible, have a night-flying capability;

- possess a payload capability that allows it to link with satellite networks for command and control purposes, as well as operating suitable visual/infrared still and video cameras in order to be able to capture and deliver needs assessment data to the National Disaster Management Organization (NDMO) swiftly and efficiently.

In effect, these criteria suggest that the RPAS should be a member of the class described as 'low altitude, long endurance' (LALE) and that it is able to operate 'beyond line of sight' (BLOS) – such as is the case for the Aerosonde and Latitude exemplars in Table 4.1.

This is not to discount the achievements that shorter range systems have already demonstrated and which are documented in a separate publication from FSD (Soeliso *et al*, 2016). These include the provision of medical payload transfers (Papua New Guinea, 2014; Malawi, 2016), post-disaster mapping (The Philippines, 2013; Nepal, 2015) and damage assessment (Vanuatu, 2015). However, the use of a LALE system would provide important additional capabilities including:

- capturing still/video photography/infrared imagery from locations that are remote (over 50 km) from the base station to support the needs assessment process;

- acting as a temporary mobile communications system by flying in a geo-stationary orbit;

- dropping a mobile communications device (such as a solar-powered satellite phone – payload up to 5 kg) into the affected area to enable direct communication with the NDMO;

- using a capability similar to the 'find your phone' function, a LALE RPAS can determine the location of an operating cell phone and initiate a call *to* this phone from, for example, the NDMO;

- overflying prospective logistic re-supply routes to ascertain if they have been impacted by, for example, fallen trees or broken bridges.

Overview of the challenges

At the process level, there will inevitably be a need to develop the most appropriate way to integrate the results of aerial observations into needs and damage assessments, search and rescue missions, and other humanitarian functions. Ideally, such RPAS data collection and dissemination would be managed by the NDMO and, preferably, using a team of GIS/remote-sensing specialists who have already been trained in the handling of RPAS-generated data.

A further, key, process-related challenge is that of ensuring that the appropriate permissions are in place that will allow the use of RPAS in the affected country with a minimum of delay. Given that the operation of RPAS is a novel challenge, and also that international and national air traffic management and safety authorities are struggling to achieve the appropriate balance between such operations and the associated safety/privacy issues, this is clearly the area that is likely to prove critical to the successful operation of RPAS in support of the logistic response.

To date, ad hoc workarounds have been brought into play – for example the Mayor of Tacloban is reported to have authorized local RPAS flights in the aftermath of the 2014 Typhoon Haiyan. However, this is no substitute for the development of an agreed protocol that can be practised in advance of a disaster event and which will support, rather than impede, the RPAS operations.

Turning to the people dimension, the actual operation of the RPAS is likely to be the least challenging of the people-related areas as it can reasonably be anticipated that the staff will have the necessary skills and expertise to conduct flying operations in a safe, effective and ethical manner, and in line with the relevant air traffic control/safety requirements. More broadly, however, it would be important for those in the affected region to understand that RPAS may be operating in the aftermath of a disaster.

This implies an education programme that covers a range of subjects including the risks and safety implications of such operations, the potential benefits, and the ways in which both local communities and NDMOs need to be ready to engage. For example, if it is planned that the RPA will drop a satellite phone for use by those affected in a disaster, the appropriate protocols must be developed and practised in advance. These would include the operation of the phone, and the ways in which meaningful information can be passed to the NDMO – for example by the use of a standardized question and answer system as well as instructions in pictorial form in the event that the operator is unable to read or uses a different language.

Finally, in relation to the cost dimension, it is understood that the capital cost of the Aerosonde Mk 4.7 in 2013 is of the order of US $100,000 (Corcoran, 2014). To this must be added that of the camera at around US $40–50,000, making the overall capital cost of a full LALE–RPAS with high-definition camera to be some US $100–150,000. By comparison, Robinson (2016) indicates that a two-seat Raven light helicopter has a capital cost of US $473,400. In terms of running costs, the crew size of a helicopter and RPAS are likely to be broadly similar, whilst the fuel consumption of a long endurance RPAS is extremely low at some 0.6 li/100 km at cruising speed.

Summary

In summary, it is perceived that the use of an LALE–RPAS has significant potential to support the logistic response to a disaster. However, a number of important hurdles remain before the concept can be operationalized, key amongst these are the development of an air traffic control regime that supports (rather than constrains) the RPAS use, and the mechanisms (both process and people-related) that translate the data from the RPAS into usable information to underpin timely and effective decision making. Further research into the ways in which the proposed use of the RPAS capabilities can be conducted safely, ethically, efficiently and effectively is, thus, needed before the concept can be more widely employed.

Hybrid cargo airships

The early-stage response to a natural disaster of any significance frequently requires the movement of supplies from outside the impacted region to meet the needs of those affected. This typically involves the transport of relief goods by freighter aircraft to a major airport near the disaster epicentre, transitional warehousing that supports the creation of truck-size loads, and distribution via a road network that is often severely disrupted both by the impact of disaster itself as well as the consequential increase in traffic, before the 'last mile' distribution to the beneficiaries takes place.

The resultant sequence of movements and associated loading/unloading requirements are not only time-consuming and costly, but are also predicated on the availability of the necessary surge capacity at the various nodes – something that can prove extremely challenging, as was demonstrated in the 2015 Nepal earthquake. The response to this disaster saw particular difficulties due to the limited number of aircraft unloading slots at the relatively small Kathmandu International Airport. Road access to the area affected by the earthquake was also extremely poor, as evidenced by one of the early operational updates from the United Nations Logistics Cluster, which stated: 'Due to the mountainous geography, infrastructure damage, collapsed bridges and damaged roads, access is reported to be extremely limited and the status of the roads in many of the regions affected is unclear' (Logcluster, 2015: 1).

Recent developments in the technology of HCAs may, however, offer a solution to these logistic challenges. In general terms, HCAs are filled with inert helium (as distinct from highly flammable hydrogen) and this provides much of the required lift, with the remainder coming from their aerodynamic shape as they fly through the air. The airships' engines are able to direct the airflow to enable vertical take-off and landing (VTOL), as well as providing normal thrust to support the actual flight mode. However, being heavier than air when on the ground, they do not require extensive ground handling equipment. This, combined with the VTOL capability, offers significantly greater flexibility in their operations when compared with fixed wing aircraft. With the advent of the next generation of HCAs that have a reported range of over 9,000 km and a payload in excess of 225 MT (see Table 4.2), and which are due into service in 2019–21, such airships clearly have significant potential to improve the efficiency, effectiveness and flexibility of post-disaster humanitarian logistic operations.

HCAs – current status

A number of prototypes of such HCAs have already flown, but improved models are now under development with 'in service' dates over the next five years being reported. For example, the LMH-1 aims to become certified by the United States Federal Aviation Administration (FAA) by the end of 2017, with delivery of the first airships in 2018 (Laskas, 2016). Table 4.2, summarizes the data provided on the websites of the relevant companies, but it will be noted that the full range of information is not available in respect of every HCA.

In summary, and as Table 4.2 clearly demonstrates, the payload and cargo volume of the largest planned HCA (ML868) is significantly greater than those of current heavy lift cargo aircraft such as the Boeing 747F series, which can carry some 140 MT. On the other hand, the HCA transit

Table 4.2   Comparative hybrid cargo airship capabilities

Company	Lockheed Martin	Hybrid Air Vehicles		Aerocraft	
Model	LMH-1	AL10	AL50	ML866	ML868
Key Dates	To be certified in 2017; delivery of 12 units 2018–21	Flight tests in 2016		Certified in 2016; delivery of 4 units 2018–21	Delivery of 18 units 2019–21
Cruising Speed (kph)	111	150	195	185	185
Cruising Speed Range (km)	2,500			5,735	9,435
Length (m)	88	92	120	170	235
Breadth (m)	43	43.5	60	55	90
Height (m)	22	26	35	36	55
Payload (MT)	21	10	60	60	226
Payload Vol (m3)	162		672	7,236	30,590
Passengers	19		60		

DATA SOURCES LMH-1: LM, 2016; AL10/AL50: HAV, 2016a, 2016b; ML866/ML868: Aerocraft, 2016

speed is much slower (185 kph v 920 kph). However, the performance of an HCA is very environmentally friendly with the International Air Transport Association (IATA) suggesting that: 'airships produce 80–90 per cent fewer emissions than conventional aircraft' (Air Cargo News, 2010: 1).

In addition to their significant payload capability, it should also be noted that it is entirely feasible for an HCA to land on an appropriately sized flat (or near flat) area – including on water, gravel, sand or swamp – before moving to a loading/unloading area that has a smaller footprint than that of the actual landing zone. Thus, for example, it is potentially possible for the HCA to land at sea and then taxi to the shore line where the cargo can be unloaded directly onto a beach or dockside. By the same token, the take-off zone does not need to be an airfield or equivalent prepared space.

On the other hand, the use of HCAs would also involve overcoming a number of negative aspects. First, a major limiting factor of HCA operations is that of altitude. As they utilize buoyancy (static lift) to obtain the majority of their lift, their load capacity decreases as altitude increases and, as a result, their optimum operating altitude is quite low at around 1,000 m. That said, the LMH-1 can operate up to 3,000 m and the ML866/8 up to 4,000 m, although it is clear the ability of an HCA to support a logistic response in a high altitude location may be constrained.

Second, as indicated above, the physical size of the HCAs and, hence, their take-off and landing areas, is significant. In the case of the LMH-1, when operating in full VTOL mode, it requires a land/launch circle of 150 m in diameter, in other words approximately double its overall length. Furthermore, this mode of operation will reduce its payload by an estimated 25–33 per cent. Alternatively, it can use a mixed mode of forward plus vertical movement (ie similar to a fixed wing aircraft) in which case a take-off/landing area 762 m x 243 m is required to meet FAA requirements. In the case of the ML868 (which only operates in VTOL mode), a circular area with a diameter of some 360 m is required for both take-off and landing. As an alternative, the use of under-slung loads is under consideration by the manufacturers of the LMH-1; however, this would reduce the payload to some 6 MT and operations would need to avoid strong wind conditions. Nevertheless, such an approach has the clear benefit of obviating the need for a landing area.

Finally, and self-evidently, the wind strength and direction will affect the operation of an HCA, with the cruising speed indicated in Table 4.2 being positively or negatively impacted by the prevailing wind. However, HCAs will operate with a suite of electronics to ensure the most efficient flight plan and this will almost certainly include a weather radar. This, together with weather prediction advice that can be transmitted in real time from the HCA's base, should help ensure an optimal course. Furthermore, by virtue of their slow speed and advanced electronic suite, they can also safely operate in low visibility conditions.

Use of HCAs to support humanitarian logistic operations

Given the above summary of the capabilities of the emerging generation of HCAs, it will be readily envisaged that there are two areas in which they would prove particularly valuable. The first is the transfer of goods from a central warehouse such as United Nations Humanitarian Response Depots (UNHRDs). In general terms, although having a significantly slower transit speed when compared to a cargo aircraft, their ability to fly directly to a field location, rather than to an international airport with subsequent transfer by truck or ship, means that the overall timeline is likely to be broadly comparable. Indeed, given their inherent flexibility, the cargo discharge point can be adjusted as necessary – even to the extent of making in-flight destination changes as the disaster response unfolds.

An alternative approach that would be particularly applicable in areas such as the Pacific nations of Fiji and Vanuatu, which have recently been severely impacted by cyclones, would see an HCA transporting supplies from the country's international airport to the affected islands – a journey that can otherwise only be supported by relatively slow coastal shipping. A similar scenario could also apply in locations such as Nepal, where the relatively poor road infrastructure could be circumvented through direct transfer by HCAs from the international airport to a given field location (subject to the altitude constraints mentioned earlier).

It is, of course, accepted that the potential use of an HCA to support the logistic response to a disaster is predicated on their availability. Given that no HCAs are currently operational it is only possible to speculate on the size of the world fleet, its location and what actual activities airships will be conducting over, say, the next 5–10 years. However, it would be reasonable to expect hubs to be formed in areas near remote mining operations (such as in Africa, Australia, North America and Eastern Europe/Asia), and from these hubs an HCA could relocate within 1–2 days to provide the movement requirements to support disasters in these regions.

Second, it is accepted that the global fleet size is likely to be very small initially, perhaps of the order of 20–30 airships, until the capability of HCAs has been demonstrated in a range of situations. Thereafter, it is entirely possible that it could grow swiftly. For example, in the case of the LMH-1, Lockheed Martin are proposing an initial production of one HCA per month (Laskas, 2016). However, given its comparatively simple non-rigid construction, this could be quickly ramped up. Thus, it is not unreasonable to suggest that by the mid to late 2020s the global fleet size could reach into the hundreds (Aviation Week, 2016).

HCA costs

A degree of caution must be exercised when considering both the capital and operating costs of both HCAs and freighter aircraft, but the following analysis is offered using the LMH-1, for which some limited data is available as shown in Table 4.3.

Table 4.3 Capital cost comparison

Aircraft	Payload (MT)	Cost (US$M)	Source
LMH-1	21	40	Wells (2016)
Boeing 747F	140	358	Ausick (2014)

Table 4.4 High level operating cost estimates

Mode	US$/MT-KM	Source
Road	0.06	BITRE (2008) indexed for inflation to 2016
Air	1.12	
HCA	0.30	Prentice *et al* (2004)

Overall, therefore, the broad order capital cost figure for the LMH-1 is some US $2 M/MT of lift, and this can be compared with the equivalent for a fixed wing freighter of around US $2.5 M/MT.

In terms of operating costs, Table 4.4 offers a similarly broad order comparison between road, HCA and air transport.

Overall, it can be seen that the difference in cost, speed and cargo capacity between the various modal combinations exemplifies the classic supply chain efficiency v effectiveness v flexibility conundrum that has challenged multiple organizations over the years.

Summary

Clearly, the use of HCAs is predicated on their successful migration from the drawing board to an operational reality, as well as the development of suitable processes (such as pre-negotiated contractual arrangements) that would enable their inclusion as part of an integrated range of responses available to the humanitarian logistician. In this regard, the potential use of an HCA will need to reflect the optimal speed v time v distance v cost balance that is appropriate in the circumstances of a particular disaster event.

It is also clear that there is no unique solution to the problem of moving large quantities of relief goods at short notice and as cheaply as possible. For example, a judicious mix of fixed wing aircraft together with HCAs may prove optimum. However, it is argued that HCAs present the humanitarian logistician with a mode of transportation that has the potential to provide a significant enhancement to the existing means of responding to a disaster by, in particular, overcoming the traditional challenges posed by supply chain choke points and disruptions to infrastructure.

Furthermore, whilst the thrust of this section of the chapter has discussed the capability of HCAs as cargo-carriers for relief supplies, it is clear that they have a broader range of potential roles including, for example, the transport of a mobile field hospital together with appropriate medical personnel or water treatment plants and their engineers. By the same token, it is theoretically entirely feasible for an HCA to act as a 'flying warehouse' and support multiple humanitarian agencies – even to the extent of incorporating a 3DP workshop and/or RPAS to conduct the 'last mile' deliveries.

Cash transfer programmes

Humanitarian organizations are finding new and increasingly efficient ways of delivering aid and assistance, notably through the use of 'digital cash'. The use of such cash transfer programmes (CTPs) is on the rise as, for example, in the case of the World Food Programme (WFP), which saw the use of cash increase from US $10 million (less than 1 per cent of total aid) to US $3 billion in the period between 2009 and 2014 (IRIN, 2014). Indeed, by the start of 2016 it was estimated that cash-based programming accounted for more than 25 per cent of WFP's total spend on assistance (WFP, 2017). Similarly, in 2000 UNHCR implemented 15 programmes that relied on cash and cash-alternatives, but by 2015 that number had increased to 60 programmes, with a budget of approximately US $465 million (UNHCR, 2015).

In the humanitarian context, CTPs speed up the delivery of aid, reduce the need for inventories and transportation capacity, and even allow beneficiaries to make their own choices rather than humanitarian organizations making these for them (Heaslip et al, 2015). For example, Ugandan mobile network operators MTN and Airtel are partnering with NGOs including Danish Church Aid (DCA), Mercy Corps and the International Rescue Committee to deliver digital cash to refugees. By the same token, after the 2004 Indian Ocean tsunami the Sri Lankan Government made people open bank accounts to facilitate a CTP, as did the Iranian Government after the Bam earthquake in 2003 (Doocy et al, 2006).

Whilst there are a range of mechanisms used to deliver cash-based responses to recipients (see Table 4.5), CTPs utilizing mobile money can take one of three basic forms: (a) fund transfers directly into the beneficiary's mobile account, (b) fund transfers via a mobile voucher for the beneficiary to redeem (or cash-out), or (c) fund transfers for a pre-determined purpose,

Table 4.5 Types of cash-based responses used in emergencies

Type of Cash-based Responses	Definition
Unconditional Cash Transfer	People are given money as a direct grant with no conditions or work requirements. There is no requirement to repay any money, and people are entitled to use the money however they wish.
Conditional Cash Transfer	The agency puts conditions on how the cash can be spent, such as reconstructing a home. Alternatively, cash might be given after recipients have met a condition, such as enrolling children in school or having them vaccinated. This type of conditionality is rare in humanitarian settings.
Vouchers	A voucher is a paper, token or electronic card that can be exchanged for a set quantity or value of goods, denominated either as a cash value or as predetermined commodities or services. Vouchers are redeemable with preselected vendors or at 'voucher fairs' set up by the implementing agency.
Cash for Work	Payment (in cash or vouchers) is provided as a wage for work, usually in public or community programmes.

SOURCE Heaslip *et al*, 2015

such as buying food (see Table 4.6). In general, mobile money is a term describing the services that allow electronic money transactions over a mobile phone. It is also referred to as mobile financial services, mobile wallets or mobile payments.

Implementing a mobile money-based CTP using any of these three approaches is complex and requires significant planning to ensure beneficiaries can access their funds quickly and in a user-friendly format. This form of humanitarian assistance has since become more popular in recent years, and new telecommunication solutions for cash transfers such as mobile money launched by Safaricom have enabled their use in various African countries (Kovács, 2014). Concern Worldwide pioneered this relief transfer mechanism in a humanitarian context in a remote area of Kenya in early 2008. Funds were transferred to registered numbers which could then be exchanged for actual money or electronically transferred to

Table 4.6   Forms of mobile money

Mobile Money	Transaction Point	Use
Fund transfers directly into beneficiary's mobile account	Agent/vendor with basic phone	Cash + mobile money services including transactions like money transfers + goods/services
Fund transfers via a mobile voucher for the beneficiary to cash-out	Agent/vendor with basic phone	Cash
Fund transfers for a predetermined purpose (eg buying food from a specific merchant)	Vendor with basic phone	Goods and services

SOURCE GSMA, 2017

another phone or used for phone credit through a system they pioneered, the M-PESA system, which does not require a bank account (Datta *et al*, 2008). Rather, this system needs a functioning telecommunication network and an agent who will exchange the digital credit for actual cash – although the mobile phone can serve as a digital wallet with some traders accepting the digital credit as payment (Datta *et al*, 2008).

Generally speaking, CTPs imply a reconfiguration of the humanitarian supply chain with consequential important contributions to the reinstatement of the local economy (Kovács, 2014; Heaslip *et al*, 2015). In humanitarian supply chains where the main activity is providing physical goods, the actors conducting the activity of distribution are commonly a local partner such as the local authorities or local NGOs (Altay and Ramirez, 2010). In the distribution of CTPs, there is a shift in this role towards an actor that can better handle the financial flow. However, a clear pre-condition is that there are functioning markets at the affected location, and that the beneficiary has access to such markets noting that, for vulnerable populations, this is not always the case.

From the beneficiaries' perspective, CTPs offer greater flexibility as they allow the recipients to choose the goods and services that are most appropriate to their personal situation. Thus, cash transfer reinstates the purchasing power of beneficiaries and, hence, changes their very role in the humanitarian supply chain – in a similar way to the use of voucher systems in Kosovo and FYROM (Matopoulos *et al*, 2014). Importantly, through CTPs, beneficiaries receive the full measure of the intended relief aid. Cash transfers also support local procurement (by beneficiaries themselves), thereby ensuring the cultural, technical, and health appropriateness of items bought. This, in turn, can help to build resilience in the local economy and also improve diversity. In short, cash transfers adhere to the oft cited principles of empowerment, dignity and choice for the beneficiaries (Bailey *et al*, 2008), whilst, for donors, cash transfers deliver benefits in traceability, efficiency, timeliness and the cost effective delivery of aid.

Cash transfer programming – a humanitarian logistic perspective

The traditional humanitarian supply chain pushes items in the immediate aftermath of a disaster event, and then gradually moves towards a pull strategy once more information becomes available. In contrast, however, CTPs enable a pull strategy to be implemented from the beginning and this, in turn, helps to ensure that the needs of the beneficiaries are met more quickly and accurately.

In a traditional humanitarian supply chain model, financial flows originate from donors to humanitarian organizations, which then use these funds to pay for material supplies that they deliver to beneficiaries. In a CTP, financial flows from donors still come to humanitarian organizations, which then assess the potential for distributing cash directly to beneficiaries. If this is possible – given, for instance, that there are items available on a market – the finance flows directly to beneficiaries, who then pay for the products and services they need. Under this model, humanitarian organizations become the brokers of these flows and the associated distributors of cash, but not the providers of the purchased materials. Their role in delivering materials thus diminishes and focuses on the provision of materials and supplies that are not readily available on the local market.

Heaslip *et al* (2015) illustrated the two extremes of 'before' and 'after' supply chains, in which the material flows are shown with full arrows, and financial flows with dashed arrows (see Figure 4.1). In the original case, humanitarian organizations procure materials and deliver these to beneficiaries. In the ultimate, unconditional cash transfer case humanitarian organizations would only deliver funding to beneficiaries who, themselves, procure from suppliers.

CTPs do not incur the transport, warehousing and intensive distribution systems and costs that form part of the traditional in-kind aid model. CTPs

Figure 4.1 Changing paradigm of the humanitarian supply chain – before and after CTPs

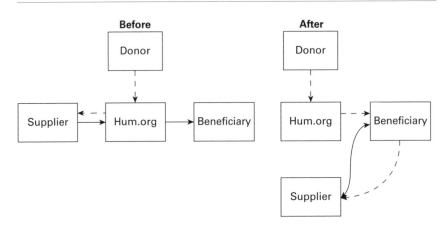

also shorten the logistical supply chain, simplify procurement and remove or lessen the need for transport and warehousing considerations, which may, in turn, shrink the humanitarian sector considerably (WFP, 2013). The functionality of such cash transfers is, however, conditional. For cash transfers to work there needs to be an available market, and the beneficiary needs access to that market.

In humanitarian supply chains where the main activity is providing physical goods, the actors conducting the activity of distribution are commonly a local partner such as local authorities or local NGOs. In the distribution of CTPs, there is a shift from this role towards that of an actor who can better handle a financial flow.

Summary

As humanitarian organizations strive to understand how best to deliver CTPs, the need for partnerships between humanitarian agencies and mobile money service providers is growing. Thus, the impact of cash-based responses on humanitarian operations cannot be understated. They alter supply chain design, the very role of beneficiaries as well as humanitarian organizations, and change the strategy of aid delivery from push to pull. Perhaps the most important factor is that they lead to the elimination of many logistical activities that previously needed to be performed by humanitarian organizations: delivering cash diminishes the need for lengthy procurement and assessment processes, pre-positioning, transportation and distribution. This has the potential to deliver significant reductions in the cost of providing a humanitarian response whilst, at the same time, it is an important move from aid to trade.

References

Aeroscraft (2016) Fleet [Online] http://aeroscraft.com/fleet-copy/4580475518 (accessed 19 July 2017)

Air Cargo News (2010) Airfreight must embrace dirigibles [Online] http://www.aircargonews.net/news/single-view/news/airfreight-must-embrace-dirigibles-says-iata.html (accessed 19 July 2017)

Altay, N and Ramirez, A (2010) Impact of disasters on firms in different sectors: Implications for supply chains, *Journal of Supply Chain Management*, 46(4), pp 59–80

Ausick, P (2014) Why a Boeing 747-8 costs $ 357 million [Online] http://247wallst.com/aerospace-defense/2014/06/03/why-a-boeing-747-8-costs-357-million/ (accessed 19 July 2017)

Aviation Week (2016) Newsfeed [Online] http://www.straightlineaviation.com/news/9-webnews/15-aviation-week-lockheed-martin-readies-lmh-1-hybrid-airship-assembly (accessed 19 July 2017)

Bailey, S, Savage, K and O'Callaghan, S (2008) *Cash Transfers in Emergencies: A synthesis of World Vision's experience and learning*, Humanitarian Policy Group at Overseas Development Institute, London

BITRE (2008) Freight rates in Australia, *Information Sheet 28* [Online] http://bitre.gov.au/publications/2008/files/is_028.pdf (accessed 19 July 2017)

Booth, W (2010) Haiti faces colossal and costly clean-up before it can rebuild, *Washington Post Foreign Service*, 7 May [Online] http://www.washingtonpost.com/wp-dyn/content/article/2010/03/06/AR2010030602544.html (accessed 17 July 2017)

Christopher, MG (2016) *Logistics and Supply Chain*, 5th edn, Pearson Education Ltd, Harlow, UK

Corcoran, M (2014) Drone journalism: Newsgathering applications of unmanned aerial vehicles (UAVs) in covering conflict, civil unrest and disaster [Online] http://www.flinders.edu.au/ehl/fms/law_files/Drone%20Journalism%20During%20Conflict,%20Civil%20Unrest%20and%20Disasters%20March%201%202014.pdf (accessed 17 July 2017)

Datta, D, Ejakait, A and Odak, M (2008) Mobile phone-based cash transfers: Lessons from the Kenya emergency response, *Humanitarian Exchange Magazine*, 40(1), pp 37–40 de Leeuw, S, Kopczak, L and Blansjaar, M (2010) What really matters in locating shared humanitarian stockpiles: Evidence from the WASH Cluster, *PRO-VE 2010*, pp 166–72

Doocy, S, Gabriel, M, Collins, S, Robinson, C and Stevenson, P (2006) Implementing cash for work programmes in post-tsunami Aceh, *Disasters*, 30(3), pp 277–96

GSMA (2017) *Landscape Report: Mobile money, humanitarian cash transfers and displaced populations*, Global Systems for Mobile Communication Association, May

HAV (Hybrid Air Vehicles) (2016a) Airlander 10 Technical Data [Online] http://www.hybridairvehicles.com/downloads/Airlander-21.pdf (accessed 19 July 2017)

HAV (Hybrid Air Vehicles) (2016b) Airlander 50 Technical Data [Online] http://www.hybridairvehicles.com/downloads/Airlander-77.pdf (accessed 19 July 2017)

Heaslip, G, Haavisto, I and Kovács, K (2015) Cash as a form of relief, in *Advances in Managing Humanitarian Operations*, eds C Zobel, N Altay and M Haselkorn, pp 59–78, International Series in Operations Research & Management Science, Springer

IRIN (2014) Latest innovations in cash transfers [Online] http://www.irinnews.org/feature/2014/07/31/latest-innovations-cash-transfers (accessed August 2017)

Kovács, G (2014) Where next? The future of humanitarian logistics, in *Humanitarian Logistics: Meeting the challenge of preparing for and responding to disasters*, 2nd edn, eds M Christopher and P Tatham, pp 275–85, Kogan Page, London

Laskas, JM (2016) Helium dreams, *The New Yorker*, 29 February [Online] http://www.newyorker.com/magazine/2016/02/29/a-new-generation-of-airships-is-born (accessed 19 July 2017)

LM (Lockheed Martin) (2016) Hybrid airships: Revolutionizing remote transport [Online] http://www.lockheedmartin.com.au/us/products/HybridAirship.html (accessed 19 July 2017)

Logcluster (United Nations Logistics Cluster) (2015) Nepal situation updates [Online] http://www.logcluster.org/search?f[0]=field_raw_op_id:24058&f[1]=field_document_type:156 (accessed 19 July 2017)

Matopoulos, A, Kovacs, G and Hayes, O (2014) Local resources and procurement practices in humanitarian supply chains: An empirical examination of large scale house reconstruction projects, *Decision Sciences*, 45(4), pp 621–46

OCHA (Office for the Coordination of Humanitarian Affairs) (2014) Unmanned aerial vehicles in humanitarian response, *OCHA Policy and Studies Series*, Occasional Paper No 10 [Online] https://docs.unocha.org/sites/dms/Documents/Unmanned%20Aerial%20Vehicles%20in%20Humanitarian%20Response%20OCHA%20July%202014.pdf (accessed 17 July 2017)

Prentice, BE, Beilock, RP and Phillips, AJ (2004) Global trade of perishables in the 21st century: The case for giant airships, *Proceedings of the 45th Annual Transportation Research Forum, Evanston, Illinois, March 21–23* [Online]

http://ageconsearch.umn.edu/bitstream/208234/2/2004_GlobalTrade_paper.pdf (accessed 19 July 2017)

Robinson (2016) R42 Raven II 2016 Estimated Operating Costs [Online] http://www.helispot.be/hs/documents/heli/r44_eoc.pdf (accessed 17 July 2017)

Soeliso, D, Meier, P, Lessard-Fontaine, A, Du Plessis, J and Stuhlberger, C (2016) Drones in humanitarian action, *Swiss Foundation for Mine Action (FSD)* [Online] http://drones.fsd.ch/wp-content/uploads/2016/11/Drones-in-Humanitarian-Action.pdf (accessed 17 July 2017)

Soesilo, D and Sandvik, KB (2016) Drones in humanitarian action: A survey on perceptions and applications, *Swiss Foundation for Mine Action* [Online] http://drones.fsd.ch/wp-content/uploads/2016/09/Drones-in-Humanitarian-Action-Survey-Analysis-FINAL21.pdf (accessed 17 July 2017)

UNHCR (2015) *Innovation: Cash-based interventions* [Online] http://www.unhcr.org/5596441c9.pdf (accessed August 2017)

Wells, J (2016) Lockheed has liftoff: Sells new airships in $480M deal, *CNBC* [Online] http://www.cnbc.com/2016/03/29/lockheed-has-liftoff-sells-new-airships-in-480m-deal.html (accessed 19 July 2017)

World Food Programme (2013) *Impact Evaluation of the Targeted Food and Cash Transfer Programme (August 2012–March 2013)*, WFP, Lilongwe

World Food Programme (2017) *WFP Strategic Plan, 2017–2021* [Online] https://docs.wfp.org/api/documents/WFP0000019573/download/?_ga=2.54782434.850199635.1503717212-1544348492.1503717212 (accessed August 2017)

The increasing importance of services in humanitarian logistics

05

GRAHAM HEASLIP

Abstract

Services have always been an essential part of logistics and they are becoming increasingly important in today's world, especially in humanitarian logistics. Considering the interaction of different kinds of organizations and the globalization of relief efforts, it is imperative that the humanitarian relief community embraces new strategies, techniques and technologies for improving productivity and quality in services operations. The service operations of the logistic function start well before a disaster strikes and continue past the occurrence of the crisis and the direct response to it. This chapter examines service operations management and its application to the field of humanitarian logistics.

Introduction

In today's logistics world freight forwarding, transportation, and other logistic contributions have become so well defined that the service component has, in effect, been productized. In other words, the intangible contributions of logistics have become so well defined and understood by customers and suppliers that they are sold as a product (Johnston, 2005). As logistics providers struggle to differentiate themselves from their competition they have sought to become more and more integrated with their customers' processes. This trend becomes apparent when we look at industry leaders who operate in the area of humanitarian logistics such as DHL, Kühne+Nagel and UPS, all of which position themselves as providers of integrated services or solutions. As logistics is receiving increasing recognition as a competitive parameter, the focus is shifting to more strategic considerations of service response and flexibility instead of simple make-or-buy decisions (Bask *et al*, 2010; Skjoett-Larsen, 2000). Thus, there are many good reasons to focus on research regarding logistics services. First, the outsourcing of logistics services is expected to increase; second, the provision of logistics services is an emerging industry that promises a positive future and new roles in supply chains and value networks. Third, value added logistics services seem to be the fastest growing part of the transport industry.

In short, the provision of services has now turned into a conscious and explicit strategy with services becoming a main differentiating factor in a totally integrated products and service offering (Baines *et al*, 2009). The value proposition often includes services as fundamental value-added activities (Gebauer *et al*, 2006; Vandermerwe and Rada, 1988) and reduces the product to being just a part of the offering (Gebauer *et al*, 2006; Oliva and Kallenberg, 2003). Indeed, some companies have found this to be a most effective way to open the door to future business (Wise and Baumgartner, 1999).

There is also a need for international humanitarian organizations (IHOs) to differentiate themselves, just as commercial companies do. For example, many humanitarian organizations do exactly the same things (provide food, water, sanitation, shelter, healthcare, education), and in doing so they seek funding and resources from the same donors (governments, institutional and private); they use the same mass media to raise awareness and funds; their marketing strategies are very similar; and they use the same transport carriers and logistics service providers (Heaslip, 2015; Heaslip, 2013; Oloruntoba and Gray, 2009). Consequently, whatever marketing strategies they employ are quickly copied by other IHOs, who in essence are in competition (Oloruntoba and Gray, 2009). Organizations trying to create or maintain differentiation in the humanitarian sector often find that whatever changes they make are greeted by counter-moves from competing relief organizations (Heaslip, 2015; Oloruntoba and Gray, 2009). For many IHOs the way to sustainable competitive advantage may not lie in changes in the product, promotion or pricing strategies of the organization, but rather in improving customer service within humanitarian logistics (HL), ancillary services, such as logistics and distribution (Oloruntoba and Gray, 2009) and servitization (Heaslip, 2015; Heaslip, 2013).

A further interesting trend in HL practice is that IHOs have started to develop services that they offer each other. The International Federation of Red Cross and Red Crescent Societies (IFRC) provides key logistics services offered to third parties, such as procurement and transportation, warehousing and handling, contingency stock, fleet service and insurance (IFRC, 2012). Contract logistics services with third and fourth parties, such as those offered by the United Nations Children's Fund (UNICEF) and IFRC, include shared facilities, outsourcing and alliances to provide a wide service mix from just-in-time (JIT) deliveries and distribution to full-scale services and supply chain solutions replacing the IHO's order processing and warehousing functions. Most of the services IHOs offer to each other fall under the realm of logistics. For example, the World Food Programme (WFP) offers customs clearance, transportation and warehousing services through the Logistics Cluster to other organizations (WFP, 2012). They currently run the 'common humanitarian transport' in Syria, and hauled over 11,000 m^3 of cargo on behalf of a dozen of IHOs within the first three months of 2013. These services are becoming rather standardized, with request forms having been developed for each ongoing operation.

Background to service operations

The word service means many different things to different people, and even within the service operations management community there is no commonly agreed definition (Sampson and Froehle, 2006). In no small way this is due to the many different industries that perceive themselves as providers of services in one form or other. Irrespective of the type of industry (finance, healthcare, education, manufacturing, shipbuilding, humanitarian aid), all organizations need to consider how best to meet their customers' service requirements. Therefore, it is important to realize that a 'service industry' is not simply, by default, any industry not engaged in the manufacturing of a tangible product (Paton and McLaughlin, 2008).

A more specific definition limits a service industry to those focused on providing customers with the product they require, and delivering that product in a manner acceptable to the customer (Taylor and Taylor,

2009). Any organization that develops their service as a core competitive strength can, and should, be considered part of the service industry (Johnson, 2008).

Vandermerwe and Rada (1988) describe how companies initially considered themselves to be in goods or services (eg product manufacture or insurance), and then moved to offering goods combined with closely related services (eg products offered with maintenance, support and finance), and finally to a position where 'firms offer "bundles" consisting of customer focussed combinations of goods, services, support, self-service and knowledge'. They termed this movement the servitization of manufacturing. In the management-related literature, servitization development is commonly traced back to the early 1990s. However, Davies *et al* (2006) point out that the industrial marketing literature suggests that pioneering applications originated in the 1960s with the introduction of 'systems selling' strategies. In the evolution of servitization, many manufacturing companies have moved dramatically into services and so caused the boundaries between products and services to become blurred.

The failure to correctly capture customer requirements is inherent in organizations that have a dominant 'product focus', as opposed to a 'customer focus'. The characteristic of the product-focused organization is one that develops a product first and then looks to match that product to a market. This differs from a customer-focused organization in that this latter type of organization strives to understand the needs of the market, and then develops the right product or service for that market (Johnston, 2008; Johnston, 2005). This is a subtle difference but one that can mean the success or failure of a service organization.

Considering the fluid and dynamic nature of many markets the need to establish a clear customer perspective is vital if an organization is to be competitive (Oloruntoba and Gray, 2009). Therefore, any organization that fails to understand and respond to the changing needs of their customers will fail to provide services that stand any chance of meeting their customers' expected levels of quality and satisfaction (Oloruntoba and Gray, 2009; Heskett, *et al*, 2008).

A traditional concept of the customer is the party that pays for goods or services, and is thus involved in a commercial transaction. Just as various segments of the target markets differ in customer requirements, customers in the humanitarian relief context have differing and varying requirements. However, an understanding of the complexity of the customer profile of IHOs could be a key towards understanding the servitization offering. Thus, Table 5.1 provides an overview of IHOs' customers.

Table 5.1 IHOs customers

Type of Customer	Function	Commercial Transaction	Authors
Beneficiaries	The end-user of the product or service whose needs or requirements must be accommodated.	None	Altay and Green, 2006; Kovács and Spens, 2007; Oloruntoba and Gray, 2009
Implementing Partner (IP)	These are specific organizations, with specific functions (such as water, shelter, etc) operating between the IHOs and the aid beneficiaries/end-users of the relief effort.	Yes between IP and IHO	Kovács and Spens, 2011; Matopoulos et al, 2014; Thomas and Mizushima, 2005
Donors (Including Governments, Institutional, Private)	Provides funding for IHOs to procure staff, relief goods, and transport them to disaster sites for relief distribution. The donor not only provides funding but may also provide supplies such as clothing, food or cooking oil; here, the donor acts like a supplier, except that the donor does not get paid.	Yes between donor and IHO None when donor acts as a supplier (in-kind donations)	Heaslip, 2013; Holguín-Veras et al, 2013; Kovács and Spens, 2009; Oloruntoba and Gray, 2009; Van Wassenhove, 2006
Other IHOs (UN Agencies, NGOs)	Can act as donors, implementing partners, or delivery partners in particular programmes or through clusters.	Yes between IHOs	Jahre and Jensen, 2010; Kovács, 2014

Servitization in humanitarian logistics

Servitization is now widely recognized as the process of creating value by adding services to products. There are a variety of forms of servitization, with its features differing for each. The literature identifies potential applications along the so-called 'product–service continuum' (Gebauer et al, 2008;

Gebauer and Friedli, 2005; Neu and Brown, 2005). This is a continuum from the traditional manufacturer where companies merely offer services as add-ons to their products, through to service providers where companies have services as the main part of their value creation process. As observed by Gebauer *et al* (2008), companies have to look at their unique opportunities and challenges at different levels of 'service infusion' and deliberately define their position. This is envisioned to be a dynamic process, with companies redefining their position over time and moving towards increasing service dominance.

Baines *et al* (2009) describe how commercial companies are moving to exploit downstream opportunities from services. They demonstrate that these opportunities fall into four categories: embedded services, comprehensive services, integrated solutions and finally distribution control. Applying these criteria to humanitarian logistics shows that IHOs are actually to the fore in adopting servitization techniques:

1 Embedded services that allow traditional downstream services to be built into the product (eg WFP stock lists for monitoring of non-food items).

2 Comprehensive services, such as those offered by DHL around its product markets (eg DHL's comprehensive logistics solution).

3 Integrated solutions, where companies look beyond their traditional product base to assess the overall needs of customers (eg the move of the United Nations Humanitarian Response Depots (UNHRDs) to network-infrastructure solutions).

4 Distribution control, as used by WFP with its high-volume, low-margin non-food items.

The first wave of servitization in HL

Initially IHOs were defined around the products they delivered, such as WFP – food; IFRC – shelter; and Médecins Sans Frontières (MSF) – health. However, the Asian tsunami in December of 2004 and the response to the Darfur crisis in 2004/2005 demonstrated the problems inherent in providing sufficient coverage in large relief operations (Jahre and Jensen, 2010). A cluster approach was proposed as a way of addressing gaps and strengthening the effectiveness of the humanitarian response, with product foci being used as the basis for this model (Kovács and Spens, 2007).

Originally there were 10 clusters: water, sanitation and hygiene (WASH); protection; nutrition; education; early recovery; emergency shelter; camp management; health; food security; and emergency telecommunications. To ensure the delivery of 'goods' for the clusters, 'common services' such as logistics were incorporated into the cluster system. The Logistics Cluster is responsible for coordination, information management, and, where appropriate, logistics service provision to ensure an effective and efficient logistics response takes place in each and every operation (Holguín-Veras *et al*, 2013). To achieve this goal, the Logistics Cluster fills gaps in logistics capacity, meets the need for logistics coordination services, and where necessary acts as 'provider of last resort'. The introduction of the Logistics Cluster led to the first wave of servitization in the humanitarian environment with, for example, moving from a focus on delivering food to delivering services (Heaslip *et al*, 2015; Heaslip, 2015, Heaslip, 2013).

With this first wave of servitization, it is as if the goods an IHO provides had become a 'qualifier', whereas the service offered has become the 'order winner'. The focus has shifted from core products towards the services, not least because offering a mixture of goods and services allows the IHO to differentiate itself and create a more satisfied and loyal customer – though with a focus on donors as the customers, rather than the beneficiaries. Figure 5.1 shows the different types of IHOs and their move to a greater level of service offerings. From this it will be seen that the traditional view of an IHO is in providing tangible relief (such as water, food and shelter),

Figure 5.1 Types of international humanitarian organization

Asset based	Skills based
Major functions	*Major functions*
Warehousing	Information consultancy
Inventory management	Supply chain management
Postponement	Financial services
Transportation distribution	Training
Traditional	**Network based**
Major functions	*Major functions*
Food	Track and trace
Water	Procurement
Sanitation	Custom clearance
Shelter	Service standardization
Health care	
Education	

Physical service ↑

Management services →

with examples of traditional IHOs including Oxfam and World Vision. Following the 2004 Asian tsunami, the asset-based IHO developed. This was primarily from the diversification of some traditional IHOs into more complex offerings. Several of the world's leading IHOs moved in this direction (for example the UNHRDs).

In the early 2000s a number of network-based IHOs appeared, most notably UNICEF and WFP. This move by IHOs to offering value-added services includes procurement services being offered by agencies such as UNICEF, the UNHRD network and the United Nations Office for Project Services (UNOPS), to other UN agencies as well as to governments (Kovács, 2014). Procurement works like a pivot in the internal supply chain process turning around requests into actual products/commodities or services to fulfil the needs. Beyond the UN family, the IFRC have developed a procurement centre and procurement portal that has been accredited by the European Commission's Civil Protection and Humanitarian Aid Operations department (ECHO), and through which third parties outside Red Cross/Red Crescent national chapters can request their services.

Other value added services are also available, for example (as mentioned earlier) the IFRC is offering its services in areas such as procurement and transportation, warehousing and handling, contingency stock, fleet service and insurance (Kovács, 2014; IFRC, 2012). In addition to these, Heaslip (2013) has demonstrated the existence of further applications of service operations in humanitarian supply chains, for example the WFP acting as a consignee in major disasters and consolidating transportation, as well as service standardization. The nature of these services necessitates creating geographically extensive and tightly integrated networks of operations. The development of 'common services' has even become one of four key points on the agenda of the Global Logistics Cluster meeting in Copenhagen in November 2014. The global strategy of the Logistics Cluster for 2013–15 (GLC, 2013) includes the point of developing a 'service catalogue' that would be available for addressing and filling gaps in logistics services in risk areas but also to build national preparedness – albeit it remains disputed which role the cluster should play in the latter.

The fourth type of IHO – the skill-based – has been a recent phenomenon. These are IHOs that provide a range of, primarily, information-based services. These encompass consultancy services (including supply chain configuration) and training. Examples of this type of IHO include the WFP, which has developed the logistics response team (LRT) training that it has offered to other organizations in the Logistics Cluster since 2007. Interestingly, an integral part of this is a 'service mindset training' for logisticians.

The second wave of servitization in HL

Until now, the role of beneficiaries as customers in humanitarian operations has been disputed (Holguín-Veras *et al*, 2013; Kovács and Spens, 2007; Van Wassenhove, 2006), not the least because of their lack of purchasing power (Heaslip *et al*, 2015). The traditional form of humanitarian relief has been to provide the people in need with goods. Beneficiaries in this model do not have a voice in the type of goods being procured for or distributed to them (Matopoulos *et al*, 2014). However, humanitarian aid is shifting towards providing cash-based assistance instead of goods (Heaslip *et al*, 2015; Kovács, 2014), thus providing beneficiaries with purchasing power. This move from a product delivery to a cash delivery represents the second wave of servitization.

The WFP's shift from food aid to food assistance in 2008 is evidence of the changing humanitarian landscape. WFP adopted a cost-conscious approach to the global economic downturn that considers: value; accountability; alternative funding models (cash); justification of spending; capacity building; innovation and performance measurement tools. Between 2009 and 2014, the use of cash by the WFP increased from US $10 million (less than 1 per cent of total aid) to US $3 billion (IRIN, 2014), and by the start of 2016 it was estimated that cash-based programming accounted for more than 25 per cent of WFP's total spend on assistance (WFP, 2017). In 2000 the United Nations High Commissioner for Refugees (UNHCR) implemented 15 programmes that relied on cash and cash-alternatives; by 2015 that number had increased to 60 programmes, with a budget of approximately US $465 million (UNHCR, 2015).

Cash transfers shorten the supply chain, simplify procurement and remove the need for many humanitarian logistics activities such as transport and warehousing, and this change in thinking may ultimately shrink the humanitarian sector considerably (WFP, 2013). In short, a shift from material to financial flows diminishes the total cost of aid whilst simultaneously empowering beneficiaries (Heaslip *et al*, 2015; Kovács, 2014). Beneficiaries receive the full measure of the intended relief aid through cash transfers as opposed to selling in-kind aid which is sold at much less than the associated logistical costs in order to meet other needs (Bailey *et al*, 2008). Cash transfers fundamentally alter the balance of power between the donor and the beneficiary as they increase the freedom of beneficiaries to decide how to use the cash (Aker, 2013). This has meant that beneficiaries have changed from a passive role to becoming active members of the humanitarian supply chain (Matopoulos *et al*, 2014).

Service developments in humanitarian logistics

Adopting a downstream position, such as the provision of installed base services, organizations have to be service oriented and value services (Oliva and Kallenberg, 2003). In humanitarian logistics this could be the tracking and tracing of relief goods. These organizations provide solutions through product–service combinations and tend to be client-centric, providing customized, desirable client outcomes organized around particular capabilities, competences and client requirements (Miller *et al*, 2002). For example, World Vision (WV) Canada has been working on a tracking and tracing system that they intend to offer to other humanitarian aid organizations for a fee (WVI, 2012). Similarly, in the immediate aftermath of the 2010 Haiti earthquake, WFP acted as a consignee for other IHOs who had not been registered in Haiti previously (Besiou *et al*, 2011). Kovács and Spens (2011) observed that IHOs have started to develop not only new technology, but also services for each other, such as specialized systems for tracking and tracing, and fleet management. At the same time, social media applications have entered the scene not just for fundraising, but also through applications such as searching for missing relatives and matching donations with demand (for example, ALAN's Aid Matrix) (Kovács and Spens, 2011). The following sections provide some examples of service development that are taking place in humanitarian logistics. The points discussed here are not in any way intended as the ultimate solution, but rather as a starting point for further discussions.

HA organizations as logistics service providers

The general notion of IHOs functioning as logistics service providers (LSPs) leads to an important perspective on IHOs in research, aside from the more common focus on how such IHOs use companies as LSPs. For example, WFP transports and distributes items belonging to IHOs, whilst UNHRD provides warehousing hubs for IHOs – in other words, in both cases they act as logistics service providers. IFRC perform a similar role with their hubs, and this is an emerging trend in the field, which demands further research.

Service standardization

Kovács and Spens (2011) identified (service) standardization and modularization, improving the interoperability of humanitarian operations, and the role of humanitarian organizations as service providers as gaps in current humanitarian logistics research. These are important issues as, in particular, they may facilitate the use of services across IHOs – for example, the Logistics Cluster's *Logistics Operational Guide* (Log Cluster, 2012), as well as the Sphere Standards (2011), and the use of items catalogues (WFP, 2012, IFRC, 2012). In a similar way, the World Health Organization (WHO) have adopted a logistics standardization for not only equipment but also standard operating procedures in Ethiopian labs (WHO, 2012).

Procurement

Another service many organizations offer is that of procurement. Van Wassenhove and Allen (2012) describe procurement as a key activity in the supply chain, representing a large proportion of total spend. Procurement works like a pivot in the internal supply chain process, turning around requests into actual products/commodities or services to fulfil the needs. UNICEF have developed a procurement service for, in particular, medical items which includes kitting and customs clearance. UNOPS, the operational arm of the United Nations, offer their procurement service to a number of governments. Outside the UN family, the IFRC have developed a procurement centre and procurement portal that has been accredited by ECHO, and through which third parties outside of national chapters can ask for their services (Heaslip *et al*, 2015). The UNHRD also offer procurement as a third party service provision, whilst the IFRC offer smaller actors expertise, supplier relationships, and potential cost savings due to the consolidated size of orders (Heaslip, 2013).

Customer contact

The importance of customer contact, the interface between the customer and the service provider, has been identified as one of the key differences between services and manufacturing operations. Chase (1981: 701) argues that 'common service systems could be grouped together according to decreasing contact under three broad headings: pure services, mixed services, and quasi-manufacturing'. Designing the service encounter to deliver high levels of customer satisfaction and quality is one of the major issues facing service organizations today. The customer's satisfaction with the product quality may be problematic, and this is even more so in a humanitarian context where the customer could range from an international non-governmental organization (INGO) such as Oxfam, to their implementing partners, to beneficiaries in a humanitarian crisis, or, to some extent, even the donors funding an operation. Beneficiaries differ from customers in that they lack purchasing power, and often even a voice in formulating their needs (Kovács and Spens, 2011). Needs assessment processes have been established to proxy for their needs, but in spite of rapid assessment teams, their expectations are only documented in relation to material needs, and not in terms of service delivery.

Concluding remarks

In summary, it is argued that IHOs need to integrate a broader servitization paradigm in order to maintain a competitive advantage. This is because the current manufacturing-based paradigm focuses almost exclusively on tangible relief products and associated 'freight' transport and storage; whereas, in reality, the practice of humanitarian logistics for disaster response and management has shifted in the direction of providing services, and as of late, cash or vouchers (Kovács, 2014; Heaslip, 2013; IFRC, 2012). Thus the execution of activities such as deliveries, repair and maintenance, customer training, problem recovery and invoicing can be incorporated into the service process (Grönroos, 2011).

Current trends in developing service offerings across IHOs are leading to a greater emphasis on service supply chains. Hand in hand with this development will be an increase in research on robustness, standardization and quality control. This is the kind of work that will significantly advance the maturity of humanitarian logistics as a field. As mentioned earlier, a service perspective not only enhances humanitarian logistics, it highlights an area of increasing importance for supply chain and logistics as a more general field. Focusing on service is a means of increasing the reliability of operations. Humanitarian logistics provides a compelling example of this need.

References

Aker, J (2013) Cash or coupons? Testing the impacts of cash versus vouchers in the Democratic Republic of Congo, Working Paper 320, Center for Global Development [Online] http://www.cgdev.org/publication/cash-or-coupons-testing-impacts-cash-versus-vouchers-democratic-republic-congo-working (accessed 8 April 2014)

Altay, N and Green, WG (2006) OR/MS research in disaster operations management, *European Journal of Operational Research*, **175**(1), pp 475–93

Baines, TS, Lightfoot, HW, Benedettini, O and Kay, JM (2009) The servitisation of manufacturing: A review of literature and reflection on future challenges, *Journal of Manufacturing Technology Management*, 20(5), pp 547–67

Bailey, S, Savage, K and O'Callaghan, S (2008) *Cash Transfers in Emergencies: A synthesis of World Vision's experience and learning,* Humanitarian Policy Group at Overseas Development Institute, London

Bask, AH, Tinnilä, M and Rajahonka M (2010) Matching service strategies, business models and modular business processes, *Business Process Management Journal*, 16(1), pp 153–80

Besiou, M, Stapleton, O and Van Wassenhove, LN (2011) System dynamics for humanitarian operations, *Journal of Humanitarian Logistics and Supply Chain Management*, 1(1), pp 78–103

Chase, RB (1981) The customer contact approach to services: Theoretical bases and practical extensions, *Operations Research*, 21(4), pp 698–705

Davies, A, Brady, T and Hobday, M (2006) Charting a path towards integrated solutions, *MIT Sloan Management Review*, 43(7), pp 39–48

Gebauer, H and Friedli, T (2005) Behavioural implications of the transition process from products to services, *Journal of Business & Industrial Marketing*, 20(2), pp 70–80

Gebauer, H, Bravo-Sanchez, C and Fleisch, E (2008) Service strategies in product manufacturing companies, *Business Strategy Series*, 9(1)

Gebauer, H, Friedli, T and Fleisch, E (2006) Success factors for achieving high service revenues in manufacturing companies, *Benchmarking: An International Journal*, 13(3), pp 374–86

GLC (2013) Global strategy 2013–2015, *Logistics Cluster* [Online] http://www.logcluster.org/sites/default/files/logistics_cluster_glcsc_strategic_plan_2012-2015_0.pdf (accessed 19 February 2015)

Grönroos, C (2011) A service perspective on business relationships: The value creation, interaction and marketing interface, *Industrial Marketing Management*, 40(2), 240–47

Heaslip, G (2013) Services operations management and humanitarian logistics, *Journal of Humanitarian Logistics and Supply Chain Management*, 3(1), pp 37–51

Heaslip, G (2015) Humanitarian logistics – an opportunity for service research, *Journal of Humanitarian Logistics and Supply Chain Management*, 5(1), pp 2–11

Heaslip, G, Haavisto, I and Kovács, K (2015) Cash as a form of relief, in *Advances in Managing Humanitarian Operations*, eds C Zobel, N Altay and M Haselkorn, pp 59–78, International Series in Operations Research & Management Science, Springer

Heskett, J, Jones, T, Loveman, G, Sasser, E and Schlesinger, L (2008) Putting the service profit chain to work, *Harvard Business Review*, 86(7/8), pp 118–29

Holguín-Veras, J, Pérez, N, Jaller, M, Van Wassenhove, LN and Aros-Vera, F (2013) On the appropriate objective function for post-disaster humanitarian logistics models, *Journal of Operations Management*, 31, pp 262–80

International Federation of Red Cross and Red Crescent Societies (2012) *Annual Report Global Logistics Service*, IFRC

IRIN (2014) Latest innovations in cash transfers [Online] http://www.irinnews.org/feature/2014/07/31/latest-innovations-cash-transfers (accessed August 2017)

Jahre, M and Jensen, LM (2010) Coordination in humanitarian logistics through clusters, *International Journal of Physical Distribution and Logistics Management*, 40(8/9), pp 657–74

Johnston, R (2005) Service operations management: From the roots up, *International Journal of Operations & Production Management*, 25(12) pp 1298–308

Johnston, R (2008) Internal service – barriers, flows and assessment, *International Journal of Service Industry Management*, 19(2), pp 210–31

Kovács, G (2014) Where next? The future of humanitarian logistics, in *Humanitarian Logistics: Meeting the challenge of preparing for and responding to disasters*, 2nd edn, eds M Christopher and P Tatham, pp 275–85, Kogan Page, London

Kovács, G and Spens, K (2007) Humanitarian logistics in disaster relief operations, *International Journal of Physical Distribution & Logistics Management*, 37(2), pp 99–114

Kovács, G and Spens, KM (2009) Identifying challenges in humanitarian logistics, *International Journal of Physical Distribution and Logistics Management*, 39(6), pp 506–28

Kovács, G and Spens, KM (2011) Humanitarian logistics and supply chain management: The start of a new journal, *Journal of Humanitarian Logistics and Supply Chain Management*, 1(1) pp 5–14

Log Cluster (2012) *Logistics Operational Guide* [Online] http://log.logcluster.org (accessed 1 December 2012)

Matopoulos, A, Kovacs, G and Hayes, O (2014) Local resources and procurement practices in humanitarian supply chains: An empirical examination of large scale house reconstruction projects, *Decision Sciences*, 45(4), pp 621–46

Miller, D, Hope, Q, Eisenstat, R, Foote, N and Galbraith, J (2002) The problem of solutions: Balancing clients and capabilities, *Business Horizons*, March/April, pp 3–12

Neu, W and Brown, S (2005) Forming successful business-to-business services in goods-dominant firms, *Journal of Service Research*, 8(1), pp 3–16

Oliva, R and Kallenberg, R (2003) Managing the transition from products to services, *International Journal of service Industry Management*, 14(2), pp 1–10

Oloruntoba, R and Gray, R (2009) Customer service in emergency relief chains, *International Journal of Physical Distribution & Logistics Management*, 39(6), pp 486–505

Paton, RA and McLaughlin, SA (2008) Service innovation and the supply chain: Managing the complexity, *European Management Journal*, 26(2), pp 77–83

Sampson, SE and Froehle, CM (2006) Foundations and implications of a proposed unified services theory, *Production and Operations Management*, **15**(2), Summer, pp 329–43

Skjoett-Larsen, T (2000) Third party logistics – from an inter-organisational point of view, *International Journal of Physical Distribution & Logistics Management*, **30**(2), pp 112–27

Sphere Standards (2011) Humanitarian charter and minimum standards for humanitarian response, *The Sphere Project* [Online] http://www.sphereproject. org/silo/files/the-sphere-handbook.zip (accessed 29 January 2018)

Taylor, A and Taylor, M (2009) Operations management research: Contemporary themes, trends and potential future directions, *International Journal of Operations and Production Management*, **29**(12), pp 1316–40

Thomas, A and Mizushima, M (2005) Logistics training: Necessity or luxury? *Forced Migration Review*, **22**, pp 60–61

UNHCR (2015) *Innovation: Cash-based Interventions* [Online] http://www.unhcr. org/5596441c9.pdf (accessed August 2017)

Van Wassenhove, LN (2006) Humanitarian aid logistics: Supply chain management in high gear, *Journal of the Operations Research Society*, **57**, pp 475–89

Van Wassenhove, L and Allen, AM (2012) *Management Report: The World of the Humanitarian Logistician*, INSEAD Humanitarian Research Group and the Humanitarian Logistics Association, INSEAD Social Innovation Centre, Fontainebleau, France

Vandermerwe, S and Rada, J (1988) Servitisation of business: Adding value by adding services, *European Management Journal*, **6**(4), pp 314–24

WHO (2012) [Online] http://www.who.int/hiv/amds/amds_impact_ethiopian_lab. pdf (accessed 6 December 2012)

Wise, R and Baumgartner, P (1999) Go downstream: The new profit imperative in manufacturing, *Harvard Business Review*, September/October, pp 133–41

World Food Programme (2012) *WFP (World Food Programme) Strategic Plan 2008–2013* [Online] http://www.wfp.org/content/wfp-strategic-plan-2008-2013 (accessed 30 July 2012)

World Food Programme (2013) *Impact Evaluation of the Targeted Food and Cash Transfer Programme (August 2012–March 2013)*, WFP, Lilongwe

World Food Programme (2017) *WFP Strategic Plan, 2017–2021* [Online] https:// docs.wfp.org/api/documents/WFP0000019573/download/?_ga=2.54782434. 850199635.1503717212-1544348492.1503717212 (accessed August 2017)

WVI (2012) World Vision International [Online] http://www.wvi.org/wvi/wviweb.nsf (accessed 1 August 2012)

An exploration of horizontal supply chain integration for humanitarian and disaster relief

**JIHEE KIM, STEPHEN PETTIT,
ANTHONY BERESFORD AND IRINA HARRIS**

Abstract

Research related to supply chain integration (SCI) in the commercial sector has been widely documented and discussed in the academic literature, and SCI is often seen as being central to the successful implementation of supply chain management. On the other hand there has been limited attention paid to SCI in the humanitarian aid and disaster relief area where the objective is moved from one of economic improvement to one of delivering aid more successfully, and thereby achieving humanitarian imperatives such as reducing the human impact of an environmental event, and in the medium term saving lives. Although there are some studies examining collaboration, cooperation and coordination in a humanitarian context, these are only partly related to full SCI. Therefore, this chapter explores the SCI activities of some major aid organizations in the context of the preparedness and immediate response phases of sudden onset natural disasters. The research is based on a qualitative comparative design approach. Data were collected from semi-structured interviews and secondary source material. The key findings are that the strategic, tactical, or operational level of SCI depends on the type of organization and the phase in which the integration occurs. It also shows the divergent needs and context surrounding these aid actors towards SCI.

Introduction

Disasters impact not only the lives of those living in the immediate area of occurrence, but also the wider economy of the country. The link between disasters, both natural and man-made, and annual economic losses increased from US $75.5 billion in the 1960s to US $659.9 billion in the 1990s. Moreover, it has been suggested that disaster occurrences will rise a further fivefold over the next five decades as a result of, for example, environmental degradation, rapid urbanization, military conflict and natural disasters (Thomas and Kopczak, 2005). Compared to man-made disasters, natural disasters account for a much smaller proportion of disaster relief operations (Van Wassenhove, 2006). However, the issue of natural disasters cannot be neglected because of the impact on the society affected. Recent events such as the Nepalese earthquake, which killed nearly 9,000 people and injured more than 22,000 (UNHCR, 2015), and Hurricane Irma, which killed 134 people and devastated a large swathe of Caribbean islands (Anon, 2017), highlight this point.

Among the diversity of natural disasters, the damage done by sudden onset natural disasters is particularly harmful. Overall annual losses ranged from US $100 billion to US $380 billion during the five year period from 2011 to 2015, and 2017 is likely to set new records for impact mainly due to devastation from exceptional North Atlantic hurricanes and Californian wildfires. Rapid onset natural disasters such as earthquakes, tsunamis, volcanic eruptions, storms, floods and mass land movements on average contribute to 90 per cent of the overall economic losses from natural disasters (Munich RE, 2015). In the period following a sudden onset natural disaster a period of flux will exist in developing a response and a number of obstacles will impact on the ability of governments and NGOs to provide an effective response. Search and rescue tasks and the delivery of aid become particularly difficult. Usually these crises create unpredictable environments which, for example, cause uncertainty and complexities in coordination, and the ability to respond may often be limited (Caunhye et al, 2012). Therefore, a study of effectiveness and efficiency in supply chain management (SCM), which can reduce uncertainty and relieve suffering, is pertinent.

One of the major factors contributing to a difficult set of circumstances is the sheer number and range of aid actors involved in the response to disaster: 'from supranational aid agencies (eg the United Nations (UN)) and governmental organizations (GOs) to big international non-governmental organizations (BINGOs) and "one-man" NGOs (Kovács and Spens, 2009). Moreover, some of them are new and inexperienced organizations in disaster relief management and there is virtually a free entry environment for volunteers (Van Wassenhove, 2006). Thus, there are multiple aid actors with various specialities on the ground and 'coordination of assistance is vital' for efficient SCM amongst them (OCHA, 2010b, cited in Larson, 2012: 2). However, for many reasons, it seems that the issues of 'coordination, collaboration and integration' among aid actors cannot be easily implemented in the area of humanitarian and disaster relief supply chain management (HDR-SCM). Many aid organizations have their own agendas and their own ways of delivering aid, and outside times of disaster relief are in direct competition with each other for funding. These factors affect their relationships and there is little collaboration among them (Thomas and Kopczak, 2005).

For these reasons, this chapter focuses on the integration of supply chains (SCs) between major aid actors, as integration has been considered as 'vital to supply chain management' (Chen *et al* 2009; Frohlich and Westbrook, 2001). The concept of SCI is widely understood as allowing 'the entire supply chain to be managed as a single process' (Council of Supply Chain Management Professionals, 2005, cited in Palomero and Chalmeta, 2014). Given the multi-dimensionality of SCI, it is therefore important to investigate the relationships that exist between aid actors and to analyse aid activities through frameworks based on diverse segments of SCI.

The primary aim of this chapter is to explore humanitarian and disaster relief supply chain integration from the different perspectives of major aid actors, in particular when they deal with sudden onset natural disasters such as earthquakes, floods, tropical storms, tsunamis and volcanic eruptions. The following research questions were developed in the context of how the horizontal supply chain integration of suppliers from different types of aid organizations (UN, NGOs, GOs) varies in the context of sudden onset of natural disasters across the different phases of the disaster management cycle:

1 What are the roles of each aid actor and how do the roles differ?

2 How do humanitarian SCM activities vary during the phases of natural disaster relief management?

3 How do major aid actors integrate their supply chains with each other?

4 What do the actors have in common and how do they differ?

Disaster types, management phases and major aid actors

Types of disasters and management phases

Responses to disaster vary by type of disaster and the requirements of the situation. Different management skills and activities are consequently required depending on the types and different phases of disaster management. First, disasters can be divided into natural disasters and man-made disasters dependent on their source and both have slow and sudden onset cases. In the case of natural disasters, they 'collectively account only for 3 per cent of disaster relief operations' (Van Wassenhove, 2006). Nonetheless, natural disaster issues cannot be neglected because they tend to have a significant impact on economies, creating enormous financial losses and human lives by killing thousands of people. Among 'the 40 deadliest disasters in the 36-year period' between 1970 and 2005, '38 out of 40 disasters were due to natural causes' (Abbott, 2008: 4). Furthermore, 'between 1990 and 1998, approximately 94 per cent of major natural disasters and more than 97 per cent of all natural disaster-related deaths occurred in developing countries' (World Bank, 2001, cited in Maon *et al*, 2009). It can therefore be said that natural disasters create more casualties, economic damage and impact on lives, particularly to those in vulnerable areas. Therefore, this chapter focuses on sudden onset natural disasters and how effective SCM can be used to improve humanitarian aid.

Looking at the pattern of disasters and disaster response over time, there are three clear phases of the disaster management processes: preparedness; immediate response; and aftermath (Lee and Zbinden, 2003; Kovács and Spens, 2007; Perry 2007; Kumar and Havey, 2013). Here, the focus is on the phases of preparedness and immediate response, rather than on the aftermath phase. Preparedness can be defined as 'activities and measures taken in advance to ensure effective response to the impact of hazards, including the issuance of timely and effective early warnings and the temporary removal of people and property from threatened locations' (UN-ISDR, 2003). The preparedness phase cannot be ignored because the more investment there is at this stage of the process, the less the overall cost of the response will be (Tatham and Pettit, 2010). Relief or response can be understood as 'the provision of assistance or intervention during or immediately after a disaster to meet the life preservation and basic subsistence needs of those people affected' (UN-ISDR, 2003). In the response phase, 'risk-taking is encouraged and mistakes are rarely punished, because the priorities are rapid access to the disaster area and minimizing suffering' (Maon *et al*, 2009). As Tatham and Kovács (2010) assert, in the case of rapid onset disasters, aid supplies should be delivered as quickly as possible, and at the same time aid actors' efforts should be coordinated as far as possible within a broader response network and within an overall plan.

Major aid actors

In disaster events, the humanitarian aid supply chain network includes a number of logisticians from various organizations and organizational types (Tatham and Kovács, 2010). Many authors typically discuss five major groups of aid providers: NGOs; the UN agencies; GOs; the military; and private businesses (ie suppliers and logistics service providers) (Kaatrud *et al*, 2003; Van Wassenhove, 2006; Kovács and Spens, 2007). Among these, this study selected three key categories: NGOs, UN agencies and GOs (Seaman, 1999), but excluded the military and private businesses. For the military, humanitarian aid provision is not prioritized among their tasks; rather it is considered as the task of relief agencies (Byman *et al*, 2000). On the other hand, private businesses pay more attention to economic objectives such as 'earning profit to increase shareholder wealth' (McLachlin *et al*, 2009). They want to function as a provider of support to NGOs and governments (Vega and Roussat, 2015). Hence, this research excludes the aforementioned two actors and focuses on a direct aid provider for the beneficiary, working at the same level with other aid actors.

There are often no clear structural or operational links between aid actors (Kovacs and Spens, 2007) and each organization has its own way of operating, different cultures, rules and entities in law (Larson, 2012; Seaman, 1999). Thus, it can be assumed that it is difficult for these actors to integrate their supply chains. Nonetheless, in the context of humanitarian and disaster relief, NGOs play a key role in, and often dominate, aid operations (Seaman, 1999; Kovacs and Spens, 2007).

Additionally, it appears that UN agencies and NGOs often work at the same status in terms of authority/control (Seaman, 1999). While UN agencies and NGOs have different perspectives and functions, they cannot be missing from humanitarian and disaster relief. In the case of the governments of neighbouring countries, there are typically two roles for them to fulfil as both donors and aid actors, and they are also regarded as key in the area of aid supply (Kaatrud *et al*, 2003). Kovács and Spens (2009) depict the different perspectives of stakeholders, namely humanitarian organizations and governmental organizations, towards challenges they meet in humanitarian and disaster relief supply chains. Regarding the competitive environment as a source of challenge, humanitarian organizations want a more coordinated environment, which can be achieved from SCI or collaboration. Furthermore, it is reasonable to assume that there might be different ideas and activities in humanitarian and disaster relief supply chain management among aid actors.

Dimensions of supply chain integration

Christopher (2011: 3) asserts that 'the focus of supply chain management is on co-operation and trust and the recognition that, properly managed, the "whole can be greater than the sum of its parts"'. SCI has been regarded as a key factor of business success and 'supply chain management excellence' (Childerhouse and Towill, 2011). This means that 'a truly integrated supply chain' functions not only to 'just reduce costs' but also to 'create value for the company, its supply chain partners and its share-holders' (Lee, 2000 cited in Palomero and Chalmeta, 2014).

SCI can improve the understanding of supply chains based on its diversity in dimensions, directions and degrees. Many authors try to explain SCI by understanding 'two key integration dimensions: "internal" and "external"' (Bernon et al, 2013). Pagell (2004) defines internal integration as 'integration across various parts of a single organization', while external integration is pertinent to cross-organizational boundaries. External integration involves many players, such as 'suppliers, manufacturers, distributors, customers, competitors and other non-competitor organizations' (Barratt, 2004; Guan and Rehme, 2012). Barratt (2004) clarifies vertical integration as being implemented in the relationships among customers, internally, and suppliers, whilst horizontal integration is related to the relationships among competitors, internally and non-competitors. Mason et al (2007) consider transport management using four different potential relationship partners, suppliers and customers on the vertical axis and complementors or competitors on the horizontal axis. In particular, to handle relatively unexpected conditions such as fluctuating demand, horizontal ties with competitors and complementors have become more important (Mason et al, 2007). Toyasaki et al (2017) also adopt this horizontal concept into 'cooperation among humanitarian organizations in inventory management of the United Nations Humanitarian Response Depot (UNHRD) network'. Likewise, this can be applied to the humanitarian and disaster relief context in this study,

Figure 6.1   Forms of supply chain integration in humanitarian and disaster relief

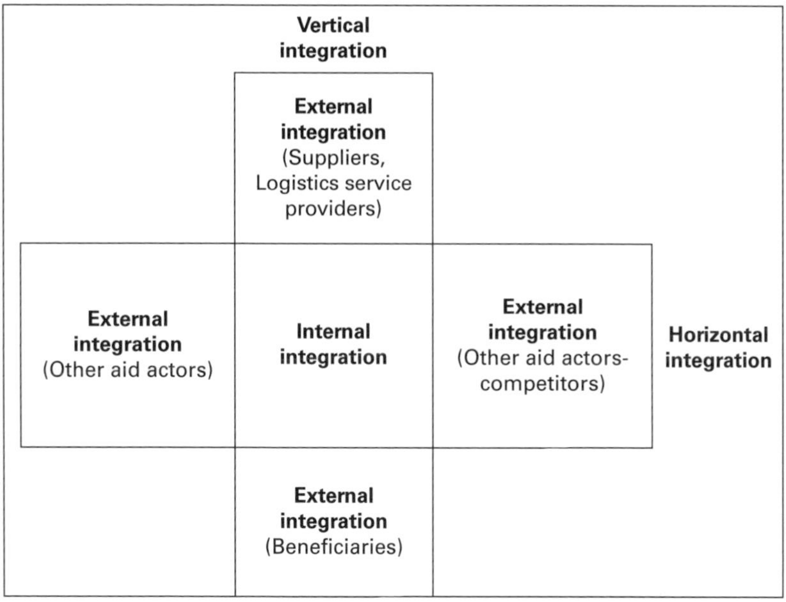

SOURCE Adapted from Barratt, 2004; Mason *et al*, 2007

as illustrated in Figure 6.1. The upstream/downstream integration partners can be converted to 'suppliers/logistics service provider' and 'beneficiaries' respectively, forming the vertical integration. In the horizontal relationships, 'other aid actors including NGOs, UN and GOs' are replaced in the position of complementary players or competitors.

In addition, some studies focus on arcs of SCI towards suppliers and customers (Frohlich and Westbrook, 2001; Childerhouse and Towill, 2011). Furthermore, some researchers view SCI from different levels: the strategic, tactical and operational levels of activities (Stevens 1989; Alfalla-Luque *et al*, 2013). Stevens (1989), for example, assumes that 'the traditional approach which focuses on the operational and planning levels' generates conflicts between different functions. Hence, although this model considers the vertical relationships with suppliers and customers, at the same time it pays attention to different internal/external functional units such as 'purchasing, distribution, market, finance, and production'. Similarly, this concept was also adapted for the area of collaboration. The notions of integration and collaboration are strongly linked because collaboration is a key component to construct the notion of integration (Mason *et al*, 2007) and integration is considered as an integral part of collaboration (Spekman *et al*, 1998). Whipple and Russell (2007) classify

Figure 6.2 Typology adapted for the humanitarian contexts

Strategic Perspective	Collaborative Process Management
Developing: objectives and policies for the supply chain; the shape of the SC in terms of key facilities and their locations; the company's competitive package; an outline organization structure and operate an integrated SC effectively.	Implying a more strategic collaboration, covering both demand and supply processes. Involving long-term joint business planning and more fully integrated SC processes across functions and organization.

⇨

- Pre-positioning partnerships
- eg strategically plan and integrate their upstream and downstream supply chains

Tactical Perspective	Collaborative Event Management
Focusing on the means of the strategic objectives. Translating the strategic objectives and policies into complementary goals. Determining the tools, approaches and resources.	Joint planning and decision making centred on critical events or issues, such as developing joint business plans or sharing information on upcoming product promotions.

⇨

- Joint needs assessment and sharing assessment information
- eg ReliefWeb (UN OCHA)

Operational Perspective	Collaborative Transaction Management
Concerning the detailed systems and procedures. Performance measuring in inventory investment, service level, throughput efficiency, supplier performance and cost.	Focusing on operational issues/tasks, targeting at solving problems and developing immediate solutions (eg expediting late deliveries).

⇨

- Close cooperation in the field
- Adapting, improvising and overcoming obstacles

SOURCE Adapted from Stevens, 1989; Whipple and Russell, 2007; Larson, 2012

three levels of collaborative relationships as: 'collaborative transaction management; collaborative event management; and collaborative process management'. Larson (2012), on the other hand, applies the concept of 'relationships' to humanitarian logistics and specifies the activities for humanitarian contexts. Comparing the activities as shown in Figure 6.2, it can be argued that these three types of relationships can be matched with the three different levels of integrated supply chains. At the strategic level, it can be clearly seen to form an integrated supply chain system to reduce the barriers across functions or units. At the tactical level, decisions or determinations are made so that important issues can be considered as much as possible in the prevailing conditions, and more detailed objectives set, derived from strategic goals. Finally, the operational level is focused on practical operations and detailed procedures which can be adjusted minute-by-minute or day-by-day.

Conceptual framework

A conceptual framework was developed by Kim *et al* (2017), as shown in Figure 6.3. In attempting to explain the main factors or constructs studied, it allows the researcher to investigate 'the same phenomenon' in a cross-case analysis (Miles *et al* 2014: 20).

First, in order to clarify the degree of supply chain integration, three levels of SCI are addressed: strategic, tactical and operational. These three levels are then used to clarify the degree of SCI in a given situation. This concept stems from 'the needs of the businesses' that requires diverse levels of consideration. For instance, solutions for conflicts that result from 'functional attitudes and goals' are usually concentrated at the operational level and are often not very effective (Stevens, 1989). Hence, it obviously seems more useful to deal with SCI issues from all three levels. The concept was further developed into a typology of collaborative relationships that are related with integration in business and further developed for humanitarian logistics by Larson (2012). Second, with respect to the disaster management phases, the current chapter focuses on the phases of preparedness and immediate response, which are regarded as relatively more important time for effective responses to events. Thus, the conceptual framework comprises two main categories on its axes: the levels of SCI and the phases of natural disaster relief management. Lastly, this framework is applied respectively to the activities and roles of NGOs, GOs and the UN.

Figure 6.3   Levels of supply chain integration in different phases

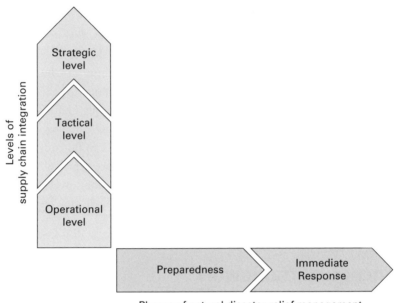

SOURCE Kim *et al*, 2017

Methodology

In order to gain an in-depth understanding of different aid actors' approaches, the research used a qualitative approach. This approach is appropriate to explain the diversity of interactions between different aid actors and describe the processes of SCI in complex situations (Kumar, 2014). Baxter and Jack (2008) suggest three ways of establishing boundaries for case studies: (a) by time and place; (b) by time and activity; and (c) by definition and context. This study bounded the cases using the last factor, and analysed them on a comparative basis. As stated earlier, the types of organization chosen were NGOs, the UN and GOs. The three cases are analysed in the context of sudden onset natural disasters. Each case has its own operational context, which is important for understanding the specific issues related to it, and which cannot be separated from the cases when explaining them. Four interviews were conducted, as depicted in Table 6.1. Each in-depth interview was with a senior operative in an aid organization with extensive experience in humanitarian and disaster relief. The overall purpose of this research is therefore to gain a better understanding of SCI, specifically in the

Table 6.1 Interviewees

No	Interviewees	Cases	Location	Position
1	NGO A	Non-governmental organizations	International/ Western Europe	Head; 28 years' experience
2	NGO B		International	Director/head; over 23 years' experience
3	UN A	United Nations	Middle East	Senior supply coordinator; 28 years' experience
4	GO A	Governmental organizations	Western Europe	Senior manager

context of humanitarian and disaster relief, rather than to simply generalize 'the rule of relationships'.

For the analysis, in vivo coding and sub-coding was used. The in vivo coding method is prevalent in qualitative data analysis and 'usually borrows the actual words and short phrases from the interviewees' own languages for coding' (see, for example, Miles *et al*, 2014). Further, the sub-coding analysis enhances the primary codes by explaining them in greater detail. These entities, created from the first cycle coding analysis, are used to expand on the conceptual framework through the second stage of analysis. In the second cycle of analysis, the pattern codes were used for a more in-depth analysis. This method helps the researcher to derive clearly condensed results from a large amount of data. Also, it is useful for cross-case analysis and the visualization of the interconnections of components, to map the categories, or to develop the conceptual framework. By using the pattern codes as the second cycle coding, the activities within SCI in each case were clarified and compared with each other. The developed framework that emerged covered the horizontal SCI activities of the selected aid actors pertinent to the focus of this chapter (Miles *et al*, 2014).

Findings: characteristics of major aid actors

Non-governmental organizations

In general, NGOs are the first responders for many rapid onset natural disasters. The only actor likely to move before an NGO is the host government's military, as they usually undertake the role of 'ensuring basic access, evacuating people and re-building infrastructure' (NGO B). This observation is consistent with findings from field research in, for example, East Africa (Choi *et al*, 2010), Myanmar (Christopher and Tatham, 2011) and Haiti (Pettit and Beresford, 2012). In the case of big international NGOs (BINGOs), they are more likely to respond with agility because their regional offices across the world can be mobilized for the disaster relief (NGO A). While NGOs meet 'the basic needs' by providing medicine, medical professionals, food assistance and recurring items, they are very keen to 'assess the problem' and identify priorities on the ground quickly as a first stage (NGO A; NGO B). Indeed, they tend to consider the need assessment very important and try to share it as much as they can (NGO A). This makes them responsive to the needs of beneficiaries. This traditional aid operation works certainly for the first week after large-scale disasters while the local market is closed. However, distribution is usually based on the physical SCs that require a high cost of setting up for air freight, transportations, warehouse management and labours (NGO A).

More recently, NGOs have considered running cash and voucher programmes as an alternative and compatible way of aid distribution. This provides money to beneficiaries and is seen as a very cost effective and innovative programme (NGO A; NGO B). NGO A explains the need for cash programmes: 'some will have more kids, some will have fewer kids and some will have grandparents. So, it is far better to give them twenty dollars so that they can go and buy for their own particular circumstance'. That is to say, NGOs often require HDR-SCM to be more flexible in order to respond more effectively to the diversity of cases and situations.

The United Nations

When beginning relief operations, the UN agencies, like most humanitarian agencies, work with 'self-initiatives', in particular in the areas where they have been running programmes or existing projects and therefore have some pre-knowledge of requirements (UN A). At the same time, they may be requested to participate in disaster relief management with other UN agencies, from international/local NGOs or in most cases from the host government (UN A). The UN usually tries to establish basic supply chains to get relief operations started quickly and provide beneficiaries elemental relief items in the very early stages. Referring to the interviews, it seems that the UN tries to 'cover all the recurring needs whether they are goods or services' (UN A). For example, in the case of the goods, there are recurring general relief items such as 'blankets, tents, and kitchen sets', while for recurring services there are common search and rescue tasks (UN A).

Further, UN agencies try to coordinate within the UN system and with other aid actors such as international or local NGOs by developing common operations and logistics approaches (UN A). Given this, it can be argued that the UN agencies are already heavily involved with a variety of aid actors working flexibly and putting more emphasis on coordination with other aid actors. With respect to this, one of the interviewees pointed out that 'they (UN agencies) have to coordinate across all the UN bodies and all the NGOs and take their information and try and collect that into one picture', that is to say, this implies that the UN often takes a lead role in coordination amongst multiple actors. This can result in slow processes or operations because the UN has to concern itself with a number of actors and donors, thus needing to build up a coordination system, sometimes from scratch.

Governmental organizations

GOs take an approach that is different from that of NGOs and the UN because their operational philosophy is fundamentally different from other humanitarian organizations. GOs are mainly led by politicians and naturally tend to prioritize the events that receive the most media coverage, or the activity that it is best able to cope with. National politics and the motivations of politicians cannot be detached from GOs as aid actors (GO A). Intrinsically, GOs can be more sensitive about political drivers and issues than other organizations. In general, GOs directly cooperate with the host government of the affected country and cannot start the emergency relief assistance without a request from the host government (GO A). Hence, their roles are more focused on primary supporters and donors to the agencies of the UN and the NGOs (GO A) who are relatively neutral in terms of politics and recognized as primary humanitarian aid actors. For instance, GOs often make a donation to UN agencies to help them start emergency relief operations in the initial phase, and also provide facilities from the stockpiles or cash directly to their NGO partners (GO A). Governments also usually control, or are deeply involved in, the appeals process, and thus play an important role in matching need with donations. In the case of the United Nations Central Emergency Response Fund (UNCERF), 99.76 per cent of financial contributions between 2006 and 2014 were gained from the member states and observers, namely the governmental organizations of 125 countries (UNCERF, 2015). This means many aid actors like UN agencies and NGOs heavily rely on GOs' donations.

At the same time, GOs send search and rescue teams at the request of the host government, and they can also make use of domestic resources such as a medical response team, fire service resources or military. This assistance is distinguished from the long-term programme of development basis. GOs tend to use their own resources and information for humanitarian and disaster relief based on regular suppliers and qualified partners. For example, at the very early stage of the immediate response phase, GOs organize their own planes, which is a very important method of transport in the first few hours after a disaster has occurred (GO A). For GOs, 'speed' is the most important factor when responding to a natural disaster, and they try to respond quickly within the first few hours. Hence, they prefer to start relief operations independently or cooperate with a limited number of partners in the early stages because it takes time to establish temporary SCs for all the aid actors (GO A). Additionally, because GOs usually have a specialized department, or simply a few staff that can respond rapidly to international disasters, it is not easy for them to coordinate with many other aid actors. Instead, they prefer working with regular partners and looking for appropriate ones that can deliver quickly and access the most vulnerable beneficiaries (GO A). These are all dependent on the local situation since GOs work flexibly depending on the specific context of the emergency.

Summary

Table 6.2 summarizes the distinctions between the three major aid actors that participated in this research, showing that their roles and activities are distinguished from each other based on different concerns and issues. NGOs are more concerned with agility and try to be more responsive to beneficiaries' conditions. Consequently, they tend to work closely with beneficiaries and find practical solutions that fit to ever-changing conditions in the affected area. However, within the group of NGOs as one of many organization types a great deal of organizations exist and their target beneficiaries and operational styles are unique. Next, the UN pay more attention to building a fundamental base of common SCs and try to function as a coordinator that makes the operations smooth and quick. For this, the UN has to collaborate with many other aid actors and donors and this can make the process slow. Lastly, GOs have to consider many facets. They need to concern themselves with the nation's political motivations or agenda and this can limit its range of aid activities and pattern of participation. At the same time, GOs need to act as a response team conducting emergency relief practices. Hence, it is suggested that GOs have to establish effective methods

Table 6.2 Characteristics of major aid actors (based on interviews and secondary data)

Category	NGO	UN	GO
Role	Usually act as a first responder working on the very front line	Often act as a key coordinator	Two roles: key donors and response teams
Concerns	Focus on agility and the needs of beneficiaries	Focus on establishing common SC to help multiple actors respond quickly	Focus on two factors: political drives and the most reasonable way of operations
Relief Activities	Try to be innovative and less costly rather than using a traditional way of operating	Try to cover all the recurring needs	Support the UN system, send a response team and work with regular qualified partners
Issues	Internal integration, different target beneficiaries	Slow process due to a number of actors and donors involved	Limited activities due to the political context and a high media profile

of disaster response involving a diverse and reliable range of humanitarian organizations in order to address the challenges of a specific disaster emergency response.

Findings: phases of natural disaster management

Preparedness

Undertaking activities in the preparedness phase is not simple and tends to have complex facets. One interviewee described the complexity of the preparedness phase where: 'in a resource poor environment, it is very hard to get people to change their lifestyles' (NGO B). Thus preparedness activities will vary depending on both the context and the on-the-ground situation. When aid actors are considering pre-positioning works, they will try to establish what are 'the most high risk contexts', and look into 'vulnerability, poverty and less sustainable likelihoods' (GO A; NGO A; NGO B). After such an evaluation, aid actors will often run preparedness activities, such as mitigation planning or preparedness programmes, through their regional offices (NGO A; GO A). These activities are generally associated with long-term development programmes because it is easier for aid actors to use existing programmes in order to improve efficiency. On the other hand, some aid actors need to conduct preparedness activities in 'low–middle income countries' where they do not have existing development programmes or regional offices (NGO B). Further, they will need to consider a wide range of issues ranging from, for example, the country's infrastructure and environmental conditions to political issues such as national disaster response policies (NGO B). Building prevention systems will have considerable associated challenges, and will need to be developed over a period of time. Consequently, for an organization's policy makers there are no easy decisions regarding how to prioritize 'resourcing and practising' (NGO B).

Despite these difficulties, most aid agencies and organizations recognize that dealing with significant natural disasters is beyond their own individual capacity and they will need to work with other agencies prior to any potential event (NGO A). Hence, the UN, NGOs and GOs often use the UN cluster system or work with each other in regular partnerships. In other words, they establish cluster coordination to optimize responses to disasters and to respond collaboratively, for instance by using a common logistics framework or hiring aid workers (UN A; NGO A). In addition to this, aid agencies may try to mitigate the impacts of repeated disasters by setting up early warning systems or evacuation plans and, in such cases, the UN and NGOs collaborate closely with the host government (NGO B; GO A).

Immediate response

Humanitarian and disaster relief supply chain management in the immediate response phase can be characterized as follows:

(a) *Temporarily and suddenly formed supply chains (NGO B; UN A; GO A).* When sudden onset natural disasters occur, in general there is no supply function in the early stage because most actors are not running regular operations in the specific affected area. However, aid agencies will usually have to make supply chains function within 24 hours at least. Thus supply chains for rapid onset natural disasters tend to be temporary, as more permanent, robust supply chains cannot be established in a short period of time.

(b) *Involvement of a wide variety of aid agencies both new and inexperienced (NGO B; UN A; GO A).* In addition, broadly the bigger, or the more unpredictable a disaster is, the more assistance the host government will require. In other words, the more serious the emergency, or the larger the disaster, the wider is the required range of humanitarian actors for the relief effort regardless of their aid speciality. This is because aid agencies that specialize in responding to natural disasters, and generally also the host government, cannot deal with all aspects of a disaster and the participation of a range of agencies is required. Additionally some agencies may not be specialized in natural disaster relief management but may have specific skill-sets that could contribute to the relief effort if managed correctly (Pettit and Beresford, 2005).

(c) *Response slowed by disrupted and damaged infrastructure (NGO A; UN A; GO A)*. Natural disasters usually create serious physical damage or destruction to infrastructure, and in the early stages of a response even tasks such as search and rescue are extremely challenging. One respondent described how disrupted operating conditions were created following Cyclone Nargis in May 2008: 'When the cyclone hit Myanmar, the water was coming from everywhere, the roofs had flown off, and the trees were lying all over the place. Once you got out of the house, the pole lines were down' (UN A). The August 2017 Sierra Leone mudslides are a further case-in-point where the consequences of the natural disaster severely disrupted the ability of agencies to respond effectively (BBC, 2017). Due to the complexity and level of disruption in emergencies such as these it is not easy to establish the foundations for effective delivery of relief and provision of help becomes almost impossible.

(d) *Need for strong coordination (NGO A; NGO B; UN A; GO A)*. In a chaotic situation, post-disaster leadership is a crucial issue. One respondent asserted the importance of the role of coordinator in disaster relief: 'it is amazing how one person (a very good coordinator) with the right back-up can make a difference' (NGO B). In many natural disaster events, the UN acts as a coordinator, organizing aid actors working together. On the other hand, the UN often also coordinates with the host so the role of the host government is very important in demonstrating leadership and greater coordination. Nonetheless, it is not easy for the host government facing the sudden onset disaster to make quick decisions and respond promptly. It often takes two or three days, sometimes even five days, for the host government to request assistance from other agencies and neighbouring countries (NGO A; GO A). There is an understandable tendency for the government in the affected country to first try to be self-sufficient, but when it becomes clear that the situation is too much for them to handle alone they call in the help of other institutions. Even countries such as China, which have extensive resources both civilian and military, resort to calling for international assistance in the biggest emergencies (Pettit and Beresford, 2012). Thus, particularly for the first week after the event, it is clear that decent coordination is a vital aspect of the response effort.

Interpretation

Non-governmental organizations

Overall, it is clear that NGOs have distinct activities during the different phases of natural disaster relief response. Particularly, in the preparedness phase, the host government plays an important role. As mentioned above, this is because the preparedness activities are often related to existing social infrastructure or national policies. Hence, preparedness programmes are frequently led by the host government, and humanitarian actors join them according to need (NGO A). Preparedness programmes are usually long-term projects, sometimes lasting several years; in many cases these are guided at arm's length by the UN. One respondent said that 'anything we did for disaster preparedness, we would report to the UN coordinator' (NGO A). This means that, in this phase, governments, the UN and NGOs share information on planning, progression, past performance and so on.

In terms of the level of SCI, NGOs tend to have activities focused on strategic and tactical aspects during the preparedness phase (see Figure 6.4). Based on studies of rapid onset disasters, they try to build a prevention system that is robust and has the capacity to be of use. They do this in tandem with the host government and other aid actors. In addition, NGOs also join global UN conferences regarding disaster preparedness, such as the UN World Conference on Disaster Risk Reduction. At the conference, 'the governments surrounding NGOs, the UN and other international organizations look at the whole agenda with respect to disaster preparedness' (NGO B). This can help NGOs to update their own agendas and adjust their policies or strategies. All these activities can be categorized under strategic SCI because they are related to strategically planning and developing objectives and policies (Stevens, 1989; Larson, 2012). At the level of tactical SCI, NGOs report the progress of preparedness to the UN coordinator. Although they cannot share resources at the operational level because each aid actor

Figure 6.4 Framework of NGOs' activities in SCI

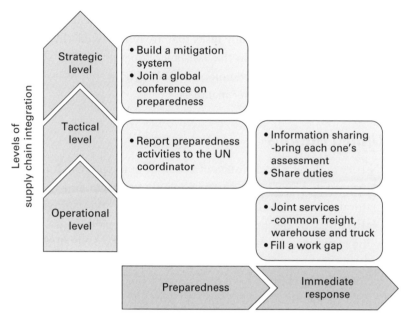

Phases of natural disaster relief management

has 'different mandates, different budget and different donors... they still try to share information and knowledge with other aid actors' (NGO A). This can help other aid actors to determine their allocation of resources.

In the immediate response phase, NGOs focus on the tactical and operational levels of SCI as described in Figure 6.4. One NGO respondent emphasized the importance of the tactical and operational levels as follows: 'pre-positioning supplies are the means to the end. If you have not got the capacity to manage the people, to access the people and to identify their needs and to distribute what they need, then the operations are not going to work' (NGO A). This is because it is common to see a large proportion of pre-positioned supplies remain in the containers, and not distributed. Thus, in this phase, NGOs try to make the operations flow smoothly and efficiently. For this, they share assessment information and divide responsibilities with other organizations to avoid unnecessary duplication. However, NGOs have 'quite limited competency' in collaborative needs assessment. Another respondent (NGO B) described the problems of common assessment: 'during my experience of humanitarian work over 25 years, it is very rare that you find common assessments done quickly and collaboratively'. Individual NGOs tend to do their own assessments. Each organization has a different mandate and distinct objective and consequently it takes a great deal of time to proceed with a commonly agreed assessment. Instead, they try to share the result of assessment for more efficient allocation of resources. Further, if there are any tasks that are not covered, they will then try to fill any identified gaps in the assistance programme. The sharing of activities may also extend to common air freighting, warehousing and sea/land transport with other cluster members.

The United Nations

The UN tries to cover a wide range of activities in the preparedness phase. It can be argued that they tend to prepare mainly for responding to a sudden onset natural disaster. Also, as Figure 6.5 illustrates, the UN conducts a broad variety of activities across all levels of SCI, through many coordinating groups in the preparedness phase. First of all, the UN 'clusters' play a pivotal role in integrating the supply chains of the various aid actors. Eleven cross-cutting clusters have been created since the 2004 tsunami for the purpose of avoiding duplication. In particular, the Logistics Cluster takes the role of providing common services such as 'a common trucking pipeline', to reduce congestion in a port, and to share useful information (Tatham and Pettit, 2010). The UN is also involved in many coordinating groups by designing a common strategy, exchanging information and data and training staff together. Furthermore, it has an agreement to temporarily share personnel with principle NGO partners for a short period.

During the immediate response phase, the UN focuses strongly on activities at the operational level. During the initial stages of a response greater coordination is required, as many of the aid actors will depend on common services until they establish their own SCs. The significance of speed of response at the beginning of the aid operation was highlighted: by a respondent who stated that 'at this stage speed is vital and this depends on common services being available' (UN A). Indeed, common services such as procurement, warehousing and transport are essential for starting relief operations quickly in chaotic situations. When SCs are stabilized and settled, relatively less coordination is required between aid actors. Generally, in affected areas there are not enough available resources and costs of relief items can become higher than usual if aid actors are competing against each other. Hence, it is important to establish a common service group to save time and costs and make the most of available resources without the hindrance of competition or waste. This is often overseen through the Logistics Cluster (led by the

Figure 6.5 Framework of UN's activities in SCI

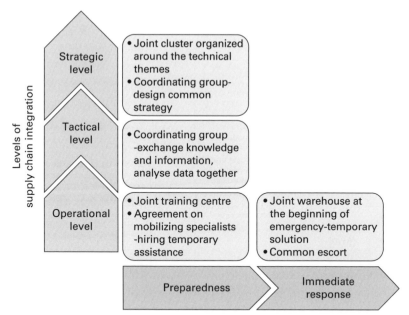

Phases of natural disaster relief management

World Food Programme (Pettit *et al*, 2011)) and then disseminated through regular coordinating groups organized in the preparatory phase. However, in a conflict area, the UN may not be able to share services with some agencies as they are required to maintain a neutral and impartial stance, and this could be compromised by the specific agendas of some agencies.

Governmental organizations

As Figure 6.6 demonstrates, GOs place great emphasis on the tactical level of SCI in the preparedness phase, while they cover the tactical and operational levels of SCI activities in the immediate response phase. These integration activities are usually conducted based on a facility network with reliable NGO partners. GOs meet these partners on a regular basis and form strong links with them during the preparedness phase.

During the immediate response phase, the role of NGO partners is very important, because these partners 'collect information and feed it back to GOs' about the needs on the ground or detailed situations (GO A). Further, for the first 72 hours to the first week after the event, usually the UN system

Figure 6.6   Framework of GOs' activities in SCI

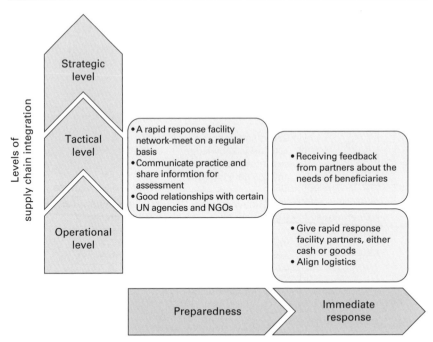

Phases of natural disaster relief management

tries to establish common service systems in supply chains. Thus, GOs first work with their regular partners to secure agility on disaster relief operations and then try to collaborate with the UN system after the common SCs are stabilized. They look at partners that 'have already presence on the ground to deliver aid items quickly and ability to get things out to people who are most vulnerable' (GO A). Based on the collated information, they provide the partners with goods from the stockpile or with cash to encourage buying from local markets.

Cross-case patterns

The case analysis highlighted that there are different needs and requirements between aid actors both temporally and across the levels of integration. However, it is also apparent that there are commonalities across the three cases. In the preparedness phase, the three groups are more focused on the strategic and tactical levels, while, in contrast, in the immediate response phase it is the tactical and operational levels that are of more concern.

Table 6.3 Common perspectives among major aid actors

Aid Actors	Tactical Perspective/ Preparedness	Operational Perspective/ Immediate Response
NGOs	• Report preparedness activities to the UN coordinator	• Joint services – common freight, warehouses and trucks • Fill a work gap
UN	• Coordinating group – exchange knowledge and information, analyse data together	• Joint warehouse at the beginning of emergency – temporary solution • Common escort
GOs	• A rapid response facility network, meet on a regular basis • Communicate practice, and share information for assessment • Good relationships with certain UN agencies and NGOs	• Give rapid response facility partners either cash or goods • Align logistics

All actors have one level of SCI in common at each phase, as shown in Table 6.3. During the preparedness phase, all three aid actors have SCI activities at the tactical level, while they have the operational level of SCI in the immediate response phase. In this phase, agencies will actively share assessment information for better decision making in resource allocation and preliminarily build a strong network between them. Immediately following a natural disaster they will try to integrate supply chains at the operational level; however, their counterparts react differently. NGOs and the UN use common services together based on the cluster system, whilst GOs tend to work closely with their own facility NGO partners and partially use joint logistics services with the other aid actors. Normally, GOs do not share warehouses or aid staff.

Indeed, it is not easy to integrate SCs with GOs at the operational level during the response phase. To some extent, this is due to the unique context surrounding GOs. As mentioned above, GOs have political agendas and are influenced by national political conditions. Their decisions and performance can be affected by the top levels of government. They may want to use their own military and they need to consider media issues. Hence, their interest in humanitarian events can be different from other actors. One respondent also explained that 'there is a very big difference between humanitarian humanitarians and political humanitarians'. Further, the issues related to SCI are fairly sensitive, particularly in conflict areas, and aid actors are generally careful when undertaking SCI in such places.

Conclusion

While SCI in commercial environments has been widely covered by academic research, the use of the concept in humanitarian situations is under-researched. The literature thus far has focused on coordination and collaboration, but the integration of supply chains requires greater focus. This chapter explored horizontal SCI between aid organizations in the context of rapid onset natural disasters, and, more specifically, the preparedness and immediate response phases. Also, there are few in-depth studies considering SCI in terms of the different levels of SCI. By using SCI levels, this chapter tries to analyse the activities of major aid actors in a systematic way. The contribution of this chapter is threefold. First, the conceptual model for HDR-SCI, originally presented in Kim *et al* (2017) integrating the notions of business SCI and humanitarian unique contexts, is further developed. Second, the contrasting characteristics and activities of major aid actors, NGOs, UN bodies, and GOs were analysed based on the multi-dimensionality of SCI. Third, different SCI activities were identified according to their use within the different phases of disaster relief management. The findings with specific reference to the research questions are summarized below.

In terms of the *roles of each aid actor and their differences (RQ1)* the research showed that each aid actor has a different perspective and context, and these factors often inhibit the successful implementation of SCI. Also, a review of emergency relief studies reconfirmed the different perspectives and stances of major aid actors during disaster relief operations. Kovács and Spens (2009) explain the different foci and concerns among individual UN agencies and international NGOs and examine the challenges by the type of organizations: international NGOs and GOs. Seaman (1999) identifies the component parts of the international relief system: UN, NGOs and governmental donors, and states concisely the features of three participating bodies. Pettit and Beresford (2005) present the conflicting pressures faced by military and non-military participants. Given the academic opinion and preliminary interviews, different roles between major aid actors were assumed and this research investigated the unique characteristics of major aid actors. The major aid actors have their contrasting roles and issues in relation to the sudden onset natural disaster relief activities. In summary, this research assumes that NGOs act as a first responder to a rapid disaster with agility, while the UN tries to encompass a wide range of responsibilities as a coordinator, and GOs carry out two roles as a primary donor and a relief participant.

With reference to *how humanitarian SCM activities vary in the phases of natural disaster relief management (RQ2)*, previous research suggests that there are clear differences in SCM activities. The literature divides disaster relief management into several phases in order to optimize relief activities. This research also found differences between the two phases; preparedness and immediate response. SCM performance during the preparedness stage is not a simple issue because it is strongly associated with national policies, infrastructure, construction and people's lifestyle. SCM activities during the immediate response are difficult to implement due to the flux and disruption caused by the challenging circumstances. The research also confirms a clear difference in the SCI activities in each case in the different phases of relief management. In the preparedness phase, there are relatively higher levels of SCI activity and in the immediate response phase the lower levels of SCI activity are more focused.

When considering *how major aid actors integrate their supply chains with each other and their commonalities and differences (RQ3&4)*, a conceptual framework was developed using three levels of SCI: strategic; tactical; and operational. This concept stemmed from Stevens (1989) and Whipple and Russell (2007) who also apply three levels to collaborative relationships in the commercial sector. In humanitarian SCM studies, Blecken (2010) uses three levels in order to identify the SCM activities of humanitarian organizations and Larson (2012) apply three levels on supply chain relationships of aid actors. This concept is useful in measuring the levels of SCI and to analyse them in a systematic way. The conceptual framework was applied to all the three cases and allowed the visualization of the SCI activities. The research found that there are more differences between SCI activities among the three cases during the preparedness phase than during the immediate response phase. This research contends that the UN tries to lead the integration activities based on the cluster systems and other coordinating groups throughout all levels of SCI. As first suggested in Kim *et al* (2017), GOs are shown to have relatively little direct involvement in operationalizing SCI. However, at the tactical level they frequently liaise with other organizations to validate inputs that steer resource allocation at an operational level. Thus it can be seen that GOs are most proactive in the preparedness and immediate response phases, rather than in the longer term recovery phase.

Acknowledgements

Our special thanks to Professor Helen Walker and Dr Anne Touboulic for providing some contacts. We also wish to thank all members of aid organizations who participated in the research. We would like to acknowledge the financial assistance provided by the Economic and Social Research Council

(ESRC). We also would like to express gratitude to our discussants at the Nineteenth International Working Seminar on Production Economics for their constructive comments.

References

Abbott, PL (2008) *Natural Disasters*, 6th edn, McGraw-Hill Higher Education, London

Alfalla-Luque, R, Medina-Lopez, C and Dey, PK (2013) Supply chain integration framework using literature review, *Production Planning & Control*, **24**(8–9), pp 800–17

Anon (2017) Hurricane Irma [Online] https://en.wikipedia.org/wiki/Hurricane_Irma

Barratt, M (2004) Understanding the meaning of collaboration in the supply chain, *Supply Chain Management: An international journal*, **9**(1), pp 30–42

Baxter, P and Jack, S (2008) Qualitative case study methodology: Study design and implementation for novice researchers, *The Qualitative Report*, **13**(4), pp 544–59

BBC (2017) Reflections on Sierra Leone's mudslide disaster [Online] http://www.bbc.co.uk/news/world-africa-40973539

Bernon, M, Upperton, J, Bastle, M and Culln, J (2013) An exploration of supply chain integration in the retail product returns process, *International Journal of Physical Distribution & Logistics Management*, **43**(7), pp 586–608

Blecken, A (2010) Supply chain process modelling for humanitarian organizations, *International Journal of Physical Distribution & Logistics Management*, **40**(8/9), pp 675–92

Byman, D, Lesser, I, Pirnie, B, Bernard, C and Wazman, M (2000) *Strengthening the Partnership: Improving military coordination relief agencies and allies in humanitarian operations*, Rand, Washington

Caunhye, AM, Nie, X and Pokharel, S (2012) Optimization models in emergency logistics: A literature review, *Socio-Economic Planning Sciences*, **46**(1), pp 4–13

Chen, H, Daugherty, PJ and Landry, TD (2009) Supply chain process integration: A theoretical framework, *Journal of Business Logistics*, **30**(2), pp 27–46

Childerhouse, P and Towill, DR (2011) Arcs of supply chain integration, *International Journal of Production Research*, **49**(24), pp 7441–68

Choi, K-Y, Beresford, AKC, Pettit, SJ and Bayusuf, F (2010) Humanitarian aid distribution in East Africa: A study in supply chain volatility and fragility, *Supply Chain Forum: An International Journal*, **11**(3), pp 20–31

Christopher, M (2011) *Logistics and Supply Chain Management*, 4th edn, Pearson, Harlow

Christopher, M and Tatham, P (2011) Introduction, in *Humanitarian Logistics*, ed M Christopher and P Tatham, pp 1–14, Kogan Page, London

Fawcett, AM and Fawcett, SE (2013) Benchmarking the state of humanitarian aid and disaster relief: A systems design perspective and research agenda, *Benchmarking: An international journal*, 20(5), pp 661–92

Frohlich, MT and Westbrook, R (2001) Arcs of integration: An international study of supply chain strategies, *Journal of Operations Management*, 19(2), pp 185–200

Guan, W and Rehme, J (2012) Vertical integration in supply chains: Driving forces and consequences for a manufacturer's downstream integration, *Supply Chain Management: An international journal*, 17(2), pp 187–201

Kaatrud, DB, Samii, R and Van Wassenhove, LN (2003) UN Joint Logistics Centre: A coordinated response to common humanitarian logistics concerns, *Forced Migration Review*, 18, pp 11–14

Kim, J, Pettit, SJ, Beresford, AKC and Harris, I (2017) Understanding humanitarian and disaster relief supply chain integration, in *The Palgrave Handbook of Humanitarian Logistics and Supply Chain Management*, ed G Kovacs, K Spens and M Moshtari, Palgrave McMillan

Kovács, G and Spens, KM (2007) Humanitarian logistics in disaster relief operations, *International Journal of Physical Distribution & Logistics Management*, 37(2), pp 99–114

Kovács, G and Spens, KM (2009) Identifying challenges in humanitarian logistics, *International Journal of Physical Distribution & Logistics Management*, 39(6), pp 506–28

Kumar, R (2014) *Research Methodology: A step-by-step guide for beginners*, 4th edn, SAGE, Los Angeles

Kumar, S and Havey, T (2013) Before and after disaster strikes: A relief supply chain decision support framework, *International Journal of Production Economics*, 145(2), pp 613–29

Larson, PD (2012) Strategic partners and strange bedfellows: Relationship building in the relief supply chain, in *Relief Supply Chain Management for Disasters*, ed G Kovács and K Spens, pp 1–15, Business Science Reference

Lee, HW and Zbinden, M (2003) Marrying logistics and technology for effective relief, *Forced Migration Review*, 18(3), pp 34–35

Maon, F, Lindgreen, A and Vanhamme, J (2009) Developing supply chains in disaster relief operations through cross-sector socially oriented collaborations: A theoretical model, *Supply Chain Management: An international journal*, 14(2), pp 149–64

Mason, R, Lalwani, C and Boughton, R (2007) Combining vertical and horizontal collaboration for transport optimisation, *Supply Chain Management: An international journal*, 12(3), pp 187–99

McLachlin, R, Larson, PD and Khan, S (2009) Not-for-profit supply chains in interrupted environments: The case of a faith-based humanitarian relief organisation, *Management Research News*, 32(11), pp 1050–64

Miles, MB, Huberman, AM and Saldana, J (2014) *Qualitative Data Analysis: A methods sourcebook*, 3rd edn, SAGE, Los Angeles and London

Munich RE (2015) *Loss Events Worldwide 2010–2014: Percentage distribution* [Online] https://www.munichre.com/touch/naturalhazards/en/homepage/index.html

Pagell, M (2004) Understanding the factors that enable and inhibit the integration of operations, purchasing and logistics, *Journal of Operations Management*, 22(5), pp 459–87

Palomero, S and Chalmeta, R (2014) A guide for supply chain integration in SMEs, *Production Planning & Control*, 25(5), pp 372–400

Perry, M (2007) Natural disaster management planning: A study of logistics managers responding to the tsunami, *International Journal of Physical Distribution & Logistics Management*, 37(5), pp 409–33

Pettit, SJ and Beresford, AK (2005) Emergency relief logistics: An evaluation of military, non-military and composite response models, *International Journal of Logistics: Research and applications*, 8(4), pp 313–31

Pettit, SJ and Beresford, AKC (2012) Humanitarian aid logistics: The Wenchuan and Haiti earthquakes compared, in *Relief Supply Chain Management for Disasters*, ed G Kovács and K Spens, pp 1–15, Business Science Reference

Pettit, SJ, Beresford, AKC, Whiting, M and Banomyong, R (2011) The 2004 Thailand tsunami reviewed: Lessons learned, in *Humanitarian Logistics*, ed M Christopher and P Tatham, pp 103–19, Kogan Page, London

Seaman, J (1999) Malnutrition in emergencies: How can we do better and where do the responsibilities lie? *Disasters*, 23(4), pp 306–15

Spekman, RE, Kamauff, JW, Jr and Myher, N (1998) An empirical investigation into supply chain management: A perspective on partnerships, *Supply Chain Management*, 3(2), pp 53–67

Stevens, GC (1989) Integrating the supply chain, *International Journal of Physical Distribution & Materials Management*, 19(8), pp 3–8

Tatham, P and Kovács, G (2010) The application of 'swift trust' to humanitarian logistics, *International Journal of Production Economics*, 126(1), pp 35–45

Tatham, PH and Pettit, SJ (2010) Transforming humanitarian logistics: The journey to supply network management, *International Journal of Physical Distribution & Logistics Management*, 40(8/9), pp 609–22

Thomas, AS and Kopczak, LR (2005) From logistics to supply chain management: The path forward in the humanitarian sector, *Fritz Institute*, 15, pp 1–15

Toyasaki, F, Arikan, E, Silbermayr, L and Sigala, F (2017) Disaster relief inventory management: Horizontal cooperation between humanitarian organizations, *Production and Operations Management*, 26(6), pp 1221–37

UNCERF (2015) *CERF pledges and contributions* [Online] http://www.unocha. org/cerf/our-donors/funding/cerf-pledges-and-contributions-2006–2015

UNHCR (2015) *Nepal: 2015 earthquakes* [Online] http://data.unhcr.org/nepal/

UN-ISDR (2003) *Terminology on Disaster Risk Reduction* (working document) [Online] http://www.adrc.asia/publications/terminology/top.htm

Van Wassenhove, LN (2006) Humanitarian aid logistics: Supply chain management in high gear, *Journal of the Operational Research Society*, 57(5), pp 475–89

Vega, D and Roussat, C (2015) Humanitarian logistics: The role of logistics service providers, *International Journal of Physical Distribution & Logistics Management*, 45(4), pp 352–75

Whipple, JM and Russell, D (2007) Building supply chain collaboration: A typology of collaborative approaches, *The International Journal of Logistics Management*, 18(2), pp 174–96

Humanitarian logistics and supply chain management in Africa

07

CHARLES MBOHWA, TATENDA CHINGONO AND PAUL BUATSI

Abstract

This chapter discusses the growing importance of humanitarian logistics and supply chain management in Africa. This discussion is within the context of many factors and processes involved in the delivery of development aid and relief during disasters and emergencies. It is a reflection of the complexity of humanitarian supply networks. The advances made towards the application of theoretical concepts in business logistics and supply chain management also provide a background to the discussion of the African experience. The emphasis here is that the context within which humanitarian interventions occur in Africa is complex, and therefore poses serious management and leadership challenges: the types of disasters, the conditions of the victims, marked political and cultural diversity, the limited and poor state of infrastructure and other resource constraints required to support and manage humanitarian interventions in a sustainable manner. In addition, the role of continental, regional and international organizations, global humanitarian agencies, civil society organizations and opinion leaders all influence the efficiency, effectiveness and, therefore, the success of interventions and also moderate the degree of cooperation and collaboration. As elsewhere, the complexity of the humanitarian supply networks in Africa, with its multiplicity of actors, raises serious logistical management and leadership challenges.

The human immunodeficiency virus infection and acquired immune deficiency syndrome (HIV/AIDS) disasters and challenges are discussed in the context of three Southern African countries, Zimbabwe, South Africa and Botswana, in the form of mini-case studies. This research chapter considers ways in which the logistics function can reduce the severity of natural disasters including fire hazards (especially wildfires), floods, HIV/AIDS, xenophobia and droughts through a strengthening of relief efforts and the employment of innovative solutions in order to empower all those concerned. The impact of the disasters and the work that has been undertaken on the continent in response is identified and highlighted. The chapter contributes to research, knowledge and discourse on humanitarian logistics and supply chains in Africa.

Definition of disasters

The general area of humanitarian supply networks is predicated on the fact that the world is increasingly plagued by disasters, thus calling for the adoption and adaptation of business supply network principles and practices in the face of humanitarian interventions. This is true for all countries and continents, and Africa is similarly affected. There are many humanitarian disasters that stretch a community's capacity to cope, leading it to become overwhelmed and not able to deal with the disaster's impact using the status quo systems. The communities thus have become vulnerable and in need of external assistance.

Africa's disasters are, in many cases, man-made. However natural disasters also occur that can have serious negative impacts on the physical infrastructure of the region resulting in the destruction of airfields and bridges, and communication and electricity networks. When this happens, there is need to have, or to be able to activate, agile supply chains that have fast response times. This can be a challenge in Africa, especially in cases where the infrastructure is non-existent and/or communications are slow. On the other hand, when slow-onset disasters occur in an African setting of this nature, the planning horizon is important and this assists humanitarian logisticians to achieve cost efficiencies (Oloruntoba and Gray, 2006).

The nature and incidence of disasters in Africa

Humanitarian disasters have recently claimed many lives, causing very costly material losses and inflicting terrible tolls on developing countries. These divert governmental attention and resources from the development that is desperately needed to enable a country to escape poverty. The costs of managing disasters in terms of humanitarian support, logistics and related supply chains have grown significantly since 2005, when the United Nations humanitarian appeal was US $3.7 billion to about US $20 billion in 2016 (*Guardian*, 2017).

The disasters are also at times generated by, and often exacerbated by, human activities. Poor land-use planning, inadequate environmental management and defective institutional and legislative arrangements can increase the risk and multiply the effects of a disaster. It is also projected that the Human Development Index for sub-Saharan Africa will fall by as much as 24 per cent by 2050 under extreme environmental disaster scenarios, pointing to a need to put in place mitigation and adaptation strategies and resilient humanitarian logistics and supply management systems. It is estimated that failure to do so has the potential to increase the number of people that can be classified as being in extreme poverty in Africa to more than 1 billion (UNDP, 2013).

Disasters in Africa include civil strife, xenophobic eruptions, population displacement (refugees or internally displaced people), earthquakes, cyclones, climate related flooding and droughts and epidemics. Additional causes of disaster are the HIV/AIDS pandemic, malaria outbreaks and tuberculosis, all of which negatively impact the sustainable development initiatives that are taking place in Africa. The increased frequency of extreme weather and climate variability/change, especially in West and Southern Africa, is also culpable (IPCC, 2012).

Dry spells affected more than 1 billion people (or 25 per cent of the world's population) between 1994 and 2013, with 41 per cent of drought disasters taking place in Africa (UNISDR, 2015). However, drought events that received a relief response accounted for only 5 per cent of all disasters. In 2011 the worst drought in 60 years hit the Horn of Africa and this placed more than 13.3 million people at risk of malnutrition and starvation. In Somalia, where decades of conflicts have worn down the country's ability to cope, the drought led to famine. This resulted in excessive demand for humanitarian assistance and required effective humanitarian logistics and resilient supply management in order to reduce the impact of the disaster. Additionally, preventive actions such as development of irrigation systems and more effective conflict resolution were needed (USAID, 2012).

South Africa is also often affected by droughts (WFF, 2016) with the country currently experiencing its most severe drought in over 35 years. This follows a number of years of poor rainfall, with 2015 being the worst recorded since 1904. In 2016 many cities across the country were left nearly dry as dam levels continued to drop due to the lack of rainfall and, as a result, many South African provinces were declared 'states of disaster' due to drought.

Wars in Africa have been another major cause of refugees and displaced people, with an estimated 30 per cent of total refugees worldwide in Sub-Saharan Africa. Some 18 million people are of concern, mainly fuelled by strife in Central Africa Republic (460,000 in neighbouring countries and 411,000 internally displaced), Southern Sudan (1.9 million people internally; 630,000 in Uganda; 338,800 in Ethiopia; 297,168 in Sudan; 88,391 in Kenya; 66,672 in the Democratic Republic of Congo; and 4,915 in the Central African Republic), Burundi (409,000 people), Nigeria (2.7 million internally displaced people and 200,000 in neighbouring countries), Mali (140,000 in neighbouring countries and 37,000 internally displaced) and Somalia (1.5 million internally displaced people and 1 million in neighbouring countries) (UNHCR, 2017a). The war in Nigeria has also caused internal displacements in neighbouring countries: 192,900 people in Cameroon; 82,260 people located in Chad's Lake Region and 184,230 people in Niger. In addition, Africa hosted 715,000 stateless people at the end of 2016 (UNHCR, 2017b).

Xenophobia is the dislike of, and actions against, foreign nationals (McDonald and Jacobs, 2005). It has also been described as any kind of fear related to an individual or group perceived as different from the person that has the phobia. Such xenophobia visibly exists between a number of population groups inside South Africa and has led to disasters that have resulted in extensive damage to property, businesses and livelihoods. As a result, many victims were assisted with transportation back to their home countries and it is clear that early intervention is required before the crises of xenophobia reach disaster levels (Lawyers for Human Rights, 2015). This has led to the development of flexible and swift humanitarian supply chains supporting the response phase to xenophobic attacks. These focus on saving lives, giving food and shelter to those who have lost their homes, and providing healthcare necessities to victims, although there is a need to monitor closely how quickly and efficiently humanitarian organizations can respond to xenophobic humanitarian disasters (Schwarz and Kessler 2010).

Nevertheless, in 2008 the worst xenophobic attacks occurred, resulting in 62 deaths and the displacement of 35,000 people (Steinberg, 2008) and, unfortunately, there is no guarantee that such eruptions will not be repeated in future. In short, xenophobia poses a constant threat as a source of future humanitarian disasters in South Africa.

The solutions to such xenophobia-related humanitarian disasters can be addressed by overcoming some of its causes, with the main ones being: the government's failure to maintain law and order and to combat violent crimes (Cronje, 2008); the perception that foreigners are winning over South African women and jobs to the disadvantage of locals (Mnyaka, 2009); poor service delivery by all levels of government; foreign nationals accepting poverty level wages (Nyamnjoh, 2006); the failure of South African foreign policy that condones election theft and dictatorship in other African countries, resulting in 'economic refugees'; corruption in immigration resulting in fake work and residency permits; porous borders that, through corruption or poor policing, result in illegal immigrants; a decline in economic growth and in job creation; jealousy and fear of foreigners in good jobs and in business (Khosa and Kalatanyi, 2014); high unemployment; and a poor education system (Cronje, 2008).

That said, the issue of foreigners stealing jobs has been disputed by others. For example, Steinberg (2008) argues that foreign nationals provide services that are valuable by filling in voids in the country rather than them merely 'stealing' jobs, whilst Nkosi (2010) indicates that some foreigners are well educated and skilled. As an example, it is reported that more than 600 teachers were recruited from Zimbabwe to teach mathematics, science and technology courses in Limpopo province due to scarcity of teachers with such skills.

Wildfires can also cause humanitarian strife. Africa has many regions that are prone to drought, and wildfires have displaced many people destroying properties in the process, with wildfires in South Africa becoming a national problem. The resultant fires, which occur during the dry summer months and the dry winter months, destroy human lives, health, the environment, homes, grasslands, farms, land, soil, forests, wildlife and bush fields. Wildfires also result in considerable volumes of water being used, destroy livelihoods, increase insurance costs, cause the extinction of some species and reduce economic growth.

The main causes are neglected camp fires, heating stoves known as 'imbawula' mostly in shunt settlements, lightning, fire debris, cigarette stumps and fireworks. Wildfires have claimed human lives as well as the evacuation of homes, with a fire in the Table Mountain region affecting

500 people and resulting in the need for smoke inhalation treatment for 52 elderly people. The fire further destroyed or damaged a hotel lodge, homes, historic wine farms and offices, with six helicopters and two planes needing to be used to control the flames. The worst wildfire disaster in South Africa, mostly caused by lightning, occurred in the Western Cape in June 2017, killing nine people, destroying more than 1,000 homes and displacing 10,000 people (Wild Fire Today, 2017).

More broadly, the Emergency Events Database (EM-DAT) demonstrates that flooding caused 43 per cent of the recorded disasters between 1994 and 2013, and impacted some 2.5 billion individuals. Not only do floods result in deaths, injuries, water contamination, damage to property and disruption of electrical services, in Madagascar the resulting locust swarms left 4 million people without adequate food. In 2014 floods devastated Morocco, and in 2015 the floods in Malawi were the worst in 50 years, with close to 300 people dead, 230,000 displaced and 638,000 affected. In Ethiopia, after the worst drought in decades, flooding followed, wiping out those crops that had survived.

Climate variability and climate change are worsening the situation, making logistical operations extremely challenging. In some cases helicopters and airfreight become the only viable rescue methods. In early 2017 Cyclone Dineo brought torrential rains to South Africa with the subsequent floods causing damage to both property and the environment, as well as leaving 10.2 million people in need of food aid. Similar events in 2017 have severely impacted Madagascar and Sierra Leone (*Guardian*, 2017).

Disasters and sustainable development in Africa

According to the African Ministerial Statement to the World Summit on Sustainable Development, the high incidence and occurrence of natural disasters in Africa poses major obstacles sustainable development efforts on the continent (UNEP, 2001: para 16). This is aggravated by the fact that, in general, there is insufficient capacity on the ground to handle, mitigate, monitor and predict natural disasters. The continent's state of disaster preparedness is, therefore, of great concern (Marjanovic and Nimpuno, 2003).

The challenges faced included mismanagement of government controlled reserves; slow accreditation of non-governmental organizations (NGOs); economic downturn and the recipients' low levels of purchasing power;

weakening currencies; crippling HIV infection rates; poor nutrition; diminished labour forces; climate/weather variability; and dispersed populations. In particular, one of the main challenges was the fear that genetically modified grains would wipe out traditional crop varieties, thereby threatening the sustainability of agriculture in the recipient countries. It was felt that, in turn, the importation of genetically engineered food products in seed form can have longer-term deleterious impacts on the local economy that would outweigh the immediate benefits.

The Red Cross Code of Conduct Principle 8 requires that attention be paid to environmental issues when designing and managing humanitarian relief operations (IFRC, 2012). However, many humanitarian response operations still impact the environment negatively and the relief and recovery operations can sometimes cause as much or more environmental damage as the initial crisis (UNEP, 2012). Self-evidently, unsustainable humanitarian operations can result in over-exploitation of already stressed natural resources and the environment.

Basic humanitarian operations can cause pollution, produce waste, concentrate resource overuse and can result in unsustainable practices like poor management/disposal of spilled fuel, used oil waste, used tyres and chemicals from logistics based operations; or the procurement of goods produced through unsustainable practices, all of which have the potential to reverse and overshadow the original good intentions. However, this aspect is often neglected given the objective of the operation, which is to address pressing humanitarian needs that can be a matter of life or death.

Other typical sustainability problems include: displacement camps that were built for short-term relief but which end up lasting for years if not decades; boreholes that run dry due to overpopulation; and large-scale deforestation (Encyclopedia of the Earth, 2009). In short, a failure to address risks such as the use of forests to provide wood for cooking can undermine humanitarian operations, resulting in further loss of life, aid dependence, displacement, and increased vulnerability. Although this is acknowledged by many NGOs and United Nations (UN) agencies, there remains a big research and action gap, since these problems and risks are largely ignored in favour of the reality of humanitarian needs and operations.

On the other hand, it is argued (URD, 2008) that sustainable humanitarian operations provide for smoother recovery. There is, therefore, a clear need to study how the humanitarian logistics and supply chain systems operations in Africa can be made to be environmentally sustainable, and the resultant knowledge needs to be incorporated in research, teaching and training curricula for humanitarian logistic operations in Africa.

The resultant lessons will have clear potential for broader applications in countries and regions of the world that face similar problems and conditions.

The HIV/AIDS epidemic in Africa

Africa has the largest numbers of HIV/AIDS victims on antiretroviral therapy, with Zimbabwe, Botswana and South Africa in the top five countries in the world. However, the best access to therapy is also in this region, and this is constantly being improved with, for example, more than 61 per cent of affected adults being treated on the programme (UNAIDS, 2016). Nevertheless, HIV/AIDS poses new logistics challenges especially given that thousands of people are newly enrolled for therapy every month, and that these figures are projected to increase. Unsurprisingly, therefore, the unpredictable and unstable supply is still not meeting demand – leading to an unacceptable situation, given that those affected need to commit to the drugs for life. Indeed, the challenge is further exacerbated as donor aid is decreasing because some African countries are now categorized as mid-level income countries, and thus organizations like the Bill & Melinda Gates Foundation are pulling out (as happened in Botswana in 2013, and as is also happening to South Africa).

The mini-case study of HIV/AIDS logistics management in Zimbabwe

Due to the many deaths, high prevalence rate and the ungovernable nature of the HIV/AIDS epidemic, the Government of Zimbabwe first declared a state of emergency in May 2002. This was subsequently extended for six years and during this period the government, in partnership with aid agencies and NGOs, established and implemented the antiretroviral programme.

Antiretroviral therapy greatly reduces HIV/AIDS-related mortality and morbidity (Kerina *et al*, 2013). However, access and uptake still remains quite low and hundreds of thousands of people are not covered, notwithstanding that the 13.7 per cent prevalence of HIV/AIDS in Zimbabwe is still one of the highest globally. On the other hand, HIV/AIDS programmes are complex, and the associated management of the supply chain for HIV/AIDS products is particularly challenging with 120 different medical commodities (together with good nutritional programmes) being required to provide the full range of prevention, detection and treatment services.

Victims of the HIV/AIDS epidemic in Zimbabwe depend mainly on two streams of medicines: private distributors (for those that can afford them), and the Zimbabwean government, which supports the general public with free services. In its effort to eradicate the epidemic, the Zimbabwean government uses the National Pharmaceutical Company (NatPharm), which is a 100 per cent state owned company that was created in 2001 to take over the functions and responsibilities of former Government Medical Stores. NatPharm is generally considered to be the most logical and cost effective method that is used by projects involving the Ministry of Health and Child Welfare. In addition, several NGOs also support the provision of HIV/AIDS-related commodities including antiretroviral (ARV) medicines, contraceptives and nutritional food aid to the people of Zimbabwe (Chingono and Mbohwa, 2017).

The mini-case study of HIV/AIDS logistics management in South Africa

South Africa has the world's biggest HIV/AIDS challenge, with an estimated 3.6 million people accessing the life-saving medication in the public healthcare sector alone. The country also has the world's largest antiretroviral therapy (ART) programme. In April 2014 more than 3 million people took part, a figure that represents 47 per cent of people living with HIV (up from 31.2 per cent in 2012). However, more than 50 per cent of those affected by HIV/AIDS are not receiving medication through the public health sector and this implies that new, unique and different supply chain management solutions are likely to be needed (South African National Aids Council, 2015).

Both the delivery of ARV medicines, as well as getting people to accept and continue to take them, are big challenges in South Africa. As a result, the poor state of the supply chain has meant that some people die due to a failure to receive medication on time or regularly. That said, the South African government has pledged to provide ART therapy to those who have been tested positive and are in dire need of the therapy, and this has helped people carry on with their lives normally and productively.

However, primary healthcare facilities in South Africa struggle to provide continuous access to medication and to other necessary supplements. These range from antibiotics to ARTs that prevent mother-to-child transmission (PMTCT), to needles and test kits for HIV. In many situations there have been stock-outs at clinics, shifting the demand to district hospitals which provide the next level of support. Fortunately, however, whilst there have been some cases of stock-outs at all levels of health-care, including hospitals, these have been rare (South African National Aids Council, 2015).

South Africa has also been involved in efforts to lower the price of HIV/AIDS commodities from suppliers in its capacity as both the largest buyer and largest market for these products. This has given the country more leverage. For example, in 2013 South Africa achieved the lowest global prices, which resulted in a 53 per cent reduction in ARTs expenditure (UNAIDS, 2013). Nevertheless, despite the enormous volume of medication involved in its HIV-treatment programme, South Africa still relies on international pharmaceutical companies for the active components in ARVs, most of which are imported from overseas. None of the local pharmaceutical companies that supply the medication to public clinics and hospitals, produces them. Instead, they buy the ingredients that go into ARVs, called active pharmaceutical ingredients (API), and formulate them into tablets. Thus, the real winners are the international pharmaceutical companies.

The mini-case study of HIV/AIDS logistics management in Botswana

The first Botswana national HIV programme was implemented in 1988 and it has since evolved over time. The famous teacher-capacity building programme launched in 2004 by the Ministry of Health in collaboration with the United Nations Development Programme (UNDP) was very successful. It focused on improving teachers' knowledge, as well as demystifying and reducing stigmatization of HIV and AIDS affected people. This was supplemented by a twice weekly Botswana television programme called 'Talk Back', which was accessed by more than 20,000 teachers and 460,000 students. The programme won many awards based on its contribution and service to HIV/AIDS response (UNDP, 2013).

Makgabaneng was also introduced as a long-running radio serial drama. This utilizes mass media to promote HIV prevention through information dissemination. The themes covered are HIV/AIDS prevention, partnership and faithfulness, the role of cultural traditions, and AIDS treatment and services. Sexual health medical services and information are provided during roadshows and health fairs, and in 2013 these reached more than 20,000 people (Botswana Ministry of Health, 2014).

In 2015 Botswana was ranked third in terms of HIV prevalence in the world at 22.2 per cent (after Lesotho and Swaziland), a figure that, although high, demonstrated a marked improvement over the 2005 level of 25.4 per cent. However, Botswana is now classified as a middle-income country (World Bank, 2017), and is thus facing a big challenge to sustain its HIV response as donors are pulling out and increasingly refocusing on lower income countries. As an example, the US President's Emergency Plan for AIDS Relief (PEPFAR) reduced its funding to Botswana by more than 50 per cent, from US $84 million in 2011 to a total of US $39 million in 2015 (World Bank, 2015).

Botswana has, however, demonstrated a very strong commitment to address HIV and AIDS, becoming an excellent example for other sub-Saharan African countries. It is the first country to provide free antiretroviral treatment to people who are living with HIV/AIDS. As a result new infections decreased from 15,000 to 9,100 between 2005 and 2013. Similarly, AIDS-related deaths decreased from 14,000 to 3,200 between 2005 and 2015 (World Bank, 2017).

Nevertheless, specific areas within HIV prevention in Botswana require further work. Condom use is both low and decreasing despite the fact that 85 per cent of condoms in Botswana are free and highly available. Also, there is a myth and cultural belief supported by traditional healers who consider HIV/ AIDS to be an 'old' Tswana disease that can be cured (Botswana Ministry of Health, 2014).

The scope and role of humanitarian logistics

With the challenges posed by diverse forms of disasters in Africa there is a growing awareness of the significance of humanitarian logistics and supply chain management. The number and impact of the most recent disasters have exposed clear shortcomings in preparedness and planning for emergencies. Logistics accounts for about 80 per cent of disaster relief operations and is critical in saving lives and disaster recovery (Van Wassenhove, 2006). Unfortunately, whilst the supply chain should be at the apex of humanitarian aid operations in Africa, in reality in many African cases it is still seen as a support function within humanitarian organizations.

Unpredictable demand and supply

Disaster relief operations are often executed in environments with a destabilized service infrastructure leading to power cuts as well as a dysfunctional transport infrastructure. Disasters and emergencies are unpredictable and so are the material, logistics and goods demands that result. The speed of humanitarian aid is dependent on the capacity and capability of logisticians to supply to the humanitarian relief effort site (Thomas, 2003: 4). Humanitarian supply chains, unlike commercial supply chains, are unique and have unanticipated demands. Poor infrastructure in Africa is often worsened by weak political systems. It is difficult to assess and balance demand and supply requirements. These pose serious challenges such as inflexibility, and distribution networks are set up too quickly and with errors (Scholten et al, 2010).

Responding to disasters is, however, not easy and is not an exact science. A research and practice gap therefore exists for developing systems that enable effective resource allocation.

The need to avoid fixed and irrelevant logistics networks

Some NGOs have turned down food donations from traditional donors that were destined for Africa. This is because the donations often support and justify the subsidization of the donor country's agricultural industry and/or the donor's underutilized logistics networks and/or, in some cases, the NGOs and recipients sell the food to the detriment of sustainable food production in the recipient countries. International food donations in one country can lead to a regional excess of food stocks and levels outside the developed fixed logistics networks. For example, food relief in Zimbabwe depended on maize meal supply from the United States through well-established logistics networks even though Malawi had excess maize supplies. Thus, unless well managed, donations can distort markets and destroy the local production volumes and capacity.

Some of the natural disasters in Africa can be resolved at a national and regional level using suppliers closer to the point of need and supporting regional and local production which, in turn, will provide an improved capacity for future interventions. Some of the African economies can, therefore, be generally better off with no donations of food at all – not least because, if dependency syndrome and/or donor fatigue sets in, prices can go up to a very high level and/or shortages can recur due to diminished capacity to meet the demand.

Critical success factors for African humanitarian aid supply chains

In the light of the challenges outlined above, it is clear that humanitarian logisticians need to focus attention on a number of key success factors that are required for efficient and effective interventions. While it is accepted that there is a clear tension between the corporate driven activities and economies in most African countries and the life-saving humanitarian logistics operations, it is nevertheless argued that the latter can learn from the former (Nyaguthie, 2008).

Inventory management systems, information and communication technology management, transport and capacity planning, human resource management, continuous improvement methodologies and collaboration and supply chain strategies are all areas where the expertise of the 'for profit' sector could be leveraged. To this list might be added the role of gender in humanitarian logistics operations in Africa where the experiences of Oxfam demonstrate that women can perform better in humanitarian development projects (Nyaguthie, 2008).

To enhance our understanding of how the operational efficiency of humanitarian supply networks might be improved, attention must be paid to the recommendations of Richey (2009: 619) that humanitarian logistics and supply chain management, recovery and preparedness be supported by the following theoretical perspectives: communication theory, the resource-based view of the firm, relationship management theory and competing values theory.

This approach is supported by other authors who argue that a range of activities require attention including: improving agility of the systems (Oloruntoba and Gray, 2006), consideration of risk management and insurance issues (Kleidt *et al*, 2009), addressing humanitarian issues (Kovács and Spens, 2007), implementing inventory management systems (Beamon and Kotleba, 2006), using facility location methodologies (Balcik and Beamon, 2008), activating collaboration and networks (Gibbons and Samaddar, 2009), and consideration of multi-level partner and non-partner integration (Perry, 2007).

To this long list might be added a further key issue that impacts on most humanitarian logistics operations in Africa, which is that of language. This reflects the reality that most countries use multiple indigenous languages together with French in Francophone Africa, Portuguese in the former Portuguese colonies and English in former English colonies (Nyaguthie, 2008).

Disaster risk management and contingency planning in Africa

In response to the challenges posed by disasters on the African continent, various countries have established public institutions that are collaborating with international development and relief agencies to engage in disaster management activities. Institutional involvement spans national governments, regional, provincial, state, district and metropolitan authorities, depending on the country involved. As an example, the Disaster Management Act: 57 (2002) of the Ekurhuleni Metropolitan Council in South Africa manages disasters using continuous and integrated multi-sectorial, multi-disciplinary process planning with related implementation measures. The aim is to: (a) prevent or reduce the risk of disasters; (b) mitigate the severity and/or consequences of disasters; (c) create emergency preparedness; (d) have rapid and effective emergency response systems; (e) develop post-disaster recovery and rehabilitation systems. Similar approaches are found in Ghana, which has established a National Platform for Disaster Risk Reduction.

Disaster response in Africa can be hindered by inadequate disaster preparedness, lack of well-developed contingency plans, and limited response capacity and capability within governments and NGOs. Contingency plans for potential disasters are essential as they: enhance an organization's capacity to pre-empt and manage effectively any eventuality; facilitate proactive approaches; increase accountability through set performance indicators and benchmarks; and promote the creation of evacuation plans and drill tests against them.

Contingency planning, as a continuous process, requires continuous monitoring of the plan as the situation evolves. Adopting such an approach would have improved the management of the 2000 Cyclone Eline in Southern Africa. By contrast, when Cyclone Favio struck Mozambique in 2007, the resultant flooding was severe, particularly in Inhambane province which was already suffering from major flooding. The Mozambique Disaster Management Authority and all local and international stakeholders had plans for handling floods and cholera prevention/outbreak. These provided early warning and increased preparedness, with the resulting impact being minimal compared to that of 2000.

Institutional frameworks and policies

Governments in Africa are also putting in place systems to improve the efficacy and effectiveness of institutional policies to deal with humanitarian logistics and supply management challenges. As such, the African Union (AU) with its New Partnership for Africa's Development (NEPAD) has developed an Africa Regional Strategy for Disaster Risk Reduction (African Union, 2004).

Development partners and international relief and development agencies such as World Vision International, Action Aid, Care International, Oxfam and ADRA (among others) are collaborating to address the challenges through policy formulation and implementation and diverse interventions on the continent. However, the above initiatives aimed at disaster risk reduction, and the multiplicity of challenges associated with these efforts, have clear implications for humanitarian logistics. This is especially true in Africa because of uncertainties surrounding the determination of both demand and supply for humanitarian relief, which frequently leans towards emergencies rather than development.

Stakeholder collaboration, communication and coordination

A disaster or emergency always attracts many players. Richey (2009) suggests that these partners are best managed by using the relationship management theory. The different players have different systems that need to be harmonized. They can consist of different governments, militaries, NGOs and agencies of the UN (Scholten *et al*, 2010). In this regard, both the 'structural' elements of supply chains as well as the 'cultural' elements are considered essential to the establishment of an effective supply chain. While the earlier discussion in this chapter clearly indicates that there is a degree of collaboration between organizations involved in humanitarian relief activities in Africa, there is clearly more work to be done here, especially in integrating the work of international organizations and NGOs with national and regional African organizations to achieve an improved level of strategic supply chain planning and implementation.

Inevitably, governments tend to channel aid through major NGOs, some of which are large enough to be global actors. However, some of the more effective ones are small regional and/or country-specific organizations (Thomas and Kopczak, 2005). Other actors are from the military, the host governments or the governments of neighbouring countries and logistics service providers. It is noted that inter-agency contingency planning is more beneficial than individual organizational operations. Collaboration is not easy, but it enables information and resource sharing, while minimizing duplication and confusion among organizations.

Technology's role in humanitarian logistics and supply chain management in Africa

The essential role of communication theory in humanitarian relief and supply chain management is one of the four theoretical thrusts proposed by Richey (2009). The quality of communications technology, effective communication, information exchange and support is key to disaster relief and humanitarian operations. The ongoing development of information and communication technology infrastructure in African countries will assist in the improvement of humanitarian supply networks in Africa.

Moreover, because humanitarian logistics operates across the disaster management cycle, improved information systems/information technology (IS/IT) can assist relief operations throughout their entire life cycle. According to Scholten *et al* (2010), supply chain technology for humanitarian aid organizations is only in the development stage, but for humanitarian supply chains to be virtually integrated, information technology is a necessity so that data can be shared between buyers and sellers.

In Africa, the deployment of modern technology in the operations of humanitarian organizations is growing, albeit there are different levels of adoption. Apart from the national and international aid agencies (Red Cross, World Vision, WHO, etc), relatively few of the local NGOs use enterprise resource planning (ERP) systems. An example of efforts to address the challenge of the technological gap is a European Union (EU) sponsored project known as Advancing ICT for Disaster Risk Management in Africa–AIDA (AIDA, 2009).

The AIDA project acquires and shares knowledge about affordable ICT solutions that support disaster risk management (DRM) in Africa. It facilitates dissemination of knowledge and best practices to different stakeholders and at-risk communities. One of its test cases in South Africa involves the Forest Fire Association (FFA) in Nelspruit, which uses alarms developed by the South African Council for Scientific and Industrial Research (CSIR) in its operations to fight wildfires. The system uses CSIR's Advanced Fire Information System based on satellite-based products, like the Meteosat Second Generation (MSG) active fire products to provide automated alerts for defined areas.

Another example in South Africa is Umoya Networks. This uses satellite networks that activate technical supporting systems for disaster management, resulting in improved response speed. In the Western Cape fire management stakeholders have deployed Africon's GEMC system, which works together with Umoya Networks systems in improving preparation for, and response to, disasters (Disaster Management Southern Africa, 2007).

The South African Disaster Management Act No 57 (2002) supports the use of technologies that use satellites, remote sensing, imagery and geographic information systems in disaster response and management. The South African National Disaster Management Centre (NDMC) has agreements with the Satellite Application Centre (SAC) to use their technologies to enhance the National Disaster Management Information System (NDMIS) (Disaster Management Southern Africa, 2007). These investments enhance the interventions of logisticians as they collaborate with other stakeholders in various African humanitarian supply networks.

The International Telecommunications Union (ITU) has memoranda of understanding with many countries and allocates frequencies for humanitarian operations. They can set up satellite telephone call centres that are available free of charge to both the affected people and to relief agencies during emergencies. This is important in Africa where information and communications infrastructure and finance is lacking. The ITU has a project of US $55 billion to enhance connectivity in Africa including broadband connections. The organization seeks partnerships with NGOs and effective coordination is required – however, a key problem is that many organizations involved in humanitarian logistics and operations see the need for coordination, but none want to be coordinated (Zavazava, 2008).

Human capacity building for disaster risk management in Africa

Training and capacity building needs in humanitarian logistics in Africa are extensive, diverse and multidisciplinary. However, capacity is lacking, and there are insufficient training units/institutions. Marjanovic and Nimpuno (2003) highlight the importance of a cooperative network approach that would help ensure more effective training and capacity building in relief management within Africa. In short, Africa needs to develop state-of-the-art continuous and long-lasting capacity development programmes, particularly in humanitarian logistics and supply chain management.

Formal training in disaster management, logistics and supply chain management

A combination of short courses to address short-term needs, focusing on fundamentals of disaster management from a practical point of view, and formal training programmes in disaster management leading to undergraduate and postgraduate qualifications is clearly needed. However, there have been some advances, such as in Ghana where systematic training programmes have been developed for public sector officials (such as the National Disaster Management Organization) who also benefit from overseas training. Officials of international relief agencies are constantly undergoing in-house training at home and abroad, while professional bodies such as the Chartered Institute of Logistics and Transport have incorporated courses in humanitarian logistics for professional certification in collaboration with the Ghana Institute of Management and Public Administration (GIMPA).

In the Republic of South Africa, the Disaster Risk Management Training and Education Centre for Africa at the University of the Free State offers postgraduate education and training. Also, the Disaster Management Institute of South Africa offers disaster management training. In response to the Disaster Management Act No 52 (2002) and the Municipal Systems Act No 32 (2000) disaster management plans are included in the municipality's integrated development plan (IDP). The Provincial Disaster Management Centres (PDMCs) then conduct disaster management/IDP training targeted at municipal politicians and officials who are engaged in disaster management.

Humanitarian logistics research, system development and improvement in Africa

Relief logistics and supply chains in Africa have many practice and research gaps. For example, is there a role for humanitarian organizations in infrastructure development and maintenance? How can the impacts of politics, insecurity and wars on humanitarian operations be minimized? Other questions include the locations of main, sub- and small warehouses and storage areas for better preparedness, cost optimization and higher impact; the development of algorithms for developing quick supply networks; whether ownership of equipment and infrastructure is necessary; finding ways to match donations and demands/needs; developing bespoke information and communication technologies for different operations; lessons from corporate, global and military logistics systems and rapid catch-up models; improving collaboration, coordination and cooperation among peers and stakeholders; the role of individual volunteers; emergency preparedness and response systems for disaster-prone areas; agile and resilient systems; routing problems; military–civil interfacing; and related legal issues (Mbohwa, 2008; Mbohwa, 2010).

Library resources

The UN Office for Disaster Risk Reduction (UNISDR) Unit for Africa donated an Inter-Agency Field Library for Disaster Reduction to the Disaster Management Institute of Southern Africa (DMISA) in July 2006. This provides a hazard, vulnerability and disaster history of each country as well as literature, and practical, technical and educational information on disaster risk reduction for practitioners, researchers, national, provincial and local leaders, regional institutions, libraries, NGOs, the UN and other international agencies as well as for educational institutions.

Challenges of humanitarian logistics in Africa

The forgoing discussions have underlined the challenges of humanitarian logistics in Africa, and the following represents a summary of these.

Poor infrastructure and resources

Africa is plagued by poor infrastructure in most parts of the continent and this hampers swift responses to disasters. However, the growth in cellular phones and access to third generation communication technologies has assisted in overcoming this challenge through their use in areas such as tele-medicine, early warning systems and improved information and communication when disasters occur.

Lack of strong institutional frameworks and policy

Institutional frameworks and disaster risk reduction policies exist in different degrees of completeness in many African countries and the effectiveness is limited in many cases (African Union, 2004). Where effective systems do exist, they are, at times, not focused on solving African challenges. For example, while firefighters in South Africa have been able to assist in Canada, Australia and other countries outside Africa, there seems to be less thrust on similar intra-Africa collaborations.

Lack of standards and indicators

Africa has yet to achieve convergence in harmonizing national policies and efforts to facilitate regional and continental interventions. These are essential for collaborative efforts in tackling disasters. In short, responses within Africa must become faster than those from outside.

Lack of coordination

There is a serious lack of coordination in humanitarian efforts in Africa, which can result in conflicting programmes and activities. For example, after a recent incidence of xenophobic activities, while the South African government was setting up temporary shelters for victims, neighbouring countries assumed denialism and started to repatriate their affected citizens.

Lack of collaboration

Lack of collaborative information sharing among stakeholders often results in the duplication of efforts and a waste of resources. Lack of collaboration affects the coordination of humanitarian efforts in Africa.

Lack of needs assessment

Needs assessment following a disaster is a key component of efficient and effective relief efforts. Unfortunately, because of the lack of expertise in

Africa, international aid agencies usually conduct needs assessments of disasters when they arrive on the scene.

Lack of appreciation of logistics and supply chain management

There is a general lack of awareness of the contribution, and hence importance, of the role of humanitarian logistics within NGOs and humanitarian aid agencies. This requires more training, especially when new challenges arise. An example is the recent wildfire outbreak in Western Cape, South Africa. Whilst the existence of the drought ravaging the country was well known, better disaster preparedness could have limited the scale and effect of the disaster, especially in Knysna.

Furthermore, despite a willingness to embrace humanitarian logistics and supply chain management in Africa, the continent has a shortage of logisticians in general. This greatly hampers efforts at leveraging humanitarian logistic principles to achieve operational effectiveness and cost efficiency. This is exacerbated by a serious lack of training in the area of humanitarian logistics and this is a major hindrance to the continent's state of disaster preparedness and management.

Conclusion

In order to provide an understanding of the context of African humanitarian supply networks, this chapter has examined the nature and incidence of disasters in Africa and their impact on sustainable development.

Given the unpredictability of disasters and their associated demand and supply needs, the enormous breadth of the role of humanitarian logistics within the African context becomes clearer. The degrees of efficiency and success of humanitarian response and recovery efforts by the multiplicity of actors that demonstrate different levels of collaboration and cooperation have been shown to be important considerations.

As such, the identification of key success factors and the grounding of humanitarian supply network management in sound management theory become important considerations within the African context, as elsewhere. The institutional developments in, and adoption of, disaster risk management, including policy development, strategic planning, interagency communication, collaboration and coordination, the adoption of a diversity of technologies to facilitate hazard analysis, vulnerability assessment, contingency planning, reporting systems as well as early warning systems, are indications of change that will increasingly enhance the efficiency of humanitarian supply networks and therefore the degree of success in humanitarian interventions.

These efforts must be complemented by the development of human capital at all levels and in all aspects of disaster management, including humanitarian logistics and supply chain management. The HIV/AIDS epidemic has been discussed in some detail with three mini-cases in Southern Africa, focusing on Zimbabwe, South Africa and Botswana. These add to knowledge and to the discourse on humanitarian logistics and supply chains in Africa for slow onset disasters.

An interesting aspect is the growing role of third generation cellular networks supported by broadband transmission systems and fibre optics technology that is enabling better flow of information systems, hence improving early warning systems, communication, information dissemination and exchange and recovery systems.

These perspectives on humanitarian logistics in Africa highlight the enormity of the challenge, but also affirm that the progress being made in various areas at all levels should result in the evolution of greater efficiency and effectiveness in the management of humanitarian supply networks in Africa. Above all, the issues discussed should guide the development of research models of humanitarian supply networks in Africa that would enhance the performance of humanitarian logisticians working for the various organizations on the continent.

References

AIDA (2009) Advancing ICT for disaster risk management in Africa, Fact Sheet FS.02, v.1, *EUMETSAT* [Online] www.eumetsat.int (accessed 7 December 2013)

African Union (2004) Africa Regional Strategy for Disaster Risk Reduction, *African Union* [Online] www.unisdr.org/files/13093_AFRICAREGIONAL DRRSTRATEGYfullPDF.pdf (accessed 7 December 2013)

Balcik, B and Beamon, BM (2008) Facility location in humanitarian relief, *International Journal of Logistics: Research & applications*, 11(2), pp 101–21

Beamon, BM and Kotleba, SA (2006) Inventory management support systems for emergency humanitarian relief operations in South Sudan, *International Journal of Logistics Management*, 17(2), pp 187–212

Botswana Ministry of Health (2014), Botswana 2013 Global AIDS Response Report [Online] http://www.unaids.org/sites/default/files/country/documents/BWA_narrative_report_2014.pdf (accessed 30 September 2017)

Chingono, TT and Mbohwa, C (2017) HIV/AIDS humanitarian supply chain management: The case of Zimbabwe, in *Transactions on Engineering Technologies*, ed SI Ao, H Kim and M Amouzegar, WCECS 2015, Springer, Singapore

Cronje, F (2008) Xenophobia: Nine causes of the current crises – news and analysis [Online] http://www.politicsweb.co.za/news-and.../xenophobia-nine causes-of-the-current crises (accessed 29 September 2017)

Disaster Management Southern Africa (2007) Using satellite imagery, remote sensing and geographic information systems for South African disaster management, *Disaster Management Southern Africa*, 4(1), October/December [Online] www.disaster.co.za/pics/DMISAJournalVol4No1SepDec2007.pdf (accessed 7 December 2013)

Encyclopedia of the Earth (2009) Virunga National Park, Democratic Republic of Congo [Online] www.eoearth.org/article/Virunga_National_Park_Democratic_Republic_of_Congo (accessed 11 November 2013)

Gibbons, DE and Samaddar, S (2009) Designing referral network structures and decision rules to streamline provision of urgent health and human services, *Decision Sciences*, 40(2), pp 351–71

Guardian (2017) Natural disasters and extreme weather [Online] https://www.theguardian.com/world/natural-disasters+africa (accessed 28 September 2017)

IFRC (2012) Code of conduct for the International Red Cross and Red Crescent movement and NGOs in disaster relief [Online] www.ifrc.org/Docs/idrl/I259EN.pdf (accessed 11 November 2012)

IPCC (2012) *Managing the Risks of Extreme Events and Disasters to Advance Climate Change Adaptation: Special report of the Intergovernmental Panel on Climate Change*, Cambridge University Press, New York [Online] www.ipcc.ch/pdf/special-reports/srex/SREX_Full_Report.pdf (accessed 2 December 2013)

Kerina, D, Stray-Pedersen, B and Muller, F (2013) HIV/AIDS: The Zimbabwean situation and trends, *American Journal of Clinical Medicine Research*, 1(1), 15–22

Khosa, L and Kalatanyi, T (2014) Challenges in operating micro-enterprises by African foreign entrepreneurs in Cape Town, South Africa, *Mediterranean Journal of Social Sciences*, 5(10), pp 205–15

Kleidt, B, Schiereck, D and Sigl-Grueb, C (2009) Rationality at the eve of destruction: Insurance stocks and huge catastrophic events, *Journal of Business Valuation and Economic Loss Analysis*, 4(2), pp 1–25

Kovács, G and Spens, KM (2007) Humanitarian logistics in disaster relief operations, *International Journal of Physical Distribution & Logistics Management*, 37(2), pp 99–114

Lawyers for Human Rights (2015) *A New Apartheid: South Africa's struggle with immigration* [Online] http://www.lhr.org.za/news/2015/new-apartheid-south-africas-struggle-immigration (accessed 4 September 2017)

Marjanovic, P and Nimpuno, K (2003) Living with risk: Toward effective disaster management training in Africa, in *Building Safer Cities: The future of disaster risk*, ed A Kreimer, M Arnold and A Carlin, The World Bank [Online] www.bvsde.paho.org/bvsacd/cd46/cap14-living.pdf (accessed 7 December 2013)

Mbohwa, C (2008) Identifying challenges and collaboration areas in humanitarian logistics: A Southern African perspective, *Proceedings of the Conference on Humanitarian Logistics – Networks for Africa*, 5–9 May 2008, Rockefeller Foundation Bellagio Study and Conference Center, Italy

Mbohwa, C (2010) Humanitarian logistics: Review and case study of Zimbabwean experiences, *Journal of Transport and Supply Chain Management*, 4(1), pp 176–97

McDonald, DA and Jacobs, S (2005) (Re) writing xenophobia: Understanding press coverage of cross-border migration in Southern Africa, *Journal of Contemporary African Studies*, 23(3), pp 295–323

Mnyaka, MMN (2009) Doctoral thesis: Xenophobia as a response to foreigners in post-apartheid South Africa and post-exilic Israel: A comparative critique in the light of the gospel and Ubuntu ethical principles [Online] http://uir.unisa.ac.za/handle/10500/1176 (accessed 8 October 2017)

National AIDS Coordinating Agency (Botswana) (2015) Progress report of the national response to the 2011 declaration of commitments on HIV and AIDS reporting period: 2014 [Online] http://www.unaids.org/sites/default/files/country/documents/BWA_narrative_report_2015.pdf (accessed 30 September 2015)

Nkosi, A (2010) Zimbabwean teachers to fill our gaps [Online] https://limpopo.educationcrises.599435 (accessed 1 September 2017)

Nyaguthie, A (2008) Oxfam-GB: The important role of humanitarian logistics, *Proceedings of the Conference on Humanitarian Logistics – Networks for Africa*, 5–9 May 2008, Rockefeller Foundation Bellagio Study and Conference Center, Italy

Nyamnjoh, FB (2006) *Insiders and Outsiders: Citizenship and xenophobia in contemporary Southern Cape*, Codesria, Daker

Oloruntoba, R and Gray, R (2006) Humanitarian aid: An agile supply chain?, *Supply Chain Management: An international journal*, 11(2), pp 115–20

Perry, M (2007) Natural disaster management planning: A study of logistics managers responding to the tsunami, *International Journal of Physical Distribution & Logistics Management*, 37(5), pp 409–33

Richey, RG (2009) The supply chain crisis and disaster pyramid: A theoretical framework for understanding preparedness and recovery, *International Journal of Physical, Distribution & Logistics Management*, 39(7), pp 619–28

Scholten, K, Sharkey-Scott, P and Fynes, B (2010) (Le)agility in humanitarian aid (NGO) supply chains, *International Journal of Physical Distribution and Logistics Management*, 40(8/9), pp 623–35

Schwarz, J and Kessler, M (2010) Humanitarian logistics: TU Berlin (Logistik) [Online] http://www.logistik.tu-berlin.de/fileadmin/fg2/2010-10-27_vortrag_kessler_Schwarz.pdf (accessed 29 August 2017)

South Africa (2002) Disaster Management Act, 57 of 2002, *Government Gazette* [Online] www.info.gov.za/view/DownloadFileAction?id=68094 (accessed 7 December 2013)

South African National AIDS Council (2015) Global AIDS response progress report [Online] http://sanac.org.za/2016/06/22/global-aids-response-progress-report-garpr-2015/ (accessed 29 September 2017)

Statistics South Africa (2017) Poverty trends in South Africa: An examination of absolute poverty between 2005 and 2015 [Online] http://www.statssa.gov.za/publications/Report-03-10-06/Report-03-10-062015.pdf (accessed 26 September 2017)

Steinberg, J (2008) South Africa's xenophobic eruption, ISS Papers, No 169, Pretoria institute for security studies [Online] https://www.files.ethz.ch/isn/98954/PAPER169.pdf (accessed 8 October 2017)

Thomas, AS (2003) Why logistics?, *Forced Migration*, **18**, p 4

Thomas, AS and Kopczak, L (2005) From logistics to supply chain management: The path forward in the humanitarian sector, *Fritz Institute*, San Francisco, CA, pp 1–15

UNAIDS (2013) Press release: Around 10 million people living with HIV now have access to antiretroviral treatment [Online] http://www.unaids.org/en/resources/presscentre/pressreleaseandstatementarchive/2013/june/20130630prtreatment (accessed 29 September 2017)

UNAIDS (2016) Prevention gap report [Online] http://www.unaids.org/en/resources/documents/2016/prevention-gap (accessed 29 September 2016)

UNDP (2013) *Human Development Report 2013 – The Rise of the South: Human progress in a diverse world*, United Nations Development Programme [Online] www.undp.org/content/dam/undp/library/corporate/HDR/2013GlobalHDR/English/HDR2013%20Report%20English.pdf (accessed 29 September 2017)

UNEP (2001) African ministerial statement to the World Summit on Sustainable Development [Online] www.unep.org/roa/docs/pdf/African%20ministerial%20statement_english_.pdf (accessed 6 December 2013)

UNEP (2012) Sudan post-conflict environmental assessment [Online] www.unep.org/sudan/ (accessed 11 November 2013)

UNHCR (2007) *Handbook for Emergencies,* 3rd edn [Online] www.unhcr.org/publ/PUBL/471db4c92.html (accessed 6 December 2013)

UNHCR (2017a) Africa [Online] http://www.unhcr.org/africa.html (accessed 28 September 2017)

UNHCR (2017b) Regional summaries: Africa [Online] http://www.unhcr.org/afr/publications/fundraising/593e4bf27/unhcr-global-report-2016-africa-regional-summary.html

UNISDR (2015) *The Human Cost of Natural Disasters: A global perspective*, UNISDR

URD (2008) Humanitarian aid on the move [Online] www.urd.org/IMG/pdf/URD_newsletter1_p_UK.pdf (accessed 11 November 2013)

USAID (2012) Working in crises and conflict [Online] www.usaid.gov/what-we-do/working-crises-and-conflict (accessed 30 September 2013)

Van Wassenhove, LN (2006) Humanitarian aid logistics: Supply chain management at high gear, *Journal of the Operational Research Society*, 57, pp 475–89

WFF (2016) Water facts and futures: Rethinking South Africa's water futures [Online] http://awsassets.wwf.org.za/downloads/wwf009_waterfactsandfutures_report_web__lowres_.pdf (accessed 29 August 2017)

Wild Fire Today (2017) Wild Fire South Africa [Online] http://wildfiretoday.com/tag/south-africa/ (accessed 8 October 2017)

World Bank (2017) Data: Botswana [Online] https://data.worldbank.org/country/botswana (accessed 30 September 2017)

Zavazava, C (2008) Bridging the last mile gap through telecommunications/ICT in disaster management, *Proceedings of the Conference on Humanitarian Logistics – Networks for Africa*, 5–9 May, 2008, Rockefeller Foundation Bellagio Study and Conference Center, Italy

An inquiry into public procurement for the civil preparedness space

A case study in Finland

08

HLEKIWE KACHALI AND ISABELL STORSJÖ

Abstract

Finland is a country with high levels of infrastructure and a public procurement system designed to ensure the availability of supplies, services and works to meet the public needs. However, societal needs and challenges still remain to be tackled, both now and in the future. The projected increase in the number and magnitude of disasters and, by extension, in the number of those affected by disasters underscores the importance of enhancing our preparedness capabilities for such events. The occurrence of emergencies and disaster events demonstrates that humanitarian operations are a critical aspect of disaster risk reduction and disaster management. Research shows that investment in preparedness activities can prevent or mitigate the effects of a crisis or disaster more effectively than efforts that are part of post-disaster operations. The government, and instruments at its disposal, can play an important role in civil preparedness. This chapter provides insight into the use of such a government instrument, public procurement, and specifically the public procurement of elements necessary for civil preparedness as a contribution to, and enhancement of, society's preparedness capabilities. Procuring for preparedness is one way of ensuring the well-being of society in all circumstances, and has the additional value of being both economic and effective.

Introduction

The increase in the severity and magnitude of disasters and, by extension, in the number of those affected (IFRC, 2016; Norris *et al*, 2008) necessitates that we enhance our preparedness capabilities for such events. Responding to emergencies and disaster events can be challenging, not least because the large number of people who are affected and the somewhat unpredictable direct and indirect consequences of such events clearly demonstrate that humanitarian operations are a critical aspect of disaster risk reduction and disaster management (European Commission, 2017).

The disaster management cycle comprises four main phases: reduction, readiness, response and recovery (O'Brien *et al*, 2010). Reduction (mitigation) is designed to minimize the effects of a disaster, while readiness (preparedness) aims at planning on how to respond should a disaster occur (Coetzee and Van Niekerk, 2012). According to United Nations Office for Disaster Risk Reduction (UNISDR, 2017), response occurs directly before, during or immediately after a disaster, and involves the provision of emergency services and public assistance. Recovery is the phase in which the immediate needs of the affected community have been met, and is therefore the stage of restoring or improving of livelihoods, health and other aspects of a disaster-affected community.

It is well established that many emergencies are not unexpected; they are a result of interactions between the physical environment, the built environment and the communities that experience them (Mileti, 2005). Governments, especially local governments, have the potential to organize society with the goal of making people less vulnerable to certain hazards. For instance, the United Nations' Hyogo Framework for Action 2005–2015 (UNISDR, 2005) calls on governments to mainstream disaster risk reduction considerations, for example by designing resilience into the planning procedures for major projects and works. This means that government actions, or inactions, can contribute directly to population disaster risk exposure and vulnerability.

Over time, disaster risk awareness has improved and investments in preparedness activities can prevent or mitigate the effects of a crisis or disaster more effectively than efforts put into post-disaster operations (European Commission, 2017). There are several aspects that can contribute to achieving the aims described in different parts of the disaster cycle; one such aspect is the role of government and of the instruments at its disposal. One of these instruments is public procurement, specifically public procurement of the elements necessary for civil preparedness as a contribution to, and enhancement of, society's preparedness capabilities.

Much work has been undertaken on preparedness and on public procurement as policy tools, but little consideration exists on the intersection of these areas. This chapter is intended for those with an interest in the different aspects of public procurement, its link to civil preparedness and, to a lesser extent, supply networks. In this work, we are presenting some of the output from CAIUS – a two-year research project on public procurement, preparedness and innovation undertaken in different sectors in Finland. The project was carried out by the Humanitarian Logistics and Supply Chain Research Institute of the Hanken School of Economics, with Finland's National Emergency Supply Agency (NESA) as a primary partner. NESA was used as the starting organization through which relevant informants were located through snowball sampling.

We used original and primary data from interviews with public procurers and experts from the healthcare, water services and energy sectors to examine the role of public procurement in civil preparedness. Our investigation sought to understand current policy and practice, what gaps and challenges may exist, and what best practice would be needed to make public procurement for civil preparedness more effective. We present public procurement within the context of regulations, processes and a desire to fulfil the societal needs of civil preparedness and mitigation. We employ findings from the Finnish context to help answer how public procurement and civil preparedness can be used in the humanitarian context writ large.

After this introduction, we briefly describe the organization of, and responsibilities for, civil preparedness in Finland as well as public procurement in relation to civil preparedness. After that, we describe the case sectors involved in the study. Thereafter, we investigate and lay out the specific challenges to actualizing public procurement for civil preparedness in the Finnish context. This is followed by an account of some best practice approaches to make public procurement for civil preparedness more effective. We end with a summary and conclusions.

Civil preparedness in Finland

Although Finnish society is considered relatively safe, there are myriad threats to Finland's welfare, economy, environment and security. The severity of these threats depends on the probability of their occurrence and the extent to which they would affect people or disrupt business-as-usual. Due to the interconnected global supply networks, Finland is susceptible to internal and external events, with a summary of possible scenarios to be found in the text box. This means that preparedness is also predicated on factors external to Finland's control. Examples of disruptions in recent years, provided by informants in the CAIUS project, included local water supply contamination and electricity disruptions after storms. In addition, epidemics such as those relating to avian flu and Ebola, as well as the Fukushima disaster in Japan, caused authorities and service providers to react and re-evaluate their risk assessments and preparedness measures.

Possible event scenarios for Finland (from the National Risk Assessment 2015)

Wide-ranging events affecting society:

- serious disruptions in energy supply;

- risks in cyber domain: utilizing the cyber domain in paralysing systems vital to society; risks associated with cybercrime; data security risks in digitalization;

- serious human infectious diseases, worldwide and in Finland's vicinity;

- a security policy related crisis that directly or indirectly affects Finland;

- a severe nuclear accident in Finland or in its vicinity;

- a 100-year risk scenario for a solar storm.

Serious regional events:

- extensive rapid flooding in or around urban areas;

- a serious chemical accident or explosion at a plant handling dangerous substances;

- a major maritime accident;

- a major aviation accident;

- a major rail transport accident;

- a major road traffic accident;

- several simultaneously occurring major forest fires;

- a major building fire at infrastructure critical to society;

- an extensive or extended disruption in water supply;

- a large-scale winter storm followed by a long cold spell;

- a severe thunderstorm;

- a terrorist act or terrorism targeting Finland;

- a serious act of targeted violence;

- violent, large-scale civil disturbances;

- a mass influx of migrants.

Civil preparedness has a long history in Finland, where it is organized both through formal delegation of responsibilities and mandates via laws and decrees, as well as being facilitated through collaboration and information-sharing, in order to ensure the availability of supplies and continuity of critical functions in strategic sectors. Today, preparedness involves multiple actors from different levels of public administration (state, regional and local), business, non-governmental organizations (NGOs) and residents. The term 'comprehensive security' is used to describe this approach of guaranteeing the well-being and security of Finnish society and its citizens in all circumstances (Ministry of Defence, 2010; The Security Committee, 2015).

One of the cornerstones of this comprehensive security approach is security of supply. The Finnish Act on Security of Supply (1390/1992) states that there should be sufficient reserves to produce necessities and steer production, distribution, consumption and trade in exceptional situations and serious disturbances, to secure the economic functions and related technical systems that are necessary for the people's livelihood, the activities of the private sector, and the country's defence. In practice, security of supply means that the availability of materials is constantly ensured through a combination of reserve stocks, obligatory stocks and state-owned stocks of critical items (NESA, 2017a).

The practical implementation of what the laws and resolutions stipulate on preparedness is managed by the National Emergency Supply Organization (NESO) which consists of the National Emergency Supply Agency (NESA), the National Emergency Supply Council, various sectors (information society; logistics; food supply; energy supply; healthcare; financial industry; industrial) and pools (pools comprise businesses belonging to the same industry subsection). Consequently, this network includes hundreds of companies, government authorities and associations (NESA, 2017b), while the NESA is tasked with the resultant planning, development and maintenance of security of supply. NESA uses several methods to do this: ensuring that security of supply is taken into account in general trade and industrial policy, maintaining the emergency stockpiling, and supporting enterprises critical to society with tools for developing their business continuity management (NESA, 2017a).

The National Emergency Supply Council assesses and reviews the general state of security of supply, while the NESO sectors steer, coordinate and monitor preparedness in their respective fields and determine the goals of the pools (NESA, 2017a). The sectors consist of representatives including authorities, industry organizations and important actors, and are tasked with steering, coordinating and managing risks and preparedness in their own field, as well as offering suggestions for broader development approaches and activities (NESA, 2017c). The business-led NESO pools are responsible for the operational preparedness in sub-fields of the sectors, and are tasked with monitoring, analysing, planning and preparing measures for the development of security of supply within their individual industries, and determining which enterprises are critical to society (NESA, 2017a). The constellation of NESO and regional and local authorities should also (according to the Government Resolution on Comprehensive Security of 5 December 2013) jointly develop preparedness systems for power, fuel, household water and food distribution as well as for the information and communication systems.

It is important to note that Finnish civil preparedness utilizes a market- and regulation-based approach within which functioning international markets, a diverse industrial base, stable public finances and a competitive national economy are considered to be premises of security of supply (Oikeusministeriö, 2013). There are structures for cooperation, and preparedness is both mandated through law, and supported by state government and expert organizations.

Public procurement for civil preparedness

While public interest may be more immediately concerned with economic and social impacts through, for example, the provision of services for populations, of key concern with respect to civil preparedness are the prevention, mitigation and continuation of societal functions. Being prepared for disruptions almost always calls for the use of regulated procurement procedures.

Research on emergency procurement has shown that procurement in crisis situations can be vulnerable to corruption, resulting in fewer resources available for life-saving operations, lower quality of products and services provided, and aid diverted from those who need it most (Schultz and Søreide,

2008). Procuring for preparedness is thus not only a way to guarantee the well-being of society in all circumstances, but can also be more economic and effective. For this reason, it behoves us to prepare for such situations ahead of time.

Inventories and the stockpiling of equipment and supplies are typical preparedness activities (Medina, 2015). Since the procurement of such inventories and stocks is carried out in normal (non-disaster) times, in the Finnish case (as in many others) the regular procurement legislation applies. In other words, there is normally enough time for public units to make procurement decisions in line with procurement legislation, whereas this is not so in case of crisis or disaster when solutions are required urgently. Public procurement refers to the process by which actors such as the state, municipalities, unincorporated state enterprises and other contracting authorities (as defined in procurement legislation), enter into public contracts with external suppliers. Public procurement uses taxpayers' money to purchase goods, services and works for the public good, and therefore the fundamental principles of public procurement provisions include transparent and efficient tendering, and equality and non-discriminatory treatment of tenderers (Ministry of Economic Affairs and Employment Finland, 2017).

Public procurement is a legislative area in which the European Union (EU) has a strong influence because of the impact on the internal market and freedom of movement. The European initiatives in public procurement started in the 1970s with the aim of controlling crime and corruption (Pekkala and Pohjonen, 2015). After Finland joined the EU in 1995, its legislation has been steered by EU directives and regulations. The Finnish (and EU) public procurement legislation makes a distinction between public procurement in general; public procurement in the utilities sectors, ie water, energy, transportation and telecommunications; and public procurement in areas of defence and security. The application of these different legislative frameworks is determined by the purpose of the procurement (eg defence and security procurement), the object to be procured (ie goods, services, works), the area in which the procuring unit operates (eg utilities sectors), and the value of the contract.

In the CAIUS project, it was clear that public procurement was carried out by individuals with varying backgrounds: some were lawyers, others had an education in procurement, while others were subject-matter experts either trained to carry out procurement or to make use of legal assistance when undertaking procurement. However, we could see, and were told by some interviewees, that overall procurement has become a more specialized function, partly due to the strict and complex public procurement legislation in Europe and Finland.

The sectors studied: energy, healthcare and water services

The case sectors for this study of energy, water services and healthcare, were purposively sampled after discussions between NESA and the researchers. Energy and water services are on the list of critical infrastructure sectors in the Government Resolution on Comprehensive Security (5 December 2013), while healthcare belongs to the category of critical production and services that need to be safeguarded.

The energy sector in Finland

Finland's electricity and gas markets were liberalized following EU initiatives, resulting in the current separation of the sector into a competitive part (operators supplying customers and producing or importing energy), and a non-competitive part (operation of the main grid) (European Commission, 2012). Finland has power transmission links to Sweden, Norway, Russia and Estonia (Finnish Energy, 2017a).

Finland uses district and electrical heating, with district heating being the most common form. The district heating network (about 15,000 kilometres) covers towns and larger population centres (Finnish Energy, 2017a). Hydroelectric power, biomass, coal, natural gas, peat, waste and oil are used to generate heat in heat-only plants, or in combined heat and power plants (CHP) (Finnish Energy, 2017b).

The water services sector in Finland

The provision of water services in Finland is primarily provided by municipality-owned public water and sewerage utilities. In the main, these water utilities are coordinated as quasi-independent enterprises within the municipality. A large part of Finland's population, about 90 per cent, is served by centralized water supply systems, while 80 per cent is connected to public sewerage systems, which are linked to wastewater treatment plants. The water services sector is affected by both changeable and extreme weather (Seppälä, 2013).

The healthcare sector in Finland

Residents in Finland have the right to universal healthcare. The healthcare sector involves numerous actors, both public and private, but the majority of hospitals are public and owned either by municipalities or joint municipalities (Ministry of Social Affairs and Health Finland, 2017a). Municipalities are responsible for the provision of primary healthcare, while for specialist care the municipalities belong to one of 21 hospital districts, and the hospital districts, in turn, to five specialist care areas (Ministry of Social Affairs and Health Finland, 2017b).

Preparedness and procurement in the case sectors

In the healthcare, energy and water services sectors in Finland, procurement is achieved by following EU or national procurement legislation, depending on the value of the purchase. The contracts typically last for one to four years in case of consumables, or for a varying period in case of a service or works contract – in other words, the supply networks are established for a certain period of time and there is no guarantee that they will continue after the end of a particular contract.

Public procurement starts with a need, which can relate to, for example, the goods required on a continuous basis in service provision or a new way of doing things that needs new facilities. The actual procurement process then usually starts between two and six months before the tender documents are published. The initial phase of the process often involves reviewing documents used in previous procurement rounds (especially for procurement of regularly consumed items and services), and/or by gathering information about the object from end-users or through market research. Some procurers even undertake a dialogue with potential suppliers on the process and requirements before deciding these. The procurement legislation offers different procedures, but the most commonly used are the open and restricted procedures.

As previously mentioned, Finland ensures security of supply through maintaining obligatory stockpiles, security stockpiles and state-owned stockpiles. When it comes to the obligatory stockpiles there are two instruments, the Finnish Act on Mandatory Reserve Supplies (979/2008) and the Finnish Act on Mandatory Reserves of Imported Fuels (1070/1994), which affect the healthcare and energy sectors respectively. These instruments require not only the public service providers, but also private sector actors such as manufacturers and importers, to keep supplies in stock that equal the amounts consumed in the past.

In the energy sector, contingency planning involves holding coal and oil fuel reserves while in the water services sector, stockpiling is for water treatment chemicals. Regarding energy, the Finnish government mandates that there must be a stock of import fuels equal to five months' average consumption. Similarly, oil and coal importers, including crude oil importers, are obliged to hold reserves of the products they import. However, crude oil importers can apply to NESA to hold up to 50 per cent of their obligatory crude reserves in the form of other oil products. Importers of other oil products can also apply to substitute their obligatory stockpiles for other finished products.

The obligatory and NESA-owned fuel stocks are in many locations in Finland, which allows for transportation methods including sea, road or railway. NESA-owned stocks cannot be stored outside Finland, but the government permits up to 30 per cent of obligatory industry-owned oil reserves to be held in the EU (International Energy Agency, 2017).

In healthcare, procurement of goods is divided into pharmaceuticals and medical and procured, supplied and supervised by different actors because of strict quality and professional requirements in the sector. Supply and distribution of pharmaceuticals is primarily through two wholesalers, and procurement is undertaken by hospital pharmacies. On the medical supplies side, there are also two larger wholesalers, but manufacturers often also have their own distribution networks. Most of the manufacturing of both pharmaceuticals and equipment takes place outside Finland, although there is some specialized equipment production in Finland. The Finnish Act on Mandatory Reserve Supplies concerns pharmaceuticals and, at the time of writing, the list contains approximately 1,390 medicinal products for which, depending on the drug, the mandatory reserve supplies need to consist of an amount equivalent to 3, 6 or 10 months of consumption for pharmaceuticals manufacturing companies and importers, and 2 weeks, or 3 or 6 months for healthcare units (Fimea, 2017a; Fimea, 2017b). Many of the products on the list are active ingredients and, as a result, procurement decisions affect what is stored and in what amount at the distributor and user locations. The storing organizations are then eligible for compensation from NESA for the required storage of goods.

The interviews also provided information on security stockpiles of emergency equipment and pandemic drugs, which are considered critical for emergencies but which may not be used to a great extent otherwise, with the amounts for these items based on estimates rather than past consumption. It is important to understand that both the obligatory stockpiles as well as a part of the security stockpiles are stored together with regular stock, and replenishment takes place through the first-in, first-out principle – however, the amounts held should stay constant.

Overall, the information from respondents showed that the availability of supplies is the main driver of many preparedness measures; however, it was also clear that certain events, such as anticipated weather events, accidents and vandalism, are accounted for in service agreements. In terms of the procurement of works, preparedness seemed to be more embedded since continuity of supply is crucial in normal times for both the water and energy units, and this translated into, for example, the quality of pipes for water piping, or construction of additional storage space for drinking water.

Challenges to effectively operationalizing public procurement in relation to civil preparedness

As previously pointed out, the Finnish approach to civil preparedness covers many levels and areas of society through a system of formal networks. Additionally, security of supply and preparedness are implemented using both carrots and sticks. While there are clear lessons to be learned from the Finnish approach to preparedness, it is not without its challenges, especially when public procurement and civil preparedness are considered together. These challenges, developed from the informant interviews, are summarized in the sections that follow and can be seen as aspects that should be given additional consideration during the procurement process and, as part of the bigger picture, represent areas that can be further improved.

Balancing different policies and outcomes in procurement processes

Neither procurement nor preparedness policies or practices stand on their own, thus their implementation is affected by regulations in other areas as well as circumstances in everyday life. The procurement activities include designing procurement procedures and evaluation criteria, and there are thus many aspects to take into consideration, including: price, usability, environmental issues, existing infrastructure and practices, etc.

For instance, in healthcare, there are strict regulations on market authorization and product approval because of patient safety concerns. These mean that the product development to market introduction lead times can be long – even for products that could be important for civil preparedness. The regulations and practices also affect potential bids with another example from healthcare procurement – but affecting the supply side – being that kitting for potential Finnish needs (although a typical practice in the humanitarian sector) was not preferred among medical equipment distributors. This is because it would, according to Finnish legislation, shift the manufacturer's responsibility from the manufacturer to the Finnish distributor. That said, kitting could be done after procurement, ie in the hospitals.

The cost of preparedness also seems to be difficult to justify in normal times. From all the sectors, we could see instances where public buyers would wish to keep more stock at the supplier-end, add inventory space for emergency situations or increase stand-by maintenance personnel. Nonetheless, implementing these measures would require investment and/or raise the price of the contracts and, in normal times, there are already many other immediate competing priorities for which the funds could be used.

Dependence on global supply chains, and limiting local factors

With only 5.5 million residents, Finland is considered a small market with its inhabitants living mainly in cities and in the southern parts of the country, although some segments of the population can also be found in remote or less reachable areas such as Finnish Lapland in the North as well as in the archipelago in the West. Finland's geographical location in Northern Europe (bordering Sweden, Norway and Russia) makes it mainly reliant on maritime and aviation supply networks, meaning that Finland makes up a part of, and is dependent on, global supply networks. Although the goal of the security of supply measures is to be able to manage serious emergencies within national means, Finland is vulnerable to the volatility of global supply, thereby making security of supply a critical issue. The production of critical goods often takes place far from Finland (sometimes in areas with a higher probability of disasters), and this has an impact on both lead times and on the perception of quality of the goods. At best, procurers have managed to take this into account by including quality criteria, penalties in case the suppliers fail to deliver, or by choosing more than one supplier for the same product (although the procurement legislation put some limitations on this practice).

At the same time as Finland is dependent on global supply chains and with regulations permitting bidders from other countries, the number of offers in a tendering process can be low – likely reflecting the country's relatively small market and dispersed population. The EU internal market allows for bidders from other countries to bid for tenders in Finland but, in practice, the local languages impose some limitations on bidders, and we saw this especially in construction of works in the water and energy sectors. In addition, supplies might be country specific, which is the case with, for example, pharmaceutical packaging. For these reasons, the actual range of alternatives may not be large and Finland may, therefore, not get the best solutions. On the other hand, both procurers and suppliers acknowledged that the small market and resource limitations have the advantage that collaboration is made easier, and decision making more flexible and swift. Importantly, Finland needs to be aware that its size may be a disadvantage in case of a shortage, when more important markets could be prioritized.

Fragmented competence, expertise and information

Respondents in the research described preparedness and procurement as being affected by functional and organizational silos, both within and outside their organizations. The mandate for preparedness is seen to lie with those responsible for risk management and other departments apart from procurement, and involving preparedness as an aspect of the procurement decision did not seem to be strategic – rather the decision on what to store and in what amounts came from legislation, or from elsewhere within or outside the organization. Some informants indicated uncertainty over what situations the mandatory stocks are actually for. We also noted that the rules on what is required to be stored are not all-encompassing, so that the obligatory storage of critical material might not correspond with devices that are in use and/or that needed to manage the critical material. Furthermore, this problem is exacerbated when the categories were procured by different divisions and also as a result of the increasing rate of change of, for example, medical equipment and drugs.

The existence of functional silos and specializations makes information exchange between procurers, subject-matter experts and preparedness experts crucial. On the positive side, we observed examples in which committees were used or opinions were sought from relevant stakeholders before decisions were taken in the procurement process. Several informants indicated that they had invested efforts into increasing the awareness of preparedness and procurement procedures in their organizations or in the sector, but that they sometimes found it hard to get the attention of other professionals as people are busy with their own tasks and responsibilities. Overall, the awareness or experience of procurement among the risk management, preparedness or sector experts interviewed varied.

Preparedness outside core operations

In all the case sectors, preparedness or business continuity plans and measures existed at all levels of government and businesses. However, the authors noted from interviews that informants frequently talked about the continued functioning of the core operations of *their* organization. Finnish society and the organizations included in the study have, however, become more embedded in an interlinked societal structure, driven by cost savings through centralization and outsourcing of support services. It thus remains an open question over how the organizations perceive the preparedness of other sectors that are vital for the continuity of their own operations, for example the supply of fuel to emergency power generators or the health of maintenance personnel. It may well be that our snowball sampling method did not allow us to capture these aspects, or that this information was not public, but we could still see that, for example, both procurement and some preparedness measures are contingent on the availability of electrical energy and other technology, but that the functioning of these technologies is taken for granted.

Innovation-oriented public procurement

One aspect of the CAIUS project was to consider innovation-oriented public procurement. Innovation could also have a role in preparedness, especially in the energy sector where policies and international agreements are driving the move away from fossil fuels. In the project, several informants expressed a view that the stockpiling obligations are outdated or reflect old technologies. Innovative solutions such as solar and wind power or new transportation modes do not seem to have been considered as alternatives in current preparedness plans. There are several reasons for this: in terms of electricity the problem is that there is no reliable technology available for storing it, and security of supply of energy is therefore managed through the storage of fossil fuels. So, despite the interest in the energy sector in renewable energy and clean technology, procurement for preparedness still needs to secure the availability of fuel for heat and power production.

Innovation can be not only in the *what* but also in the *how* – how things are done or how things are procured. Several informants from different sectors gave examples, mainly from outside Finland, of new ways of doing things, such as outsourcing the operations of power plants, or sharing the costs and risks of new expensive drugs between the hospital and pharmaceutical manufacturer. These solutions were, however, considered to be problematic to implement under the existing procurement legislation, and the potential impact on the security of supply was not even factored into the discussion. Procurers and suppliers alike noted that the perceived inflexibility of the procurement legislation results in minimal risk being taken by procurers who, as a result, default to previously tried solutions as opposed to unproven innovative alternatives. At the same time, however, both the EU and the Finnish government have emphasized that innovation must have a greater role in public procurement.

Best practice approaches to operationalizing public procurement for civil preparedness

Informants alluded to there being several positive aspects in the intersecting areas of public procurement and civil preparedness. They pointed to the existence of processes, procedures and regulations acting as a baseline standard for actors engaged in public procurement activities. Regulations and procedures were seen as a way of ensuring a fair and efficient process. Furthermore, informants reported that the public procurement process allowed for the more effective use of public resources and could also result in improved quality in the provision of public services. Another advantage is that the process allowed for choice between multiple suppliers whilst also enabling cooperation and collaboration between public and private actors. This means that organizations that have specialist knowledge can provide goods, services and works for public benefit.

The resultant recommendations from the research included here provide a common foundation for the different sectors; however, their operationalization may differ for each sector and even for organizations within the same sector. It should be noted that the recommendations are interrelated, ie the challenges and recommendations do not directly map one to one.

Integrated and strategic procurement for preparedness

Importantly, one aspect of civil preparedness and humanitarian response is that it is linked to systems already in existence for other purposes and with local stakeholders. In order to appreciate preparedness and response, it is necessary to understand the systems they are linked to, as well as the priorities, needs, core capabilities and how different actors interact. In the Finnish case, preparedness is connected to the structure of service provision, administration, politics, decision making and business life, including in the case sectors.

It is also critical for the different stakeholders to understand what can be achieved within existing laws, regulations and processes. As much as there are different parts of the ecosystem or chain that are designed to provide support for different functions, the trick lies in using these different arms to achieve *overall* success. Currently, the different parts of the system do not seem to be used to their full advantage in procuring for preparedness. Organizations could look at public procurement from the perspective of how to do business, and incorporate this into organizational strategy, planning and risk management. In fact, emerging from several of the interviews with procurers was an explanation that preparedness seems to have become somewhat automated through the requirements to keep safety levels in inventory, and was not considered a strategic aspect of procurement decisions. Thus, it is argued that actors need to have a more holistic picture, and to work with the overlapping structures as far as possible. Lastly, risk management in public procurement requires more attention; there did not seem to be a clear, overarching risk management system in procurement that took into account how risks were analysed, rated and categorized.

Including supply chain and life cycle considerations in procuring for preparedness

Public procurement leads to a contract for a certain period of time, while civil preparedness is an ongoing and evolving concern. In order to improve procurement for preparedness, we would argue that there is room to improve consideration of product life cycles and supply chain aspects. The procurers should (and some of them already do) ask questions like 'Where do materials come from?', 'How long does it take before it arrives?', 'Should there be more than one supplier?', etc, when designing the procurement process and documents.

In all three case sectors, it is evident that there has been substantial investment in infrastructure, eg power plants, dams and hospitals. Looking ahead, public procurement for preparedness in these sectors calls for harmonization of secure supply with sustainability and affordability. The lifetime and desired return on investment can have an impact on the willingness to change to new technologies or solutions, or to accommodate new threats. This applies not only to energy and water purification plants, but also to the size of medical equipment. For example, procurers considered whether innovative solutions would fit into the existing walls of a hospital, or if they could be integrated with existing systems and ways of working.

Data and information management

The Finnish approach to preparedness gives the National Emergency Supply Organization the right to receive information from businesses and private sector organizations about production capacity, locations, staff resources and other circumstances relevant to achieving security of supply. We could, however, see examples where information has been gathered when it was originally needed, but has not been updated since. In terms of procurement, the actors involved in various stages of the process all seem to be collecting vast amounts of data and information. This begs the question: what parts of this information can be used for the purposes of preparedness? What are the different ways of looking at this information or data, and how can we translate this knowledge into practice?

Capacity and participation

Successful public procurement for preparedness requires a wide range of skills and capabilities that procurers do not always possess. For instance, in order to be understood and used effectively, the intricate processes and legislation demand knowledge and supporting functions. This suggests a closer working relationship between the different specializations: for example, the procurement, legal, subject matter and preparedness experts.

Both suppliers and procurers need to acknowledge and understand the existence of threats to the functioning of society and how their own organizations could contribute to civil preparedness. However, public procurement for preparedness should be more inclusive, for example in setting requirements, writing bids and proposals. From the supplier perspective, a contribution to public procurement can occur if and when businesses recognize that their offerings are important not only to their consumers, staff, shareholders and financiers, but also to society at large.

Summary and conclusions

Finland is a relatively wealthy country with high levels of infrastructure and a procurement system in place to ensure availability of supplies, services and works to meet the public needs. Despite all of Finland's advantages and the goals that have been attained, there still exist societal needs and challenges to be tackled, both now and in the future. Some of these demands, such as better civil preparedness, can be met via better use of existing instruments such as public procurement. The procurement system can be employed to prepare for events that could potentially impact society and its well-being.

Overall, the coordination of the disaster management cycle related to the provision of public services can be modelled on decisions associated with the procurement, transport, stockpiling, and maintenance of infrastructure and required supplies and services. These are all aspects that affect the case sectors investigated for this work. The sectors are dependent on each other to varying extents and they also affect other sectors, for example agriculture.

Realization of the full potential of this need for a supply network for civil preparedness requires dialogue between procurers, end-users and personnel involved in preparedness. In our study preparedness was, in most cases, only routinely translated into procurement by ensuring stockpile safety levels and stand-by requirements for maintenance staff. It seems that preparedness staff struggle with having their voice heard in non-disaster or 'business-as-usual' times, and the issue of cost may weigh heavier than additional or even holistic security. In short, we believe that there is a clear case for the use of civil preparedness aspects as evaluation criteria in the regular public procurement processes.

Acknowledgements

The authors would like to thank the Jane and Aatos Erkko Foundation for their funding of this important work.

Special thanks to all the people who gave of their valuable time and expertise at various stages of this project. The Hanken project team included Gyöngyi Kovács, Hlekiwe Kachali, Isabell Storsjö, Eija Meriläinen, Ira Haavisto and Kimmo Kaasinen. In addition, a number of assistants and part-time workers helped out with different tasks in the project. Without them, this would not have been possible.

References

Coetzee, C and Van Niekerk, D (2012) Tracking the evolution of the disaster management cycle: A general system theory approach, *Jàmbá: Journal of Disaster Risk Studies*, 4(1) [Online] https://doi.org/10.4102/jamba.v4i1.54

European Commission (2012) European Commission – competition – energy – overview [Online] http://ec.europa.eu/competition/sectors/energy/overview_en.html (accessed 9 August 2017)

European Commission (2017) Disaster risk reduction [Online] http://ec.europa.eu/echo/what/humanitarian-aid/risk-reduction_en (accessed 6 August 2017)

Fimea (2017a) List of products to be stocked as mandatory reserve supplies – Fimea [Online] http://www.fimea.fi/web/en/supervision/mandatory_reserve_supplies/list_of_products_to_be_stocked_as_mandatory_reserve_supplies (accessed 10 August 2017)

Fimea (2017b) Reports on quantities to be stocked as mandatory reserve supplies – Fimea [Online] http://www.fimea.fi/web/en/supervision/mandatory_reserve_supplies/reports_on_quantities_to_be_stocked_as_mandatory_reserve_supplies (accessed 10 August 2017)

Finnish Energy (2017a) Energy networks [Online] https://energia.fi/en/information_about_energy_sector/energy_networks (accessed 9 August 2017)

Finnish Energy (2017b) District heat production is produced close to the customer [Online] https://energia.fi/en/information_about_energy_sector/energy_production/district_heat_production (accessed 10 August 2017)

IFRC (2016) *World Disasters Report – Resilience: Saving lives today, investing for tomorrow*, Geneva

International Energy Agency (2017) Finland – oil stocks [Online] http://www.iea.org/countries/membercountries/finland/oilstocks/ (accessed 16 August 2017)

Medina, A (2015) Promoting a culture of disaster preparedness, *Journal of Business Continuity & Emergency Planning*, 9(3), pp 281–90

Mileti, DS (2005) Disasters by design, in *Economics and Wind*, ed BT Ewing and JB Kruse, pp 1–12, Nova Science Publisher

Ministry of Defence (2010) Security Strategy for Society – Government Resolution 16.12.2010, Ministry of Defence, Finland, Helsinki

Ministry of Economic Affairs and Employment Finland (2017) Public Procurement [Online] http://tem.fi/en/public-procurement (accessed 8 August 2017)

Ministry of Social Affairs and Health Finland (2017a) Hospitals and specialised medical care [Online] http://stm.fi/en/hospitals-and-specialised-medical-care (accessed 10 August 2017)

Ministry of Social Affairs and Health Finland (2017b) Sairaanhoitopiirit ja erityisvastuualueet [Online] http://stm.fi/sairaanhoitopiirit-erityisvastuualueet (accessed 10 August 2017)

NESA (2017a) Methodology and tools [Online] http://www.nesa.fi/security-of-supply/methodology-and-tools/ (accessed 9 October 2016)

NESA (2017b) Organisation [Online] https://www.nesa.fi/organisation/ (accessed 1 August 2017)

NESA (2017c) Sektorit ja poolit - Huoltovarmuuskeskus [Online] https://www.huoltovarmuuskeskus.fi/organisaatio/sektorit-ja-poolit/ (accessed 1 August 2017)

Norris, FH, Stevens, SP, Pfefferbaum, B, Wyche, KF and Pfefferbaum, RL (2008) Community resilience as a metaphor, theory, set of capacities, and strategy for disaster readiness, *American Journal of Community Psychology*, **41**(1–2), pp 127–50

O'Brien, G, O'Keefe, P, Gadema, Z and Swords, J (2010) Approaching disaster management through social learning, *Disaster Prevention and Management: An International Journal*, **19**(4), pp 498–508

Oikeusministeriö (2013) *Valtioneuvoston Päätös Huoltovarmuuden Tavoitteista (5.12.2013 857/2013)*, Suomen Säädöskokoelma, Finland

Pekkala, E and Pohjonen, M (2015) *Hankintojen Kilpailuttaminen Ja Sopimusehdot*, 6th edn, Tietosanoma, Helsinki

Schultz, J and Søreide, T (2008) Corruption in emergency procurement, *Disasters*, **32**(4), pp 516–36

Seppälä, O (2013) IWA yearbook 2013 [Online] http://www.vesiyhdistys.fi/english.html (accessed 12 October 2016)

The Security Committee (2015) *Secure Finland: Information on comprehensive security in Finland*, The Security Committee

UNISDR (2005) *Hyogo Framework for Action 2005–2015: Building the resilience of nations and communities to disasters*, UNISDR

UNISDR (2017) Terminology [Online] http://www.unisdr.org/we/inform/terminology#letter-r (accessed 9 August 2017)

Supply chain and logistics competencies for the humanitarian logistician

09

GRAHAM HEASLIP, ALAIN VAILLANCOURT, PETER TATHAM AND GYÖNGYI KOVÁCS

Abstract

This general aim of upskilling the workforce has been taken forward in the logistics domain, where the ability of managers to put in place and operate an agile supply chain in the complex and unstable post-disaster international context clearly requires a high level of professional skills, competence and knowledge. However, there is, as yet, a dearth of research on the essential competencies for those working in this role. This chapter therefore proposes a humanitarian logistics competency framework (HLCF) to assist in the professional development of humanitarian logisticians. The resultant framework can be used both as a way of enabling individual humanitarian logisticians to develop the necessary competencies to be successful at their current and future career levels, and also to enable humanitarian organizations to map their own competency frameworks to a common standard. This will, in turn, assist in workforce mobility and support the overall concept of a certified humanitarian logistics professional.

Introduction

The need for appropriately skilled staff is, self-evidently, of great importance in helping to ensure the efficiency and effectiveness of any logistic organization. However, this need is further emphasized in the humanitarian context by the generally accepted statistic that the cost of the end-to-end processes (procurement, transport into the affected country, warehousing, transport within the country, and last mile distribution) represent some 60–80 per cent of the income of responding agencies. This, in turn, clearly raises the question of what skills are needed to be a successful humanitarian logistician. The aim of this chapter is, therefore, to review existing supply chain and logistics competency models, discuss their application to the challenges faced by humanitarian logisticians, and offer a high-level competency framework that could become the basis of a reference model to be used by multiple humanitarian agencies.

In doing so, it will be appreciated that the terminology surrounding the discussion and use of competencies can vary between countries and organizations. Thus, to avoid confusion, we adopt the definitions used by the Chartered Institute of Personnel and Development (CIPD). The CIPD defines a *competency framework* as

> a structure that sets out and defines each individual competency that is a behavioural or technical skill (such as people management or stock taking capacities) required by individuals working in an organization or part of an organization to carry out a specific task with a list of N competencies being associated with a specific task (pharmacy management, trucking supervisor…)
>
> (CIPD, 2014: 2)

These competencies can then be assembled in *competency domains*, which are groups or clusters of specific competencies within a given competency framework.

Logistic competencies from a business perspective

Within the commercial supply chain management literature, a broad spectrum of research has been undertaken into the whole area of competencies, and the general conclusion is that there is a clear need for both technical and general management skills, with the latter including those related to areas such as leadership, communication, interpersonal relations management and problem solving. This approach can be summarized through the 'T-shaped' model that was first introduced by Dorothy Leonard-Barton in 1995, and in which technical skills form the vertical leg, and general management the horizontal arm. Importantly, the literature is clear that, as an individual rises within a managerial structure, the prominence of the latter increases.

This interest in competency management has not only been taken up by firms trying to become more competitive but also by governments such as those in both the United States and United Kingdom that have developed initiatives such as the standard attainment tests (SATs), the National Skills Standards Board, and the National Council for Vocational Qualifications (NVQs) with the aim of addressing the decline in international business performance and the need for efficient and effective managers. In addition, given that the goal of competencies is to support an organization's performance objectives, not only should these be linked to the institution's strategic goals (Sanchez and Levin, 2009), but also it should be recognized that both organizational-level and employee-level competencies will (or should) exist (Cardy and Selvarajan, 2006) – with the latter being the focus of this chapter.

However, in developing the framework offered in this chapter, the authors fully recognize that, whilst performance management in humanitarian logistics has certain similarities with that of its general business counterpart, there are also some clear differences – for example, those relating to the different financial flows (from donor via agency to recipient rather than customer to supplier), and to the ultimate goal (saving life/reducing hardship versus profit). Thus, simply 'cutting and pasting' model(s) from the business to the humanitarian context is clearly not a sensible approach – rather, such models or approaches need to be suitably adapted to reflect the different demands of the disaster response/development arena.

Logistic competencies from a humanitarian perspective

Drawing on the existing business-related supply chain skills and competencies literature, a number of authors have considered how the models contained therein might be applied to a humanitarian logistics context. For example, Kovács and Tatham (2010), Kovács *et al* (2012), and Bölsche *et al* (2013) all draw on the T-shaped model, which aims to create a profile where 'managers have an in-depth expertise in one discipline combined with enough breadth to see the connection with others' (Mangan and Christopher, 2005: 181). In doing so, Kovács and her colleagues undertook an analysis of advertisements for humanitarian logisticians, whilst Bölsche *et al* used the European Qualification Framework to identify relevant skills and competencies.

These latter authors also emphasized the need for continuous training, a theme that was taken up by Allen *et al* (2013) who identified the link between the needs and the individual's management responsibilities and, in a result similar to that of Mangan and Christopher (2005), confirmed that, as these responsibilities increase, there is a need for a greater focus on general management skills and, hence, training. Conversely, logisticians with fewer management responsibilities are more likely to need technical logistics training.

A comparison of competency frameworks

In short, there is general agreement over the high-level construct of a humanitarian competency framework – first, it must distinguish between the technical and managerial competencies, and second, it should be designed in such a way as to differentiate between the managerial levels within an organization and their associated competency requirements. In order to develop the resulting competency framework a number of different sources were used:

(a) First, a systematic review of the academic literature resulted in consideration of 22 journal articles that are relevant to logistics skills and competencies, of which three were specifically related to the humanitarian sector.

(b) Second, the competency framework from (i) People that Deliver (PTD) – an agency that focuses on delivering medical supplies through sustainable supply chains in developing countries (PTD, 2015) – and (ii) Oxfam's logistics staff were analysed.

(c) Third, a number of interviews conducted with senior humanitarian logisticians in order both to confirm the proposed groupings and their labels, and to understand the differences in the significance of various competency domains in light of their importance at a particular managerial level. The final sample consisted of eight respondents, two from UN agencies, one employee from an international humanitarian organization and five employees from international non-governmental organizations (NGOs). The respondents were selected by means of stratified sampling, ie in such a way as to cover organizations across different types of operational mandates, including: multi-country, food, water, shelter, education and health. A further criterion for inclusion was that respondents had to have a minimum of 10 years of experience in humanitarian logistics (HL) (rather than in logistics/supply chain management in general). Being senior humanitarian logisticians with such a length of experience, they had all worked in both field and country offices as well as in headquarters, and were thus able to bring all of these perspectives into the discussions.

The first stage of the resultant analysis is summarized in Figure 9.1 and Table 9.1, which groups the competencies that were identified into general areas based on the input from the various sources. A definition of each

Figure 9.1 The application of the 'T-shaped' model to the humanitarian logistic context

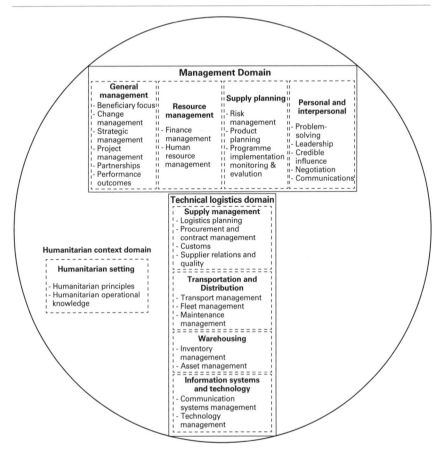

ble 9.1   Competency areas and their sub-components highlighted for each source

e competencies umanitarian istician must have...	Competency area: PTD	Competency area: Oxfam	Academic: Literature	Interviews
eneral management				
o lead and manage a team	Project management; understands the complementarity of SCM systems	Internal coordination; partnership; external coordination; developing and maintaining collaborative relationships; operating safely and securely in a humanitarian response; supply and logistics operational policies and procedures; achieving results effectively	Risk and profit management; economics and financial knowledge; business skills; strategic ability; initiative and enterprise skills; compliance and legal knowledge of labour and tax laws; trends in globalization; international finance and trade; customer orientation; market trends	Change management; work collaboratively; performance outcomes; project management; customer (beneficiary) service
source management				
o manage money, people and ormation to ensure that their tems work effectively	Manage resources and financial activities; recruitment; training and team management/supervision	Financial responsibility: funding; human resources	Finance/cost control	Finance; human resource management
pply planning				
o be able to develop the erational plan for the ely provision of the correct plies in a humanitarian vironment.	Prepare for product supply during disasters and emergencies; select the appropriate product specifications and quality; understand special considerations for the product; manage forecasting; quality assurance; and risk management activities	Assessment planning and design; project cycle – relating to supply and logistics; programme implementation; monitoring and evaluation	Planning, evaluation, and analysis of supply sources	
rsonal and interpersonal				
o manage their ponsibilities and create a ure career path	Basic generic skills (eg literacy, numeracy, technology); communication; problem-solving; professional and ethical values; leadership abilities; abides by rules/ laws/legislation	Understanding humanitarian contexts and application of humanitarian principles; leadership in humanitarian response; managing yourself in a pressured and changing environment	Communication and teamwork; leadership and negotiation; negotiation skills; problem-solving and personality traits; interpersonal skills; managerial and personal characteristics	Communications; problem solving; humanitarian principles; leadership
pply management				
o procure the relevant plies needed for the manitarian environment	Manage procurement costs and budget; build and maintain supplier relationships; manage tendering processes and supplier agreements; undertake contract management and risk and quality management; assure quality of products; manage donations of products; undertake or manage manufacturing or compounding of products; undertake or manage re-packing of products; manage outsourcing of SCM functions; understand use of products	Procurement	International trading/ procurement; SCM knowledge	Procurement and contract management
ansportation/distribution				
o transport and distribute plies within the manitarian environment	Manage import and export of products; supply commodities to facilities; manage transport for commodities; dispense or provide commodities to patients/users (ie ensuring the product goes where appropriate)	Import and export procedures; transport and distribution; fleet management	Operational skills; logistics analysis; planning and awareness	Logistics planning
arehousing				
to store and manage supplies thin the humanitarian vironment	Manage storage facilities; manage warehousing and inventory management; undertake or manage re-packing of products	Warehousing; asset management	Storage and warehousing; manage consumables and assets	
formation systems				
to manage information tems within the manitarian environment	Knowledge of logistic management information system (LMIS)		Information technology and quantitative analysis; networking/ computing knowledge; information integration; communication systems management	Technology

domain is offered in Table 9.2. It will be noted that, in doing so, the basic 'T-shaped' model has been adjusted to incorporate an additional 'humanitarian context' domain. Whilst, arguably, a similar contextual domain could well apply in a multitude of business environments, the interviewees particularly stressed the importance of individuals appreciating the overarching humanitarian nature of their work. Examples include an appreciation of the particular behaviours that are required for humanitarian work, such as an application of humanitarian principles, understanding the beneficiaries' needs and legal frameworks.

In terms of core competency requirements, the main theme that emerged from the interviews was in the areas of management and leadership, which was mentioned by the majority of respondents. Interview respondents, being senior humanitarian logisticians, stressed general management skills over technical ones – a perspective that reinforces the relevance of the T-shaped model. Similar differences could be detected in the secondary data where, in the case of Oxfam, the emphasis on general management can be explained by a large scale of general management requirements for more senior staff. In the PTD framework there is a strong emphasis on procurement, which is to be expected given that the focus of PTD is on medical supplies, where achievement of appropriate quality is paramount.

Specific competencies aggregated by domains also differ. For instance, project management is often highlighted as being very important in humanitarian logistics, while it is not of major concern in the business-centric academic literature. The focus on competency for project management in humanitarian logistics reflects the funding structure of organizations which, typically, receive grants from major donors for specifically defined projects, and which are linked to political agendas and/or budget cycles/reporting requirements. Although some private funding is available, institutional donors usually have strict guidelines that orientate the different stages and activities of humanitarian organizations towards a specific goal. As a result, it can be seen that project management is more relevant as a competency for humanitarian logisticians than for their counterparts in the private sector.

Another major difference between business logistics and humanitarian logistics is the emphasis on coordination and collaboration between organizations. Because of their lack of resources and their associated need to eliminate the duplication of effort, humanitarian organizations often try to shape their response to meet their perception of the emerging challenge. As a result, whether it is for development, disaster relief or conflicts, humanitarian organizations will often work through clusters to share capabilities and knowledge. This approach creates a stronger emphasis on creating ties to manage and integrate multiple supply chains efficiently and effectively. Coordination and collaboration are also important competencies to help in developing a good understanding of the local context and links to local social networks and, in this way, they play an important role in the effective delivery of aid.

Another issue that promotes a high need for coordination and collaboration is the presence of a dysfunctional infrastructure. When operations are undertaken after an extreme disaster that damages or destroys infrastructure and impedes logistics activities, or in a remote area with inadequate or non-existent infrastructure, capacity will often be shared by organizations in order to overcome bottlenecks. This represents a clear distinction from the profit-seeking nature of commercial organizations, which have fewer incentives to collaborate and coordinate with other firms when compared with humanitarian organizations, which are driven by beneficiary needs and donor funding.

Working in dysfunctional environments also creates a distinction between the competencies required in business and humanitarian sectors as they relate to the handling of stress. This type of personal capability is found in the context of human resource for managers to help diffuse stress in their staff and in self-stress management. Humanitarian logisticians working and living in an unstable (and sometimes dangerous) environment – especially when operating in conflict areas – require good stress management to address the specific issues of security, as well as the inevitable frequency and speed of changes to plans and responses.

A final distinction between humanitarian and business logistics competencies is the emphasis on long-term planning that is more often found in the business literature. Indeed, the lack of quantitative and qualitative analysis and strategy competencies for humanitarian logisticians clearly demonstrates the difficulties that result from an unknown demand pattern in terms of quantity, location and timing. Such issues tend to stifle planning and strategy making. Furthermore, transactional humanitarian logistics activities that focus on delivery to beneficiaries do not emphasize an added-value supply chain approach that is frequently at the core of a business strategy. This often results in humanitarian logisticians undertaking a broad support role, which can include additional responsibilities in the field such as premise management, telecommunications management and security management.

In summary, there are clear distinctions between the humanitarian and business competency requirements, and as a result a separate competency domain that stands outside the T-shape model is proposed, namely a humanitarian competency. Thus such competencies might include a clear understanding of the humanitarian principles (humanity, impartiality, neutrality and independence) and their operational implications, of ethics and of values that support diversity. In addition, such a domain should include considerations related to operating in the field, such as personal resilience, responsiveness in crisis and security management.

The humanitarian logistics competency framework

Whilst the T-shaped model for humanitarian logistics at Figure 9.1 is the starting point for the humanitarian logistics competency framework (HLCF), as discussed earlier, a competency framework exists not only to document the competencies needed in a profession but also to demonstrate changes in the emphasis on particular competencies during career progression. Moreover, in the area of HL there are some clear differences between the required competencies across the phases of disaster relief as well as between field logisticians at the one end of a spectrum, and logisticians in a headquarters and/or those managing clusters at the other.

To increase the challenge and complexity in this area, there is good evidence of a high turnover of humanitarian workers in field operations (Heaslip, 2013), which has clear potential to result in much tacit field experience and knowledge being lost from the institutional memory. Since there is no 'structured knowledge system that allows information to be shared among people and for it to be transmitted from one occurrence to another' (Cozzolino, 2012: 28), there is an absence of both information and learning from past disasters and failed/successful solutions. The resultant HLCF is, therefore, designed to help overcome this challenge both by being globally applicable and also by addressing the diversity of operational requirements encountered by logisticians.

Importantly, the number of staff at a given level can fluctuate significantly as, for example, entry level staff may be recruited on a time-limited contract in order to respond to a particular disaster. Even logisticians with higher management responsibilities may be on an 'on call' roster of a humanitarian organization and, thus, only be activated when additional support is needed. Therefore, notwithstanding differences in responsibilities, career progression may not be as clear in HL as in a business context – hence the importance of a competency-based model is reinforced.

Given that the main goal of competencies is to support the performance objectives of the organization, it is important to link competencies to strategic goals (Rodriguez *et al*, 2002). To reach these goals, organizations will often have different hierarchies of competencies, with organizational-level competencies and employee-level competencies existing in parallel (Whitehead *et al*, 2014). Organizations will therefore need to map their competency requirements, diagnose any gaps and address these through competency development in order to achieve their performance goals (Dischinger *et al*, 2006).

Applying these principles to the HLCF, we first defined various levels in the career progression of humanitarian logisticians. Whilst their names and salary categories differ across organizations, Table 9.2 presents these at an aggregate level, and gives examples of staff for each. These four descriptors range from Level 0 to Level 3, reflecting a progressive increase in complexity and skill.

The resultant management responsibility levels are summarized in Table 9.2. In general, these are based on the PTD framework, but it should be noted that PTD does not have a 'Level 0' category. This reflects the organization's particular focus – health supply chains – in which almost all staff will have a degree of expertise as part of their training as, for example, pharmacists.

In developing the resulting framework, within each of the nine competency groups (Figure 9.1; Table 9.1), the first stage was to present the individual competencies with a brief description of what the competency covers. The next step was to develop behavioural indicators for each element within the identified competency. Behavioural indicators are

Table 9.2 Managerial responsibility levels

Management Responsibility	Description
Level 0	Entry level staff who possess some of the behavioural competencies but in a different (eg commercial) context. Other examples include locally recruited staff who are also at entry level.
Level 1	Staff who can operate unsupervised on routine tasks at, for example, a field level.
Level 2	Staff who can operate on unanticipated tasks and/or at a level that requires the integration of multiple (potentially conflicting) inputs (eg at a regional level).
Level 3	Senior and experienced staff in significant leadership positions.

Table 9.3   The competency domain of supply management

Competency Group	Supply Management		
Competency Name	Logistics Planning (Plan to Achieve Priority Outcomes and Respond Flexibly to Changing Circumstances)		
Level 0	Level 1	Level 2	Level 3
Plan and coordinate allocated logistics activities	Take into account future aims and goals of the team/ unit and HA organization when prioritizing logistic work	Understand the links between logistics, the HA organization and the donor agenda	Establish broad logistical objectives
Reprioritize own work activities on a regular basis to achieve set logistics goals	Initiate, prioritize, consult on and develop team/unit goals, strategies and plans for logistics	Ensure logistic plan goals are clear and appropriate, including contingency provisions	Understand the HA organization's current and potential future role within the humanitarian community
Contribute to the development of team work plans and goal setting	Anticipate and assess the impact of changes, such as donor policy/economic conditions, on team/unit objectives and initiate appropriate responses	Monitor progress of initiatives and make necessary adjustments	Ensure effective governance frameworks and guidance enable high-quality strategic logistics strategy
Understand team objectives and how own work relates to achieving these	Ensure current work plans and activities support and are consistent with logistical initiatives	Anticipate and assess the impact of changes, such as government policy, donor and/or economic conditions, to logistics plans and initiatives, and respond appropriately	Consider emerging trends

(continued)

Table 9.3 (Continued)

Competency Group	Supply Management		
Competency Name	Logistics Planning (Plan to Achieve Priority Outcomes and Respond Flexibly to Changing Circumstances)		
Level 0	Level 1	Level 2	Level 3
	Evaluate achievements and adjust future plans accordingly	Consider the implications of a wide range of complex issues, and shift logistics priorities when necessary	Drive initiatives in an environment of ongoing
		Undertake planning to transition the organization through change initiatives and evaluate progress and outcome to inform future planning	

an expression of what an individual does, and are observed when effective performers apply motives, traits, and skills to a relevant task (PTD, 2015). We undertook this element of the analysis using Bloom's taxonomy of learning behaviour as a guide (Bloom, 1956). For example, in the domain of supply management and for the competency area of logistics planning, each behavioural indicator was allocated to one of four levels, corresponding to progressive levels of management responsibility within the sector. Expressing competencies in the form of such behavioural indicators facilitates the use of a framework as a tool for assessing ability and performance. The resultant HLCF entry for the competency group of supply management is contained in Table 9.3.

Similar tables have been developed for each of the nine competency groups (see Figure 9.1 and Table 9.1), but space constraints preclude their inclusion within this chapter. Nevertheless, they are available from the authors.

Summary

One of the key aims of the research described in this chapter is to support the overall goal of improving the professionalization of those engaged in humanitarian logistics. By developing a generic competency framework it is envisaged that individual humanitarian organizations will be able to map their existing individual competency frameworks onto this with two key benefits. First, it is entirely possible that some organizations will recognize gaps in their own frameworks that merit additional training and education for their staff. Second, mapping individual frameworks onto the generic one has the potential to allow for improved mobility of individuals between organizations.

Although every effort has been made to identify all essential competencies, it is fully accepted that the list may not be exhaustive due to the various limitations of the current research. It is also noted that the competencies highlighted through expert interviews may well have been biased towards each individual's area of expertise, prior experience, or organizational role, and also reflect international rather than national perspectives. It is also accepted that further research is required to increase the understanding of the skills needed at different levels of the job or in different locations. Current research does not differentiate between staff working at the country office level, in headquarters or field-based appointments, and this is a clear gap in the literature. Thus, one might anticipate yet further granularity as the research progresses although, at the same time, the current framework contains over 500 entries and there is clearly a balance to be struck here.

Nevertheless, the model is commended to the humanitarian community in the hope that it will provide a solid baseline to support the overall drive to deliver more efficient and effective logistics through an upskilling of those undertaking this vital work. The move to a competency-based approach is a logical step that has the potential to strengthen the humanitarian logistics sector and to build human resource capacity.

References

Allen, AM, Kovács, G, Masini, A, Vaillancourt, A and Van Wassenhove, L (2013) Exploring the link between the humanitarian logistician and training needs, *Journal of Humanitarian Logistics and Supply Chain Management*, 3(2), pp 129–48

Bloom, BS (1956) *Taxonomy of Educational Objectives: The classification of educational goals – Handbook I: Cognitive domain*, McKay, New York

Bölsche, D, Klumpp, M and Abidi, H (2013) Specific competencies in humanitarian logistics education, *Journal of Humanitarian Logistics and Supply Chain Management*, 3(2), pp 99–128

Cardy, RL and Selvarajan, TT (2006) Competencies: Alternative frameworks for competitive advantage, *Business Horizons*, **49**, pp 235–45

CIPD (2014) Competence and competency frameworks, Chartered Institute of Personnel and Development [Online] http://www.cipd.co.uk/hr-resources/ factsheets/competence-competency-frameworks.aspx

Cozzolino, A (2012) *Humanitarian Logistics: Cross-sector cooperation in disaster relief management*, Springer, New York and London

Dischinger, J, Closs, DJ, McCulloch, E, Speier, C, Grenoble, W and Marshal, LD (2006) The emerging supply chain management profession, *Supply Chain Management Review*, **10**(1), pp 62–68

Heaslip, G (2013) Services operations management and humanitarian logistics, *Journal of Humanitarian Logistics and Supply Chain Management*, **3**(1), pp 37–51

Kovács, G and Tatham, PH (2010) What is special about a humanitarian logistician? A survey of logistic skills and performance, *Supply Chain Forum: An international journal*, **11**(3), pp 32–41

Kovács, G, Tatham, PH and Larson, PD (2012) What skills are needed to be a humanitarian logistician? *Journal of Business Logistics*, **33**(3), pp 245–58

Mangan, J and Christopher, M (2005) Management development and the supply chain manager of the future, *The International Journal of Logistic Management*, **16**(2), pp 178–91

PTD (2015) Health supply chain competency framework for managers and leaders, People that Deliver

Rodriguez, D, Patel, R, Bright, A, Gregory, A and Gowing, MK (2002) Developing competency models to promote integrated human resources practices, *Human Resource Management*, **41**(3), pp 309–24

Sanchez, JI and Levin, EL (2009) What is (or should be) the difference between competency modeling and traditional job analysis? *Human Resource Management Review*, **19**, pp 54–63

Tatham, PH and Kovacs, G (2010) The application of 'swift trust' to humanitarian logistics, *International Journal of Production Economics*, **126**, pp 35–45

Tatham, PH and Pettit, SJ (2010) Humanitarian logistics: The journey of supply network management, *International Journal of Physical Distribution and Logistics Management*, **40**(8/9), pp 609–22

Thomas, A and Mizushima, M (2005) Logistics training: Necessity or luxury?, *Forced Migration Review*, **22**, pp 60–61

Trunick, PA (2005) Special report: Delivering relief to tsunami victims, *Logistics Today*, **46**(2), pp 1–3

Van Wassenhove, L (2006) Humanitarian aid logistics: Supply chain management in high gear, *The Journal of the Operational Research Society*, **57**(5), pp 475–89

Whitehead, C, Selleger, V, van de Kreeke, J and Hodges, B (2014) The 'missing person' in roles-based competency models: A historical, cross-national, contrastive case study, *Medical Education*, **48**(8), pp 785–95

Application of centre-of-gravity analysis in network design for pre-positioning of emergency relief items

10

GERARD DE VILLIERS

Abstract

The efficiency of emergency relief depends to a large extent on the availability of the right goods at the right time in the right condition and in sufficient quantities at the right place. There is usually very little time to reorder incorrect items or replenish inadequate quantities but, at the same time, the emergency response supply chain should not be burdened with unnecessary stock, especially in the wrong place. Centre-of-gravity analysis has been used very effectively in commercial network design, and the purpose of this chapter is to indicate the usefulness of this technique in emergency response. The chapter starts with defining humanitarian logistics, the planning hierarchy and a discussion of network design. It continues with an overview of disaster event locations and describes the importance of establishing pre-positioning facilities for emergency relief items at the correct locations. The current United Nations Humanitarian Response Depot (UNHRD) network is discussed and the centre-of-gravity technique explained. The location of disaster events in Africa is used as a case study to suggest how centre-of-gravity analysis can usefully be applied, and the chapter ends with brief reference to channel strategies and how each strategy should be aligned with an appropriate network.

Introduction

Commercial supply chains consist of a network of nodes and links between origins and destinations. The nodes consist mainly of intermodal terminals and freight logistics hubs that provide intermediate locations where logistics value is added to the movement of freight. Examples of logistics value add at freight logistics hubs include consolidation or deconsolidation, picking, packing, storing in customized warehousing facilities and related activities to provide for delivering into the market. This is often referred to as the 'last mile' and it is probably the most important link in the supply chain, as it is the most expensive due to relatively small loads to be delivered in congested destinations where economies of scale are not possible. Hence it is important to place these facilities at locations that provide cost-effective delivery to the market.

Pre-positioning of relief items at cost-effective locations is similarly important in humanitarian supply chains, and the same principles apply in ensuring that the 'last mile' to the field is as cost-effective as possible for emergency relief. Appropriate network design is needed and, although global pre-positioning facilities are currently in place, there is a need to look carefully at the location of such regional facilities in order to reduce costs of the humanitarian supply chains while increasing the yield of scarce resources committed to emergency relief.

Humanitarian logistics

Humanitarian logistics consists of the same elements or functions of business logistics, such as transport, warehousing, inventory management, procurement, logistics information systems, order management, materials handling, packing and reverse logistics. 'Customers', though, should rather be replaced by 'beneficiaries' but, in principle, the definition is the same. Figure 10.1 provides a useful framework that incorporates all the components of the humanitarian logistic challenge.

Figure 10.1 Humanitarian logistics and supply chain management

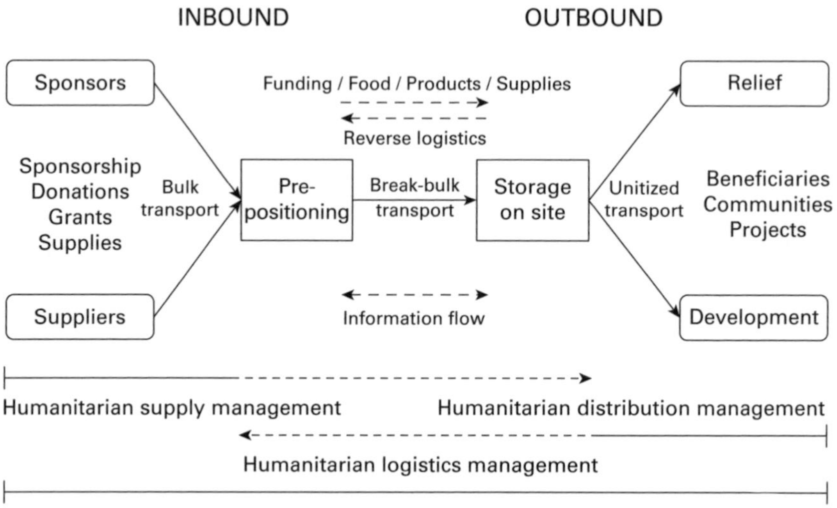

SOURCE De Villiers *et al*, 2017: 349

The upstream (or inbound) side consists of sponsors and suppliers providing sponsorship, donations, grants or supplies such as food and non-food items. The funding, food, products and supplies move downstream through the supply chain from the inbound to the outbound side while information flows in both directions. Reverse logistics refers to returns, recalls and any other packaging material or vehicles that have to be returned from the field or disposed of once the programme or project has been completed.

Planning hierarchy

The planning hierarchy (Stock and Lambert, 2001: 702–04) is very useful in providing a framework for humanitarian logistics planning. Figure 10.2 provides an adapted version of this planning hierarchy to include *inter alia* procurement as well as freight forwarding between the functional and operational levels, plus some minor editing to expand description of some of the key areas.

The importance of this framework for the discussion is the sequence in which planning should happen. It should start at the strategic level, and follows in a specific order through the structural, functional and operational levels as indicated by the arrow, to ensure that the resultant structure

Figure 10.2 Planning hierarchy

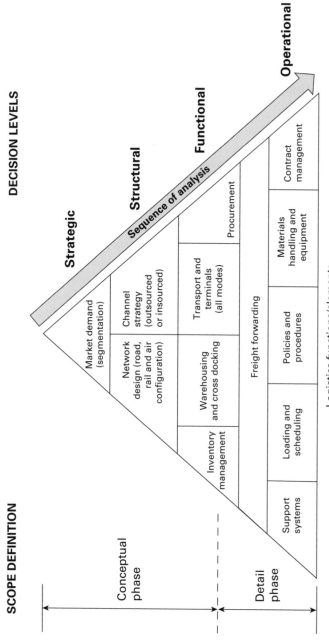

SCOPE DEFINITION

DECISION LEVELS

Strategic

Structural

Functional

Operational

Sequence of analysis

Conceptual phase

Detail phase

Market demand (segmentation)

Channel strategy (outsourced or insourced)

Network design (road, rail and air configuration)

Transport and terminals (all modes)

Procurement

Inventory management

Warehousing and cross docking

Freight forwarding

Policies and procedures

Materials handling and equipment

Contract management

Support systems

Loading and scheduling

Logistics functions/elements

PLANNING HIERARCHY

SOURCE Adapted from Stock and Lambert, 2001: 703

follows the strategy. The pinnacle of the triangle or hierarchy starts with the specific requirements of the customer or the beneficiary in the operational theatre, based on an analysis of the requirements in the field. Once the demand is determined and future growth estimated, the planning process should proceed to network design and channel strategy on the structural level. Network design addresses questions such as the number and location of facilities, for example the pre-positioning facilities and centralization versus decentralization, as discussed in the next section.

Network design

De Villiers *et al* (2017: 348) suggest that, on the outbound side of the humanitarian supply chain, the first stop for food, products or supplies that enter the humanitarian supply chain is highly likely to be a pre-positioning facility from where they will be moved to local storage on site, except for direct deliveries immediately after the disaster when urgency will necessitate a shorter supply chain. The customers on the outbound side are split between relief and development, and are referred to as beneficiaries, communities or projects. There is usually little or no production-related logistics activity in this supply chain, except maybe 'kitting' of sanitary kits or meals ready to eat (MREs).

The location of these pre-positioning facilities should be determined by appropriate network design, such as centre-of-gravity analysis, to ensure that the most cost-effective sites are chosen. There are a number of different network design options available, but the two most common types are *decentralization* and *centralization*. The first concept, decentralization, is presented in Figure 10.3 and indicates a number of global warehouses at the origin and a number of warehouses at the destination.

The second concept, centralization, is presented in Figure 10.4 for consolidation of warehousing at the origin, and in Figure 10.5 for consolidation of warehousing at the destination.

There is no easy answer as to which network is the best, and it is argued that total logistics costs should be used to determine the least cost network design, based on centre-of-gravity analysis. An example of the trade-off between logistics costs is the reality that centralization usually incurs higher delivery transport costs, while decentralization incurs lower delivery transport costs due to closer proximity to the market. The opposite is true for

Figure 10.3   Decentralized distribution network

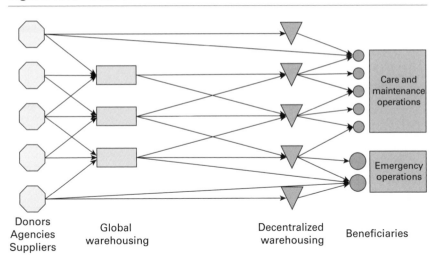

Donors Agencies Suppliers   Global warehousing   Decentralized warehousing   Beneficiaries

Figure 10.4   Centralized distribution network – consolidated warehousing at the origin

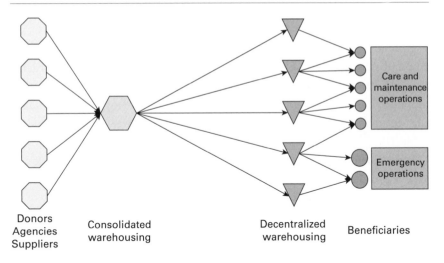

Donors Agencies Suppliers   Consolidated warehousing   Decentralized warehousing   Beneficiaries

warehousing costs, as centralization usually incurs lower warehousing costs, while decentralization incurs higher warehousing costs due to the higher number of facilities. Inventory carrying costs should also be included in the analyses and, based on the square root law of inventories, the costs are likely to reduce significantly with centralization. (The square root law states that total safety stock can be approximated by multiplying the total inventory by the square root of the number of future warehouse locations divided by

Figure 10.5   Centralized distribution network – consolidated warehousing at the destination

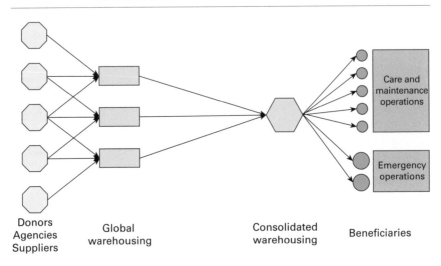

Donors
Agencies
Suppliers

Global
warehousing

Consolidated
warehousing

Beneficiaries

the current number. X2 = (X1) * $\sqrt{(n2/n1)}$ where: n1 = number of existing facilities; n2 = number of future facilities; X1 = existing inventory; X2 = future inventory.)

Roh and Kim (2016: 7–9) provide an interesting perspective on the inbound side and suggest that once a disaster occurs, humanitarian organizations can acquire relief supplies from three main sources, namely local suppliers, global suppliers and pre-positioned warehousing. The advantages and disadvantages of procuring from these three sources are indicated in Table 10.1.

It is clear from this discussion that the design of the logistics network can have a profound impact on the total logistics costs, and hence the yield of scarce resources committed to emergency relief.

Location of disaster events

The design of an appropriate logistics network should start at the location of disaster events and, although the exact locations are mostly unknown, it is possible to determine the most likely locations for typical disasters such as earthquakes, as these are mostly linked to geological formations, for which the locations are known. Similarly, there are areas or regions on a global scale where hurricanes, typhoons, droughts and other natural disasters seem to happen regularly.

Table 10.1   Advantages and disadvantages of relief procurement

Procurement	Advantages	Disadvantages
Local Procurement	Low transport cost Prompt deliveries Local economy support	Risk strategy to operate solely Unavailability of enough quantity and quality needed Creates shortage in the local market
Global Procurement	Increase the availability of large quantities of high-quality supplies	Longer delivery times Higher transportation cost Supplies not delivered to affected area during the initial critical days due to bidding process
Pre-positioned Stock	Deliver sufficient relief aid within a relatively short time frame Less expensive than post-disaster supply procurement Increase the ability of mobilization Efficient (low cost, less duplication of efforts, less waste of resource) Effective (quick response, satisfied demand)	Financially prohibitive Complex Too many uncertainties Only few can operate Impossible to depend solely in case of large-scale disasters Capacity limitations

SOURCE Roh and Kim, 2016: 8

The Emergency Events Database of the Centre for Research on Epidemiology of Disasters (CRED) at the Université catholique de Louvain (EM-DAT, 2017b), maintains an extensive and detailed database of disaster events and Figure 10.6 provides a very interesting indication of the location of natural disasters from 1986 to 2015.

The impact of such disaster events can be reduced significantly with proper mitigation measures such as early warning, and World Vision has developed a crisis country cluster map, clearly identifying zones in the world where disasters historically are common, and what type of disaster

Figure 10.6 Location of natural disasters, 1986 to 2015

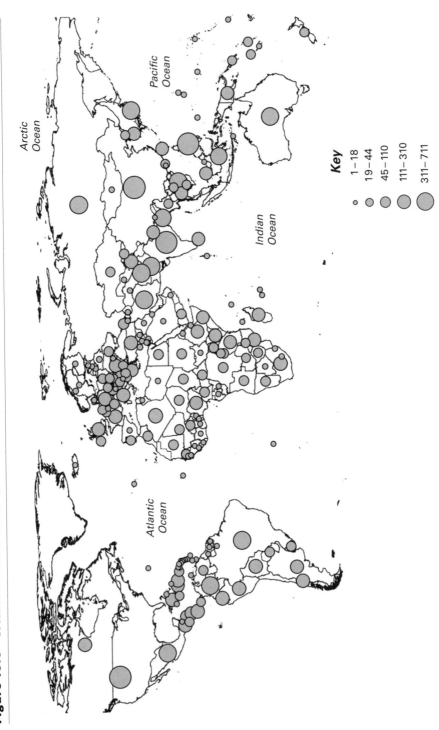

Key

1–18
19–44
45–110
111–310
311–711

Figure 10.7 Crisis country clusters

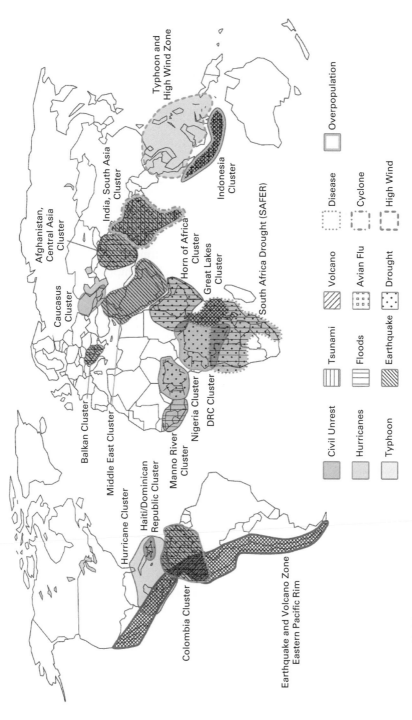

Afghanistan, Central Asia Cluster

Caucasus Cluster

India, South Asia Cluster

Typhoon and High Wind Zone

Horn of Africa Cluster

Great Lakes Cluster

Indonesia Cluster

South Africa Drought (SAFER)

Balkan Cluster

Middle East Cluster

Nigeria Cluster

DRC Cluster

Manno River Cluster

Hurricane Cluster

Haiti/Dominican Republic Cluster

Colombia Cluster

Earthquake and Volcano Zone Eastern Pacific Rim

Civil Unrest

Hurricanes

Typhoon

Tsunami

Floods

Earthquake

Volcano

Avian Flu

Drought

Disease

Cyclone

High Wind

Overpopulation

SOURCE World Vision, 2010: 16 (© World Vision International 2010, reproduced with permission) to expect (World Vision, 2010: 16). This is indicated in Figure 10.7 and clearly shows not only areas prone to natural disasters such as hurricanes, typhoons, floods, and droughts, but also locations of potential civil unrest and overpopulation.

The monitoring of historical occurrences and information available from research such as the crisis country cluster provides very good indications where emergency relief items should be pre-positioned for effective deployment to the disaster areas.

Typical emergency relief items to be pre-positioned

Experience in emergency response has over time provided a better indication of the specific items to be stored as well as improved estimates of the required quantities. Duran *et al* (2011: 8) found in their work done for CARE that the following relief items should be stored in pre-positioning facilities: food, water and sanitation kits, hot weather tents, cold weather tents, household kits and hygiene kits.

De Villiers (2008: 2) mentioned that World Vision carries a similar assortment that includes programme stock and support stock as follows:

- Programme stock: Shelters (tarpaulins, blankets, etc), water and sanitation (drilling equipment, tanks, etc) and food (high energy biscuits, etc).

- Support stock: Electronic equipment (satellite communication devices, computers, etc), security items (bullet proof vests, helmets, etc), team support (prefabricated offices, staff tents, etc), transportation (vehicles, etc), medical equipment (cholera kits, surgical kits, etc) and storage kits (mobile depot, etc).

The TLI White Paper (NUS, 2016: 4) elaborates on the matter and suggests that pre-positioning critical relief supplies in strategic locations can be an effective strategy to improve the capacities in delivering sufficient relief aid within a relatively short lead time, including improvement of logistics infrastructure and processes.

The White Paper mentions that these emergency response facilities will be capable of providing further supporting services such as the handling and consolidation of humanitarian cargo for distribution of relief goods in the disaster affected areas. According to the TLI research, the main functional benefits of an established network of distribution centres (DCs) include:

- improvement of capacity of governments and all humanitarian actors to respond to emergencies in a timely and cost-effective manner;

- enablement of timely and coordinated receipt and dispatch of relief assistance via air, sea and surface transport;

- improvement of the immediate availability of relief items, eliminating else needed long lead times for the mobilization of resources, and minimizing potential risk of supply disruptions, increasing the overall resilience of the disaster relief supply chain;

- enhancement of capacity building to support operations of repackaging;

- establishment of practical training venues for logistics stakeholders and emergency responders; and

- reduction of operational costs.

UNHRD network

The United Nations Humanitarian Response Depot network (UNHRD, 2017) was established in 2000 and is managed by the United Nations World Food Programme (WFP). It currently consists of a network of six strategically located depots that procure, store and transport emergency supplies on behalf of the humanitarian community. It focuses on emergency preparedness and response, and enables the strategic stockpiling of relief items and equipment for its 85 partners including UN agencies, governmental and non-governmental organizations. The depots provide a full range of comprehensive supply-chain solutions and are located in Italy, the United Arab Emirates, Ghana, Panama, Malaysia and Spain, as indicated in Figure 10.8.

By pre-positioning relief items at these locations, UN agencies, governmental and non-governmental organizations can respond faster and more efficiently to people in need. The mandate of the UNHRD network includes (UNHRD, 2009: Slide 3):

- 24/48 hours emergency response;

- to support WFP in meeting its corporate goal of being prepared to respond to four large-scale emergencies at any given time; and

- to support the emergency response efforts of the UN, international, governmental and non-governmental organizations.

Figure 10.8 Location of UNHRD facilities

SOURCE UNHRD, 2017

Centre-of-gravity analysis technique[1]

The design of a suitable logistics network and the development of appropriate channel strategies in multiple markets and multiple suppliers are daunting tasks, and some modelling is needed to assist with the complex calculations. Coyle *et al* (2008: 542–49) call centre-of-gravity analysis the 'grid technique' and suggest the technique is a useful, simplistic heuristic modelling approach for determining the least-cost facility location. This modelling can easily be done by spreadsheets and does not require dedicated optimization software.

Centre-of-gravity analysis is used to determine the least-cost location of a fixed facility (distribution centre, warehouse, depot or terminal) for moving raw materials, finished goods or relief items in the network. The technique assumes sources of raw materials, markets and disaster areas are fixed, and that supply and demand are known. The coordinates of each supply and demand point are needed to present the points in geographical format on a map and to calculate the transport costs of all movements.

The technique is shown graphically in Figure 10.9. If all the points are plotted at their respective coordinates on a map and respective supply or demand volumes (represented by weights) are connected through small holes to a central ring on the surface, the ring will come to rest in the centre of gravity (Schoeman, 2017: 40).

The analysis is based on the differential transport costs of raw materials or relief items from the manufacturing facilities or suppliers to one or more fixed facility such as distribution centres (primary transport), and finished goods from these facilities directly to destinations in the market, such as

Figure 10.9   Centre-of-gravity technique

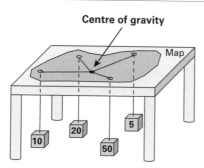

SOURCE Schoeman, 2017: 40

retail outlets (secondary transport). The results of the analysis provide a theoretical indication of the least cost location of the centralized facility.

Bowersox and Closs (1996: 554–61) provide four analytical techniques for calculating the centre of gravity:

- ton–centre solution (weight–centre solution);
- mile–centre solution (distance–centre solution);
- ton–mile–centre solution (weight–distance–centre solution); and
- time–ton–mile–centre solution (time–weight–distance–centre solution).

The ton–centre solution (weight–centre solution) is the basic centre-of-gravity calculation and the centre of movement represents the least cost location. The mathematical formula is presented in Equation 1.

$$x = \frac{\sum_{i=1}^{n} x_i F_i}{\sum_{i=1}^{n} F_i}, \quad y = \frac{\sum_{i=1}^{n} y_i F_i}{\sum_{i=1}^{n} F_i} \tag{1}$$

Where:

x, y = Coordinates for the centre of gravity
x_i, y_i = Coordinates for all origins and destinations
F_i = Supply or demand (ton)

The mile–centre solution (distance–centre solution) determines the geographical point that minimizes the combined distance to all points. The ton–mile and time–ton–mile–centre solutions are the most accurate reflections of reality and should be used where possible. They can incorporate a number of variables that need to be considered, such as transport rates ($/ton.km) that are likely to be different for primary and secondary transport. Similarly, a differential parameter for congestion in urban areas that reflects the additional time required can be used. This parameter could range from high value for high congestion to a low factor for low congestion. The mathematical formula of a hybrid between the two solutions (adapted from Bowersox and Closs, 1996: 554–61) is shown in Equation 2.

$$x_k = \frac{\sum_{i=1}^{n} x_i F_i R_i C_i / d_i}{\sum_{i=1}^{n} F_i R_i C_i / d_i}, \quad y_k = \frac{\sum_{i=1}^{n} y_i F_i R_i C_i / d_i}{\sum_{i=1}^{n} F_i R_i C_i / d_i} \tag{2}$$

Where:

x_k, y_k = Coordinates for iteration k (in km)
x_i, y_i = Coordinates for all origins and destinations (in km)

F_i = Supply or demand (ton)
R_i = Transport rate (\$/ton.km)
C_i = Congestion factor (relative value)
d_i = Distance between points for each iteration

This calculation requires an iterative process to determine the increasingly improved location, based on the lowest cost. The distance between the locations in each iteration reduces every time a better location is found, and the objective is to find the spot where the costs are the lowest. The measurement of distance between two points is done by the formula in Equation 3.

$$d_i = \sqrt{(x_i - x_k)^2 + (y_i - y_k)^2}$$ (3)

Where:

x_k, y_k = Coordinates for iteration k (in km)
x_i, y_i = Coordinates for all origins and destinations (in km)
d_i = Distance between points for each iteration

In summary, centre-of-gravity analysis is based on the differential transport costs from the supply points to one or more distribution centres or terminals (primary transport), and from the distribution centres or terminals directly to the destinations (secondary transport). The result of the analysis provides a theoretical indication of the least cost location of a distribution centre, terminal or pre-positioning facility. Qualitative factors to be considered to accommodate the complexities of the real world include road accessibility, rail accessibility, environmental and geotechnical conditions, land-use and spatial development guidelines.

The centre-of-gravity analysis does not provide the final answer, but it provides a scientifically calculated indication of where to start looking for a possible location. Calculations are done for the base year volumes of freight as well as for the anticipated future flows to identify possible trends that might influence the choice of location.

Centre-of-gravity analysis application

It was mentioned earlier that the Emergency Events Database (EM-DAT, 2017b) contains useful information on various disasters that have taken place over many years across the world. This section provides a practical application of the centre-of-gravity analysis technique and focuses on the natural disaster events in Africa from January 2014 to June 2017. These include the following categories of events:

- Geophysical: A hazard originating from solid earth. This term is used interchangeably with the term 'geological hazard'.

- Meteorological: A hazard caused by short-lived, micro- to meso-scale extreme weather and atmospheric conditions that last from minutes to days.

- Hydrological: A hazard caused by the occurrence, movement and distribution of surface and subsurface freshwater and saltwater.

- Climatological: A hazard caused by the long-lived, meso- to macro-scale atmospheric processes ranging from intra-seasonal to multi-decade climate variability.

- Biological: A hazard caused by the exposure to living organisms and their toxic substances (eg venom, mould) or vector-borne diseases that they may carry. Examples are venomous wildlife and insects, poisonous plants and mosquitos carrying disease-causing agents such as parasites, bacteria or viruses (eg malaria).

- Extra-terrestrial: A hazard caused by asteroids, meteoroids and comets as they pass near the Earth, enter the Earth's atmosphere and/or strike the Earth, and by changes in interplanetary conditions that affect the Earth's magnetosphere, ionosphere and thermosphere.

Table 10.2 indicates an extract of 10 of the 43 countries in Africa that experienced some form of natural disaster in the period under consideration.

Table 10.2 CRED disaster centre-of-gravity analysis – Africa

No	Country name	No of Events	Location	Region	Lon°	Lat°
1	Benin	1	Porto Nova	West	2.63	6.50
2	Réunion	1	Saint-Denis	South	55.45	−20.89
3	Togo	1	Lomé	West	1.23	6.17
4	Zambia	1	Lusaka	South	28.32	−15.39
5	Botswana	2	Gaborone	South	25.92	−24.63
39	Kenya	9	Nairobi	East	36.82	−1.29
40	Somalia	10	Mogadishu	East	45.31	2.05
41	Niger	11	Niamey	West	2.12	13.51
42	Tanzania	11	Dodoma	East	35.75	−6.16
43	DRC	12	Kisangani	East	25.20	0.52
	Centre-of-Gravity				21.00	−0.12
	Total number of events	200				

Figure 10.10 Centre-of-gravity analysis of all natural disaster events in Africa (January 2014 to June 2017)

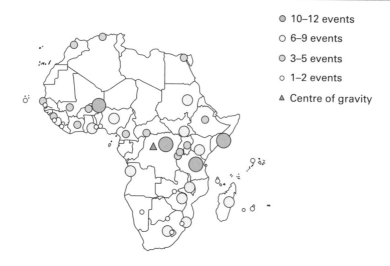

The coordinates of each location were used to provide the locations for plotting the number of natural disaster events on a map of Africa, as indicated in Figure 10.10. The legend indicates four categories as well as the centre of gravity of the mentioned disaster events. The result represents a centralized centre of gravity for all disaster events and is located just west of Kisangani in the Democratic Republic of the Congo, a location that is not ideal as accessibility in this remote area is a huge challenge.

However, the locations of all events, as indicated in Figure 10.10, suggest that there could be merit in splitting the continent into three regions or clusters as follows: West, South and East Africa. Such a regional or decentralized network will improve accessibility and mobility significantly and result in a more responsive network of pre-positioning facilities, as shown in Figure 10.11.

The resultant centres of gravity for the three regions are indicated in Figure 10.12.

The centre of gravity for West Africa is located at Ouagadougou, the capital of Burkina Faso. The centre of gravity for the South African region is at Bulawayo in Zimbabwe and the third centre of gravity, for East Africa, is located at Nakuru in Kenya.

If the two outlying countries of Morocco (Rabat) and Algeria (Algiers) are ignored, the centre of gravity for West Africa moves closer to Accra in Ghana, where UNHRD currently has a depot. If the outlying countries

Figure 10.11 Potential regional clusters of natural disasters in Africa (January 2014 to June 2017)

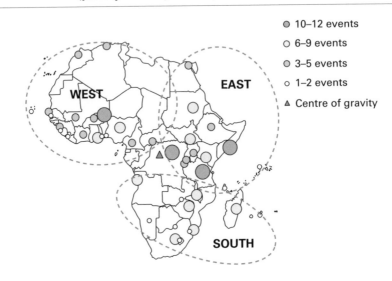

Figure 10.12 Centre-of-gravity analysis for potential regional clusters of natural disasters in Africa

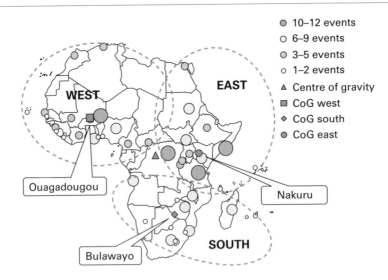

of Angola (Luanda) and Réunion (Saint-Denis) are ignored, the centre of gravity for South Africa will probably stay close to Bulawayo, although it might make sense to move it slightly south to Johannesburg in South Africa, due to better global accessibility. If the outlying country of Egypt (Cairo) is ignored, the centre of gravity for East Africa will move closer to Nairobi.

It is important to reiterate that the centres of gravity do not necessarily provide the answer to where the facilities should be located, but rather the starting point on a macro level from where the best location could be found. The calculations are based on optimization of transport costs, and should be complemented with qualitative indicators before final decisions are made.

The results suggest that the three regions should have pre-positioning facilities located at:

- West: Accra (Ghana);
- South: Johannesburg (South Africa);
- East: Nairobi (Kenya).

This might not be a surprise to those active in emergency response in Africa, although it provides at least comfort that the UNHRD depot at Accra is at the correct location. What is maybe more important is that, if similar facilities could be established at the centres of gravity for the southern and eastern regions, emergency response could be achieved much more efficiently.

Once the locations have been determined on the macro level, further analyses will be required on the micro level to ensure that qualitative factors as mentioned earlier, are taken into account.

Channel strategy[2]

Channel strategy refers to the configuration of supply chains to provide for the required service levels at acceptable costs, and the purpose of this last section is to indicate the close relationship between network design and channel strategy.

Although the main focus of this chapter is pre-positioning for emergency response, it is important to mention that humanitarian logistics does not only deal with disasters. Different supply chains exist for different services, such as emergency relief or response, food distribution, distribution of gifts-in-kind and development projects. For example, long-term droughts that might require food and medical supplies can be managed with predictable and known demand. Little safety stock is needed, and inventory demand is mostly dependent with sufficient time to negotiate cost-effective logistics services. This is not the case when unpredictable earthquakes happen, and independent demand requires sufficient safety stock to be carried in suitable pre-positioning locations.

Gattorna (2010: 51–56) has done much work in the development of supply chain frameworks and he suggests that there are typically four generic supply chains (or strategies):

- *Continuous replenishment supply chain*: Very predictable demand from known customers; easily managed through tight collaboration with these collaborative customers; focus on retention of customer relationships.

- *Lean supply chain*: Regular pattern of demand; quite predictable and forecastable although may be seasonal; tend to be mature low risk products/services; focus on efficiency.

- *Agile supply chain*: Usually unplanned at least until the last possible moment. May result from promotions; new product launches; fashion marketing; unplanned stock-outs; or unforeseen opportunities. Focus on the service–cost equation.

- *Fully flexible supply chain*: Unplanned and unplannable demand due to unknown customers with exceptional, sometimes emergency, requests. Focus on providing creative solutions at a premium price.

This last type is further split between a business event strategy in an entrepreneurial environment, and a humanitarian response strategy in an emergency environment. Gattorna (2010: 251–60) recommends that the emergency response or humanitarian supply chain should not only be agile, but fully flexible. In disaster situations, there is usually an initial event (or series of events) that dictates the requirement for a fully flexible supply chain, although it changes from the critical response phase into the ongoing rebuilding phase.

The immediate aim is to quickly provide life-saving essentials to the survivors, who often have no choice of buyer behaviour, but rather accept 'whatever is provided'. In the next stage, when basic living requirements are restored, and in the subsequent rebuilding phase, survivors will exhibit a greater range of buyer behaviours as the situation permits. This situation occurs when an entire complex of supply chains needs to be created from scratch because of a major disruption to normal living and business due to situations such as war, terrorist attacks, famine and natural disasters such as earthquakes, tsunamis or cyclones.

De Villiers *et al* (2017: 353–54) match the four generic supply chains of Gattorna with typical supply chains in humanitarian situations, as indicated in Table 10.3.

Emergency relief or response clearly requires a fully flexible supply chain, while food distribution needs a lean supply chain, possibly because of known

Table 10.3 Matching humanitarian situations with generic supply chains

Humanitarian Situation	Generic Supply Chain
Emergency relief or response	Fully flexible supply chain
Food distribution	Lean supply chain
Distribution of gifts-in-kind	Continuous replenishment supply chain
Development projects	Agile supply chain

SOURCE De Villiers *et al*, 2017: 354

Table 10.4 Supply chain strategies and network design

Supply Chain Strategy	Channels of Distribution (Network Design)
Continuous replenishment supply chain	Either direct or via trusted outlets
Lean supply chain	Wide distribution through multiple channels for maximum accessibility
Agile supply chain	Fewer, more direct channels to access consumers
Fully flexible supply chain – business event	Limited and very targeted
Fully flexible supply chain – humanitarian	As many as needed in a given situation

SOURCE Gattorna, 2010: 79–86

demand from historic take-off. Gifts-in-kind usually provide for predictable demand due to long-term relationships and regular supply of school books or medicines, while development projects often necessitate agility in order to be able to respond to unplanned or unforeseen demand.

Finally, management of the strategies requires different approaches to activities and challenges in the supply chains in general and network design in particular. Gattorna (2010: 79–86) provides a comparative analysis of the different strategies and his opinion on the differences in channels of distribution (or network design) is indicated in Table 10.4.

The generic supply chain strategies and associated logistics networks all contribute to the objective of developing and implementing a supply chain that will be able to compete effectively on cost, service levels and whatever other performance indicators require. The solution is not 'one size fits all' but a process to develop a customized supply chain with the support of modelling techniques such as centre-of-gravity analysis.

Conclusion

The purpose of this chapter was to discuss the centre-of-gravity analysis technique and explain its usefulness in determining the locations for the pre-positioning of emergency relief items. The application of this technique in humanitarian logistics is indeed similar to the application in commercial supply chains and it promises significant improvement in emergency relief response.

Much information is available in databases such as the EM-DAT Emergency Events Database (EM-DAT, 2017b) and it is relatively easy to use the available information to start looking for the ideal location for the establishment of global, regional or local pre-positioning facilities.

Notes

1 This section is based on the author's contribution to Chapter 2 in Schoeman, 2017: 40–42.

2 This section is based on the author's contribution to Chapter 2 in Schoeman, 2017: 45–47.

References

Bowersox, DJ and Closs, DJ (1996) *Logistical Management: The integrated supply chain process*, McGraw-Hill, Singapore

Coyle, JJ, Langley, CJ, Gibson, BJ, Novack, RA and Bardi, EJ (2008) *Supply Chain Management: A logistics perspective*, South-Western Cengage Learning, Mason

De Villiers, G (2008) Supply chain management in humanitarian and emergency relief, *SAPICS 2008*, Sun City

De Villiers, G, Nieman, G and Niemann, W (2017) *Strategic Logistics Management: A supply chain management approach*, Van Schaik Publishers, Pretoria

Duran, S, Gutierrez, MA and Keskinocak, P (2011) Pre-positioning of emergency items worldwide for CARE International, *Interfaces*, **41**(3), pp 223–37

EM-DAT (2017a) Map of natural disasters [Online] http://www.emdat.be/ (accessed 29 July 2017)

EM-DAT (2017b) The emergency events database, Université catholique de Louvain (UCL) – Cred. D Guha-Sapir [Online] http://www.emdat.be/ (accessed 29 July 2017)

Gattorna, JL (2010) *Dynamic Supply Chains: Delivering value through people*, 2nd edn, Pearson Education Limited, London

National University of Singapore (NUS) (2016) Decision support preparedness: Requirements for a network of emergency response facilities in Indonesia, *TLI Asia Pacific White Papers Series*, 16 January HL, Singapore

Roh, S and Kim, C (2016) Humanitarian relief logistics: Pre-positioning warehouse strategy, *KMI International Journal of Maritime Affairs and Fisheries*, 8(2)

Schoeman, IM (2017) *Transportation, Land Use and Integration: Applications in developing countries*, WIT Press, Southampton

Stock, JR and Lambert, DM (2001) *Strategic Logistics Management*, McGraw-Hill, New York

UNHRD (2009) *United Nations Humanitarian Response Depot (HRD) Network*, UNHRD Customer Service

UNHRD (2017) About us [Online] http://unhrd.org/page/about-us (accessed 29 July 2017)

World Vision (2010) *HEA Ministry Guiding Philosophy: Principles and values for humanitarian action*, Los Angeles

Humanitarian logistics – the functional challenges facing field offices

11

IRA HAAVISTO, PETER TATHAM, HANNA-RIITTA
HARILAINEN, CÉCILE L'HERMITTE, MAGNUS
LARSSON AND ALAIN VAILLANCOURT

Abstract

The aim of this chapter is to identify a number of operational challenges that field offices in humanitarian response organizations struggle with. Humanitarian logistics challenges are often identified by researchers as broad and extensive and hard to solve while, in parallel, field office employees often define their struggles as concrete and related to daily *ad hoc* fire-fighting. Thus we attempt to bridge the gap between current humanitarian logistics research and field challenges using the United Nations High Commissioner for Refugees (UNHCR) as a case study.

Operational challenges in humanitarian response

What are humanitarian actors actually struggling with? What are researchers actually focusing on in their research? According to previous studies, the humanitarian logistics literature has identified multiple challenges, which include: collaboration and coordination (Balcik *et al*, 2010), contextual factors related to unpredictability (Kovács and Spens, 2009), related to lack of resources (Gustavsson, 2003) and lack of planning (Jahre *et al*, 2016) – albeit this literature has been criticized for failing to link theory and practice (Altay and Green, 2006; Natarajarathinam *et al*, 2009; Kunz and Reiner, 2012). However, when researchers are asked about challenges in the humanitarian setting, they often focus on a high strategic level, for example on coordination between actors or collaboration between international responders and local community partners. The challenges stated can also be related to funding, to accountability and even to sustainability.

In contrast, aid workers are more focused on the day-to-day operations and on the search for practical and easily applicable solutions that would improve these operations (Pedraza-Martinez *et al*, 2013). Thus, when humanitarian responders who are currently working in the field are asked about their challenges, the struggles that they discuss are often at a very practical level. Examples include best practice when operating in uncertain and harsh conditions or finding adequate resources such as durable vehicles and functioning generators. As a result of these differences between academic research and field practice, the humanitarian community often tends to ignore (and sometimes even mistrust) the work of academics (Pedraza-Martinez *et al*, 2013).

Thus as a contribution towards bridging this clear gap, this chapter will analyse three specific types of operational challenges (transportation, warehousing and inventory management (WIM), and procurement) as portrayed by humanitarian logistics researchers and as presented by UNHCR staff in three field locations (Athens, Beirut and Addis Ababa).

Functional challenges in humanitarian response

As shown in Table 11.1, all three areas have been the subject of humanitarian logistics research, but whilst the results are perceived to have been valuable in an academic sense, the findings are not easily generalizable and are difficult to put in place in another (other than the studied) field setting – thus their 'impact' has been less impressive.

With this introduction in mind, the next section presents a case organization (UNHCR) and highlights a number of challenges identified by UNHCR staff, noting that although some of these challenges do, indeed, appear in the humanitarian logistics literature, they have not been studied in any depth in academic research.

Table 11.1   Functional challenges

Transportation	Fleet management	Pedraza-Martinez and Van Wassenhove (2012); Martinez *et al* (2011); Van Wassenhove and Pedraza-Martinez (2012).
	Routing	Ukkusuri and Yushimito (2008); Campbell *et al* (2008); Neis *et al* (2010); Huang *et al* (2012); Hamedi *et al* (2012); Beresford *et al* (2016).
	Distribution	Liberatore *et al* (2014); Balcik *et al* (2008); Luis *et al* (2012); Vitoriano *et al* (2011); Banomyong and Grant (2016).
Warehousing and Inventory Management	Facility location	Balcik and Beamon (2008); Gatignon *et al* (2010); Roh *et al* (2013); Beamon and Kotleba (2006); Duran *et al* (2011) (pre-positioning).
	Inventory management	Beamon and Kotleba (2006); Ozbay and Ozguven (2007); Natarajan and Swaminathan (2014).
Procurement	Procurement process	Falasca and Zobel (2011); Ertem *et al* (2010); Pazirandeh (2011); Trestrail *et al* (2009); Bagchi *et al* (2011); Duran *et al* (2013).
	Collaboration	Tomasini and Van Wassenhove (2009); Herlin and Pazirandeh (2015); Pazirandeh and Herlin (2014).

Case study: UNHCR

The main mission of the UNHCR is that of 'saving lives, protecting rights and building a better future for refugees, forcibly displaced communities and stateless people' (UNHCR, 2016). It currently has field staff located in 130 countries and mostly serves people on the move, both refugees and internally displaced people (IDPs) (UNHCR, 2016), and unsurprisingly, the breadth and depth of this challenge has grown over recent years. Furthermore, since the UNHCR is responding to multiple current crises, the organization has a good understanding of the main operational humanitarian logistics challenges – albeit, it is fully acknowledged that, as in the case of any humanitarian organization, its internal structure as well as its strategies and policies influence both the nature of these operational challenges, and the ways in which it responds. With this in mind, the key issues highlighted in the remainder of this chapter are perceived to reflect the challenges that humanitarian responders in large international humanitarian organizations typically face today.

It is fully accepted that other responding actors, such as smaller local non-governmental organizations (NGOs), governmental actors, military organizations or private sector actors may well face a different range of challenges. However, since international humanitarian organizations are present in most (if not all) of the larger humanitarian responses, and also since most actors involved in a response are, to a greater or lesser extent, dependent on each other due to intertwined operations, the findings in this case study are aimed at providing a comprehensive view of a number of challenges that any responding actor will have to take into account when responding to a disaster or crisis.

Methodology

The data for this study was gathered through a series of semi-structured interviews of 30 UNHCR representatives and other related organizations. These respondents hold roles such as head of supply, supply officer, procurement officer, supply assistant, supply associate, senior supply associate, senior supply officer, programme officer and senior supply chain planning advisor. The data was gathered in four locations during the period September–November 2016. One of the locations was the organization's HQ (Budapest, 15–16 September) whilst the remaining three were field locations (Beirut, 19–23 September; Athens 3–7 October; Addis Ababa 7–11 November). In each case, the respondents were asked to identify the main operational challenges that they face, and to offer a concrete example of such a challenge.

General finding from the field interviews

The main operational challenges as identified by those interviewed relate to: *inadequate infrastructure, security concerns, poor emergency response preparedness (ERP), coordination* (particularly lack of transparency between actors as well as between intra-organizational departments), and the lack of, or inadequate, *information sharing*. Above all, the paucity of *planning* would appear to be the core reason underpinning most of the other issues. Table 11.2 offers a summary of these challenges as they relate to the three areas of transportation, WIM and procurement, each of which will then be discussed in turn.

Table 11.2   Challenges identified during the case study interviews

Functional areas	Identified Challenge
Procurement	Procurement processes
	Supplier selection and development
	Market distortion
	Internal roles and responsibilities
	Demand forecasting and re-order management
Transportation	Contracting options
	International transportation (information sharing, coordination and integration)
	Customs
	Access and accessibility
	Security
WIM	Inventory management (stock-outs)
	Facility security
	Facility operational capacity
	Internal collaboration local/international staff
	ERP coordination
	Inventory reporting and updates

Function specific challenges – procurement

This section presents the main challenges that were identified within the functional theme of 'procurement'.

First, it was noted that various terms related to procurement, such as sourcing, purchasing and buying, are often used interchangeably. This reflects a clear difference from academic usage where when, viewed from a process perspective, *procurement* is the umbrella term that covers the whole process from needs identification of the internal customers to the follow-up at the supplier end. *Sourcing* (including specification of need, searching for sources of supply, selecting the suppliers, and contracting with them) is often considered to be the more strategic part of the procurement. *Buying*, on the other hand, is the more operational process of ordering goods/services against a previously established 'frame' agreement that was developed during the sourcing phase.

In the UNHCR context, once the need for goods or services has been identified, the supply team is responsible for reviewing all the options for acquiring these goods or services. The process differs slightly from that found in a typical commercial organization and could be likened to the 'make-or-buy' decision where the choice is between manufacturing a product in-house or purchasing it from an external supplier. Thus, the alternatives for acquiring goods and services from the UNHCR distribution network are:

- another operation/UNHCR warehouses where there is a surplus;
- stockpiles (noting that these are primarily designated for use in emergency operations);
- items in the pipeline (which were originally destined for another operation);
- in-kind donations;
- purchasing from a commercial source;
- delegating procurement to a partner or implementing organization.

It is the responsibility of the supply team to explore the availability and suitability of each of the above options, taking into consideration various factors, such as the resultant costs, transport and import options, and the delivery time. The team then advises on the most cost-effective options that align with the aims of the operation, noting that 'a decision to buy' should only be taken when all other options have been considered.

It is interesting to note that the research underpinning this chapter found a number of differences in the challenges identified in those field offices that are in the midst of managing UNHCR's response to a complex disaster, when compared with those field offices enjoying more stability in their operative environment.

For example, in the case of the Beirut supply office, it was having to manage the difficulties associated with the huge influx of refugees from Syria. Operations in the Beirut office had increased dramatically and, to some extent, were characterized by uncoordinated and *ad hoc* solutions when providing relief and aid assistance to the persons of concern (PoCs). (UNHCR no longer uses the term 'beneficiaries' when referring to those who the organization is assisting, preferring 'persons of concern'. In a similar way, Oxfam now uses the phrase 'people we work with'.) However, during 2016 the mission in Beirut had been able to make inroads into the constant 'fire-fighting' to resolve problems and had managed to implement several long-term solutions. In this respect, interviewees acknowledged that planning had previously not been conducted in a structured manner, and its absence was reflected in many activities. As an example, procurement plans were only established in 2016 and had, in effect, been absent during the crucial three previous years of emergency response.

In a similar way, those interviewed in the Athens office noted that the reality of the situation that they were dealing with resulted in multiple short-notice changes. These contradicted the generally mandated approach to procurement, which often needed long lead times both because of rigorous procurement processes as well as long transportation and delivery times. Larger procurements were similarly stated to be time-consuming, with four to eight weeks (as a conservative estimate) being required to get a valid contract established.

Those interviewed also remarked on the heavy administrative burden when procuring both supplies and services, albeit staff were well aware of the importance of following rigorous procurement policies and processes to ensure accountability. A similar observation was made in the Addis Ababa office, where the absence of knowledgeable, experienced, motivated and high-performing staff was stated to be the underlying cause of a number of procurement problems.

A further practical challenge to efficient and effective procurement was that of coordination and collaboration with other actors. As an example, the Athens supply office was struggling with the continuously changing requirements emanating from the Greek government. On the one hand, the operation in Greece is at a large scale, but in parallel the requirements were stated to be changing monthly and, as a result, operational planning was significantly compromised.

In summary, and in the context of a complex disaster characterized by the challenges of reaching the PoCs and by a high increase in demand, UNHCR seems to be faced with conflicting goals of accountability (and, hence, the need for rigorous processes) and speed. Reaching the right balance is further challenged by the shortages of adequate human resources that would allow for solid long-term planning in parallel with the ability to meet *ad hoc* and swiftly changing demands.

The following additional challenges were identified:

- compliance with the procurement regulations and processes during the emergency phase;
- compliance with the mandated planning procedures in the face of continuously changing demands;
- keeping records and systems updated at all times;

- establishing well-functioning frame agreements for third party logistic (3PL) services;
- establishing key performance indicators (KPIs) as part of the tendering process;
- obtaining accurate and comprehensive input in respect of technical specifications and quantities;
- arranging qualified supply staff at short notice, and undertaking any additional training needed.

Function specific challenges – transportation

The transportation function is an integral part of supply chain management, as it represents the physical link between a number of supply chain nodes from the origin of the goods, via a number of intermediate locations, to their final destination. In other words, transportation supports movements of cargo along the supply chain from one place to another, and interconnects a variety of nodes such as the points of purchase, warehouses and distribution nodes. Transportation is, therefore, closely related to other supply chain functions, such as procurement and warehousing. Indeed, as the major link between these functions, it plays a fundamental role in supply chain integration. For example, transportation moves the goods from a supplier to a warehouse, from a warehouse to a depot, and from a depot to the point of distribution. Within this framework, the role of transportation is to ensure that the right goods are delivered to the right place, at the right time, in the right condition and at an acceptable cost. If transport does not fulfil this role, eg if transportation delays occur, the downstream supply chain operations are negatively affected.

Since the flow of supplies cuts across the above-mentioned functions, cross-functional communication and coordination are essential to achieve seamless supply chain processes. In other words, for the right supplies to be made available to the right place at the right time, in the right condition and at an acceptable cost, it is fundamental that the individual functions do not work in silos but rather as integrated supply chain components, each supporting the other. Therefore, unsurprisingly, the importance of inter-functional information sharing, coordination and integration were recurring themes in the UNHCR interviews.

Indeed, given that transportation in the UNHCR context refers to international transportation, regional transportation and distribution, the large variety of transport-related challenges range from difficult access to beneficiaries, to the existence of different contracting options, international transportation and customs-related issues, infrastructure problems (such as the low quality of the road network), and security concerns. From a theoretical perspective, these should be overcome or mitigated by the transport planning process which includes, among other things, the timely identification of the possible constraints and risks that may impede the movement of goods, the assessment of the capabilities and resources available in the country of operation, the arrangement for any additional skills and capacity needed, and the integration of a variety of transport activities (eg movements of goods using multiple modes, cargo handling, transshipment, customs clearance, the reception of the goods at the delivery point, etc).

In practice, however, the interviews conducted in Beirut, Athens and Addis Ababa emphasized a range of issues. The logistics staff in Beirut highlighted a number of criteria to be considered in the selection of third-party transporters and customs clearing agents. In particular, given that UNHRC frequently contracts the services of local/national transporters, field workers need to be provided with a clear set of criteria to ensure that the most suitable and competent transport service provider is selected. Such criteria should include, for example, strong quality and reliability records (eg in terms of timely delivery and consistent performance), as well as prior experience in working with UN agencies. Following a successful award of contract, framework agreements need to be established with two transporters (one core provider, and one back-up) to ensure that enough transport capacity is available to meet peaks in demand following an emergency response.

Turning to the selection of a customs clearing agent, important criteria include the existence of a good reputation and a proven professional track record in clearing humanitarian goods effectively. Effective customs operations are also closely related to the agent's ability to maintain good contacts with the relevant ministries and authorities, and to the provision of the customs-related documentation in a timely manner.

In Athens, the use of integrated 3PL services provided by a single vendor and covering WIM, transport and customs supports effective logistics operations. The contract covers nationwide transportation services, including onto and within the islands. As Greece is a member of the European Union (EU), customs regulations mainly apply to goods imported from outside the EU. The customs-related problems mentioned during the interviews with UNHCR's logistics staff included the timely clearance of the imported goods at the beginning of the mission.

UNHCR's transport operations in Ethiopia (a landlocked country) involve the regional movements of goods (eg from Djibouti or Nairobi to Addis Ababa for incoming international consignments), as well as in-country transport (eg between Addis Ababa and the local warehouses).

Challenges in the Addis Ababa office were identified to be:

- inaccurate and/or incomplete documentation for international shipments;
- port congestion (eg at the Port of Djibouti);
- problems with third parties (eg the unavailability of customs inspectors or other officials);
- demurrage;
- shortage of trucks when the Ethiopian government mobilizes them and gives priority to specific cargo (eg fertilizers).

In addition, customs rules are very strict in Ethiopia and UNHCR is not treated differently from any other importer (eg a duty-free permit needs to be obtained for each individual shipment). Other customs-related issues encountered by UNHCR in Ethiopia include frequent changes in the customs rules and regulations, a high turnover of customs staff, meticulous customs processes, as well as challenges with different requirements for different types of goods (eg medical supplies, vehicles, etc).

Another transport challenge refers to in-kind donations, where the donor delivers the supplies only to the port of entry and UNHCR is tasked with distributing large consignments in a very short time frame, all across the mission area. This can be a challenge in many ways, not least in respect of its impact on staffing requirements.

Function specific challenges – WIM

Warehouses create both a physical decoupling point in the supply chain where orders can be grouped or split, as well as a temporal decoupling point where items can be withheld for use at a later date. Warehousing usually follows a basic set of inventory management processes to organize the goods at the warehouse, but it also can provide value-adding activities such as packing, kitting, quality control, labelling and returns management.

Humanitarian supply chains will often include temporary warehouses during emergencies. The use of mobile storage units helps the achievement of shorter delivery times by being located closer to the PoCs, as well as improving flexibility and, in some cases, solving a shortage of local warehouse capacity. Such temporary warehouses include quick rotation locations in which goods move in and out on a daily basis as they reach the affected population. Another warehouse option is that of a temporary collection site that consists of any form of space available to be used as a stockpile before the items are sorted and sent to an appropriate warehouse.

When managing an emergency, UNHCR will often require some level of surge capacity, which leads to the opening of one or more warehouses to accommodate incoming goods at the beginning of the operations. Once the situation has stabilized there is an opportunity to review and reorganize the warehouse decisions. Finally, a draw down in the operation will lead to a requirement for the closure of one or more of the warehouses that are being used.

It is important to choose a WIM contractor who has capacity to deal with both small and also very large quantities of material, thus the contractor needs to be able to respond to flexible requirements. Unfortunately, it was reported that once a contract has been established, the day-to-day communication between UNHCR and the WIM contractor can be very basic, using, for example, e-mails with attachments for information and documentation exchange. In parallel, the UNHCR administration routines and requirements for documentation and reporting are heavy and time-consuming for the WIM contractor and there is a high risk of typing errors in the day-to-day inputs to the UNHCR inventory system. As an example, information on volume and weight for the different items is kept separately and not integrated into the system, which does not facilitate the optimization of resources. Unsurprisingly, the training of staff on the documentation requirements was identified as important for the management of field warehouses, whether this activity is carried out by implementing partners or UNHCR staff.

The WIM services for the UNHCR Greece mission are, as mentioned above, integrated into the 3PL contract. This includes management of the field warehouses on the islands, as well as the main warehouses in Athens and Thessaloniki. The 3PL contract is arranged in a flexible way that supports the short notice handling and storage of both small volumes as well as very large quantities. However, once again, information on the volumes and weights of the commodities is only partly integrated in the system.

Although some problems are present in the UNHCR Addis Ababa office, several good practices were identified. The Addis Ababa office places significant emphasis on tracking and reacting to upcoming expiry dates through coordination with field staff to prioritize items with an upcoming expiry date. However, a number of challenges were identified, including the lack of staff capacity; the absence of a formalized information sharing which, in turn, resulted in an absence of planning. This lack of planning was manifest through a reduction in the clarity over warehouse capacity and location requirements, and the optimal reordering process with orders being linked to funding availability rather than stock levels. This was perceived by the research team to be a fundamental area in which the UNHCR system could be improved.

A further aspect of the overall supply chain management process was that relating to decisions on warehouse locations, which are actually undertaken by the programme office in consultation with protection officers (whose remit covers the safety and security of the PoCs) together with information from organizations that assists in the needs forecasting process. Whilst, clearly, these are all important considerations, it is argued that these factors only represent some of the variables that need to be integrated into the overall supply chain optimization process.

Summary

Whilst the humanitarian logistics literature identifies a number of operational challenges, such as coordination and collaboration (Balcik *et al*, 2010), as well as disaster and context-specific challenges (Kovács and Spens, 2009), this chapter presents a number of functional or operational challenges as they are portrayed in three field office locations for one international humanitarian organization (UNHCR).

A common challenge for all the field offices (Athens, Beirut and Addis Ababa), as well as a common challenge for all three functional areas (transportation, procurement and WIM) was identified to be the lack or shortage of planning. The lack of time and resources for planning negatively influenced all the other activities and resulted in, for example, a paucity of proper information sharing as well as in meeting the supply requirements.

A further common denominator was the difficult balance to be struck between multiple rigorous and time-consuming administrative processes and the goal of efficiency and speed.

Thus, based on the 'real' challenges that this study has identified from the interviews with those working in the field, the authors echo the call of Leiras *et al* (2014) who encourage those involved to strive to tackle not only the 'grandiose' problems faced by humanitarian logisticians, but also those encountered on a daily basis from a field perspective.

References

Altay, N and Green, WG (2006) OR/MS research in disaster operations management, *European Journal of Operational Research*, **175**(1), pp 475–93

Bagchi, A, Paul, JA and Maloni, M (2011) Improving bid efficiency for humanitarian food aid procurement, *International Journal of Production Economics*, **134**(1), pp 238–45

Balcik, B and Beamon, BM (2008) Facility location in humanitarian relief, *International Journal of Logistics*, **11**(2), pp 101–21

Balcik, B, Beamon, BM and Smilowitz, K (2008) Last mile distribution in humanitarian relief, *Journal of Intelligent Transportation Systems*, **12**(2), pp 51–63

Balcik, B, Beamon, BM, Krejci, CC, Muramatsu, KM and Ramirez, M (2010) Coordination in humanitarian relief chains: Practices, challenges and opportunities, *International Journal of Production Economics*, **126**(1), pp 22–34

Banomyong, R and Grant, DB (2016) Transport in humanitarian supply chains, in *Supply Chain Management for Humanitarians*, ed I Haavisto, G Kovács and K Spens, pp 191–208, Kogan Page, Philadelphia

Beamon, BM and Kotleba, SA (2006) Inventory modelling for complex emergencies in humanitarian relief operations, *International Journal of Logistics: Research and applications*, **9**(1), pp 1–18

Beresford, A, Pettit, S and Al-Hashimi, Z (2016) Humanitarian aid supply corridors, in *Supply Chain Management for Humanitarians*, ed I Haavisto, G Kovács and K Spens, pp 209–21, Kogan Page, Philadelphia

Campbell, AM, Vandenbussche, D and Hermann, W (2008) Routing for relief efforts, *Transportation Science*, **42**(2), pp 127–45

Duran, S, Gutierrez, MA and Keskinocak, P (2011) Pre-positioning of emergency items for CARE international, *Interfaces*, **41**(3), pp 223–37

Duran, BS and Odell, PL (2013) *Cluster Analysis: A survey*, vol 100, Springer Science & Business Media

Ertem, MA, Buyurgan, N and Rossetti, MD (2010) Multiple-buyer procurement auctions framework for humanitarian supply chain management, *International Journal of Physical Distribution & Logistics Management*, **40**(3), pp 202–27

Falasca, M and Zobel, CW (2011) A two-stage procurement model for humanitarian relief supply chains, *Journal of Humanitarian Logistics and Supply Chain Management*, **1**(2), pp 151–69

Gatignon, A, Van Wassenhove, LN and Charles, A (2010) The Yogyakarta earthquake: Humanitarian relief through IFRC's decentralized supply chain, *International Journal of Production Economics*, **126**(1), pp 102–10

Gustavsson, L (2003) Humanitarian logistics: Context and challenges, *Forced Migration Review*, 18(6), pp 6–8

Hamedi, M, Haghani, A and Yang, S (2012) Reliable transportation of humanitarian supplies in disaster response: Model and heuristic, *Procedia-Social and Behavioral Sciences*, 54, pp 1205–19

Herlin, H and Pazirandeh, A (2015) Avoiding the pitfalls of cooperative purchasing through control and coordination: Insights from a humanitarian context, *International Journal of Procurement Management*, 8(3), pp 303–25

Huang, M, Smilowitz, K and Balcik, B (2012) Models for relief routing: Equity, efficiency and efficacy, *Transportation Research Part E: Logistics and Transportation Review*, 48(1), pp 2–18

Jahre, M, Pazirandeh, A and Van Wassenhove, LN (2016) Defining logistics preparedness: A framework and research agenda, *Journal of Humanitarian Logistics and Supply Chain Management*, 6(3), pp 372–98

Kovács, G and Spens, K (2009) Identifying challenges in humanitarian logistics, *International Journal of Physical Distribution & Logistics Management*, 39(6), pp 506–28

Kovács, G and Spens, K (2011) Trends and developments in humanitarian logistics: A gap analysis, *International Journal of Physical Distribution & Logistics Management*, 41(1), pp 32–45

Kunz, N and Reiner, G (2012) A meta-analysis of humanitarian logistics research, *Journal of Humanitarian Logistics and Supply Chain Management*, 2(2), pp 116–47

Leiras, A, de Brito Jr, I, Queiroz Peres, E, Rejane Bertazzo, T and Yoshizaki, H (2014) Literature review of humanitarian logistics research: Trends and challenges, *Journal of Humanitarian Logistics and Supply Chain Management*, 4(1), pp 95–130

Liberatore, F, Ortuño, MT, Tirado, G, Vitoriano, B and Scaparra, MP (2014) A hierarchical compromise model for the joint optimization of recovery operations and distribution of emergency goods in humanitarian logistics, *Computers & Operations Research*, 42, pp 3–13

Luis, E, Dolinskaya, IS and Smilowitz, KR (2012) Disaster relief routing: Integrating research and practice, *Socio-economic planning sciences*, 46(1), pp 88–97

Martinez, AJP, Stapleton, O and Van Wassenhove, LN (2011) Field vehicle fleet management in humanitarian operations: A case-based approach, *Journal of Operations Management*, 29(5), 404–21

Natarajan, KV and Swaminathan, JM (2014) Inventory management in humanitarian operations: Impact of amount, schedule, and uncertainty in funding, *Manufacturing & Service Operations Management*, 16(4), pp 595–603

Natarajarathinam, M, Capar, I and Narayanan, A (2009) Managing supply chains in times of crisis: A review of literature and insights, *International Journal of Physical Distribution and Logistics Management*, **39**(7), pp 535–73

Neis, P, Singler, P and Zipf, A (2010) *Collaborative mapping and emergency routing for disaster logistics–case studies from the Haiti earthquake and the UN Portal for Afrika*, pp 1–6 [Online] http://www.geog.uni-heidelberg.de/md/chemgeo/geog/gis/un-osm-emergency-routing.gi-forum2010.full.pdf

Ozbay, K and Ozguven, E (2007) Stochastic humanitarian inventory control model for disaster planning, *Transportation Research Record: Journal of the Transportation Research Board*, (2022), pp 63–75

Pazirandeh, A (2011) Sourcing in global health supply chains for developing countries: Literature review and a decision making framework, *International Journal of Physical Distribution and Logistics Management*, **41**(4), pp 364–84

Pazirandeh, A and Herlin, H (2014) Unfruitful cooperative purchasing: A case of humanitarian purchasing power, *Journal of Humanitarian Logistics and Supply Chain Management*, **4**(1), pp 24–42

Pedraza-Martinez, AJ and Van Wassenhove, LN (2012) Transportation and vehicle fleet management in humanitarian logistics: Challenges for future research, *EURO Journal on Transportation and Logistics*, **1**(1–2), pp 185–96

Pedraza-Martinez, AJ, Stapleton, O and Van Wassenhove, LN (2013) On the use of evidence in humanitarian logistics research, *Disasters*, **37**(1), S51–S67

Roh, SY, Jang, HM and Han, CH (2013) Warehouse location decision factors in humanitarian relief logistics, *The Asian Journal of Shipping and Logistics*, **29**(1), pp 103–20

Tomasini, R and Van Wassenhove, LN (2009) *Humanitarian logistics*, Springer

Trestrail, J, Paul, J and Maloni, M (2009) Improving bid pricing for humanitarian logistics, *International Journal of Physical Distribution & Logistics Management*, **39**(5), pp 428–41

Van Wassenhove, LN and Pedraza-Martinez, AJ (2012) Using OR to adapt supply chain management best practices to humanitarian logistics, *International Transactions in Operational Research*, **19**(1–2), pp 307–22

Vitoriano, B, Ortuño, MT, Tirado, G and Montero, J (2011) A multi-criteria optimization model for humanitarian aid distribution, *Journal of Global Optimization*, **51**(2), pp 189–208

Ukkusuri, S and Yushimito, W (2008) Location routing approach for the humanitarian prepositioning problem, *Transportation Research Record: Journal of the Transportation Research Board*, (2089), pp 18–25

UNHCR (2016) The UN refugee agency: Statistics and operational figures [Online] http://www.unhcr.org/figures-at-a-glance.html (accessed 20 August 2017)

Supply chain improvement at ShelterBox

A case study of the application of lean principles and techniques in a disaster relief organization

DAVID TAYLOR AND DARREN MOSS

Abstract

This case study reports on an initiative to introduce best practice in supply chain management at ShelterBox, a medium sized non-governmental organization (NGO) specializing in the provision of emergency shelter in disaster zones. The scope of the project covers all aspects of supply chain activity from acquisition of materials through to delivery to beneficiaries, and describes the strategic and operational changes implemented. The improvement approach was based on the application of the lean principles and techniques, which have been developed and widely applied in commercial sectors but, hitherto, have had limited application in humanitarian environments. The initiative commenced in 2014 and was initially led by external consultants, but over a period of three years was increasingly progressed and shaped by the ShelterBox internal management team. Lean approaches have now become part of the organization's operational DNA and will continue to inform ongoing efforts to improve supply chain efficiency and effectiveness into the future.

ShelterBox background

ShelterBox is a medium-sized international disaster relief charity that provides temporary shelter and life-saving supplies to displaced families. Each iconic, green ShelterBox typically contains a tent or tarpaulins, water purification equipment, blankets, tools and other necessities to help a family survive after a disaster.

ShelterBox was founded in 2000 in the town of Helston in the United Kingdom (UK). The first consignment of 143 boxes was sent to victims of the 2001 Gujarat earthquake. The charity significantly expanded its work in response to the 2004 Indian Ocean tsunami, providing 12,000 boxes to support some 60,000 people. Since then the charity has steadily grown in both income and numbers of families served. In Haiti in 2010, ShelterBox provided shelter for 28,000 families, or approximately 25 per cent of all tents delivered in areas surrounding Port Au Prince. By 2016 some 20,000

Figure 12.1 Typical contents of a ShelterBox

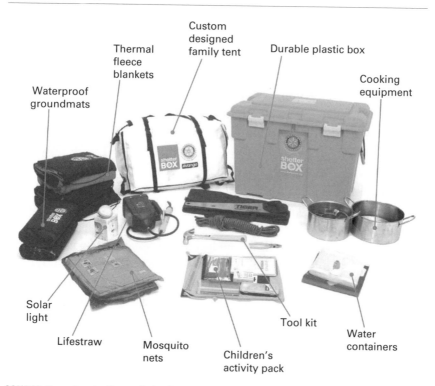

SOURCE Reproduced with permission from ShelterBox

families were served annually in disasters across the world. The ShelterBox strategic plan aims to serve 200,000 families (approximately 1 million people) by 2025, with a target income of £40 million.

- *The Rotary Club connection*: At the time of its inception in 2000 ShelterBox was adopted by its local Rotary Club in Cornwall as a millennium project. Since then, Rotary organizations across Britain and around the world have supported ShelterBox. In 2016 Rotary International designated ShelterBox as its global 'project partner' for disaster relief, an agreement that formalized the 16-year bond between the two organizations. Rotary clubs are not only an important source of income for ShelterBox, but also provide volunteers to assist in disaster relief operations.

- *ShelterBox volunteers*: A central part of the ShelterBox model has been in the use of volunteers to staff ShelterBox response teams (SRTs). There are some 200 volunteers spread around the world who have been selected and trained in disaster response. They are typically deployed in teams of two or three to organize the distribution of aid in disaster zones; sometimes supported by full-time operations staff from the UK headquarters (HQ), sometimes operating independently but in close communication with HQ.

- *A 'can-do' organization*: The founder of ShelterBox was from a military background, and in consequence many of the staff in the operations department have been drawn from the military. There is a logic to this policy in that the deployment of relief into disaster zones has many similar characteristics to military operations, requiring urgent action, in unfamiliar territory, often operating in challenging, dangerous and disrupted environments. As ShelterBox has grown, its staff have prided themselves on a militaristic, 'can-do' approach that is not bureaucratic, responds quickly and just gets the job done.

- *The context of the supply chain project*: ShelterBox experienced relatively rapid growth from its inception in the year 2000 where it had a restricted range of around 10 products supplied from a small Helston warehouse, to a situation in 2014 where it had a product range of over 100 items, purchased from some 20 suppliers, with stocks to the value of £5.5 million, 40 per cent of which were located in the UK with the rest held in 26 locations spread across 18 different countries. Senior management identified a need to review purchasing activities, and LCP Consulting Ltd were contracted for a three-month assignment. Recommendations followed, which led to a strengthening of procurement practices, more formalized buying procedures, clarification of purchasing roles and authorities within ShelterBox, and the appointment of an experienced purchasing manager. Improvement in purchasing efficiency resulted, but it was clear that consideration of purchasing activity in isolation would only have limited impact. It was suggested that more significant improvements in efficiency and effectiveness could be achieved if a wider review of the supply chain operations was undertaken. This recommendation was accepted by ShelterBox management, and a supply chain improvement project was initiated.

The organizational context for supply chain improvement

The situation in ShelterBox at the outset of the project presented several challenges from a supply chain management perspective:

- There was no appreciation of the concept of an integrated supply chain. Activities along the chain operated in silos: purchasing, inventory management, warehousing, logistics, field distribution etc.

- There was no one in the organization with specific expertise in supply chain management.

- There was no reference to supply chain management within the annual strategic plans other than the setting of ever-higher inventory levels.

- There was a lack of data on supply chain activity. The 'can-do' philosophy in the operations department meant that there was an emphasis on getting the deployments done, with little concern to collect data that would enable evaluation of supply chain performance and subsequent improvement. Furthermore, the data that did exist was often confused, incomplete and contradictory.

- Moreover, there was no real recognition that management of the supply chain from acquisition of equipment to its delivery to beneficiaries in disaster zones was *the core activity* of the organization.

The aim of the supply chain improvement project was, therefore, twofold:

- to ensure that the ShelterBox supply chain was organized in the most efficient and effective way so as to serve the maximum number of beneficiaries, in the most appropriate manner, with the available resources;

- to ensure the most efficient and appropriate use of the financial resources provided by donors.

Lean thinking: the basis of the adopted methodology

The underlying logic for the analysis and improvement of supply chain operations was based on the application of lean principles and techniques. Lean is based on the methodologies developed by Toyota, the world's leading auto manufacturer, over a period of 50 years. Lean is now adopted as best practice across many industries and commercial sectors, and a wide range of lean tools and techniques are available for analysis and process improvement. However, to date, there has been relatively little application of lean within the humanitarian aid sector.

At the heart of lean are two key ideas. First, understanding and delivering *value* to the end-user of the product or service and, second, *elimination of waste* or 'non-value-adding activities' from the processes that are in place to deliver that value. The Five Lean Principles (Womack and Jones, 2003) provide a top-level framework for approaching supply chain improvement:

1 Understand what is *value* from the point of view of the customer.

2 Identify all the steps in the *value chain* (or value chains) that are used to source, organize and deliver products to the customers and categorize all steps as either value adding or non-value adding.

3 Aim for *flow* through the value chain, by eliminating or reducing non-value adding steps so that product moves from one value adding activity to the next without interruption, delays or detours.

4 Aim for a *pull* system, whereby the product delivered is what is required by the customers, when it is required, in the quantity and condition required.

5 Aim for *perfection*, by setting ambitious targets and continually trying to reduce waste of product, time or money in the value chain processes.

The initial overview of ShelterBox supply chain activity: the big picture map

The starting point was the development of a 'big picture map' (BPM) to give an overview of the structure of the ShelterBox supply network. It includes details of the key suppliers of aid materials, their locations and relative importance in terms of purchasing expenditure; global inventory locations together with respective stock levels; transportation partners and their relative importance; and, importantly, details of the various disasters served in terms of locations, number of beneficiaries and expenditures. For ShelterBox, in common with most disaster relief organizations, the disasters served change from year to year, so BPMs were created for three consecutive years. These indicated that the upstream features of the network were relatively stable (ie key suppliers, inventory locations), whilst destinations, transport routes and modes and methods of distribution varied with the location and type of disaster served. The BPM was supplemented by the development of a supply chain costing framework, which had hitherto been absent at ShelterBox as financial reporting was based on traditional accounting frameworks.

The BPM was useful for a number of reasons. It provided a concise and visual summary of all supply chain activity on one sheet; it provided a quantified assessment of each process in the supply chain; it showed interrelationships between the various processes and activities along the chain and the extent to which these were aligned. The quantification of performance of both individual elements within the supply network and of the supply network as a whole provided a basis for setting improvement targets for future years and evaluating performance year on year.

The BPM also highlighted a number of significant strategic and operational issues including:

- a need for clarification of the organization's strategic objectives and scope of activity in order to set a framework for supply planning;
- the need to better understand the demand for ShelterBox equipment and services;
- the need to better understand what is 'value' from the point of view of the beneficiaries;
- the need to balance the capabilities of the key elements in the ShelterBox supply chain, in terms of supplier capabilities, inventory levels and field-deployment capability;
- the need for an organization-wide information technology system to facilitate supply chain monitoring and planning;
- a requirement for detailed evaluation of the performance of individual deployments;
- the need to ensure that all staff were clear as to supply chain strategy and objectives, and how they could contribute to their achievement.

Internal project teams were established to address each of these issues.

Clarifying the strategic direction and scope of ShelterBox activity

Within the complexities and wide-ranging needs of disaster relief and subsequent recovery, where was the ShelterBox niche? What was it trying to achieve? What equipment should be supplied? In which regions should it operate? Should it respond to all disasters? What was the timescale for involvement?

At its outset, ShelterBox started with a restricted range of products which were focused on emergency shelter, but over the years the scope of activities had expanded. The range of equipment had increased as staff and volunteers regularly identified more items that could potentially be of use within disaster zones. This presented increasing challenges for inventory investment and control, particularly with multiple stock locations around the world. The length of time that ShelterBox was involved in disaster zones had also expanded. There had never been a clear definition of the 'emergency phase' of a disaster. In consequence ShelterBox was increasingly involved in activity in the later stages of disasters, ie the recovery and rebuild phases (Pettit and Beresford, 2005). In some disaster zones ShelterBox was still providing relief six, nine or even twelve months after the onset of a disaster.

The needs in disaster situations are always complex and wide-ranging. Mission creep is a danger for any NGO, but particularly for a smaller organization with limited resources. The problem is that, in trying to do more and more, there is a danger of being less and less effective in any of the specific activities. Recommendations were therefore made to more tightly define the scope and aims of ShelterBox activity, which would then provide a clear framework for developing supply chain policies.

It was agreed that ShelterBox would revert to its roots and refocus on the provision of a restricted range of shelter types and associated non-food items (NFIs) required during the emergency phase of a disaster. The 'emergency phase' was arbitrarily defined as the first three months after the occurrence of a rapid-onset natural disaster or in the first three months after the decision to deploy in a slow-onset or protracted disaster situation. The logic being that, after a period of three months, in most circumstances beneficiaries would have arranged some form of shelter and would no longer be in need of *emergency* shelter. As part of a systematic approach to supply chain improvement it was deemed important in the first instance for ShelterBox to concentrate on becoming excellent in its core activity, ie the provision of emergency shelter, before branching into wider remits such as 'build back better' or disaster prevention, albeit that these are laudable objectives.

Definition of the time frame for response and the required range of equipment created a clear framework for supply chain planning both in terms of ensuring the specified range of materials was available and also in determining the required response capabilities.

Understanding demand

Demand volume

A key question in any supply chain planning process is 'what is the volume of demand we are trying to serve?' Once the required demand has been established, it is then possible to determine the required capabilities across the supply chain to meet that demand.

The global demand for humanitarian assistance is enormous. In 2016 it was estimated that worldwide there were some 60 million displaced people. Forecasts suggest this will grow to close to 200 million in 2030 (UNHCR, 2106). For a medium-sized relief organization such as ShelterBox, the global shelter requirement is, in practice, not a particularly relevant figure in terms of supply chain planning. Indeed even in the context of many individual disasters, the total number of families affected typically far outstrips ShelterBox's resources. The key question is, therefore, not what is the absolute demand in terms of number of families needing shelter, but rather what is the ShelterBox capability to respond?

Traditionally ShelterBox had viewed this as being governed simultaneously by available donor income and available stocks of relief items, a policy that meant stock levels had continued to grow year-on-year as income increased. Certainly, donor income will always be a fundamental issue, but within the context of any given level of income what determines the supply chain response capability? Analysis of capacities along the supply chain highlighted that, in reality, the restricting factor or bottleneck was not inventory availability (as had been previously assumed), but the capabilities to distribute aid once it had arrived in the country of need. It was thus determined that initial supply chain capacity planning would be based not on any notion of overall demand, but on an assessment of the organization's field distribution capabilities. A project was therefore initiated to determine the realistic deployment/distribution capabilities first through ShelterBox's own-account efforts, and second through other partner NGOs. Disasters were categorized as either 'core' being funded from regular funding streams, or 'major' where large-scale events triggered specific funding appeals. The outcome of this work was that the following response capabilities were set as targets:

- to meet the emergency shelter needs of 1,000 households in each of the first three months of a core disaster;

- to serve two core disasters simultaneously;

- in addition, to have a surge capability to meet the needs of 3,000 households per month in each of the first three months of a major disaster.

These response targets effectively created a surrogate for demand in terms of supply chain capacity planning, and the lean concept of 'line-balancing' was introduced to ensure all functions along the supply chain were designed to meet these targets.

Demand geography

A second aspect in understanding demand is to determine where in the world aid is likely to be required. This directly affects the key issues of stock locations and the required transport capabilities. A project was therefore initiated to determine disaster risk areas. The primary source of information used was the INFORM Index for Risk Management (INFORM, 2016). This evaluates and ranks countries throughout the world in terms of their risk from humanitarian crises set against their national response capacities. In addition, maps were produced identifying the regions of the world where ShelterBox had deployed in the previous five years to indicate areas in which the organization had specific experience. The outcome was the production of a list of countries and regions in which ShelterBox would be most likely to respond. This evaluation was subsequently used in planning pre-positioned stock locations and in prioritizing work to better understand beneficiary value.

Understanding beneficiary value

The first lean principle quite deliberately focuses on the need to understand what value is from the point of view of customers, who, in the aid environment, are the beneficiaries. ShelterBox had long understood that different groups of beneficiaries had different value propositions (ie different requirements) depending on their circumstances, and that a one-solution-fits-all approach was inappropriate. However, there had been no systematic approach to determine these differences. A project was therefore initiated to gain an in-depth understanding of beneficiary needs in different situations – for example: hot versus cold climates; mountain versus lowland terrain; refugee camp versus settlement rebuild; varying cultural/religious contexts. Initially desk research was undertaken consulting various sources including: previous needs assessments carried out by ShelterBox, reports by other aid agencies, as well as published demographic and climate data. This was followed up and deepened by direct surveys of previous beneficiaries in prioritized, high-risk locations.

Understanding beneficiary value is seen as an ongoing task, acknowledging that requirements will change over time and that there is a continuous need to gain a deeper understanding of how best to meet beneficiary requirements and thereby provide value. However, in the short term, the beneficiary value analysis had an immediate impact in determining the range of equipment required in different regions and circumstances, which in turn informed purchasing and inventory policies.

Ensuring materials availability

The three areas of work described above (clarifying the scope of ShelterBox activity, defining the required response capability, and understanding the beneficiary value proposition) established a framework and objectives for supply chain planning. In doing so, it was acknowledged that all three of these areas would change and evolve over time in response to varying resources at ShelterBox and varying beneficiary circumstances. However, setting some clear and, wherever possible, quantified parameters at a particular point in time provided terms of reference for an improved approach to supply chain planning.

The next section of work was to address three interrelated issues that affected the availability of equipment and materials:

- sourcing material supplies and supplier management;
- inventory policy;
- international transport from inventory sources to countries of disaster.

Equipment sourcing and supplier management

At the outset of the project, materials acquisition at ShelterBox was, to say the least, *ad hoc*. Indeed the project was triggered by a recognition of the need to improve purchasing strategies. Purchasing of materials fell into three broad categories:

- *Single source products*: A number of products were single sourced, perhaps most significantly a proprietary designed and branded ShelterBox tent. This led to a situation where the supplier was in a position to dictate terms, in particular requiring large volume purchases and restricted manufacturing schedules. This resulted in ShelterBox at times holding excessive volumes of inventory, whilst at other times having shortages because of long lead times from order placement to delivery.

- *Supplies from humanitarian aid wholesalers*: Globally, there are a number of recognized and accredited companies each supplying a wide range of humanitarian products from locations in different parts of the world. ShelterBox purchased from a number of these suppliers on an as-required basis. Prices and product availability would vary depending on supply and demand. In common with most other smaller NGOs, ShelterBox would frequently incur difficulties in obtaining materials during major disasters when demand from all NGOs is high, which further contributed to the propensity for high stockholding at ShelterBox.

- *Purchases from non-humanitarian suppliers*: Some products, such as toolkits and camping stoves, had been sourced from general commercial suppliers. Purchasing was often in significant volumes to gain price discounts, further contributing to high stocks.

As part of defining the terms of reference for supply chain activity, a smaller and more consistent range of key items was specified, all of which would be non-proprietary relief items meeting either International Federation of Red Cross and Red Crescent Societies (IFRC) or United Nations High Commissioner for Refugees (UNHCR) specifications. A number of the major humanitarian wholesalers were then approached to discuss possible sourcing arrangements. The outcome was that two suppliers were selected, each of which could supply the full range of required products, some of which they manufactured in-house, and some of which were outsourced. They also offered regional coverage, with warehouses in the Far East, Middle East, Europe and Africa. A partnership approach was developed with these suppliers that included a number of key elements:

- ShelterBox provided details of the required response capability, ie the requirement to provide equipment for 1,000 families per month over a three-month period in the defined risk regions, together with ramp-up capability to 3,000 families in times of major disaster.

- Suppliers provided lead times for supply from warehouse stocks into the specified areas of need, and also details of replenishment lead times from point of manufacture into their respective warehouses.

- Agreements were made regarding the levels of reserved stock to be held by suppliers and by ShelterBox, and the terms on which this stock should be held.

- A pricing policy was adopted acknowledging that suppliers needed to make an acceptable level of profit, whilst ShelterBox would not be subject to short-term price fluctuation or inflated pricing in times of major disaster.

The aim of the partnership approach was to create a more stable supply base for ShelterBox, with assurances regarding product availability, quality and fair pricing, and with a reciprocal commitment from ShelterBox to channel current and future demand to the partner suppliers. At the same time, the use of a dual sourcing approach ensured competition and security of supply in case of problems with either supplier. Interestingly, the CEO of one of the partners remarked that the ShelterBox initiative to develop a partnership was the first time in 25 years of trading in the humanitarian sector that he had encountered such an approach, which he found refreshing when compared with the more usual, price-focused and frequently adversarial tactics that typified many trading relationships in the aid environment.

Pre-positioning and inventory management

At the outset of the supply chain project in 2014, ShelterBox had approximately £5 million worth of stock, and the plan was to increase stockholdings to £10 million by 2016 in line with projected income growth. Stock was held at some 26 locations around the globe, which could be grouped as follows:

- The biggest single stockholding was in the two warehouses adjacent to the UK headquarters, where picking and packing operations took place.

- At the five United Nations Humanitarian Response Depots (UNHRDs) in Dubai, Panama, Subang, Accra and Las Palmas stocks were held in pre-packed shelter boxes, each containing a standard set of equipment.

- Stock was held at a variety of locations where free warehousing had been offered, some by other NGOs, some by international transportation providers, and some by Rotary organizations.

- Stock was held at 'legacy locations' where aid had been deployed to a region but not distributed, and left in the country in the hope that it might be used in subsequent disasters.

These stock locations had evolved over time without ever having been part of an overall plan. A project was therefore initiated to determine the most appropriate global stock locations and to reduce stock levels commensurate with achieving required service targets. The information from the projects on beneficiary value, geographical demand, supplier capabilities and required response capability informed the analysis.

The following potential stock locations were considered:

- at or close to points of manufacture operated by the two chosen supply partners;
- at regional warehouses in the Middle East, East Africa and Eastern Europe operated by the two partner suppliers;
- at three UNHRDs in Panama, Las Palmas and Accra to give coverage in areas not accessible from the supplier locations.

A decision model was developed that evaluated the most appropriate locations to serve each disaster risk zone together with the most appropriate mode and routing of transport. The model took account of total lead times and total costs from point of manufacture to delivery at port/ airport of entry into the relevant country. Realistic details of transport costs and supply lead times were provided by the partner suppliers and the UNHRDs, together with their respective freight agents. The priority was to ensure the product could be delivered in the required time frames; the secondary requirement was to minimize the overall cost to serve. The model determined which stock location and transport solution would be most appropriate in each of the three months of the response phase. The decision model was subsequently developed to be a real-time tool that could be used to determine the most appropriate sourcing and methods of transport at the time of a disaster.

Improving deployment capability

Having identified the field deployment capability as the immediate capacity constraint within the supply chain, a project was initiated to address this issue. The ShelterBox model had developed based on volunteers in SRTs taking responsibility for field deployment, coordinated and supported remotely by a small operations team of about eight staff at headquarters. This model had a number of problems in terms of the management of both volunteers and HQ staff. Volunteers could not always be relied on to be available when required, which meant that, in some instances, aid could not be deployed because of lack of staff. Although all SRTs had received standard training, in practice individuals had widely differing levels of experience and capabilities which, in some cases, resulted in suboptimal decisions in the field. The small HQ staff team meant that responsibility for a particular deployment often shifted between staff members during the course of a disaster, with no one having overall accountability. It also meant that frequently no full-time HQ staff were available for field deployment, so field activities were entirely dependent on volunteers. Significant operational changes resulted from the review:

- The number of full-time operations staff at headquarters was tripled. These were formed into three teams, with individual teams given responsibility for specific deployments.

- HQ staff would always be directly involved in the field throughout each deployment, with responsibility to coordinate and direct volunteers.

- HQ staff and volunteers would increasingly be trained to specialize in particular functions such as needs assessment, liaison with local authorities and logistics – whereas previously both staff and volunteers had essentially been generalists.

The outcome was a steady improvement in the reliability, availability, capability and professionalism of ShelterBox field staff.

Development of an organization-wide information technology system

In order to develop a coordinated approach to supply chain management a critical requirement was to establish an integrated information technology, data capture and data management system. The requirement was for a *'rapid development tool'* which could be readily applied and adapted to ShelterBox's immediate needs and, critically, one which had the capability to be further developed in-house by ShelterBox's staff as future circumstances evolved. A market review led to the selection of a system developed by Mendix (www.mendix.com). Prior to installing the system a root and branch review of all information management processes was carried out in order to remove duplication and eliminate non-value-adding tasks. The system was then used to manage the key operations-related tasks and processes and, where possible, to reduce and automate data capture. An important element was the ability to link directly to mobile apps used by field staff during disasters. This enabled real time data collection during deployments, giving ShelterBox greater insight into their responses, and an ability to make better informed decisions regarding beneficiary needs as well as the activities of other stakeholders such as in-country authorities, the Shelter cluster and other NGOs. The information technology tool was also integrated with the existing finance, stock management and fundraising systems, thus reducing the overall implementation cost.

Improved evaluation and management of individual deployments

The term 'supply chain management' is something of a misnomer as it suggests a linear, sequential set of processes between suppliers and customers. It is more helpful to think in terms of a supply network as, in practice, the situation in most organizations (including ShelterBox) is more complex, with multiple sources of supply, multiple beneficiary groups and a variety of intermediaries. Value chain analysis (VCA) provides a method of breaking into this complexity and focusing clearly on the processes that are required to bring products and value to end-customers. A value chain is defined as all the steps in the processes required to bring specific products from specific sources of supply through to specific end-customers. Within any supply network there will be numerous value chains. VCA is one of the fundamental techniques from the lean toolbox and involves a number of elements:

- mapping all the steps from the start to the end of the process;
- developing quantified measures to evaluate the efficiency and effectiveness of the individual steps within the process and of the process as a whole;
- identifying 'waste' and 'non-value adding' elements within the process;
- developing a prioritized action plan to improve process performance and reduce waste.

VCA was developed in the commercial context where supply chains, once established, are usually long lived and relatively stable and are, therefore, readily available for observation, analysis and systematic improvement. Well-established approaches are available for mapping and improving commercial chains (for example see Jones and Womack, 2002; Martichenko and Von Grabe, 2010). The challenge was to adapt these VCA techniques to disaster response where value chains are variable, temporary and, in many cases, quite short lived. A two-stage approach was adopted. First, post-event, retrospective analysis of previous responses was undertaken in order to develop an appropriate structure for the disaster response value chain analysis (DRVCA), and second, responses were mapped in real time as they occurred.

The first step in DRVCA is the development of a value chain 'current state map'. The aim of the map is to diagrammatically capture the most relevant features of the process. The map is structured on a number of levels:

- *The timeline*: The fulcrum of the DRVCA is a timeline that covers the period of the response. In relation to a rapid-onset natural disaster (eg an earthquake), the starting point for the timeline is the date at which the event occurs. In relation to slow onset disasters (eg flooding or conflict) the starting point is the date at which ShelterBox makes the decision to intervene. The timeline provides the critical reference point against which response activities are monitored.

- *The physical flow of goods*: Using a series of standard visual symbols, the movement of relief materials from sources of supply through to final distribution are tracked against the timeline, and evaluated using relevant performance indicators.

- *Staff deployment*: Similarly, the deployment of ShelterBox response teams is tracked, together with the objectives, accomplishments and costs of each team.

- *Coordination with other agencies*: As ShelterBox often works in conjunction with other relief agencies, the key interactions with partners are recorded.

- *Information flows*: Mapping of the information flow shows when, where and what information is collected; how, when and where it is transmitted; and for what purpose it is used. Mapping information flows is vital, as information availability and veracity are frequent causes of supply chain problems and delay.

- *Decision processes*: The efficacy of a deployment is fundamentally dependent on the timing and appropriateness of decisions regarding the structure and modus operandi of the value chain. Key decisions are mapped.

- *Key performance indicators*: A critical aspect of VCA is quantification of performance. Key performance indicators (KPIs) are developed to evaluate the efficiency and effectiveness of the individual processes within the chain. In addition, a restricted number of top level KPIs is developed to summarize the performance of the chain as a whole. Parameters include the number of families served, the timeliness of aid delivery, the number of staff deployed, the total cost of deployment and the number of shelters undistributed at the end of the deployment. These top level KPIs allow comparison between deployments, and also provide a basis for setting improvement targets.

The adoption of VCA as the methodology for evaluating deployments led to immediate benefits at ShelterBox. In the first instance, retrospective analysis of previous deployments identified a number of recurrent issues. For example: a lack of coordination between deployment of staff and deployment of equipment, meaning that staff teams were often in the field waiting for materials to arrive; delays in equipment transportation due to documentation problems; unacceptable levels of undistributed equipment at the end of the deployment; and the absence of standard procedures for needs assessment. Plans were put in place to address these and various other common issues.

Once the structure for the DRVCA was established, the next step was to move to real-time monitoring of deployments. The new IT system facilitated the capture of the relevant data from across the value chain thus enabling the current state map to evolve day-by-day during the course of a disaster. Furthermore, the production of the current state map was automated and displayed live on screens within the operations department. As a result, management had a concise, visual, overview of all relevant activity in the deployment, meaning that problems could be identified quickly and adjustments made to the relevant processes.

The core activity, indeed the raison d'être of ShelterBox, is to deliver specific sets of relief equipment, to specific groups of beneficiaries, in specific disasters. DRVCA provides an approach that directly addresses this core process in terms of planning, evaluation and improvement. As far as the authors are aware, ShelterBox is the first disaster relief organization to apply VCA, and the methodology described above continues to evolve with its application to each successive deployment.

Culture change

At the outset of the supply chain project there was little understanding in ShelterBox of the need for, and potential benefits of, an integrated approach to supply chain management, and certainly no appreciation of the potential benefits that lean concepts and tools could bring to a disaster relief organization. Furthermore, a recurrent complaint from staff was that they were unclear as to the strategic direction of the organization, and were disillusioned with a continual procession of improvement initiatives that seemed to have no coherent context. A variety of approaches were adopted in order to create a receptive context for the required organizational changes.

The overarching change strategy was the use of 'policy deployment' (Akao, 2004) which is another lean tool based on visual management. At the simplest level, policy deployment is manifest as a diagram that summarizes and quantifies the strategic aims and objectives, and cascades these down into operational activities, operational targets and improvement projects. The diagram is produced in a standardized format and displayed as a wallchart in each relevant department, so that staff can see how their daily operational activities, as well as the various improvement initiatives, contribute to achieving both supply chain and wider corporate objectives.

Another initiative in achieving change was the adoption of a standard approach to managing improvement initiatives. ShelterBox had always had a plethora of improvement projects but, typically, these were not well organized, lacked structure, were slow to progress, and were often never completed. A project management procedure, originated by Toyota and known as 'A3 management' (Shook, 2009) was introduced. This provides a standardized methodology for innovating, planning and problem-solving. Rigorous project plans are produced on A3 size paper which succinctly describe the background to the issue, current conditions, required outcomes, recommendations and implementation plans. Use of A3s brought a discipline to the improvement process.

A further significant factor in achieving change was the recruitment from the commercial world of a number of staff, including a new operations director. These individuals brought best practices and different thinking from environments beyond disaster relief and questioned some of the established practices that inevitably existed. New staff with specific humanitarian logistics expertise were also attracted from other aid organizations. At the same time, retention of many long-serving members of the operations team meant that the 'can-do' characteristic of ShelterBox's culture was not lost. As a result, an organizational culture slowly developed that was prepared to challenge its methods of operating, strive for continuous improvement in both strategy and operations, whilst simultaneously ensuring that responsiveness and minimal bureaucracy continued as key strengths. The urgency of individual deployments and the rapidly changing needs and circumstances in the wider disaster relief environment mean that such a culture is imperative for an organization such as ShelterBox.

Conclusion

This chapter has described the overall logic and structure used to bring a more cohesive approach to supply chain planning and improvement at ShelterBox, together with details of some of the specific initiatives that have been adopted.

The programme started with a three-month project in which consultants were engaged to review purchasing policies at ShelterBox. This was subsequently extended into a review of the wider supply chain which, over a period of some three years, moved from being seen as a supply chain improvement project, to becoming an ongoing supply chain transformational process that slowly became embedded in the organization's culture.

The logic of the improvement process was based on the Five Lean Principles and implemented using some of the many lean tools and techniques that have been developed and used in many commercial organizations throughout the world.

The first lean principle states that an organization needs to understand *value* from the point of view of the customer. ShelterBox now has a process in place to gain an ever-deeper understanding of beneficiary value for different groups of people in different environments and circumstances. It is also recognized that the value proposition will continually change both as needs and potential solutions develop.

The second lean principle highlights the need to understand the *value chain*, in other words all the steps necessary to bring relief products from sources of manufacture to families in disaster zones. A top level, big picture map visualized the ShelterBox supply network and, in so doing, highlighted a number of strategic issues and potential improvement opportunities. The supply network is comprised of many individual value chains that serve specific disasters with the specific products required. A disaster relief value chain analysis methodology was developed, and this now enables ShelterBox to undertake comprehensive, real-time, monitoring of individual deployments. This not only facilitates better management of deployments as they occur, but also provides relevant and consistent data for retrospective analysis and improvement of future responses.

The third lean principle of *flow* sets a clear objective when designing the supply chain so that the chain as a whole, and the individual functions within it, are configured to allow materials to move from origin to destination without delay, detours or other avoidable wastes. A variety of initiatives were introduced aimed at improving material flow, ranging from the strategic such as supplier partnerships and revised inventory positioning, to operational improvements in individual deployments such as better coordination of field staff and equipment delivery and improved procedures for management of documentation.

The fourth lean principle of *pull* sets the objective of only providing what beneficiaries actually require, when and where needed. It contrasts to 'push' systems, which have characterized many disaster responses and have resulted in well-documented accounts of inappropriate products, arriving at inappropriate times, in inappropriate volumes. The fundamental requirement in operating a pull system is the need to understand demand. The work on understanding beneficiary value contributes one element in understanding demand by determining the range of products required. The geography of disaster risk adds a second element to the demand picture, whilst a third element is the need to understand the volume of product required. For a small NGO such as ShelterBox, the total demand for aid typically far outstrips the resources available. The notion of deployment capacity was, therefore, used as a surrogate for demand when planning balanced supply chain capabilities.

The fifth lean principle sets the ambition of *perfection*. Initiatives adopted in this supply chain work slowly, engendering a culture of setting stretched targets and continuous improvement amongst staff at all levels within ShelterBox. Policy deployment created a clear vision of organizational and supply chain aims and how these could be achieved, backed by practical lean improvement techniques such as A3 project management. The introduction of new staff drawn from a variety of professional backgrounds, and from organizations in both the commercial and humanitarian sectors, also helped to invigorate the organization.

It is now recognized that supply chain management is the core activity at ShelterBox. Acquisition of materials and their delivery to beneficiaries is the raison d'être of the organization. The other functions in the organization, ranging from the vitally important fundraising through to financial management, human resources and external communications are all there in support of aid delivery. Continually improving supply chain performance at ShelterBox has twin benefits, not only enabling more beneficiaries to be served more effectively, but also providing evidence to donors of the efficient and judicious use of resources, which, in turn, will give confidence to ensure continued and increased financial support.

The ShelterBox 2017 strategic plan includes two ambitious aims: that ShelterBox will become the most effective and efficient provider of emergency shelter within the humanitarian sector; and that ShelterBox will be a leader in developing and sharing best practice in disaster relief. The work described in this chapter contributes to the achievement of both these aims.

Acknowledgements

The authors would like to thank the following: Michael Johns, Chief Operating Officer and Finance Director, ShelterBox, for having the foresight to instigate this initiative and his continuous encouragement throughout; Professor Alan Braithwaite, Chairman of LCP Consulting Ltd, for acting as a sounding board and source of wise advice throughout the project; Alf Evans, Head of Operations, ShelterBox, together with all of the operations team for embracing change.

References

Akao, Y (2004) *Hoshin Kanri: Policy deployment for successful TQM*, Productivity Press

INFORM (2016) Index for risk management published by the Interagency Standing Committee Task Team for Preparedness and Resilience and the European Commission [Online] http://www.inform-index.org/

Jones, D and Womack, J (2002) *Seeing the Whole: Mapping the extended value stream*, The Lean Enterprise Institute, Cambridge, MA

Martichenko, R and Von Grabe, K (2010) *Building a Lean Fulfilment Stream*, The Lean Enterprise Institute, USA

Pettit, S and Beresford, A (2005) Emergency relief logistics: An evaluation of military, non-military and composite response models, *International Journal of Logistics: Research and Applications*, 8(4)

Shook, J (2009) *Managing to Learn: Using the A3 management process to solve problems, gain agreement, mentor and lead*, The Lean Enterprise Institute, Cambridge, MA

UNHCR (2016) Figures at a glance [Online] http://www.unhcr.org/uk/figures-at-a-glance.html

Womack, J and Jones, D (2003) *Lean Thinking: Banish waste and create wealth in your corporation*, Simon and Schuster, New York

Emergency management and logistics responsiveness

13

A study of the Christchurch earthquakes, 2011

MARK WILSON, SHAUN FOGARTY, WALTER GLASS AND PAUL CHILDERHOUSE

Abstract

Effective emergency management in readiness and response phases before and after a disaster can often mean the difference between life and death. A key enabling factor is the logistics of deploying personnel, life-saving equipment and humanitarian materiél, and relief supplies to and within affected areas. Yet logistics as a function is often subordinated to other seemingly more pressing activities during a disaster and also in emergency management doctrine in general. As such, we examine New Zealand's civil defence and emergency management (CDEM) logistics capabilities and its response to an actual disaster event. We conducted a survey of 84 CDEM managers and specialists at national, regional and local levels. We supported this with a further seven face-to-face interviews with senior CDEM managers and triangulated our data against a review of secondary sources and academic literature. The devastating series of earthquakes that began in Christchurch on 22 February 2011 is the context we used to analyse the performance of the New Zealand's CDEM sector and its humanitarian logistics response function. We found that while New Zealand possesses a robust framework of emergency management legislation, a National CDEM Plan and related policies, the implementation and performance against this framework was fraught with deficiencies. At the time we highlighted a number of areas that required urgent policy attention to reduce future risk, and we revisit these to see what's changed. We argue that our findings have clear implications for emergency management and humanitarian logistics in developed countries.

Introduction

Emergency management (EM) is the creation of policies and plans of action to be implemented during a crisis or emergency in order to mitigate risk and socioeconomic loss for communities and countries. Within this broad EM framework is the study of humanitarian logistics (HL) that has steadily grown as a discipline over recent decades. HL examines the challenges of planning, implementing and controlling the efficient flow and storage of materiél and information from point of origin to point of consumption to provide relief to suffering populations. The range of HL activities is wide and will depend very much on the nature and the extent of the disaster, these factors being very difficult to predict. While the field has centred mainly on the domain of developing countries, a growing focus is on how so-called first world countries apply HL (Kovács and Tatham, 2009; New Zealand Government, 2010). An interesting question in this regard is whether the HL concepts and principles that have been evaluated for developing countries are equally applicable to developed nations, especially as these latter countries are generally viewed as being self-sufficient in managing disaster events with little need for external HL support. This was true for the Hurricane Katrina disaster in 2005, where the response and rebuild was very much a domestic effort. Yet, as an analysis of this event shows, there will always be room for improving disaster response and emergency relief systems (Lodree *et al*, 2012).

While a degree of self-sufficiency is desirable, on occasion events can be overwhelming. The Japanese tsunami in 2011 required significant international support and the reliance on the logistical efforts of global supply chains. This was also the case in New Zealand after the 2011 Christchurch earthquakes when many partner and friendly nations responded with assistance (McLean *et al*, 2012). It seems that the frequency of such events is increasing; however, more recent data demonstrates an actual decrease in the number of disasters worldwide, from a high of 433 in 2005 to 301 in 2016, and a commensurate decrease in fatalities and economic costs (Centre for Research on the Epidemiology of Disasters, 2016). Yet, they also note a regional increase in disasters in Asia in 2014–16. Thus, the field of HL will continue to be an important discipline to study.

Our intent is to assess New Zealand's CDEM logistics capabilities and its HL response to the 22 February 2011 magnitude 6.2 earthquake (and thousands of aftershocks) that devastated the city of Christchurch and its 320,000 inhabitants, killing 185 people and injuring another 6,000. The building and infrastructure damage was enormous, with an estimated US $40 billion of damage, making it the fifth most expensive insurance event in history. Eighty per cent of the city's water and sewerage systems were damaged, and 80–90 per cent of the buildings in the central business district needed to be demolished. Our interest is to examine how well HL operated during the critical few weeks after this event and to see if there are any gaps in the policy, doctrine and application of the EM framework. This work helps address the call for empirical studies of real life humanitarian logistics operations (Holguín-Veras, et al, 2012). Given that 'the scale and diversity of procurement and other logistics requirements after the February earthquake went far beyond anything that had been envisaged in local CDEM planning or even at a National level' (McLean et al, 2012: 158), we argue that there are some key lessons to be learned. As a result, we offer some insights to help emergency managers and HL planners build future capabilities for a more effective HL response.

The importance of the logistical response

Humanitarian logistics is a multifaceted and complex process. The function encompasses a vast range of activities including, but not limited to: preparedness, planning, procurement, contracting, all modes of transportation, warehousing, inventory management, information technology (IT), reverse logistics, base camps, accommodation provision, refugee/welfare centres, catering, food delivery, water distribution, global freight, shipping, containerization, consolidation and deconsolidation, tracking-and-tracing, and customs clearance. Logistics as a function is perhaps the most complex of all emergency management responses, yet it seems to be the 'poor cousin' when compared to other functions such as operations, planning and welfare. Indeed, logistics provides immediate short-term relief by saving lives, meeting basic human needs and protecting property. In a developing country, HL is the most expensive element, making up 80 per cent of the cost of a disaster relief event (Van Wassenhove, 2006). While this figure would be less in a developed country, the cost of relief logistic operations is not insignificant.

It is generally considered that the disaster phases of 'preparedness' and 'response' are where HL plays its most important role. In the preparedness (readiness) phase there are five building blocks that, if addressed effectively, can be the critical success elements of any disaster management event (see Figure 13.1). These five blocks interrelate and form the key dimensions that constitute 'preparedness', and later when added to the 'response phase', form the conceptual link between planning and response phases. Indeed, we note that logistics lies at the centre of this model and, based on the level of complexity of operations, how well this particular function is managed will have a major impact on the overall outcome.

In terms of managing this complexity, there is much that emergency managers can learn from business logisticians and vice versa, particularly in relation to contingency planning and building agile systems to quickly react to the changing environment. Previous work has identified five main strategies to help improve the management of HL (Thomas and Kopczak, 2005: 107–08). Of these, three deal directly with professionalization and drawing from commercial experience, these being: developing a professional logistics community, investing in standardized training and certification, and developing technological solutions. More recent work has also identified the need for professionalization in training and use of technology in

Figure 13.1 Five building blocks of preparedness

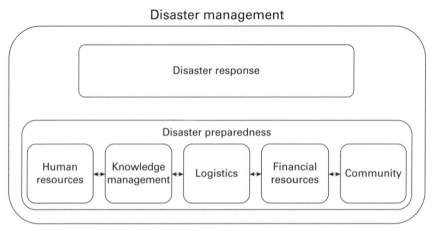

SOURCE Adapted from Tomasini and Van Wassenhove, 2009

disasters for health workers. It is argued that this training effort should mix commercial logistics best practice tempered with a deep understanding of the HL competencies needed for complex emergencies and disaster response (Herrgard, *et al*, 2016).

Indeed, commercial supply chain expertise, particularly the efficiencies of modern supply chain management (SCM) systems, can highlight the agile focus required to reduce delays, remove waste and streamline responsiveness. This is especially applicable to developed countries, which, in general, possess robust and extensive logistics systems, infrastructure, and also the presence of a number of local and global multifunctional logistics companies that could and should be called upon. For example, Lodree *et al* (2012) note the independent efforts of The Home Depot and Wal-Mart during Hurricane Katrina by pre-positioning essential commodities when the scale of the event began to be appreciated. They argue that these actions by commercial firms stood in stark contrast to the slow and uncoordinated efforts of the US Government's Federal Emergency Management Agency (FEMA). Hence, the 'agility' of a country's CDEM sector should also be a consideration and this agility is greatly facilitated by collaboration between commercial and humanitarian logisticians. This imperative also highlights the need for collaboration between those EM agencies, actors and organizations that have been charged with logistics. Indeed, this collaboration is seen as a key ingredient to success within HL (Cross, 2011; Seipel, 2011).

In order to consider the interplay that occurs across the spectrum of HL readiness and response, it is important to understand that a variety of organizations play different but critical roles. Cozzolino (2012) demonstrates this with a humanitarian relationship model (Figure 13.2) in which she highlights the various connections that exist between and across the different categories of emergency organizations. This model aptly demonstrates the complexity of linkages necessary between central/local governments, military, emergency organizations, aid agencies and the NGO community. It is interesting to note that commercial logistics companies are also a key element in this model, reflecting their extensive networks, assets, professionals and efficient supply chain approach.

Government, NGO, military and civilian cooperation

One of the key areas in assessing the logistical effectiveness of any nation's CDEM preparedness is the nature of inter-agency cooperation. In many cases non-governmental organizations (NGOs) constitute the main interface between the relief system and the beneficiaries, and often play the more

Figure 13.2   The emergency management relationship model

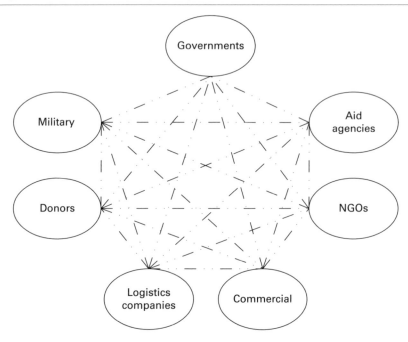

prominent role at the relief end of the supply chain alongside a nation's military forces. Seipel (2011) describes the cultural and operational challenges facing the NGO and military communities when attempting to cooperate with each other. Larson (2011) outlines how the four key principles of many NGOs – humanity, neutrality, impartiality and independence – will often become the obstacles that create challenges for interagency cooperation. He also argues that Kovács and Tatham (2009), while promoting the role of local chapters or national societies, have neglected the fact that many humanitarian NGOs are engaged primarily in 'development' aid as distinct from relief aid. Due to these challenges, Seipel (2011) has little faith in an integrated approach between NGOs, the military and private business in logistics unless there is a change of philosophy. Overcoming these philosophical differences will be an important step towards more effective supply chains in humanitarian aid operations, and that one 'actor' in any scenario should take lead 'ownership' or responsibility in order to facilitate coordination. Who takes this lead role has often proved a sticking point in civilian/military/commercial relationships.

Yet, encouragingly, NGOs, military and commercial entities have been dealing with each other at an increasing rate, particularly since the Boxing Day Asian tsunami of 2004. This cooperation does achieve success, particularly when staff are trained professionally in logistics and supply chain management technology and operations. Blansjaar and van der Merwe (2011) support this by highlighting the developments in various agencies, including OXFAM and the World Food Programme (WFP), who have increasingly provided professional development for their supply chain staff. Seipel (2011) also calls on the military to increase their understanding of the philosophical mindsets of the vast array of NGOs and commercial entities with which they may be dealing, and also professionally respect the agenda that many of these organizations work under. Cross (2011) goes further when examining this issue in relation to British military relations with NGOs. He promotes the need for military personnel to be embedded into other agencies such as the Department for International Development (DFID) and local councils to ensure that the British military can better assimilate into the operational response to domestic and international crises.

New Zealand's CDEM policy framework

The New Zealand government has adopted a 'whole of government' (WoG) approach to humanitarian assistance where all branches of government are mandated to collaborate in any emergency. Two key principles derived from international norms guide this WoG approach: first, maintenance of State sovereignty and, second, respect for international humanitarian law and instruments. Fortunately, prior to the 2011 Christchurch earthquakes, New Zealand had implemented a robust framework of legislation, policies and documents in relation to CDEM preparedness, response and recovery. The main Civil Defence Emergency Management Act (2002) (New Zealand Government, 2002) provides the powers, strategy and response frameworks. Essentially, the Act establishes a hierarchy of approving and responding authorities from local (localized emergency), to group (regional or provincial emergency – there are currently 16 regional CDEM groups that cover the whole of New Zealand) to the national level, all headed by the Minister's Office (MCDEM). Included in the Act, among other areas, is the formation of director's guidelines (a form of *aide memoire*) to assist those responsible for various functions during an emergency. Yet, it is interesting to note that a logistics director's guideline did not exist prior to the 2011 Christchurch earthquakes. That is not to say that emergency managers did not think of HL at all, they just had not thought about it enough. This, in many ways, reflected the low esteem and 'poor cousin' status of this important function.

Another important feature of the CDEM Act (2002) was the formation of what are known as lifeline utility groups. These groups are made up of public and private utility operators such as power, water and telecommunications companies that collaborate with scientists and emergency managers to improve the resilience of infrastructure, as well as contributing to emergency preparation and responses. The Act imposes certain obligations on those named members (see Part B, Schedule 1 of the Act). These duties relate to having plans for building in resilience, participating in preparedness and EM exercises, and responding during emergency events with a coordinated inter-agency approach. Yet the Act does not require the commitment of any resources or assets beyond what is needed to maintain their own services, albeit at a reduced level. A notable exclusion from previous versions of the CDEM plan was the fast moving consumer goods (FMCG) companies (such as supermarket chains) that supply nearly 95 per cent of New Zealand's food. This is an interesting oversight, as food is one of those essential relief supplies delivered by HL.

Hence, it is against this framework that we examine New Zealand's level of logistical performance during the 2011 Christchurch earthquakes and its preparedness for future events. While we note that recent reviews and assessments have documented a variety of deficiencies or concerns which indicate that the application of these policies can be held to question in a wider sense (McLean *et al*, 2011; MCDEM, 2012a, 2012b, 2012c; NZDF 2012), our concern is specifically with respect to HL. Thus, we derive the following main questions:

- How well was HL managed and coordinated at the various CDEM levels during the 2011 Christchurch earthquakes?
- How was the logistics/supply chain management expertise of the lifeline utility groups, Defence Forces and commercial companies utilized during the response phase?

Survey, interviews and reviews

To answer these important questions, we first surveyed a wide cross-section of 84 professionals across the CDEM sector. Second, a series of one-on-one in-depth interviews was conducted with a further seven leading figures within the CDEM sector. We then compared our findings against reputable secondary sources such as policy reviews and post-event reports. The people with whom we talked were chosen based on their professional experience within the CDEM sector and, where possible, consisted of individuals who

Table 13.1　Survey respondents by CDEM sector

	CDEM	Police	NZDF	OGA	Commercial Industry	NGO	Total
Respondents:	57	5	5	10	3	4	84
Percentage:	68%	6%	6%	12%	3.5%	4.5%	100%

NOTE CDEM = civil defence and emergency management agencies; NZDF = New Zealand Defence Force; OGA = other government agencies; NGO = non-governmental organizations

Table 13.2　Anonymized list of the in-depth interviews

Organization	Leadership level
1 Department of Prime Minister and Cabinet	Executive level
2 Ministry of Civil Defence Emergency Management	Executive level
3 Regional Civil Defence Emergency Management	Executive level
4 New Zealand Defence Force	Executive level
5 Regional Lifelines Group	Senior management
6 Major NGO in New Zealand	Executive level
7 Ministry of Civil Defence Emergency Management	Senior management

had first-hand experience in natural disaster events. Table 13.1 details the categories of respondents and the percentage that each group contributed to the final total.

An important aim of the senior leadership interviews was to either validate or offer contrary opinions on the data generated from our initial survey. An overview of those interviewed and a high-level description of their position is provided in Table 13.2.

Humanitarian logistics management and response

While the overall study encompassed a much wider view of CDEM activities, we limit our comments here to the survey/interview results that relate to our main questions noted above. Turning to the first question, we ask how well was logistics managed and coordinated at the various levels of CDEM during the 2011 Christchurch earthquakes?

Humanitarian logistics management

Our analysis of the CDEM community in New Zealand shows that there is a weak understanding of what 'logistics' means and how the community should attempt to understand the terminology associated with this critical function. Key logistics management functions were examined for their effectiveness, as well as taking a 'bigger picture' understanding of logistics assets that have the potential to be called upon. The survey contained a number of questions related to logistics management and coordination, as well as a number of secondary supporting questions that also contributed to our views. Figure 13.3 shows the responses to the question related to the general management of logistics in the planning and response phases.

At the national level, respondents generally felt logistics was handled satisfactorily despite the lack of clear formal doctrine and policy. At the group level, the management of logistics was regarded as similar or slightly better, and comments reflected the ability of regional logistics arrangements to be established and tested. It was at the local level where the general management of logistics was seen as more satisfactory than the other two levels, most likely due to coordination being more straightforward locally. Survey comments provided a number of themes. Most notable was that logistics was often seen as the 'poor cousin' within the CDEM sector, and is often regarded as secondary to the other main functions such as plans and operations. Forward planning of logistics (in the preparedness phase) was also identified as an area of under-performance, particularly at the local

Figure 13.3   How well do you consider logistics to be managed generally at the various CDEM levels?

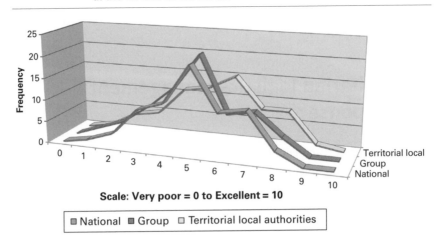

Scale: Very poor = 0 to Excellent = 10

■ National ■ Group □ Territorial local authorities

level where respondents felt that it was not afforded sufficient priority or resourcing. This view is consistent with the results of other survey questions reporting that respondents regarded the logistics 'planning function' as rather less than satisfactory.

Interviews with senior officials acknowledged that logistics is commonly the weak link within CDEM as it is often not well understood or given priority due to its inherent supporting role to operations and plans. One CDEM official stated that maintaining situational awareness of the supply chain could often be very challenging. Purchasing and distribution were regarded as key areas where CDEM logistics can make an important impact. It was also stated that situational awareness of equipment, and the supply chain procedures with which to procure and distribute items, are areas that require further work (this section in the current guide to the National CDEM Plan is under development). A consistent view of respondents was that speed of response was the 'make or break' for any logistical effort. This view is supported in the literature, noting the need for speed in deployment and supply chain awareness, not just in humanitarian events, but also in commercial logistics operations (Van Wassenhove, 2006). Indeed, speed and urgency in collaboration amongst initial responders is the real weak point of most CDEM logistics responses (James, 2008).

Further results indicate that logistics is seen as 'under-committed' or 'poorly resourced' alongside other CDEM functions. One survey question explored this in finer detail by asking, '*When comparing logistics to the other functions within the Coordinated Incident Management System* (operations, plans, welfare), *how would you rate the attention/resourcing it receives against what it requires?*' Sixty-five per cent of respondents considered that logistics garners lower levels of attention than the operations, planning, or welfare functions of CDEM. There was also a common view that a review of national CDEM logistics is required, and that a section needed to be included in the National CDEM Plan as a matter of urgency.

The respected McLean Review (McLean *et al*, 2012) of the Christchurch earthquake response was also critical of the lack of a logistics doctrinal section to the plan, and recommended that this be attended to as a matter of urgency. The Ministry of CDEM accepted this recommendation, and it was also widely acknowledged at the time by CDEM leadership that a logistics director's guideline was way overdue (MCDEM, 2012d: 12; the various iterations of this logistics director's guidelines have been reviewed and referenced as part of this study). This does, however, cast a stark spotlight on the culture and attitudes within the CDEM sector prior to the 2011 earthquakes that caused this vital omission in overall policy.

These observations are consistent with another theme that emerged relating to the lack of trained logistics professionals. Within CDEM this often eventuates from a deficiency in actual training or the appointment of inexperienced or untrained staff to logistics roles where 'a gap' needed to be filled. Often these staff members (from the council, police or other agencies), particularly at the local level, will have dual responsibilities where their 'business as usual' roles take precedence over their CDEM roles.

Assessment of the humanitarian logistics response

Given this lack of overarching logistics doctrine and policy and its relatively low priority, we asked, how well did CDEM logistics respond during an actual crisis? The survey asked questions that were related specifically to the 2011 Christchurch earthquakes and the coordination of logistics from a general perspective. Respondents were asked whether they agreed with the statement shown in Figure 13.4. The results demonstrate that an overwhelming 94 per cent of respondents agreed with the statement, with over one-quarter (26 per cent) of them giving the highest grading of 10 for 'strongly agree' showing that there was much room for improvement. This is a stark assessment.

Specific comments focused on the need for better freight reception, loading and distribution, and the critical requirement for experienced staff to be appointed to these responsibilities. A theme from respondents was that

Figure 13.4 Could logistics have been better coordinated during the 22 February 2011 Christchurch earthquake?

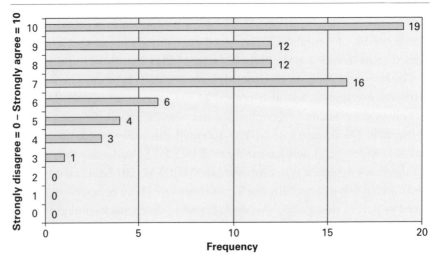

military logistics staff could play an important secondment role in relation to these functions, as could experienced logistics and SCM staff from the commercial sector. Related to the movement of equipment, a number of comments were offered which reflected concerns over the inadequate information management systems used to handle logistical requirements and tracking. This observation aligned to observations made in McLean Review (McLean *et al*, 2012), which was critical of the disparate nature of the logistics function during the response phase.

The survey also asked questions relating to the coordination and management of logistics at the three CDEM levels during the earthquakes. Just over half (51 per cent) of respondents considered logistics at the national level was below the average, while at the group level logistics coordination and management were considered to be slightly worse, with 56 per cent of respondents giving a rating of satisfactory or below satisfactory. However, local level logistics coordination and management fared slightly better, with 57 per cent of respondents considering that logistics was of a satisfactory or better standard. Recent research also argues that decentralized logistics systems are better able to respond to emergencies due to dispersion, flexibility and easier coordination (Charles *et al*, 2016). Overall, these results highlight a less than impressive HL response when the policies and plans were actually implemented on a large scale.

An oddity within the management structures put in place at the time of the Christchurch earthquakes was the *ad hoc* combining of the group level Emergency Coordination Centre (ECC) and the local level Emergency Operations Centre (EOC), into a combined operations centre called the Christchurch Response Centre (CRC). This clearly went against emergency management doctrine and had the effect of co-locating the Canterbury CDEM group logistics staff and the Christchurch City Council CEDM (local) logistics staff within the same organization. Yet, each staff group was given different responsibilities, namely the planning and operations functions respectively. These important functions were thus siloed within the same headquarters, and staff lacked familiarity with other staff and procedures.

We enquired about the efficacy of this in the survey by asking if a single emergency operations centre would assist in avoiding duplication and improve collaboration. Interestingly, despite the problems experienced, we found that 70 per cent of respondents agreed with this statement, with 45 per cent rating it between 8 to 10 (strongly disagree = 0, to strongly agree = 10). Thus the results were supportive of this concept in theory, despite it contradicting established doctrine and aggravating the dysfunctional and siloed aspects of the CRC organizational structure. However, it is interesting to note that the McLean Review (McLean *et al*, 2012) eventually recommends that, given the opportunities that the Canterbury rebuild (as opposed to response) presents, a single combined EOC should be established for future CDEM operations in Canterbury.

Overall, the data shows that the CDEM logistics response to the Christchurch earthquakes were less than satisfactory. It notes that HL efforts were reactionary as staff tried to cope as best they could to overcome issues that centred on the lack of logistics preparedness, the lack of a logistics director's guideline and procedures, unfamiliarity, siloed functions and the confusing *ad hoc* organizational structure of the CRC.

Utilization of logistics and SCM assets and expertise

The second part of our study focused on the use, or not, of the logistics and supply chain assets and management expertise of defence, NGOs and/or commercial companies during the response phase of the earthquakes. We were attempting to see if CDEM managers and policy were maximizing the use of logistics assets and expertise that resided in other sectors. Given the deficiencies noted in the previous section, we believe this to be a very pertinent topic.

Utilizing logistics and SCM expertise

The survey posed a number of questions directly related to this issue. We asked, '*How good is the level of understanding of logistics assets available domestically and internationally in the region that could be planned for in readiness and requested in response to a CDEM event?*' While 16 per cent regarded this understanding as satisfactory, a sizeable number of respondents (47 per cent) indicated that they felt this understanding was less than satisfactory. The general opinion voiced in the comments was that the location and utility of logistics assets/skills, and the associated corporate knowledge, was not well understood across the CDEM sector for both the preparation and response phases. Only a few individuals across the CDEM sector possess such knowledge, thus creating an institutional risk should they ever leave. Some respondents felt strongly that the centralized Emergency Management Information System (EMIS) should be the prime repository for this knowledge, but strong processes would need to be established to ensure the collection and sustainment of up-to-date information. This is particularly true for plant and equipment that are needed for a response but are privately held in commercial companies and lifeline utilities. Although some work has since been completed by CDEM groups to conduct surveys of assets in regions, to date, a sector-wide system to provide a high level of visibility of assets and skills does not exist in New Zealand.

Following on from this, we questioned if logistics personnel, skills and expertise from the defence, NGO and commercial sectors were utilized and optimized before and during a disaster event? We asked respondents, '*From a CDEM perspective, is good use made of the logistics expertise within the defence/NGO/commercial sector?*' A clear majority of 64 per cent rated this as unsatisfactory or poor. Many respondents, as well as some of those interviewed later, considered that this is an area where CDEM logistics could advance rapidly if there was greater use of commercial and private expertise from logistics and supply chain professionals. For example, some of the common themes reflected in survey comments were:

'No I don't think it is something that is utilized well. There is expertise out there but the CDEM sector have not worked together sufficiently yet to plan for utilizing their services better in a time of need.' (Interview 2)

'I believe it is getting better since the Canterbury event but I still believe that there is a huge gap between CDEM and the logistics professionals.' (Interview 4)

A senior executive interviewed from the Department of the Prime Minister was strongly of the view that all public and commercial expertise should be harnessed wherever possible.

'Logistics is the strongest form of resilience that we have as a country. We should be thinking how to improve resilience and what could we do to make sure logistics functions well.' (Interview 1)

This view is supported by the Fritz Institute (Thomas and Kopczak, 2005) who argue that corporate logisticians should be key contributors by sharing successful approaches to interacting as a community. Here, FMCG companies (such as supermarket chains) can play a critical role (Larson, 2011). There are two major FMCG companies in New Zealand, Progressive Enterprises and Foodstuffs Ltd, that dominate the country's food supply chains. It is worth noting that interviewees reflected on the strong communication and collaborative support that formed between these two major providers (otherwise fierce competitors) in recognition of the potential for food shortages in the population following the Christchurch earthquakes.

Progressive Enterprises lost most of its South Island storage capacity as a result of damage to its main distribution centre in Christchurch, and as a result had to manage distribution from its North Island hub. Foodstuffs had to manage the entire South Island from their secondary Dunedin satellite warehouse.

By virtue of professional communication and cooperation the FMCG companies generally managed to deliver most of what was needed to their customers, but not without overcoming some very challenging distribution and warehousing hurdles. Of note was that the main railway link (North) was not operational until three weeks after the February earthquakes. Holguín-Veras *et al* (2012) observe that, while it is much easier to transport supplies *to* large urban areas (as was the case in Christchurch where the national road network was mostly functional), it is the 'last mile' distribution *within* the city that was hugely problematic. Indeed, much of their success can be put down to the expert management and professional staff-work that played out during the first few days and weeks after the earthquakes. This cooperation greatly facilitated the health and wellbeing of the citizens and also, to a large degree, negated the need to mobilize food aid supply chains through the CDEM framework or to ask NGO aid agencies for help.

What is interesting is that one of these FMCGs companies was approached early on by CDEM officials (personal communication, 2016) with the view that they might have to take over the management and distribution of food supplies to the city. It is extremely fortunate that they retreated from this position as one could only imagine the havoc that partially trained CDEM logistics staff (and not enough of them anyway) would have caused trying to run an unfamiliar, complex and highly efficient commercial supply chain system! Indeed, what was evident was the relatively limited connections CDEM had with these FMCGs and the laissez faire approach adopted by CDEM highlighted by: 'They'll let us know if they need help' (survey comment). This awkwardness was due in part to FMCG companies, at that time, not being included under the lifeline utilities framework. Thus, relationship building, contingency planning and exercises are all areas where emergency managers and the wider CDEM sector can play a lead coordinating role with commercial entities.

We would argue that, in general, this points to a major weakness in the CDEM response plans and capabilities. Communication and tactful collaboration between key entities, while mitigating commercial sensitivities, is the space that national and group CDEM, together with lifeline groups, should actively engage in the quest for improving readiness and response to major disasters. What is concerning is that neither of the two FMCG companies mentioned above are included as lifeline group entities, nor does the CDEM Act (2002) stipulate FMCG food companies as organizations that should be. Currently, the two FMCGs are listed as 'voluntary' lifeline utility members but with no statutory obligations. This is an area that could be easily addressed with a degree of enhanced relationship management. As one survey respondent offered:

> 'There is a need to develop a logistics advisory group at the CDEM group level, along the same lines of the existing welfare or lifeline groups. To involve organizations within the group area with a supply and distribution specialty, ie Fonterra, Foodstuffs [one of the two FMCGs], Air NZ, freight companies.' (Survey comment)

The McLean Review (McLean *et al*, 2012) also noted this theme of under-utilizing the commercial expertise available in New Zealand. It cited the example of the General Manager for Toll Logistics New Zealand Ltd, who assisted the Christchurch Response Centre only by chance when he offered his services as a volunteer. His efforts were eventually described as making a significant contribution to procurement and transportation during the disaster event (McLean *et al*, 2012). In summary, we note some serious deficiencies here in the CDEM framework in terms of utilizing defence, NGO and commercial expertise at all levels.

Coordination with lifeline utility groups

Another key survey question asked respondents to consider the role that lifeline groups can play in the CDEM's readiness and response phases. The question asked was, '*From a logistics perspective how well integrated are CDEM and lifeline utilities at the national and group levels?*' The regional lifeline groups have generally been established to mirror the 16 regional CDEM groups throughout New Zealand. Part B, Schedule 1 to the CDEM Act details which utilities are subject to the provision of the Act, and defines their legislative responsibilities. Survey results show that respondents consider the integration between CDEM and lifeline groups to be more positive than not. At the national level 28 per cent believed the relationship is satisfactory, while a further 47 per cent believed it to be either good or very good.

At the group level, acknowledging that some groups will have better relationships with lifeline groups than others, 20 per cent considered the relationship to be satisfactory, while 62 per cent rated the logistics integration as either good or very good. It is not surprising that this should be the case at the group level as both CDEM and lifeline groups are mandated to have workable contingency plans at the regional level that have 'buy-in' from both sides. Yet, many stated that much more, that went beyond the minimal mandated requirements of the Act, needed to be done. Respondents who provided supporting comments stated views consistent with the following themes:

> 'I know the lifelines function is improving. This is a key relationship in terms of logistics.' (Survey comment)
>
> 'Lifeline utilities and CDEM should be working much more closely in planning and exercises. This deficiency is very hard to bridge when not in response mode.' (Survey comment)

The reality, however, is that the proactive input and the commitment levels of lifeline utility companies has to be actively nurtured and promoted. This has yet to be fully implemented and is another area of weakness in the overall CDEM framework.

Discussion and recommendations

In the New Zealand context, and the 2011 Christchurch earthquake response in particular, logistics is clearly seen by those in the wider emergency management sector as the 'poor cousin' of other CDEM functions. The study shows this problem is well recognized and acknowledged within CDEM, but little seems to be done to change this position (McLean *et al*, 2012). If not addressed over the longer term, logistics will continue to suffer the same problems of under-performance and lack of coordination that occurred following the Christchurch earthquakes.

Lack of understanding and appreciation of the importance of logistics is reflected in the inadequate professional development provided to those holding logistics appointments. A common observation by respondents was that people without appropriate logistical skills often fill the logistics roles. Indeed, an individual observation (personal communication, 2016) was that often the manning of the 'logistics desk' at the National Crisis Management Centre (Beehive) was done by people from the police or fire service or aged volunteers – all of whom appeared woefully unskilled in logistics and supply chain management, despite their good intentions. It was observed that many CDEM staff were not interested in the logistics role as most EM people want to be on the frontline as befits their training and, perhaps, their self-image. The exception to this was the Defence Force staff who had been well trained, but did not possess civilian or commercial experience. The observation was that there were no commercial logisticians amongst the CDEM staff. They concluded that there was little or no forward planning for logistics and supply chain management skills, and that the MCDEM did not possess the expertise in-house. This supports our analysis that professional development is deficient in various areas, particularly logistics. Breaking this circle should be a priority for CDEM leadership across the three levels of management. Indeed, it seems nonsensical that logistics does not receive the level of importance it warrants.

The reputation and professional effectiveness of logistics as a CDEM function needs to be addressed urgently. Fortunately some concrete measures have been put in place recently, such as the long desired CDEM logistics director's guideline. This guideline has evolved over time from the initial two page outline, to the current 116 page guideline (DGL 17/5 dated June 2015, MCDEM, 2015). This guide provides an overview of the logistics function, the nine sub-functions and how these are applied in the CDEM context. It also provides guidance in terms of roles, responsibilities and suggested templates and processes. Whilst this is a clear improvement over the pre-earthquake situation, we note that the position of logistics manager is 'non-statutory' (p.3), meaning that the role carries limited powers. Furthermore, there is no mention at all in the guideline of the need for CDEM to pre-position emergency supplies and warehouses around the country or even centrally. The lack of any policy or strategic directive relating to emergency relief supply is surprising and runs counter to initiatives in other developed countries such as Queensland in Australia (Wilson et al, 2018).

To help address these issues, we argue for the establishment of a logistics advisory group within CDEM, similar to that in other CDEM functions, which will enhance the ability to make progress. This group would be responsible for advice, advocacy and the dissemination of logistics policy, guidelines and training. Once logistics guidelines have been developed, these need to be implemented through controllers and relevant CDEM staff to ensure the processes and plans are put in place. Any logistics processes need to have support and engagement from all CDEM staff, NGOs, commercial and essential lifeline utility companies if they are to have any chance of success (Lee, 2010). A key task for this advisory group would be ensuring that adequately trained and experienced logistics and supply chain management staff are available at all times both within CDEM, and also drawn from lifeline utility groups, Defence Forces, NGOs and commercial entities as needed.

The importance of utilizing the expertise of the commercial sector was noted in the survey. New Zealand is a market-driven economy that relies heavily on the commercial sector to manage the 'backbone' of the country's infrastructure. Government departments are no longer resourced with surplus assets or staff with which to respond to a major disaster event. Apart from the Defence Force (which has also significantly diminished in size over the past decade), commercial companies are the ones who are looked to for a response with appropriate equipment and expertise during a time of need. This was the case during the Christchurch earthquakes where commercial electricity, water, transport, heavy equipment and FMCG grocery companies were, perhaps overly, relied upon as first responders. Therefore, managing CDEM's relationship with these organizations is crucial, but it is also just as important during the readiness phase of CDEM strategy. The McLean Review (McLean *et al*, 2012) was highly critical in this regard noting that the commercial sector's logistics expertise was scarcely used in the Christchurch earthquake response, and had a senior commercial logistician not volunteered his time, the commercial sector may hardly have been used at all.

Across New Zealand many commercial lifeline utility companies have excellent logistics and supply chain management expertise. They also have a detailed knowledge of what high-value logistics assets/equipment they possess and where this could be accessed. It is not suggested that CDEM should own these assets, although there is legislation that allows for requisitioning if required. Rather, a general understanding of the assets' location, and whether they can be utilized during a major disaster event, would provide a high level of situational awareness, which is essential for senior leadership decision making. Gaining this visibility (through the EMIS) would also provide access to the expertise that now sits largely within the commercial sector or the Defence Forces. *A priori* arrangements need to be in place to share and collaborate, not just in the response phase of a disaster as it is within this readiness phase that preparation, training, exercises and desktop simulations occur, ensuring that every stakeholder is well prepared for a variety of potential events.

We would further argue that greater clarity be given to the roles and responsibilities of those essential services that are, or should be, designated as lifeline unities. It is interesting to note that the Canterbury CDEM site (Canterbury CDEM, 2014) listed the following lifeline utility groups for the Canterbury Region at the time the major earthquakes took place:

- all local body authorities (local governing councils), this includes:
  - potable water supply;
  - wastewater (sewerage);

- stormwater or drainage;
- roading;
- solid waste;

- New Zealand Transport Agency (NZTA);

- Christchurch International Airport Ltd;

- the two ports – Littleton Port Coy and Primeport in Timaru;

- railways – Toll Rail Ltd;

- power generator companies and power distributor companies;

- major petroleum companies (Mobil, BP, etc);

- LPG gas companies;

- telecommunication providers;

- state-owned television and radio stations.

While this list would seem to cover most, if not all, of the essential services, assets and supplies needed to sustain a large metropolitan population, we note one glaring omission. We found that while water, power, fuel, mobility and communication are covered, there was no mention of food! Interestingly, the original Act did not see the need to include the two major FMCG companies – Progressive Enterprises and Foodstuffs Cooperative. This we consider to be a somewhat serious oversight, yet the National CDEM Office justified the omission by arguing that these commercial companies would be able to respond and support the population on their own and this attitude was confirmed by our research. This seems somewhat *ad hoc,* and given the centrality of food for survival, to place the task of managing this vital humanitarian need outside of the CDEM framework smacks of a lack of imagination.

Our interviews with the logistics manager for Progressive Enterprises (personal communication, 2016) and also the GM supply chain for Foodstuffs Cooperative (personal communication, 2017) confirmed this. They also confirmed that neither companies were part of any preparation or planning with the CDEM sector, nor considered as lifeline utilities. This is not to suggest that these two companies did not respond adequately, nor fully cooperate with the CDEM sector when asked, indeed they did so willingly. In fact, both companies incurred significant non-recoverable expenses assisting in the response. What is interesting is that the FMCG sector and both these companies have now been 'invited' to join the lifeline utility (regional) grouping (Canterbury CDEM, 2014). However, the plan notes that participation is still voluntary. In our opinion, it would seem justified that these two major FMCG companies be mandated to participate in the national lifeline utility group, and henceforth be integrated into future CDEM planning and preparedness policies and procedures.

Given our findings, we offer the following main areas as needing the most urgent attention:

1 Formation of a logistics advisory group at the national level (doctrine, policy, training and publications).

2 Equalize the status and resourcing of the logistics function vis-à-vis operations, plans and other major functions.

3 Integration of commercial/defence/NGO logistics expertise and business best practices throughout the three levels of CDEM.

4 Professionalization of logistics and supply chain management training and development for all CDEM logistics staff.

5 Mandate the two major FMCG companies in New Zealand as essential lifeline utilities.

Our findings validate the earlier work by Thomas and Kopczak (2005) concerning the need for effective management and organization of HL. The commentary by James (2008) and Tomasini and Van Wassenhove (2009) regarding the need for performance indicators and lead-time reduction is also substantiated and endorsed.

Much has been written regarding the need to utilize the logistics and supply chain management expertise of the commercial sector. Our findings also reinforce Seipel's (2011) research, highlighting the need to proactively manage the engagement between agencies, NGOs and the commercial organizations.

It is hoped that the results of this study will not only add to the debate, but also make a very meaningful contribution to enhancing New Zealand's emergency management logistics capabilities. Indeed, post the 2011 Christchurch earthquakes, the Department of the Prime Minister and Cabinet (DPMC) created a new National Security System (NSS) to guide the response to emergencies and threats (New Zealand Government, 2011). The NSS sets out the ministerial level responsibilities for a coordinated WoG response and helps guide decision making in highly complex, life-threating situations. This grouping of ministers is called the Cabinet Committee on Domestic and External Security Coordination (DESC). The various working groups and CEOs of commercial utility companies (lifeline groups) all report to the DESC. The New Zealand Defence Forces have developed their own doctrine within this NSS framework.

As such, we acknowledge that many of the issues we have highlighted in this study were not new nor a surprise to those within the CDEM sector. It would be wrong to suggest that they were ignorant of these and have not considered their implications, as work on these areas has been ongoing since at least 2005 (personal communication, 2016). What we bemoan is the slow progress of development of logistics policy and professional development, and the persistent attitude toward HL as an awkward relative that people cannot easily dismiss, but would rather not talk to.

Finally, we found that New Zealand did, indeed, possess a robust CDEM framework and policies prior to the 2011 Christchurch earthquakes following the introduction of the CDEM Act in 2002. This Act was revised in 2008 but, as we have seen, still falls somewhat short in the areas of HL operations in the response phase, and also the omission of food as a HL lifeline commodity. The Act will be revised and reissued again before the end of 2018. It is hoped that this time the lessons from the Christchurch earthquakes will have been fully incorporated into CDEM arrangements, thus addressing the HL shortfalls noted in this study.

References

Blansjaar, M and van der Merwe, C (2011) The importance of information technology in humanitarian supply chains: Opportunities and challenges in the Helios project, in *Humanitarian Logistics: Meeting the challenge of preparing for and responding to disasters*, ed MG Christopher and PH Tatham, pp 47–63, Kogan Page, London

Canterbury Civil Defence and Emergency Management (CDEM) Group (2014) Canterbury Civil Defence Emergency Management – Group Plan [Online] http://cdemcanterbury.govt.nz/media/34987/canterbury-cdem-group-plan-2014.pdf (accessed 17 August 2017)

Centre for Research on the Epidemiology of Disasters (CRED) (2016) *Cred Crunch 45* [Online] http://cred.be/sites/default/files/CredCrunch45.pdf (accessed 28 August 2017)

Charles, A, Lauras, M, Van Wassenhove, LN, and Dupont, L (2016) Designing an efficient humanitarian supply network, *Journal of Operations Management*, 47, pp 58–70

Cozzolino, A (2012) *Humanitarian Logistics: Cross-sector cooperation in disaster relief management*, Springer, Berlin

Cross, T (2011) Disaster agencies and military forces – not such strange bedfellows after all! In *Humanitarian Logistics: Meeting the challenge of preparing for and responding to disasters*, ed MG Christopher and PH Tatham, pp 233–48, Kogan Page, London

Herrgard, MM, Rabe, APJ, Lo, S, Ragazzoni, L and Burke, FM (2016) Building resilience by professionalization of healthcare workers through technological innovations, *International Journal of Disaster Risk Reduction*, **22**, pp 246–48

Holguín-Veras, J, Jaller, M, Van Wassenhove, LN, Perez, N and Wachtendorf, T (2012) On the unique features of post-disaster humanitarian logistics, *Journal of Operations Management*, 30(7/8), pp 494–506

James, E (2008) *Managing Humanitarian Relief: An operational guide for NGOs*, Practical Action/Intermediate Technology, Warwickshire, UK

Kovács, G and Tatham, PH (2009) Responding to disruptions in the supply network – from dormant to action, *Journal of Business Logistics*, 30(2), pp 215–29

Larson, P (2011) Risky business: What humanitarians can learn from business logisticians – and vice versa, in *Humanitarian Logistics: Meeting the challenge of preparing for and responding to disasters*, ed MG Christopher and PH Tatham, pp 15–31, Kogan Page, London

Lee, B-Y (2010) Working together, building capacity: A case study of civil defence emergency management in New Zealand, *Journal of Disaster Research*, 5(5), pp 565–76

Lodree, EJ, Ballard, KN and Song, CH (2012) Pre-positioning hurricane supplies in a commercial supply chain, *Socio-Economic Planning Sciences*, 46(4), pp 291–305

McLean, I, Oughton, D, Ellis, S, Wakelin, B and Rubin, CB (2012) *Review of the Civil Defence Emergency Management Response to the 22 February Christchurch Earthquake*, The McLean Report, New Zealand Government

MCDEM (2012a) *CDEM Capability Assessment Report: Part 1, April 2012*, Ministry of Civil Defence and Emergency Management, Wellington, NZ

MCDEM (2012b) *CDEM Capability Assessment Report: Part 2, April 2012*, Ministry of Civil Defence and Emergency Management, Wellington, NZ

MCDEM (2012c) *Corrective Action Plan – following the review of the civil defence emergency management response to the 22 February 2011 Christchurch earthquake*, Ministry of Civil Defence and Emergency Management, Wellington, NZ

MCDEM (2012d) *Cabinet Paper: Review of the civil defence emergency management response to the 22 February 2011 Christchurch earthquake*, Ministry of Civil Defence and Emergency Management, Wellington, NZ

MCDEM (2015) *Logistics in CDEM: Directors guidelines for civil defence and emergency management groups* (DGL 17/5, dated June 2015) [Online] http://www.civildefence.govt.nz/assets/Uploads/logistics-dgl/DGL-17-15-Logistics.pdf (accessed 20 July 2017)

NZDF (2012) Humanitarian assistance and disaster relief aide-memoire – September 2012, New Zealand Defence Force, Wellington, NZ

New Zealand Government (2002) *Civil Defence Emergency Management Act, 2002* Wellington, NZ [Online] http://www.legislation.govt.nz/ (accessed 14 Jul 2016)

New Zealand Government (2010) *Defence White Paper 2010* [Online] http://www.defence.govt.nz/reports-publications/defence-white-paper-2010/contents.html (accessed 13 Aug 2014)

New Zealand Government (2011) *New Zealand's National Security System* [Online] http://www.dpmc.govt.nz/sites/all/files/publications/national-security-system.pdf (accessed 20 Aug 2015)

Seipel, J (2011) The impossible interface? Combining humanitarian logistics and military supply chain capabilities, in *Humanitarian Logistics: Meeting the challenge of preparing for and responding to disasters*, ed MG Christopher and PH Tatham, pp 215–31, Kogan Page, London

Thomas, A and Kopczak, L (2005) *From Logistics to Supply Chain Management: The path forward in the humanitarian sector*, Technical Report Fritz Institute, San Francisco, CA, USA

Tomasini, RM and Van Wassenhove, LN (2009) *Humanitarian Logistics*, Palgrave Macmillan, Houndmills, Basingstoke, UK

Van Wassenhove, LN (2006) Blackett memorial lecture: Humanitarian aid logistics: Supply chain management in high gear *Journal of Operational Research Society*, 57(7), pp 475–89

Wilson, MJ, Tatham, PH, Payne, J, L'Hermitte, C and Shapland, M (2018) The challenge of emergency logistics: Best practice relief supply, *Journal of Humanitarian Logistics and Supply Chain Management* (forthcoming)

What next for humanitarian logistics?

14

A practitioner's perspective

GEORGE FENTON AND REBECCA LEWIN

Abstract

This chapter considers the current state of humanitarian logistics from the personal perspectives of a number of practitioners. It considers developments within the last decade, revisits their readily identifiable advantages and discusses the possibly less obvious disadvantages, and means to address these.

The chapter goes on to discuss the potential influence of several emerging issues such as the limitations of using only internal means to measure logistics performance, and also value for money (VfM), arguing in favour of a sector-wide and comparative process.

The rapidly expanding cash transfer programme (CTP) approach is highlighted, together with the need to update the profile and capabilities of humanitarian logisticians (and logistics) in order to accommodate this method of assistance and achieve its large-scale potential via the use of new technologies.

Introduction

Over the past decade 'humanitarian logistics' has become a recognized term and a critical service in disaster response.[1] Humanitarian logisticians face many challenges, due in part to the frequency, intensity and impact of disasters, but also because investment in building capacity and recognition for the profession is still limited. There is also an opportunity to build on more recently recognized synergies between commercial and humanitarian logistics activities. The quality, capability and effectiveness of any humanitarian programme will be directly proportional to the capacity, competence and preparedness of its logistics teams; 'last mile' operational assistance must be adaptable and flexible if the international aid community is to remain effective and relevant (Fenton, 2013).

Painting the current picture of humanitarian logistics requires a broad canvas but it is perhaps helpful to focus on the 'rights' supply chain planning model: the right product, to the right place, at the right time and at the right cost. There are of course differing opinions as to the appropriate number of rights – but these four are the most commonly used. (The rights model could also have a negative impact when considered for non-emergency operations as it may imply responsiveness rather than essential collaborative planning among partners.) This chapter explores the personal reflections of humanitarian logisticians with respect to emerging developments, challenges, ideas and opportunities, and raises a number of important questions regarding the evolution of humanitarian logistics both as a critical function within humanitarian response and also as a developing sector in its own right.

The right product

Historically, one of the more complex aspects of humanitarian logistics – ensuring that the right products or services reach those for whom they are intended – has been challenging. Inadequate specifications provided by those requesting an item, often coupled with a lack of clarity regarding the required delivery time, creates a dilemma: whether to refine the specification and deliver late, or to deliver on time with a best-guess specification. Asking the requester for a more detailed specification may risk the riposte 'you're the logistician, I don't know technical specs, I just know that they need blankets now'. The result not only risks wasting resources by delivering the right thing at the wrong time (or the wrong thing at the right time) but also a worsening of relationships between those requesting and those supplying and, more critically, failing to serve adequately those in need.

Fortunately, things have moved markedly in the right direction. The number of emergency item catalogues, be they from Oxfam, MSF, UNICEF or the Red Cross (to name but a few), has greatly improved the process. Now the requester can see options and specifications for any commodity.

Some catalogues even provide background information (such as fumigation recommendations for certain food stuffs) or suggestions for linked items ('would you like a kitchen set to accompany that stove'?). Across the sector, humanitarian logistics services have not quite reached the predictive marketing capabilities akin to some of the more successful internet-based companies, but catalogues and procurement portals may be leading us in that direction.

Simple catalogues work best and in turn support relief item standardization, which works well for logisticians because advance knowledge of the standard packaging size, quantity, dimensions and weight of an item will, of course, allow for far more efficient supply chain planning. Standardization works well for suppliers too, as knowledge of relief item specifications agreed between aid organizations, or even within an organization, will encourage investment in stock holdings. Indeed, one step further is the option to tender globally to establish long-term supply contracts that introduce confidence that inventory accurately meets commodity specifications, packaging and labelling and customs documentation requirements. Thereafter, a disaster of sufficient magnitude – such as the 2015 Nepal earthquake – will trigger the rapid mobilization of 'standard' relief items, with all the time-consuming procurement and administration processes having been concluded in advance.

Considerable effort and resources have gone into the development and maintenance of these catalogues. For the majority of the items agreed specifications mean that logisticians can usually be sure that product quality will be consistent – but will these products also be the 'right' ones? What we see increasingly is that the more rigid the specifications, the less flexibility logisticians have in their sourcing decisions as fewer and fewer vendors are able to compete to provide the supplies. As this chapter will go on to explore, over-specification of emergency relief items can also result in an imposition of unattainable standards rather than an acceptance of locally appropriate items.

We are now seeing an increase in the number of small to medium size disasters and the 2015 data from the Centre for the Research on the Epidemiology of Disasters (CRED) (CRED, 2016) indicates that natural disasters have had a devastating impact on human society. In 2015 a total of 376 natural disasters were registered – a figure that showed an increase from the 2014 figure, which represented the lowest number since the beginning of the century (330), and which saw 22,765 deaths and generated 110.3 million victims worldwide. Over the last decade, China, the United States, India, the Philippines and Indonesia constitute together the top five countries that are most frequently hit by natural disasters. Year after year, these countries appear prominently in the list of countries experiencing the highest number of disaster events. It is therefore prudent to plan for the worst.

Standard product specifications and global contracts for, say, pre-positioning of stock or for vendor managed inventory, are now well matched with preparedness activities for disasters of a magnitude (and media profile) that generate the funds required for large-scale mobilization. The Philippines Typhoon Haiyan emergency response operation (November 2013) and the 2017 Hurricane Irma response in the Caribbean (unofficially, the fourth-costliest hurricane on record) are examples of this. However, the small to medium disasters, with little to no profile and funding, are less suited to the deployment of these globally 'standard' items. In the aftermath of such events pre-positioned stock can still be mobilized from global locations, but the costs involved in moving smaller consignments over large distances are often prohibitive.

The solution is increasingly to invest in more numerous, but smaller, pre-positioned stock-holdings, with shorter and less costly supply chains, that are amenable for situations when funds are at a premium. This, in turn, opens up the possibility of supporting local capacities for disaster response and to source from regional, national and local suppliers with the added benefit of providing support to the local economy, which also ensures that supplies are familiar with the intended beneficiaries. However, there are several challenges: what if the preferred local specification, familiar to the local populace, does not meet the global specifications? Should logisticians refuse to purchase locally and instead import items that meet global specifications and which may be of a higher quality? Consider the spun aluminium cooking sets used throughout many disaster-prone regions, and contrast these with the more expensive stainless steel version that meets a global specification. Adherence to the latter disadvantages many local suppliers from bidding in a global, regional or national tender. In some instances the recipient might prefer to receive cash in order to buy instead a product that they are familiar with using. While stainless steel may be more hygienic than aluminium, this matters little if, as has been observed, the beneficiaries sell the pots. Similar arguments might be made for common shelter and hygiene items.

Provided that the 'do no harm' principle is always applied (as is the case for many unacceptable locally produced pharmaceuticals), there should be flexibility in sourcing policies. It is therefore important for logisticians to gain skills and experience in retail market analysis and monitoring.

Whether global or local, the ethical and environmental performance of suppliers or traders, as well as their suppliers and subcontractors, should be considered (see Joint UNEP/OCHA Environment Unit, 2014). Although work on this important issue is ongoing, the humanitarian logistics network does not yet have a common approach. For example, compliance with the United Kingdom's Modern Slavery Act (which received Royal Assent on Thursday 26 March 2015) is now critical as global supply chains are at high risk for modern slavery exploitation. Also the increase in third and fourth parties means that supply chain verification is more and more challenging as the vendor is far removed from the whole chain. What is needed is a minimum standard applicable to all suppliers, wherever they fit in the supply chain, a global or regional register of supplier audits and a common approach to supporting suppliers to reach, or exceed, the agreed minimum standards.

Most aid organizations acknowledge that one of their greatest challenges is the unexpected, as in the humanitarian sector there is very little predictability. To help overcome part of this problem a number of aid organizations have been pre-positioning relief supplies globally, regionally or nationally. In early 2016 this activity was augmented through the development of the Emergency Supplies Prepositioning Strategy (ESUPS), which is supported by an inter-agency working group. ESUPS aims to overcome challenges associated with the need for data on global stockpiles of emergency supplies before disasters strike. Understanding who has what and where will better enable the humanitarian community to pre-positioned emergency relief items in the right quantities, in the right places to contribute to the efficient delivery of life-saving items to the affected populations. This also enhances the aim of the ESUPS Working Group, which is to coordinate pre-positioning strategies. Data from the United Nations Office for the Coordination of Humanitarian Affairs (OCHA) indicated that, as of January 2017, there were 52 major stockpile holders of emergency supplies located in 47 cities across 29 countries.

Some supplies are managed independently whereas other mechanisms are collaborative, such as the United Nations Humanitarian Response Depots (UNHRDs), which are a network of warehouse facilities around the world. From these locations agencies can respond within 72 hours to a major disaster. This United Nations (UN) common service has now been in operation for over 15 years and although its services have worked well, the level of inventory utilization has generally been limited. The strategy for the Global Logistics Cluster, hosted by the UN World Food Programme (WFP), further underpins emergency supplies and logistics preparedness and crises response. However, the humanitarian landscape is changing and emergency response is increasingly tackled at a national rather than international level.

Therefore, a thorough analysis of logistics preparedness and pre-positioning impact and sustainability within countries most prone to sudden onset disasters is now needed to determine the potential to coordinate more effectively the storage and delivery of emergency relief items over the next decade. For example, it would be helpful to review regional and national markets, warehouse locations, supply lead times during response operations that have supported life-saving assistance, effectiveness of overall emergency needs and applicability to recovery programmes.

As logistics accounts for a significant proportion of emergency programme costs, donors are increasingly encouraging consolidated supply chains that all actors can use. As has been demonstrated in the November 2013 Typhoon Haiyan emergency operations in the Philippines, governments will increase the use of military and civil defence logistics assets for operational reasons, but also to leverage funds to maintain such capabilities. Commercial companies will continue to enter the humanitarian aid market attracted by the corporate social responsibility (CSR) benefits, lucrative profit margins for customized services and the commercial leverage of their own businesses. However, all of these inputs are unlikely to address the essential, specialized, capability for local 'last mile' logistics to deliver goods and services directly to those who are in need of assistance (Fenton, 2013).

It is vital to understand that the definition of 'last mile' is not from port or airport to a convenient warehouse. It is quite literally the last mile, and that makes humanitarian logistics quite different from its commercial counterpart. This can mean having to use any means of transport available including bicycles, donkeys, camels and elephants. Even in the best of times, a country's infrastructure can be unreliable and, when disaster strikes, can be badly damaged or destroyed.

The right cost

As government aid budgets are squeezed, more and more aid organizations are turning to the private sector for money and expertise. Whether it is the Gates Foundation, corporations financing aid via their CSR programmes, or individuals donating to disaster responses, it is increasingly clear that private giving is a vital element of the aid landscape. Furthermore, although initial experiments with outsourcing of key tasks, such as procurement, have been found to be beneficial, this does not (yet) address the long-term resource gap and professionalization challenge facing the humanitarian logistics community.

Such issues are just as salient for the commercial sector as they are for aid organizations. Indeed there is a need for greater understanding between the private sector (both international and national companies), the UN, non-governmental organizations (NGOs), national public sector entities and local civil society. The first step is communication and dialogue; barriers that have existed have started to fall away as humanitarian and commercial logisticians are realizing that they have a lot in common. However, the aid community has yet to recognize fully logistics as a core competence, so training and professionalism have suffered as a result. But the picture has started to change over the past 10 years as we have gone from the perception that a humanitarian logistician might be a former commercial truck driver wanting to work in the NGO world, to today where many international NGOs (INGOs) require humanitarian logisticians to have an accredited professional qualification. However, some aid organizations are still behind the commercial world in recognizing the strategic importance of logistics and supply chain management at all levels of society.

Cost considerations permeate nearly every aspect of the design and execution of an efficient and effective supply chain, starting well before the disaster itself. Organizations might laud themselves at the lower unit costs gained through pre-positioning and the economies of scale achieved via, for example, the bulk procurement of inventory – lower unit costs are, indeed, tangible and desirable. They may find, however, that those savings do not actually carry over when lifetime costs are calculated. Does the lower unit cost more than outweigh the incremental storage costs accrued each month? Consider a time period largely bereft of sizeable responses where stock may be held for months or even years. Notwithstanding the issues of stock rotation and shelf life (largely handled well in professionally managed warehouses), the dilemma may be one more of strategy than cost. Does the current strategy accept that the payment of regular storage fees is the price to pay to guarantee availability 365 days a year? Is there a mandate to accept these costs in order to meet strategic goals of readiness? If that is the case, then equally organizations need to be clear and transparent that large-scale international pre-positioning meets objectives other than simply lower unit costs. It must also be made clear that the ready availability of relief items does not factor into, and unduly influence, assessments and the resulting programme design – either due to the 'every problem is a nail when your only tool is a hammer' scenario, or the need to cost recover fixed and variable storage charges that influence not only the selection of items required, but also the sourcing decisions for those items. Here, aid organizations must clearly consider the issue of truly and fully encompassing value for money.

Funding and reporting mechanisms aside, the potential for a rapid push of items in the early stage of a major response is undoubtedly appropriate provided that a clear decision is taken to move away from the push to the pull phase as soon as is feasible. Early assessments and resulting plans of action that set in motion a sizeable in-kind supply chain, and take away any possibility for modification as the situation on the ground changes, should be a thing of the past.

The right place

Academics now study ways of sourcing relief items closer to a potential event and the pre-positioning of these nationally rather than globally or regionally. The aim is to take cost, import restrictions and time out of the supply chain while encouraging resilience in the local economy (Taylor, 2011).

Over the past decade, the humanitarian logistics sector has, in most instances, demonstrated that it can quickly deliver commonly used relief items at agreed specifications to where they are needed. However, this has usually been achieved on a largely *ad hoc* basis, as the aid sector finds it challenging to enable the conditions to consolidate effectively its supply chains. There are many reasons for this, but most issues relate to agencies' differing funding sources, and also to poor donor coordination. Across multiple agencies, identical items are often sourced from the same suppliers with the same packaging destined for the same point of entry to respond to the same crisis. The ingredients are, nevertheless, present to promote unified rather than parallel supply chains, yet this is something rarely seen even though the advantages seem plain to any humanitarian logistician, whether working to deliver life-saving assistance or longer term development programme support.

Herein lies the challenge: for a number of agencies, their logistics resource is a support function. Not meant in any detrimental sense, but simply a reflection that logisticians are often overlooked as an important team to engage in the all-important needs assessment, which hopefully identifies, with the beneficiaries themselves, not only what is needed but also when, and potentially from where – for example local vendors. Thereafter, logisticians are consulted to make sense of the resulting plan of action and often inaccurately formulated budget. The programme teams identify what is needed, where and when; the logisticians figure out how to meet the need whilst delivering the most effective and efficient, donor compliant, supply chain. It would appear that no matter how much the logisticians might lobby for collaborative supply planning and unified supply chains, it would be remarkable if the same items were identified by different programme teams within different agencies as being needed all in the same place at the same time. Unified, coordinated or collaborative supply chains may still be desirable, but their starting point could well reside less with the logisticians and more with coordinated needs assessments and more effective plans of action.

This challenge can only be overcome with slow and incremental changes in the culture of emergency work, away from panicked and questionably effective responsiveness and towards short-term forecasting and collaborative design. Advances in technology can also contribute to this change but, currently, there is no system-wide framework for judging relative severity and aligning decisions about response accordingly. The result is typically a patchwork of macro and micro-level analysis, which is hard to aggregate, rarely provides a comprehensive overview, and serves as an inadequate basis for decisions about the prioritization of a response (Darcy and Hofmann, 2003).

Keeping up with the pace of change in technology development poses considerable challenges. NGOs and donors cite a lack of awareness about what new technologies are available and lack the time to procure and adapt these to field needs. New competencies within the humanitarian (logistics) community are emerging to bridge the gap between programme implementation and technology providers in order to ensure that technology solutions respond to the needs and reality of humanitarian response (Smith, 2012).

Digitalization provides the opportunity to analyse quickly, standardize and communicate assessment findings. Interactive dashboards tailored to context allow different users to focus on the information that they find most relevant, supporting critical analysis and the ability to prioritize resources. Sample size and consistency would improve as more agencies use the tools developed, thus helping to benchmark and build a more in-depth picture towards impact and response.

In a bid to support this approach and help to overcome the coordinated assessment challenge, World Vision International's design monitoring and evaluation team has developed a simple, smartphone-enabled, basic rapid assessment tool (BRAT) that can be used by emergency response team members. Global Medic's RescUAV project demonstrates the value of using small, unmanned aerial vehicles (UAVs), also known as drones, to provide assessment information. Through UAV technology they can gather better information that is used to make aid delivery more efficient, by providing search and rescue guidance, situational awareness and emergency mapping (RescUAV has responded in the Philippines in 2014, Nepal in 2015, Ecuador in 2016 and Columbia in 2017– see giw2017.org/innovations/rescuav). Now, critical assessment information can be gathered not only for programme planning purposes but also simultaneously for logistics operations. Primary data can be gathered in an accelerated time frame that provides an emergency response with decision-making information on both the disaster context and immediate needs in households and communities. Such tools have been designed to be flexible and easy to use and contextualize, and can be used in the very earliest days of a disaster response, before the cluster system may have been set up or joint needs assessments launched. Mobile technologies can also be used where the context of a disaster is dynamic, say where people are moving or a major change affects the population's recovery, for example when the national authorities allocate a new area for resettlement, etc.

Unified or not, all logisticians will be looking at their supply chains and asking whether they are genuinely efficient and effective. Some may have the information management systems, such as the BRAT, to provide data and metrics with which to effect some degree of measurement and reporting. The key performance indicators (KPIs) need not be complicated or numerous; a starting point may simply be whether the right item was delivered to the right place at the right time and at an acceptable cost. That said, it is important not to lose sight of the critical need to assure, and measure, effective programme outcomes. Therefore the challenge is not so much defining the required data, collecting and analysing it to give the required operational information, but more what the logistician does with the information. Initially data could serve to identify trends within their own organization, but how do logisticians know whether they are delivering items for half the cost and twice as fast as another agency, or at twice the cost and half the speed?

For several years, the Fritz Institute has been collaborating with organizations such as the British Red Cross Society (April 2007), USAID/OFDA (December 2003 to March 2004), and the International Rescue Committee (November 2003) to conduct supply chain assessments. These assessments demonstrated how critically important to the improved and long-term effectiveness of humanitarian organizations it is to establish and disseminate sector-wide humanitarian supply chain management performance measures.

A follow-up survey concerning the status of humanitarian supply chain KPIs revealed that the majority of aid organizations have no KPIs in place, but of those that do, almost 50 per cent say that metrics are not linked to their organizations' programmes or mandate, whilst almost all organizations say that they would like to establish KPIs. Following discussions at the 2012 Fritz Institute Humanitarian Logistics Conference (Fritz Institute, 2012), a small group of international aid agencies agreed to move forward on this issue, citing the need to set up effective performance tracking and improvement processes to manage their costs more effectively. Critically, many larger organizations have been hindered by their inability to gauge their own performance against others, which therefore impedes their capacity to measure efficiency.

Value for money (VfM) has rapidly gained prominence in the documentation of humanitarian agencies and donors alike. Until recently this was largely considered to be about procurement by ensuring that competitive tendering processes had been conducted to provide evidence of VfM. This approach fails on at least two fronts. The first is akin to that described for KPIs – measuring your own performance using only your data will not let you assess your performance in relation to the sector, any more than declaring that an organization can deliver VfM simply because it follows its own procedures. The second readjusts the perspective of VfM to consider the scenario where the logistician could deliver class-leading performance in terms of cost whilst meeting all the required delivery dates and specifications. But if in so doing, the agency could have achieved the desired impact by a more efficient means, then VfM has not been achieved. Therefore good project design is critical to ensure that all elements of assistance are planned to maximize cost efficiency.

By way of example, consider an efficient humanitarian supply chain in Haiti that was able to continue to deliver hygiene parcels six months after the January 2010 earthquake, when the local markets were re-established in February, and CTPs established in March. When regarded in terms of the whole, end-to-end programme, such a supply chain is not delivering VfM. It may have done something right, but it did not necessarily do the right thing.

Therein lies the crux: VfM needs to be measured and reported as more than best practice in procurement. All the functions within an operation must determine not only the options required to assure efficient and effective impact, but also how peer organizations are delivering their interventions, and at what cost. Some donors now consider VfM as a key aspect of awarding grants. It is not too far-fetched to see a donor, in receipt of multiple proposals for responding to a crisis, applying their own comparative evaluation of VfM in their grant allocation process. If this pertains, it may be preferable for agencies to agree a methodology for comparing and adjusting in order to deliver collective VfM. Otherwise, there is a risk that a donor methodology will either be enforced, or indeed donors themselves will actually direct or manage operations in order to assure *their* perception of what can often be complex and contextual 'value for money'.

The right time

While the global economy is growing, so too is the world's population. There has been substantial progress in demographic trends including significant reductions in child mortality and malnutrition. These welcome gains have not yet been matched with reduced fertility rates and so, particularly across Africa, populations are growing rapidly and have more than tripled during the second half of the 20th century, to 811 million. Some, such as Joseph Chamie from the New York-based Centre for Migration Studies, claim that this is an underestimate and the figure based on census projections may now exceed 1 billion (Chamie, 2011). Population growth is seen particularly in urban centres where standard population growth rate has been further augmented with migration from rural areas. The 2014 revision of the world urbanization prospects by the United Nations Department of Economic and Social Affairs (UN DESA) Population Division notes that the largest urban growth will take place in India, China and Nigeria. These three countries will account for 37 per cent of the projected growth of the world's urban population between 2014 and 2050. By 2050, India is projected to add 404 million urban dwellers, China 292 million and Nigeria 212 million. The results of population increases are already affecting the ways in which humanitarian assistance needs to be provided. Humanitarian logisticians must now develop skills and capacity to respond to major emergencies in urban settings. For example, the Japan tsunami (March 2011) and Eastern India cyclone response (October 2013) operations are perhaps the tip of the iceberg. The September 2017 earthquake that hit central Mexico was, perhaps, a sombre warning of what could occur should the epicentre have been the densely populated mega-city of Mexico City. The question is, therefore, how well is the humanitarian logistics sector prepared for establishing and delivering through an urban supply chain?

Increasing urbanization poses multiple challenges to the delivery of material (as well as financial or service) assistance. For example, solutions to quickly minimize traffic congestion in order to increase the efficiency of emergency urban freight delivery, which in turn will improve resource allocation efficiency and lower delivery times, will be needed.

Urban logistics should focus on service level and contract performance analysis. Information sharing and service contract design will help to enhance collaboration and coordination. Service level contracts have proven to be an effective tool to motivate logistics service providers (LSPs) to enhance their service quality. The key will be to figure out how to do this as part of preparedness measures so that appropriate emergency delivery services can be activated during a crisis. Therefore, to encourage collaborative urban logistics service planning, a framework to share information and contract guidelines is required to ensure effective coordination among beneficiaries and aid organizations (the customers) and suppliers and service providers to the market – in this situation 'the market' being an emergency response operation.

For the mega disaster, the aid sector can now rapidly mobilize, and deliver to point of entry, globally prepared stocks of relief supplies. It is the last mile that typically presents a challenge, and the more densely populated and therefore more congested and disrupted the destination, the bigger the challenge. Compounding this scenario is the consideration that urban populations tend to have fewer opportunities for coping strategies, certainly in comparison with rural dwellers. This, coupled with reduced capacity to store, for instance, a month's worth of supplies at a time, adds to the strains on the supply chain. Supply chains need to be more agile, more flexible and better able to respond to frequent but smaller distribution patterns.

It may be standardized, or even outdated, 'supply chain' approaches that exacerbate the challenge: typically a single point of entry, with warehousing usually clustered around a seaport or airport (that passes for a central base of operations), with all on-forwarding emanating from there. Less common is a 'supply network' approach, with distribution hubs around the periphery of a city, fed from the point (or preferably points) of entry, with multiple routes from these hubs to final distribution points.

What prevents logisticians from establishing such a set-up as the sector is generally willing and able to try innovations? It may be a simple question of resources. Multiple holding locations and multiple routes require multiples of staff/volunteers at the time when they are both in short supply and normally under severe pressure in terms of workload and cost efficiency. Of course, capacity building and preparedness activities might yield benefits, but only if the network approach is considered from the outset and plans are then implemented accordingly.

Multi-drop scenarios should be supported by the commercial sector, as this is their daily routine in non-emergency times. Again, the potential exists but requires advance planning for contracts, service level agreements and coordination, and a clear differentiation between mandates, roles and responsibilities.

Both the humanitarian and commercial logistics sectors could be seen to have identical objectives – improving the supply chain to deliver maximum dividends to shareholders – with just the dividends (dollars versus blankets) and shareholders (holder of shares versus those affected by the crisis) that differentiates. In reality, the finer differences, such as the willingness of individuals to approach a humanitarian agency knowing that their legal status is unlikely to be challenged, their details won't be forwarded to the authorities, and knowledgeable individuals will be able to help beyond a straightforward distribution or, at the very least, signpost where help can be found. As such, cooperation with commercial sector last mile logistics has real potential, but wholesale delegation or sub-contracting the role less so.

Commercial supply chains are becoming more vulnerable, partly due to the implementation of 'just in time' techniques and globalization policies. Although humanitarian logistics has much in common with commercial logistics, good practices from the corporate world have not fully crossed over. Furthermore, given that disasters are now more frequently affecting the developed world and are having a direct and often dramatic effect on global business, there is also much that can be learned by companies from humanitarian logisticians about how to operate creatively in chaotic environments and with markedly restricted resources. Supply chain risk management (SCRM) may be the most critical area for humanitarians to learn from the business sector, argues Paul Larson from the University of Manitoba. He notes that humanitarian action is the ultimate risky business (Larson, 2011). Whether a volcanic ash cloud, war or pandemic is causing a crisis, SCRM is about minimizing interruptions either through avoidance or effective response. Humanitarian logisticians need the latest technical knowledge and business techniques and should develop risk management skills, rather than be forced simply to take risks.

Perhaps more than most other single factors, it is the combination of item, place, quality and quantity that challenges timing. Depending on the relative weighting afforded to each factor, the pressure to deliver sub-optimal goods because they are available immediately, or deliver to areas in lesser need because they can be reached more easily, or to deliver late, or over a prolonged period, because the timetable is driven by the lead-time for the right item – all contribute to a less-than-optimal response. An example that can be drawn on here is that of supply chain feedback loops: say the design of emergency shelters that require parts that are unavailable locally and must be imported with a two-month lead time. Such valuable supply information should have an effective feedback loop to prompt a change in shelter design, and ultimately result in faster service delivery to beneficiaries.

The 'hybrid logistician'

To support its evolution, there is a need to open up the humanitarian logistics profession to specialists from the private and public sectors who can bring in new skills and thinking. Through what has been termed the 'humanitarian passport initiative' (essentially a portfolio of verified evidence, either physical or digital document, that demonstrates competence in a range of skills) work has begun to define suitable career pathways to facilitate this requirement. Research suggests that aspiring humanitarian logisticians, when compared to those in commercial roles, need to possess a broad range of skills and should consider the importance of contextual knowledge before entering the profession, as should academics before attempting to conduct research in this field. There is a strong requirement for technical and functional knowledge and educators need to place a stronger emphasis on appropriate training in the technical and programmatic aspects of the role, in logistics administration and on educating future humanitarian logisticians in how to train others (Kovács and Tatham, 2010).

Several initiatives have influenced the development of the sector. Of note, are the practical logistics training courses run by the Bioforce Institute – an organization that aims to increase the impact and relevance of emergency action and development programmes – and the Fritz Institute/Chartered Institute of Logistics and Transport (CILT) UK Certificate in Humanitarian Logistics (CHL), which has become a highly regarded qualification.[2] The creation of the Humanitarian Logistics Association (HLA), which was registered in 2009 as the first professional association within the aid sector, serves as a catalyst to enhance the professionalization of humanitarian logistics and the recognition of its strategic role in the effective delivery of relief during humanitarian crises. The association supports training initiatives, best practice exchange and representation for a growing worldwide community of practice; it now has nearly 2,000 members based in 106 countries. Still in the development phase, the HLA has the backing of the UK's CILT and has partnered with training agency RedR UK to provide technical advice and support to a new generation of humanitarian logisticians.

Humanitarian logisticians need to develop competence in a range of skills and technologies, including information management, market assessments, and cash and voucher distribution, as well as the more typical procurement, transport, tracking and tracing, customs clearance and warehouse management functions. Not only must they demonstrate technical competence but they must also show broader competence as humanitarian professionals.[3]

For example, they could be expected to support economic recovery projects that may include activities such as infrastructure rehabilitation, loans or grants to traders, transport subsidies, etc. Market-based programmes aim to help protect, rehabilitate and strengthen the livelihoods of people affected by crisis. It is important for humanitarian logisticians to develop skills to support such interventions as these increasingly will include value chain or supply chain projects. They also need skills to work with local partners to help capacity building, for example to address the risk management skills gap identified above.

The complexities and constraints of managing an effective supply operation cannot be underestimated. Indeed the concept of a humanitarian intervention is now fundamentally challenging the more 'traditional' direct provision of food and non-food items (NFIs) to those in need. While the range of relief items has always been varied, from water tanks to goats, medicines to tools and equipment, food to fishing nets, now the very nature of goods and services in the humanitarian sector is changing. What if disaster-affected people don't need material assistance? Are logisticians still needed?

The challenge is clear: programme activities and modalities are changing. It is therefore critical for aid organizations to examine the likely impact now and prepare a fit for purpose workforce for the future. Several emerging trends and their impact on the role of humanitarian logistics include:

- cash as a modality;
- engaging in markets;
- emergency and development work along a continuum (often comprising the same workforce).

Where the local market serving a disaster-affected community has capacity and access to appropriate supplies, aid organizations can and should provide financial assistance, not only because this approach is rapidly becoming the modality of choice for many donors, but more importantly because it is a method to support market resilience. Rather than undermining market conditions by bringing in commodities and services from outside, conditional or unconditional financial transfers, either electronic or in the form of vouchers or cash, is a modality which strives to re-establish normal commercial transactions as quickly as possible after a disaster. Generating opportunities for beneficiaries to access markets so that they can get what they need is a seemingly obvious intervention.

It is easy to think of cash programming as being coupled to livelihoods, food aid or NFI zones. But what humanitarian organizations have seen in the last few years is an emergence of cash programming within new sectorial themes, including, for instance, access to water through the issuing of vouchers and private sector led water-trucking enterprises. Unconditional digital cash transfers are now more widely used for humanitarian assistance and the trend is rapidly increasing. The argument about whether or not cash transfers should form part of humanitarian action has largely been won. What is less clear, however, is whether or not cash is being provided as efficiently or effectively as it could be and at the right scale, and whether cash transfers have transformative implications for the future of humanitarian aid [including managing supply chains], given that they challenge the main ways that aid has been delivered over the past several decades (Harvey and Bailey, 2015). Humanitarian assistance should be 'market aware' so that local markets are looked at and accounted for in the design, implementation and monitoring of humanitarian interventions. Market analysis is, therefore, an essential precursor to defining response modalities and response options, and to identifying opportunities to support local markets and the supply chains that underpin them.

The impact this has on logistics is complex. The *modus operandi* has been designed and described, in significant detail, around the direct delivery of 'goods' but has now reached a point where a revision of these new modalities is needed. It will be a challenge moving forward to design procedures and a control framework that enables effective delivery and accountability whilst appropriately managing risk. What should procedures and controls look like in a humanitarian programme delivery mechanism of cash? What other programme activities may be changing towards cash modalities, and how can humanitarian logisticians prepare for these changes?

Market engagement has taken on several new dimensions in emergency work. Instead of being driven towards those markets where logistics can most easily and quickly meet supply demands, the market is now being considered as an integral part of an affected community and a critical driver both in the short-term recovery of beneficiaries and in the long-term sustainability of humanitarian impact. International surge capacity will always be needed for events such as the Asian tsunamis, the Haiti and Nepal earthquakes, Pakistan floods and Philippines typhoons, but increasingly aid organizations are responding to more mid-sized emergencies where the volume of supplies needed does not always exceed the national markets' capacities. In these scenarios, there is now the opportunity to make more strategic decisions about market engagement and the use of donor funds in order to create valuable micro-economic impact.

The local purchase of supplies has already started to impact 'standard' international specifications for NFIs. Spending locally to rebuild the market and ensure the local appropriateness of what is procured for beneficiaries is important. What is the right international versus local procurement balance, and how will this balance be further challenged as local spend is increased?

The aid sector has developed numerous market assessment tools, many of which have now had several years of testing, but there is a widely acknowledged market analysis gap that inhibits effective decision making and subsequent market intervention monitoring. How do logisticians and procurement managers decide what to buy and where to buy? How do they determine, rapidly and per commodity, whether the disaster-affected market really has the capacity to meet supply needs? Operating models will need to be changed to enable financial and procurement processes to be flexible and adaptable in situations where local markets can no longer provide supplies sustainably.

Scaling up cash-transfers is a critical issue for organizations as they must develop capability to use more complex cash delivery mechanisms, eg banks, post offices and mobile phones. Building on research into programme design and 'value for money', it will be important to explore options for creating tools that help to compare the cost-effectiveness of different electronic cash transfer mechanisms in relation to their impact on programme objectives as well as their impact on financial inclusion and longer-term beneficiary protection.

Another dimension to consider is the categorization of traders (local suppliers) as beneficiaries. That is, those small-scale local traders within a beneficiary group who are, themselves, seriously affected by the emergency and who have ceased or reduced trading as a result. In these cases, supply chain interventions need to be geared towards 'market support' activities, which have started to include loans or grants to boost market activity. Here the classic definition of the 'private sector' is called into question. How can logistics best place itself to adapt to trader beneficiaries and to other private sector actors in the humanitarian markets?

Aid interventions must aim to generate sustainable outcomes that span development and crisis response activities. Preparedness and resilience work are important, broad ranging, aspects of this objective. In the context of this discussion, there is an emerging role for the continuous monitoring of markets in disaster-prone countries. Making greater, faster and more effective use of market data will help logisticians make informed decisions about pre-positioning, surge capacity and specific commodity weaknesses in the most vulnerable countries. Appropriate economic analysis and methods to strengthen linkages to private sector actors will need to be explored.

Recognizing the huge pressures for donor agencies, institutions or organizations to pledge, and be seen to pledge, in support of the latest high-profile disaster can be moderated by adjusting the appeals from in-kind (for the earliest stages) to cash-for-kind as the operation moves on. If the markets are not re-established in a timely fashion, the cash-for-kind can be readily converted to in-kind supplies and these fed into the existing supply chain. However, if the local markets are recovering to the point where they can deliver against the assessed need, then the cash-for-kind can be retained as cash and used, either for local procurement by the agency or feeding into some form of cash transfer programming (CTP) to the beneficiaries.

So what does this mean for humanitarian logisticians of the future? They need to be market savvy, able to assess the impact of an emergency on local market conditions and to understand the connections of a 'target' market to the upward national and international supply chains. They need to be able to monitor commodity variations and market triggers to be prepared for a large range of response scenarios. They need to be agile and able to switch modalities where needed; moving with ease and with prior preparation and planning between the use of 'cash', vouchers, cash for work (CFW) and local, national and international commodity supply, reacting swiftly to changes in market circumstances. Logisticians need to be able to work across functional silos to redefine the nature of 'programme logistics' in order to dispel the perception that it is simply a programme or project service, and must become an integral and essential component in the delivery of humanitarian assistance. Most importantly, such assistance will increasingly be in the form of financial transfers (cash) to beneficiaries. However, to quote Donald Rumsfeld: 'there are known knowns and unknown unknowns'. Do logisticians know enough about the 'cash' provider market and how it works? To up-skill a diverse global workforce, with varying pre-existing skill levels, will be a significant challenge. It is, therefore, important to consider the need for aid organizations to find new ways to partner with private companies that can provide the technical inputs on a sustainable, for profit, basis. The role then of humanitarian logisticians and supply chain managers would be to identify need, facilitate supply and monitor quality, performance and risk.

Perhaps technology can provide some solutions and opportunities – particularly on the African continent. In 2003 a report by the United Nations Conference on Trade and Development (UNCTAD) stated that the ability to create, acquire and adapt new technologies is a critical requirement for competing successfully in the global marketplace. Their report lamented how far Africa in general lagged behind other developing nations in Asia. Since then Africa has been catching up quickly. One company,

BlogSpot, noted that in the first decade of the century internet subscriptions in Africa grew by 1,030 per cent compared to a world average of 290 per cent. Across Africa today 75 per cent of the population own phones and 25 per cent have access to the internet – although this drops to 1 per cent in Ethiopia and South Sudan. Thousands of kilometres of fibre optic cable now join Africa, Europe and the Middle East. There are now more than 23 countries with high-speed internet services, including Gambia, South Africa and Nigeria.

It is interesting to note that in Somaliland, where regulation is very unrestrictive, companies have been able to exploit the space that this provides for innovation. Now Somaliland has one of the world's highest rates of digital transactions using the cash-free Zaad service. This is used to receive remittances, pay even very small amounts and has reduced risks of theft. Some 250,000 subscribe and use this service. In the cities of Somaliland, the future has arrived: cash is disappearing, credit cards are unnecessary, and daily shopping is speedy and digital. Almost every merchant, even hawkers on the street, accept payment by cellphone (York, 2013). A recent survey found that the average customer made 34 transactions per month – a higher rate than almost anywhere else in the world.

This is an innovation that will transform the continent as well as the way in which humanitarian logisticians and supply chain managers operate. Africa is already leading the world in the use of mobile money, and its growth is accelerating. In countries such as Kenya, Tanzania and Uganda, mobile-money accounts have become much more widespread than bank accounts. More than 38.5 million Kenyans (nearly the entire adult population) are using mobile-money services, mainly to transfer money to family members or business partners in distant locations, but increasingly for bill payments and small loans.

Mobile money has also drastically reduced the cost of crime and security for consumers, private companies and government offices. The Coca-Cola branch in Somaliland, for example, is the only cashless Coca-Cola company in Africa. About 80 per cent of its sales to retail distributors are performed through Zaad, while the remainder are achieved via electronic bank transfers.

The mobile-money system grew out of Somaliland's heavy dependence on remittances from Somalis who work abroad – an estimated US $1 billion annually. Remittances are increasingly sent home electronically, and mobile money became a natural outgrowth. The biggest African user of mobile money is Kenya, where the most popular service, M-Pesa, has 31 million subscribers through the leading cellphone company, Safaricom. It was originally mainly used by migrant workers to transfer money home to their families, but now it is widely used to receive salaries and pay bills and school fees.

Clearly a mindset change is needed; as a community of practice, logisticians pride themselves on being able to deliver 'goods' in enormous quantities, with great precision and, crucially, at an unparalleled speed. What lies ahead for the humanitarian logistics community will be the need to gain confidence with a new definition of success, one where market recovery and resilience is the target and where surge capacity is a fall-back measure, not the default. Perhaps it is not a question of maintaining an identity, but rather maintaining a critical surge capacity and skills in a new era with more complex economic targets becoming the biggest humanitarian logistics challenge yet.

A future scenario might then see the initiation of regional stock pre-positioning to support the initial emergency 'push' phase when local markets are either not functioning or to overcome a situation where the items required (such as family tents) were never available in the market before the crisis. This demands more commodity-specific supply strategy; rather than 'buy local or not' as a blanket decision, logisticians will be asked to look in greater granularity at what can best be sourced where and when, while considering local market capacity and monitoring it for signs of recovery so that supply strategy can be modified as early as feasible to allow local supply to become the norm. Assistance should be structured so that it supports flexibility, either to continue the in-kind pipeline when local conditions require, or to allow a managed transition from in-kind to cash as and when the local market can support demand.

Beneficiaries may receive a smart card (with a closed information database for protection and acceptance purposes) with which they can access in-kind items from a distribution centre (their allocation recorded onto the card). Thereafter, they may be able to access locally available materials (such as shelter items) from vendors with the card acting as a voucher, and finally draw from banks or remittance offices a fixed amount of cash credited to the card to be used for unconditional support. Depending on the duration and evolution of the response, the same card can be recredited – perhaps even by several collaborating agencies – for more of the same services, or for new types of support as appropriate.

Since the global financial crisis, funding for humanitarian assistance has been dwindling. Although logisticians may increasingly be asked to take on work beyond their original, more technical, mandate with the shrinking funding pool, the question is: how do they undertake all aspects of this ever increasing portfolio effectively? More innovative capabilities are certainly needed. Logisticians are central to effective, fast disaster relief as they serve as a bridge between disaster preparedness and response, between procurement and final distribution, and between headquarters and the field programmes. As logistics operations are inherently costly and since logisticians must track goods through the supply chain, the function is often the repository of data that can be analysed to provide post-event learning. Such data reflects all aspects of execution, from the effectiveness of suppliers and transportation providers, to the cost and timeliness of emergency responses, to the appropriateness of donated goods and the management of information.

The role of the humanitarian logistician, far from being reduced with the onset and introduction of CTP, is expanding to include building preparedness mechanisms with local actors and establishing contracts with local suppliers. While the need for large-scale supply chain preparedness and pre-positioning of standard goods will remain, consistent validation and monitoring of suppliers will enable variations in specifications. The humanitarian logistician will be central to the evolution of the response programme and integral to the relief teams in facilitating not what is required, when or where, but rather feeding in the most effective and efficient means by which to meet those requirements. The future suggests that skills needed by the next generation of humanitarian logisticians will include not only the means to manage complex supply chains and the procurement of locally sourced goods and services, but also the capability to manage pre- and post-crisis market assessments and methodologies to generate comparative KPIs that guide programmes towards the achievement of qualitative and cost-efficient assistance. Logisticians will have an integral role in programming to ensure that the means to meet what beneficiaries actually need is delivered, rather than hoping that they need what aid pipelines happen to be able to deliver.

It should be noted that, despite advances in the use of technology and changing approaches to the provision of humanitarian assistance, there will be an ongoing need for the in-field presence of experienced international logisticians, particularly in complex humanitarian crises such as South Sudan where a 2017 evaluation of the UN WFP's operations identified that the transport, storage and handling component of the emergency response accounted for US $563 million per year or 55 per cent of the total budget (WFP, 2017).

In May 2016 the international community gathered at the World Humanitarian Summit (WHS) with the purpose of achieving 'better, safer and more efficient aid' through the fulfilment of the Agenda for Humanity's five core responsibilities: 1) global leadership to prevent and end conflict, 2) uphold the norms that safeguard humanity, 3) leave no one behind, 4) change people's lives – from delivering aid to ending need, and 5) invest in humanity.

Although humanitarian supply chains have made great improvements in recent years, they still face challenges with localizing response capacities, striking the correct balance between international support and national response, and investing in preparedness to improve the quality, duration and cost effectiveness of emergency responses.

A report, *Delivering in a Moving World*, that was written with inputs from a wide range of humanitarian logistics practitioners was presented at the WHS (WFP, 2016). It posed critical questions and provided recommendations for implementation based on humanitarian response case studies, including the Nepal earthquake response, the West Africa Ebola outbreak, Super Typhoon Haiyan, and others. The intent was to raise awareness within the international aid system of the importance and strategic value of humanitarian logistics.

The definition of the four 'rights' is changing, not just in terms of the right product, place, time and cost, but also towards a deeper synergy between do no harm and how aid organizations spend donor funds responsibly in order to achieve the greatest market impact.

Notes

1 Developed from the original version written in 2014 by George Fenton, Mike Goodhand and Rebecca Lewin (nee Vince).

2 The Certificate in Humanitarian Logistics course was launched in September 2006 and teaches the base principles of logistics and supply chain operations in the humanitarian context in order to increase the proficiency and expertise of humanitarian logisticians working at an operational level. Over 2,000 students have so far enrolled.

3 According to the Consortium of British Humanitarian Agencies (now the START Network) core humanitarian competency framework, humanitarian workers need to demonstrate competence in: understanding humanitarian contexts and how to apply humanitarian principles; achieving results; developing and maintaining collaborative relationships; operating safely and securely; self-management in a pressured and changing environment; and leadership in humanitarian response.

References

Centre for the Research on the Epidemiology of Disasters (CRED) (2016) Annual disaster statistical review 2015 [Online] www.CRED.BE (accessed 6 November 2017)

Chamie, J (2011) Global population of 10 billion by 2100? – not so fast, Yale Global [Online] https://yaleglobal.yale.edu/content/global-population-10-billion-2100-not-so-fast (accessed 7 November 2017)

Darcy, J and Hofmann, C-A (2003) According to need? Needs assessment and decision-making in the humanitarian sector, *Humanitarian Policy Group (HPG) Report No 15*, September

Fenton, G (2013) An evolving sector: Managing humanitarian supply chains, in *Managing Humanitarian Supply Chains: Strategies, Practices and Research*, ed B Hellingrath, D Link and A Widera, pp 64–71, DVV Media Group GmbH

Fritz Institute (2012) Humanitarian logistics conference 2012: The changing face of logistics within the humanitarian sector, June 2012 [Online] http://www.fritzinstitute.org/prgSC-HLC2012-proceedings.htm (accessed 17 November 2017)

Harvey, P and Bailey, S (2015) Cash transfer programming and the humanitarian system: Background note for the High Level Panel on Humanitarian Cash Transfers, March 2015 [Online] http://www.seepnetwork.org/cash-transfer-programming-and-the-humanitarian-system--background-note-for-the-high-level-panel-on-humanitarian-cash-transfers-resources-1643.php (accessed 17 November 2017)

Joint UNEP/OCHA Environment Unit (2014) *Environment and Humanitarian Action: Increasing effectiveness, sustainability and accountability* [Online] https://www.unocha.org/sites/unocha/files/EHA per cent20Study per cent20webfinal_1.pdf (accessed 16 November 2017)

Kovács, G and Tatham, PH (2010) What is special about a humanitarian logistician? A survey of logistic skills and performance, *Supply Chain Forum: An international journal*, **11**(2), pp 32–41

Larson, PD (2011) Risky business: What humanitarians can learn from business logisticians – and vice versa, in *Humanitarian Logistics: Meeting the challenge of preparing for and responding to disasters*, ed MG Christopher, and PH Tatham, Kogan Page, London

Smith, G (2012) New technologies in cash transfer programming and humanitarian assistance, *Humanitarian Exchange*, **54**, pp 15–17

Taylor, DH (2011) The application of value chain analysis for the evaluation of alternative supply chain strategies for the provision of humanitarian aid to Africa, in *Relief Supply Chain Management for Disasters: Humanitarian, Aid and Emergency Logistics*, ed G Kovács and KM Spens, IGI, Hersey, PA

World Food Programme (WFP) (2016) Delivering in a moving world: Looking to our supply chains to meet the increasing scale, cost and complexity of humanitarian needs [Online] http://www.logcluster.org/sites/default/files/whs_humanitarian_supply_chain_paper_final_24_may.pdf

World Food Programme (WFP) (2017) *Country Portfolio Evaluation South Sudan: An evaluation of WFP's portfolio (2011–2016)*, Volume II: Annexes, WFP

York, G (2013) How mobile phones are making cash obsolete in Africa, *The Globe and Mail*, 21 June [Online] http://www.theglobeandmail.com/news/world/how-mobile-phones-are-making-cash-obsolete-in-africa/article12756675/ (accessed 23 Dec 2013)

Where next? 15

A glimpse of the future of humanitarian logistics

GYÖNGYI KOVÁCS

Abstract

Instead of any famous last words, this chapter aims to assess the state of the art of humanitarian logistics, and to point out some future trends in this field. As in the previous edition of the book, the chapter will start with an assessment of the implementation status of its prior predictions before turning to current trends and its promised glimpse of the future of humanitarian logistics.

Humanitarian logistics is a maturing discipline. As with maturing disciplines, it is both rediscovering its roots, as well as embracing larger, systemic changes. Countless such changes exist: some due to larger external factors (not just climate change and conflicts, but also migration and pandemics), others stemming from innovation. But, contrary to expectations, only a few examples exist of research setting the pace for practice.

Introduction

Humanitarian logistics is a maturing discipline, in practice, professionalization and in research. The roots of the discipline are obviously to be found in the ideology of humanitarianism, the practice of disaster relief and emergency response, and the logistics and supply chain activities needed for this practice. The narrowest view of humanitarian logistics confines it to both:

(a) humanitarian activities in the sense of disaster relief; and

(b) logistics activities in the sense of transportation and warehousing.

This said, humanitarianism as an ideology extends to other areas as well, from development aid overall to, for example, the application of humanitarian principles in health care, or education, in other words, ensuring that lives are saved or sustained overall. In practice, some humanitarian organizations may have very specific mandates that extend to 'development' versus 'disaster relief', and/or follow a 'natural' versus 'man-made' disaster divide, and/or focus on specific groups of people (eg children, refugees, internally displaced people), and/or focus on specific functions of aid (eg water and sanitation, education, food, health care), to name but a few. Plus, as discussed in Chapter 5, there is an increased need for differentiation across humanitarian organizations. On the other hand, some humanitarian organizations cater to various needs including those needs that span the disaster – development divide or cycle, though in such cases 'humanitarian' may refer to the disaster relief side of activities.

The same goes for how the term 'logistics' is understood – referring here to the enormous literature on definitions and the debate of logistics versus supply chain management – and to how humanitarian organizations see or place logistics in their organization. The range goes from humanitarian organizations perceiving themselves as logistics organizations and likening themselves to third or fourth party logistics providers, to 'logistics' covering all supply chain functions from strategic to operational levels, to logistics being perceived narrowly as transportation. Some organizations separate logistics from supply, and even those that have put these two in the same function may still separate it from 'programmes' – which defines the scope of an operation – and/or from 'relief distribution' – which carries out distribution in the last mile (Makepeace *et al*, 2017). As long as such silos prevail, the question of for whom we are conducting research is as actual as ever. For example, ample research endeavours exist in the area of 'last mile' distribution – yet this is often not up to the humanitarian logistician to organize.

At the same time, while stressing the end-to-end supply chain view, the definition of boundaries (the ends) is equally unclear. Some humanitarian organizations focus on the activities from receiving goods themselves to delivering them to the next port, or their implementing partner's next facility. That is not in line with any of the definitions of a supply chain that would include several, if not all, echelons of suppliers and customers. The last edition of this book, and this very chapter, talked of the importance of including implementing partners (IPs; sometimes just called cooperation partners or CPs) downstream, yet such research is still scant.

Why am I taking up this discussion again while, at the same time, stating that the discipline is maturing? The scope of the discipline is a topic that may never be resolved. It is nevertheless important to be aware of the range of definitions, and of the standpoint of one's counterpart, in practice, education, and research. Yet, while the trend is towards supply chain management decisions becoming more strategic in the humanitarian area, and also towards logistics being understood in the sense of supply (chain) decisions overall, the strong focus on disaster relief, emergency response and crisis management prevails. This book, including this chapter, follows such trends in how it sees humanitarian logistics. For example, when it comes to disasters, the book touches on development aid primarily in cases where disasters just cannot be confined to a short-term disruption (such as refugee crises), and in cases where development aid and disaster relief overlap. At the same time, the focus is not only on the implications of natural hazards, but also on other crises, from pandemics to wars. Sadly, that is where the bulk of the work in this area lies right now, and there is no end in sight. Altogether, we may therefore need to reconsider the scope of humanitarian logistics.

The focus of this chapter is naturally on the changes and trends; the future to come. This will be done again by first, revisiting the topics put forward in the last edition, and then reflecting on the current indications of the future development of this area.

Revisiting old predictions

'What will happen next' was an important perspective considered in the first edition of this book. Back then in 2011, five main trends were put forward:

1 A shift in focus from inter-agency coordination towards relationship management in the supply chain.

2 A renewed emphasis on the sustainability of aid.

3 The development of specialized humanitarian logistics services that organizations offer each other.

4 An emphasis on process as well as product and packaging standardization and modularization.

5 The use of new technologies to capture data.

Then came the second edition (2014), adding on a further number of trends:

6 A shift in focus towards cash transfer programmes (CTPs).

7 A stronger focus on supply chain visibility as well as visibility across humanitarian organizations.

8 An extension of professionalization endeavours to include (implementing) partners.

9 A stronger focus on interoperability across humanitarian organizations.

10 A heightened focus on security.

At the same time, even larger changes such as population trends, migration, and climate change, were expected to alter the demand for humanitarian aid. Climate change in particular has been linked to the frequency and intensity of, in particular, hydro-meteorological disasters, but also to changes in disaster patterns. The 2017 hurricane season, and the extent of its devastation, is an example of changes in frequency and intensity of such hydro-meteorological disasters.

So where do we stand with all of these trends now? *Inter-agency coordination* has, in fact, resurfaced as a topic (see Chapter 6), not least due to tricky situations in conflict zones and the need for a common logistics operating picture (Tatham *et al*, 2017a). The other main reason for this is the strong emphasis on interoperability, which is further supported by agreements on standards, but also joint platforms for, for example, social media monitoring and other information and communications technology (ICT) endeavours overall. At the same time, the focus on purchasing consortia, or collaborative procurement, has all but disappeared – which is not to say it doesn't exist; rather, it has taken new forms. Most interestingly, collaborative platforms – eg the United Nations Global Marketplace (UNGM) system for UN agencies – allow organizations to piggyback on one another's contracts. At the same time, many humanitarian organizations have started offering *procurement services* to one another (see Chapter 5). However, it is not clear to what extent this has actually been achieved, nor whether suppliers themselves are even aware of this clause in their relationships, as research is yet to catch on to this topic. On the other hand, relationship management remains tricky with regard to the public procurement regulations that humanitarian organizations need to abide by. Not surprisingly, as discussed in Chapter 8, they also cause much headache in light of humanitarian innovation.

Whilst there is much discussion on the *sustainability of aid*, more recently some large humanitarian organizations are also looking into sustainability reporting and standards, from codes of conduct (see Chapter 1) to International Organization for Standardization (ISO) standards to the Global Reporting Initiative (GRI) which, on the UN side, is referred to as 'greening the blue'. As with industry in the beginning, the focus is on greening one's own operations and, to some extent, how to offset emissions. While there are some great examples of large-scale endeavours (eg solar-powered refugee camps), this focus is yet to be extended to the supply chain both upstream and downstream.

But sustainability can mean many things in the humanitarian context. Another hot topic in this regard is capacity building and resilience. Here, the focus has shifted somewhat from big international non-governmental organizations (BINGOs) coming to the rescue, to these organizations supporting existing national structures by scaling them up (see Figure 15.1).

Scalability refers to humanitarian supply chains adding to the surge capacity of local ones. To do so requires extensive knowledge, and also integration of the one with the other; as well as early warning systems that can activate such surge capacity in time (see Annala *et al*, 2014). Activating a dormant supply chain is subject to order and delivery lead times, as well as pre-positioning (see Chapter 10), given that – and with particular regard to public procurement – the very tendering processes may take time if framework contracts have not been established well in advance. The concept of scalability may provide some answers to resource mobilization and activation of dormant supply chains, including perhaps the aspects of the utilization of (also commercial) logistics assets, and the decentralization of logistics systems as highlighted in Chapter 13. At the same time, horizontal integration across governmental and non-governmental organizations (NGOs) (as well as UN agencies) in the

Figure 15.1 Scalability: adding surge capacity to local supply chains

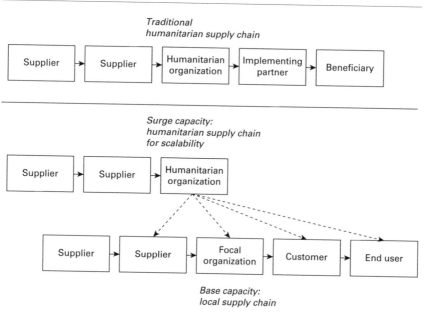

various phases of disaster relief (see Chapter 6) is key for successfully scaling up supply chains facing a surge in needs.

Service development has become the norm in humanitarian logistics (see Chapter 5). Incredibly, many organizations can be included in just one delivery through service tiering; especially when it comes to cross-border operations in conflicts. Figure 15.2 depicts the various logistics service providers and cooperation or implementing partners in a cross-border delivery to a conflict zone where even vehicles need to be switched – and reloaded – at borders. This is a simple diagram for deliveries in the last mile, which can be much more complex if considering transportation consolidation, and the involvement of fourth party logistics providers to freight forwarders in various steps in the material flow.

Great leaps forward have been taken in *standardization* and modularization especially in health kits, increasing their interoperability. Other areas lag behind, partly due to different standards across countries to begin with. A different answer to working with low stock keeping units (SKUs) of large varieties may be offered by three-dimensional (3D) printing, which the water, sanitation and hygiene (WASH) cluster is the first to embrace (Tatham *et al*, 2015; and Chapter 4). Furthermore, the wider use of enterprise resource planning (ERP) systems has led to more process standardization in humanitarian logistics. At the same time, as the Sphere standards are being revisited, the work in process standardization has just begun (see Chapter 1).

Perhaps the biggest change can be observed in the technologies to *capture data*, and the use of ICT overall (see Chapter 3). Though one needs to be mindful of the digital divide – after all, it is the most vulnerable who don't have access to smartphones and the internet; and the most affected who are in the very areas where the communication infrastructure is down after a disaster – the number of efforts to build platforms to integrate and triangulate social media messages is mushrooming; just see the latest Information Systems for Crisis Response and Management (ISCRAM) proceedings for a sense of their emerging variety (Comes *et al*, 2017). Big data analysis has entered the humanitarian scene, and even led to the rise of a new type of 'digital humanitarians' (Meier, 2015; Prasad *et al*, 2016). There are even crowdsourcing efforts of both data and funding, open data efforts, and new humanitarian data centres, as well as countless new consultancies in this area. The data they capture ranges from infrastructure assessments after a disaster, to needs versus supplies, population movements, vehicle tracking, to the constant monitoring of various incidents in conflicts. Technologies to capture data also vary; social media is but one source among different types of satellite imagery, drones, wearable devices, and 360 degree cameras.

Figure 15.2 Service tiering of a cross-border delivery

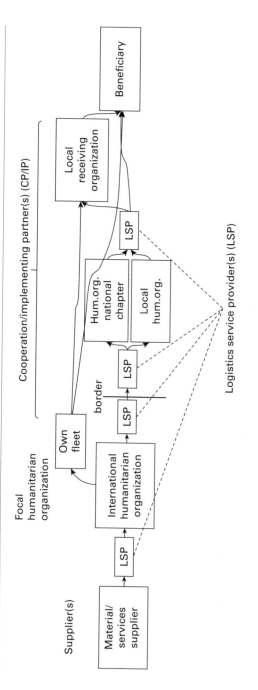

But while the current focus is still on the challenge of sorting out and validating big data, the even bigger revolution for decision making is yet to come. The bottleneck still lies in the timeliness of having the data available for the particular decision that needs to be taken. And, as is aptly pointed out in Chapter 3, keeping technologies simple will also make them robust for use in a disaster.

At the same time, *cash transfer programmes* (CTPs) have now been implemented on an ever-larger scale (see Chapter 2) through what has been called the 'second wave of servitization' in humanitarian logistics (Chapter 5). As with any innovation or technology in humanitarian logistics, CTPs require a redesign of the humanitarian supply chain (see Chapter 4). Yet while they are catching up in size and scale, and while some humanitarian organizations have even downsized their logistics and supply staff, more recently they have regained some appreciation. Cash is, after all, not a solution to all the problems, and the ability to fall back on delivering products and services lies in the hands of humanitarian logisticians (see Chapter 14). Even the assessment of current markets is a supply chain mapping exercise; although, rather confusingly, it is referred to as the 'market chain' and/or 'market system' within cash transfer programming. Overall, this is an area of increasing focus, and dealing with cash as a commodity raises its own questions for financial regulators overseeing such transactions.

As for *supply chain visibility*, financial tracking systems have been implemented across humanitarian programmes and organizations. Yet, interestingly, they stop short at the very understanding of who a humanitarian organization considers to be their next 'customer' (for a list, see Chapter 5). Thus, if the task is to deliver to a port of entry, the tracking follows up until then; if the task is to deliver to an implementing partner, it stops at that handover. Ports of entry, implementing partners, etc, work as proxies for items having been used for the right programmes and the right beneficiaries. This questions whether financial tracking requirements actually increase the accountability of humanitarian organizations or just the feeling of control of donors. As also pointed out in Chapter 2, more strings attached to funding may increase control but, potentially, reduce effectiveness and efficiency. In the end, it is still in the hands of monitoring and evaluation programmes to establish the link to beneficiaries and to confirm that they have actually received the products and services. Tracking and tracing, on the other hand, has become a hot topic also in light of tracking the actual movements of commodities, assets (vehicles, convoys) as well as humanitarian staff. The reasoning is one of security and protection of staff and assets (Kachali *et al*, 2017). But such tracking is a complex endeavour in light of service tiering and, thereby, the many handovers of materials along a delivery. Yet other aspects of supply chain visibility, eg across humanitarian organizations, have been promised through the rise of ERP systems, but this promise is yet to be fulfilled.

In the last edition of the book, there was also a prediction that the *extension of professionalization* endeavours would include (implementing) partners. Some first attempts have been made in this regard, eg the United Nations Children's Fund (UNICEF) offering courses on warehouse and inventory management both for their own staff and also for their partners (governments, ministries, NGOs). Capacity building and community resilience building efforts have continued and need to continue, but they also need to reflect the benefits and challenges of supply chain scalability (see Chapter 7). The most prominent current undertakings are the development of models that specify the competencies that are required for various levels of jobs in humanitarian logistics (see Chapter 9), as well as the assembly of a 'body of knowledge' (hosted by the Humanitarian Logistics Association: www.humanitarianlogistics.org) that should enable practitioners anywhere to look up best practices and act accordingly.

As discussed earlier, the desire for *interoperability* underpins the development of technological platforms. Furthermore, various types of kits – whether inter-agency kits or the ShelterBox described in Chapter 12 – allow for standardization in procurement and joint pre-positioning, as well as in working with the same kits across various humanitarian organizations and their implementing partners. Also, standard units such as the Red Cross family's emergency response units (ERUs) support the interoperability of different national chapters' teams in a specific response (Jahre and Fabbe-Costes, 2015). Interoperability, and the recognition of the interconnectedness of different sectors and clusters, is key for preparedness and civil protection in the first place (see Chapter 8). Sectorial interdependencies also require some thought in further innovation; after all, innovation in one sector may undermine operations in another (Haavisto and Kovács, 2015). Much more could be done to develop interoperable solutions in kits, systems, and processes. One would also expect more efforts in this regard due to the high rotation of humanitarian staff across humanitarian organizations, who are familiar with one another's products, services, processes and standards.

Security remains a headache to all humanitarian operations, given that targeted attacks on humanitarians, hospitals and humanitarian convoys are no longer unheard of. Humanitarians are not a target! Security is key for humanitarian operations to work at all, and without it humanitarians cannot even access specific regions and beneficiaries; not to speak of the accessibility of their services by the most vulnerable. The very securing of humanitarians and humanitarian operations raises many questions, from ethical, to legal, to privacy ones (Kroener *et al*, 2017), but also questions of the security of the actual security system (against hacking and targeting), and how any security-related system or activity conforms with the humanitarian principles. Security considerations not only extend to violence and warfare, but also to, for example, quarantine and working with hazardous contaminated materials in health care. A case in point is the security for the humanitarian logisticians who were in charge of securing burials for the deceased in the Ebola crisis. While there is much literature in the public health domain in respect of facility location and ambulance routing, there is (as noted in Chapter 7) relatively little research focused on pandemic response. Medical humanitarian logistics is not a new area per se; but rarely are epidemiological considerations applied in humanitarian logistics.

In conclusion, much has been done in the various areas that were outlined in previous editions of this book as emerging ones – but much still remains to be done. Apart from these, another question that remains is to consider what else there is to come.

Where next?

This book is going to print at the time of the 23rd annual 'conference of the parties' (COP23) under the UN Framework Convention on Climate Change (UNFCCC) in Bonn. Raising the flag on climate justice just increases in importance. What will be done, or left undone, is a good predictor of humanitarian needs in the future. There are direct needs of dislocation and migration due to the disappearance not only of islands but island nations; secondary effects on the frequency and impact of extreme weather events; and their tertiary effects of further hunger, migration and related crises. Further effects are not necessarily local; just as civil protection cannot be dealt with in isolation due to the dependence on global supply chains (see Chapter 8), global events also have their cascades and repercussions all around the globe.

The 2016 refugee 'crisis' in the European Union (EU) has sparked off a debate around the interrelation of disasters and crises all around the world; see Figure 15.3 for an illustration of such interdependencies from the EU perspective. As pointed out in Chapter 7, dislocation is not a one-off but often a semi-permanent feature, with refugee settlements persisting decades later. Apart from the political repercussions of *migration,* of understanding

Figure 15.3 Global events with local impact all around the globe

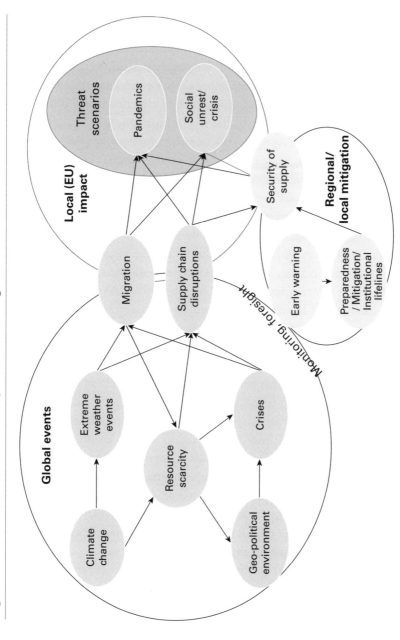

migration patterns, and for actually stopping their causes rather than effects, migration also raises important questions for humanitarian logistics. How should one cater for populations on the move, especially when they are hiding and constantly reroute themselves based on the threats they perceive on their journey?

The effects of climate change cannot be understated. We have just experienced a hurricane season that, in some cases, devastated up to 95 per cent of certain islands, and we are expecting similar patterns in the current typhoon season. Arguably, of course, it is not only climate change but society that is to blame for the impact of the recent hurricane season (Kelman, 2017). From a logistical perspective, the impact is there to be dealt with nonetheless. Consequently, while chasing new trends, *humanitarian logistics is back to basics*. Debris collection (Çelik *et al*, 2015) is as important as ever for access to beneficiaries in disaster locations, and many challenges also remain in the different functional areas of humanitarian logistics (see Chapter 11). There is, therefore, a case to be made for revisiting performance measurement, and the key performance indicators in the humanitarian supply chain.

At the same time, conflicts and crises and their security implications have made it increasingly difficult for humanitarian organizations to *access* the locations of beneficiaries in need. Though access can be negotiated for convoys, more often than not it has become a function of outsourcing to logistics service providers, with final relief distribution being in the hands of local implementing partners. The typical focal organization of humanitarian logistics research, on the other hand, has remained the international humanitarian organization. Any last mile research would do better if it included implementing partners, logistics service providers, and also if it considered *service tiering in the last mile*. Both from an external as well as an organization-internal perspective, the question that remains is what humanitarian logisticians can actually do. Perhaps it is not only implementing partners, but also other internal functions and departments that would need to be included in logistical decision making. 'Programmes' calling the shots alone may lead to logisticians just doing as they are told; with even larger consequences for the efficiency, effectiveness, and equity of the actual programme.

Contracting out the last mile comes with further repercussions. There is an overall *transparency conundrum* in humanitarian logistics, whether to:

(a) contract out to implementing partners;

(b) control the operation – eg through humanitarian organizations reintegrating deliveries in Yemen, chartering their own dhows; or

(c) change the system through various innovations (see Chapter 4).

Interestingly, the same transparency conundrum that is much emphasized upstream in commercial supply chains (with the current biggest issue being modern slavery) is more important downstream in the humanitarian supply chain.

Innovations for the humanitarian sector have been much in the limelight, whether 3D printing, the use of drones, zeppelins, or even the combination of several of them to deliver 'flying maggots' (Tatham *et al*, 2017b). There are many large-scale endeavours, and even supporting schemes for innovation, from the Humanitarian Innovation Fund, to accelerators such as the Global Humanitarian Lab, to dedicated innovation units at many humanitarian organizations. However, a common challenge for them all is public procurement regulations; while wanting to foster innovation and engage in partnerships to do so, buying from such partners is compromised by the very partnership prior to a tender. Public procurement for innovation is a hot topic outside the humanitarian area as well, but would need to be embraced more thoroughly by the sector.

Concluding remarks

As fields mature, they rediscover their roots. The field of humanitarian logistics is maturing, and the rediscovery of basics is both a consequence and an urgent necessity that stems from recent events. But many challenges in logistics functions still remain to be solved; and much more needs to be done in terms of focusing on specific logistics concepts, functions and challenges in the humanitarian context. Maturing also brings more theoretical development; although, interestingly in this regard, humanitarian logistics follows its mother disciplines of logistics, operations management and supply chain management in that it borrows theory rather than developing it (Tabaklar *et al*, 2015). The second edition of this book ended with a prediction of the maturing of the discipline leading to research setting the pace, and while some of this development can be seen in the humanitarian innovation literature (Comes *et al*, 2017) by and large this has not yet occurred.

At the same time, humanitarian logistics faces some new challenges. Climate change, security and urbanization have been identified as challenges previously; but now one could add migration as well as pandemics to the list. From a logistic perspective, the question is one of catering to people on the move and/or while avoiding further contagion. The dynamics of catering to a moving population is an interesting logistical challenge; but the question of contagion cannot be solved by logisticians alone. Sadly,

Tabaklar *et al* (2015) also found very little cross-fertilization across relevant disciplines to humanitarian logistics, but ideally the field would need to integrate considerations of epidemiology, meteorology, crisis management, and disaster management, to name but a few relevant disciplines.

Humanitarian logistics also faces other systemic changes. Apart from the innovations described in many chapters of this book, social media has already supported the rise of beneficiary-to-beneficiary delivery of aid; what other trends such as co-creation and the sharing economy bring to this sector, remains to be seen.

Acknowledgements

This research could not have been achieved without the kind support of the H2020-BES-2015 project 700510 'Integrated system for real-time TRACKing and collective intelligence in civilian humanitarian missions (iTRACK)'.

References

Annala, L, Tabaklar, T, Haavisto, I, Kovács, G, and McDowell, S (2014) Supply chain scalability, in *NOFOMA 2014 Proceedings Competitiveness through Supply Chain Management and Global Logistics,* ed B Gammelgaard, G Prockl, A Kinra, J Aastrup, P Holm Andreasen, H-J Schramm, J Hsuan, M Malouf, and A Wieland, pp 297–313, Copenhagen, Denmark

Çelik, M, Ergun, Ö and Keskinocak, P (2015) The post-disaster debris clearance problem under incomplete information, *Operations Research,* 63(1), pp 65–85

Comes, T, Bénaben, F, Hanachi, C, Lauras, M and Montarnal, A (eds) (2017) Agility is coming, *ISCRAM 2017 Proceedings,* Mines-Albi, France [Online] http://idl.iscram.org/files/tinacomes/2017/1440_TinaComes_etal2017.pdf (accessed 29 January 2017)

Haavisto, I and Kovács, G (2015) A framework for cascading innovation upstream the humanitarian supply chain through procurement processes, *Procedia Engineering,* 107(7), pp 140–45

Jahre, M and Fabbe-Costes, N (2015) How standards and modularity can improve humanitarian supply chain responsiveness: The case of emergency response units, *Journal of Humanitarian Logistics and Supply Chain Management,* 5(3), pp 348–86

Kachali, H, Kovács, G and Grant, D (2017) Determining tracking and tracing user requirements in conflict zones, *EUROMA 2017 Conference Proceedings*, Edinburgh, UK, July 2017, paper 42899

Kelman, I (2017) Don't blame climate change for the Hurricane Harvey disaster – blame society, *The Conversation*, 29 August [Online] http://theconversation.com/dont-blame-climate-change-for-the-hurricane-harvey-disaster-blame-society-83163

Kroener, I, Watson, H and Muraszkiewicz, J (2017) Agility in crisis management information systems requires an iterative and flexible approach to assessing ethical, legal and social issues, in Agility is coming, *ISCRAM 2017 Proceedings*, ed T Comes, F Bénaben, C Hanachi, M Lauras and A Montarnal, pp 247–55, Mines-Albi, France

Makepeace, D, Tatham, PH and Wu, Y (2017) Internal integration in humanitarian supply chain management: Perspectives at the logistics–programmes interface, *Journal of Humanitarian Logistics and Supply Chain Management*, 7(1), pp 26–56

Meier, P (2015) *Digital Humanitarians: How big data is changing the face of humanitarian response*, CRC Press, Boca Raton, FL

Prasad, S, Zakaria, R and Altay, N (2016) Big data in humanitarian supply chain networks: A resource dependence perspective, *Annals of Operations Research*, pp 1–31

Tabaklar, T, Halldórsson, Á, Kovács, G and Spens, KM (2015) Borrowing theories in humanitarian supply chain management, *Journal of Humanitarian Logistics and Supply Chain Management*, 5(3), pp 281–99

Tatham, P, Loy, J and Peretti, U (2015) Three dimensional printing – a key tool for the humanitarian logistician? *Journal of Humanitarian Logistics and Supply Chain Management*, 5(2), 188–208

Tatham, PH, Spens, KM and Kovács, G (2017a) The humanitarian common logistics operating picture: A solution to the inter-agency coordination challenge? *Disasters*, 41(1), pp 77–100

Tatham, PH, Stadler, F, Murray, A and Shaban, RZ (2017b) Flying maggots: A smart logistic solution to an enduring medical challenge, *Journal of Humanitarian Logistics and Supply Chain Management*, 7(2), pp 172–93

INDEX